Global Networks

Global Networks

Computers and International Communication

edited by
Linda M. Harasim

The MIT Press
Cambridge, Massachusetts
London, England

First MIT Press paperback edition, 1994

This book was set in Stone Serif and Stone Sans by .eps Electronic Publishing Services and was printed and bound in the United States of America.

Library of Congress Cataloging-in-Publication Data

Global networks : computers and international communication / edited by
  Linda M. Harasim
     p. cm.
  Includes bibliographical references and index.
  ISBN 0-262-08222-5 (HB), 0-262-58137-X (PB)
    1. Wide area networks (Computer networks)—Social aspects. 2. Telematics.
3. Computers and civilization. I. Harasim, Linda M. (Linda Marie), 1949– .
TK5105.87.G57 1993
303.48′33—dc20   92-47473
                                                                                        CIP

For Tanikka and Tasya

Contents

Preface

Global networks are increasingly a part of our work and social life today. To illuminate and guide our participation in this process of transformation, this book examines global networking from a multiplicity of viewpoints: social, educational, political, and work-related. The interdisciplinary nature of the book is itself a networking of themes, analyzing the subject from diverse but interrelated perspectives. The contributors to this volume, all experts in their fields, provide timely and critical analyses of networking from different disciplines as well as from different geographic viewpoints: North America, South America, Asia, Africa, Australia, and Europe.

At another level, the book is a testament to global networking, since the process of producing it involved networking the contributors over a period of four months in what came to be known as the GAN: the Global Authoring Network. The GAN used computer networks to link contributors in a group review of each chapter (see chap. 21 by Harasim and Walls for a discussion of the process). The networkers were networked. New linkages and connectivities among networking theorists and practitioners were established.

I thank the contributors to this volume, who shared their ideas, research, and expertise as well as their commitment to a vision of how global networking can make the world a better place. It has been a pleasure to work with you, to learn from you, and to have your contributions in this volume. The process of networking with the chapter authors on the GAN contributed to enhancing our unity of purpose and vision for the book as well as enhancing the sense of the personalities behind the chapters. It was a lot of work, but there were many good times as our conversations on the network brought smiles, laughs, and new insights. Through our network interactions, the book came alive. I especially thank Jan Walls, an enthusiastic supporter of the book and the GAN from the outset. For those authors unable to participate on the GAN, I had the opportunity and pleasure of working with you using a variety of new communication media that enabled significant dialogue between us about the book.

In addition to the chapter authors, the GAN benefited from the participation of Bobbi Smith who assisted me in organizing the GAN and who took an active role in discussing the chapters; from Ian Chunn who helped to launch the GAN and also took part in the discussions; from the participation of Jon Boede, Grete Pasch, and Tracy LaQuey Parker; and from students in my graduate class who discussed many of the chapters in our online seminars (Bruce Girard, Neil Guy, Betty Laughy, Michael Hayward, Jane Mackay, Cyndia Pilkington, and David Smith).

I am grateful for the assistance of Stephen Buckley: his word processing skills, his commitment to this project, and his facility in global networking made him a much valued part of the team. I also owe many thanks to Bob Prior, Sandra Minkkinen, Lorrie LeJeune, and Beth LaFortune Gies of the MIT Press for their interest in this book and their valuable editorial guidance.

Finally, I thank my personal network who supported me through the process of initiating, implementing, and completing this book: my mother, Mary Harasim, and my grandmother, Katherine Myronyk, who were always a source of encouragement; Luiza Leite who helped keep my life organized; and especially my husband, Lucio, and my two daughters, Tanikka and Tasya, my most important sources of inspiration.

I   *Overview*

1 Global Networks: An Introduction

Linda M. Harasim

> . . . after more than a century of electronic technology, we have extended our central nervous system itself in a global embrace, abolishing both space and time as far as our planet is concerned.
> —Marshall McLuhan, *Understanding Media*

Global networks are communication networks, media that connect people with other people. Historically, the introduction of new communication tools has transformed humanity. From the development of oral language to literacy, print, and now telecommunications, communication technologies have opened new doors for human contact and new avenues for social, intellectual, economic, and political growth. Global networks, the use of computers for international communication, will further enhance and expand how humans connect, communicate, and create community.

McLuhan foresaw global connectivity decades ago. But whereas the broadcast media of McLuhan's time and vision implied populations of passive consumers, today's computer communication networks enable communities of active participants. Global networks are not only tools but offer a venue for the global village, a matrix where the world can meet. The extension of human community onto a global scale is unprecedented; we are challenged to understand the scope and implications of such powerful social transformations in order to take part in shaping, socializing, and ensuring the accessibility of networks for the global community.

Global Networks addresses that challenge. As one of the first books to explore this new social phenomenon, *Global Networks* presents the most current thinking and practice by leaders in the field. *Global Net-*

works examines the state of the art from different international and interdisciplinary perspectives. The authors explore how the internationalization of electronic network infrastructure fits into a context of global social networking. The focus is not on the technology per se, but on issues related to its social adoption, application, impact and future.

Global Networks looks at how technology becomes a social space, considers the kind of space it can and ought to become, and debates the issues and implications that attend the reinvention of social connectivity in a new realm. Perspectives from communication theory, network design, policy, social science, education, organizational theory, linguistics, and computer science explore the human side of network environments.

This book is an invitation to learn about and become involved in the new realm of human communication and community on global networks.

Historical Context

The past 150 years have brought fundamental and rapid transformation of society by communication technologies. In this brief time span, major innovations that radically changed how humans communicate have become integrated into our daily reality. Telecommunications are a fundamental component of political, economic, and personal life today. Yet, until recently human encounter was place-dependent. Communication across distance was only possible by such technologies as talking drums or smoke signals, relatively immediate but limited to messages that were terse and susceptible to error. More detail and accuracy could be conveyed by messengers traveling by foot, boat, horse, or other beast of burden.

Messages from distant locations could take weeks or years to arrive and were used to communicate affairs of state, nobility, church, and commerce. These communication forms were not interactive and not available to common people. The voyages of Marco Polo, conveying letters from the Church of Rome to the Emperor of China, took decades. Transmission of messages was very slow and expensive even up to 150 years ago. As Arthur C. Clarke noted: "When Queen Victoria came to the throne in 1837, she had no swifter means of sending messages to the far parts of her empire than had Julius Caesar—or, for that matter, Moses. . . . The galloping horse and the sailing ship remained the swiftest means of transport, as they had for five thousand years" (Clarke, 1992, 3–4).

The events of the telecommunication revolution have come together within a few years and with tremendous societal implications. In the 1840s, the first steps of change arrived with the introduction of the telegraph (assisted by the development of the Morse code in 1844). In 1875, Alexander Graham Bell invented the telephone. It was only in 1956 that the first submarine telephone cable was laid successfully. The first telecommunications satellite was in 1960, a balloon; it was only in 1962 that the first efficient civil telecommunications satellite, Telstar, was launched into orbit. The lightwave (or fiber optic) communications system was first utilized in 1977.

The foundations of global networking are thus recent, astonishingly so given the degree of the transformations that have been adopted and integrated so intimately into the fiber of humanity. The ability to make and receive a long-distance telephone call is now possible for people in most parts of the planet, and for many it is considered an essential service, perhaps a basic right.

Global networking is another dimension of change, opportunity, and challenge. The first large-scale packet switched network, the ARPANET, was implemented in 1969, and electronic mail on the network soon followed. Now, little more than two decades later, global networks link millions of users around the planet, and the rate of adoption is growing dramatically.

For participants of global networks, these technologies are already as integral to their work and community as the telephone and the postal service, and perhaps more so. Even our language and ways to express human interaction are changing to reflect the new realms of experience enabled by computer networking. It has become necessary to coin such terms as face-to-face (f2f or f-t-f), awkward as they are, to distinguish real-time, real-place meetings from those held on the network, also known as "online" or in "cyberspace." Mail sent electronically, "email," is wryly distinguished from "snail mail," regular postal delivery.

What are the technologies that form today's global networks?

Global networks are based upon systems such as electronic mail, bulletin boards, and computer conferencing, interconnecting users locally, regionally, and globally for business, research, education, and social interaction.

Here is a brief introduction to the networking technologies discussed in *Global Networks:* electronic mail, computer conferencing, and televirtuality.

Electronic Mail

Electronic mail (or email) on computer networks has in its history of little over two decades laid the basis for global connectivity. This feat has been accomplished with the most modest of means: using computers to exchange place-independent, asynchronous, text-based messages. Electronic mail systems support one-to-one (personal) and one-to-many (broadcast) communication. User groups and bulletin board services support group communication. Using a personal computer and modem linked by a telephone line to a computer network, people send and receive messages across the hallway or across the planet.

Today electronic mail networks reach millions of people, at their offices, in their classrooms, at home, or on the road via portable computers. While many offices have local area networks (LANs) for messaging among employees in the same workplace, these are increasingly linked to the wide area networks (WANs), the basis for global networks.

A global network is an interconnection of many smaller email networks. The main global networks referred to in this book are: Internet, BITNET, USENET, FidoNet, and AT&T Mail. The first four are sometimes referred to as forming a *matrix,* Latin for mother.

Internet is a meganetwork, a network of networks connecting over two thousand smaller networks. The Internet provides access to email, bulletin boards, databases, library catalogues, chat lines, multiuser domains, discussion groups, and, for scientists and researchers, access to supercomputers. BITNET (Because It's Time Network) connects academic institutions in over thirty countries and offers mailing lists (discussion groups on various topics), email, and short real-time interactions. USENET (User's Network) is a series of *newsgroups* or discussion groups supported by a worldwide voluntary member network, with approximately 37,000 nodes in universities, government, business, and military sites (some commercial services and FidoNet bulletin boards also carry the newsgroups). FidoNet has been called the "people's network" because it is open to anyone and usually carries no fee. FidoNet consists of over twenty thousand individual bulletin boards connected across six continents, to facilitate private email, public conferences (group discussions), and file transfers. AT&T Mail is a worldwide, commercial email service that connects subscribers to each other and to the USENET/UUCP network.

Computer Conferencing

Computer conferencing systems are based on communication software specifically designed to facilitate collaboration among all sizes of groups, from two-person dialogues to conferences with hundreds or thousands of participants. People can join conferences on topics of personal interest; all messages to that conference are organized and stored sequentially in one's inbox. The system coordinates the messages. The term "computer conference" is used in the book as a generic descriptor of a type of communication networking software, distinct from user groups on email systems.

Computer conferencing systems provide groups with spaces or conferences that can be tailored to their needs. The tailoring of group communication structures is an important element in creating a particular social system, enabling the shaping and definition of the social space. Specific spaces can be organized by group membership and topic.

Computer conferencing systems, like electronic mail networks, are text-based. Multimedia communication networks combining text, graphics, scanned images, audio and/or video are becoming available. Ishii (chap. 8) describes issues in developing one, and the use of hypermedia networks for new forms of social organization is addressed by Kumon and Aizu (chap. 19).

Televirtuality

Of all forms of networks, perhaps the one to most fire our imaginations with the possibility of engaging the whole person is virtual reality (VR). VR offers the possibility of building and entering a customized three-dimensional environment in which the user is enveloped in a surrogate reality.

The use of VR for entertainment or work demands extraordinarily high data capacity to carry the video and graphic signals. And, most of the experimental work on VR networking or televirtuality involves digital pipelines to carry the data. Televirtuality, the ability to share a three-dimensional environment over a telecommunications network, is still in the experimental stages. But as Jacobson (chap. 20) observes, the technical challenges, however daunting, are more easily resolved than the social challenges that attend televirtuality.

The Global Village: Concepts and Prophets

Concepts of global networking have been around for some time. The most popular sources of discussion have circulated around the term "global villagization."

The term "global village" was coined in the 1960s by Marshall McLuhan, a University of Toronto professor. Adoption of the term, like the global technologies themselves, has spread worldwide. Yet McLuhan was not the first to contemplate human interconnectivity on a global scale. McLuhan attributed the inspiration for his term to Nathaniel Hawthorne, who in 1851 had written:

Is it a fact . . . that, by means of electricity, the world of matter has become a great nerve, vibrating thousands of miles in a breathless point of time? Rather, the round globe is a vast head, a brain, instinct with intelligence! Or, shall we say, it is itself a thought, nothing but thought, and no longer the substance which we deemed it! (Hawthorne, *The House of the Seven Gables*)

The possibility of the interconnected world raises the fundamental question: what kind of world will the global village offer? One of the major themes that emerged in literary texts considering this scenario is that of cultural consolidation and, ultimately, homogenization. In 1925 Aldous Huxley presented the following exchange in *Those Barren Leaves:*

"It's comforting to think," said Chelifer, "that modern civilisation is doing its best to re-establish the tribal regime, but on an enormous, national and even international scale. Cheap print, wireless telephones, trains, motor cars, gramophones and all the rest are making it possible to consolidate tribes, not of a few thousands, but of millions. . . . In a few generations it may be that the whole planet will be covered by one vast American-speaking tribe, composed of innumerable individuals, all thinking and acting in exactly the same way, like the characters in a novel by Sinclair Lewis . . ."

Cyberspace, a term coined by science fiction writer William Gibson, connotes a future world mediated by computer networks, with direct and total access—mental and sensorial—to a parallel world of pure digitized information and communication.

Cyberspace. A consensual hallucination experienced daily by billions of legitimate operators, in every nation. . . . A graphic representation of data abstracted from the banks of every computer in the human system. Unthinkable complexity. Lines of light ranged in the nonspace of the mind, clusters and constellations of data. Like city lights, receding . . ." (1984, 51)

The challenges of a global future were not lost on these early literary explorers. What were the implications of life in a global village? Especially if that global village were on a network?

These challenges, and more, are being confronted by the first wave of travelers and settlers in the global networks.

Organization of This Book

Global Networks explores the new realms of the global network worlds and considers issues involved in socializing and globalizing cyberspace. The major theme weaving through the book is global networks as a social space, shaped for and by human communication and community.

Global Networks is organized along four perspectives:

1. Overview: From Technology to Community

2. Issues in Globalizing Networks

3. Applications of Global Networking

4. Visions for the Future

Part 1: Overview: From Technology to Community

The first part of the book, the Overview, introduces and examines the social nature of global networks. Chapters in the Overview section look at networlds and network communities to explore human interaction on the networks as technology becomes community.

Chapter 2, by Linda Harasim, launches the theme of social relationships on the networks. Computer networks have become new environments or networlds for business, educational, and social communication. The key questions addressed are what kind of communication does the network support and how can the network be shaped to enhance and improve human communication? Attention is paid to both the need to shape the internal contours of the networlds as well as the importance of developing informed social policy governing the global use of networks.

Chapter 3, by John Quarterman, examines how technology becomes community. As Quarterman argues, networks are not just technology. Faster networks lead to new services, then new uses, then communities. These communities cross national, organizational, and time boundaries, forming global matrices of people facilitated by the global Matrix. This chapter discusses aspects of the history and near future of selected international networks (the ARPANET, the Internet, UUCP, USENET, and BITNET) to illustrate patterns of globalization.

The final chapter of the Overview section is a personal tour of life in one networld community, the WELL. Howard Rheingold describes the WELL as a community not of common location but of common interest, in which the people with whom one interacts most strongly are selected more by commonality of interests and goals than by geographical proximity. Chapter 4 presents an insider's view of life on the WELL and identifies issues that both enhance as well as challenge community life in virtual space.

Part 2: Issues in Globalizing Networks

In part 2, issues related to policy, organizational communication, and cross-cultural communication are explored from several perspectives.

In chapter 5, Anne Branscomb identifies key questions encountered in drawing proprietary boundaries within electronic space, establishing legal jurisdictions, and applying legal and regulatory schemes that are appropriate for the new legal frontiers. The chapter presents contemporary cases and discusses the numerous efforts underway to harmonize national laws with global networks.

Chapter 6, by Lee Sproull and Sara Kiesler, focuses on the impacts and implications of global networks on work. Electronic interactions differ significantly from face-to-face exchanges. The implications for the structure of organizations and the conduct of work is profound. This chapter considers how computer networks can affect the nature of work and the relationships between managers and employees in order to help people better exploit the opportunities that networks offer and to avoid or mitigate the potential pitfalls of networked organizations.

In chapter 7, Marvin Manheim focuses on how an organization can use information technology to gain competitive advantage in an era of globalization. The chapter presents several hypotheses about critical issues facing globally competing companies and concludes that systems designed to support teams working on critical tasks will have the greatest strategic return to a globally competing company. An approach to designed and implemented task-focused, team-specific systems is outlined.

In chapter 8, Hiroshi Ishii presents the case of the importance of cultural issues in the design of computer networking tools. Tools designed for Computer-Supported Cooperative Work (CSCW), Ishii argues, should be viewed as cultural tools as well as computer tools. This chapter describes differences in social protocols between two cultures, American and Japanese, in decision making processes and face-to-face meetings and the implications of cross-cultural issues for groupware design and CSCW research to facilitate global communication and cooperative work.

The cultural nature of communication and relationships in a global network is further explored by Jan Walls in chapter 9. As Walls notes, shared sociolinguistic experience creates and reinforces shared expectations in interpersonal communication (most often intracultural), including shared language and discourse habits. The chapter explores what happens when globalizing networks bring together people whose discourse habits and expectations have been created by different (i.e., cross-cultural) socio-linguistic experience.

Chapter 10, by Michael Kirby and Catherine Murray, examines the opportunities global networks provide for new assaults on data security, which will require international initiatives to harmonize national laws. Various principles to be recommended in the upcoming OECD (Organization for Economic Cooperation and Development) *Guidelines on Information Security* are discussed. But the thesis of the chapter is that we remain at risk—less from illegitimate intrusions into data security than from the frailty of international institutions and incapacity of democratic processes to keep pace with the social implications of technology.

Part 3: Applications of Global Networking

Part 3 presents and analyzes case studies of practical experiences. The contributors to this section are all pioneers in global networking and present their experiences within a framework that can provide lessons for other organizations in implementing their own networking ventures.

In chapter 11, Andrew Feenberg describes a pioneering venture as the basis for identifying lessons for future applications. In the ten years of its activity in global networking, the Western Behavioral Sciences Institute built a community of executives from twenty-one countries. Feenberg generalizes from the history of the WBSI to explain how other organizations can proceed in building similar networks.

Chapter 12, by Robin Mason, looks at the role of networking in facilitating the creation of the "European village." The European Commission is funding a wide variety of projects using computer conferencing, an initiative that has lent support to private and institutional applications of the medium in training, education, and business communication. This chapter provides a general overview of the phenomenal growth of electronic networking in Europe, illustrated by examples of networking activities to illuminate particular European issues.

Chapter 13, by Margaret Riel, presents a case and a model for global networking in the classroom. Learning circles on the AT&T Learning Network provide an instructional strategy for global education. Students use communication technology to work with their counterparts in distant locations. This chapter describes how learning circles address the objectives of global education and what students in elementary and secondary schools are able to accomplish using a globalizing communication technology embedded in an educational program.

In chapter 14, Beryl Bellman, Alex Tindimubona, and Armando Arias, Jr. describe a globalized computer network that combines computer conferencing, videotex, electronic mail, and computer phone to create a distributed educational, scientific, and social development research network linking universities in North America, Latin America, and Africa. The chapter explores issues in the building of a sustainable network combining academic, social development, and commercial interests and support.

Jeffrey Shapard, in chapter 15, notes that Japan is a nation of islands, natural as well as electronic. Shapard's chapter explores the relationship of language and character codes with isolation on computer systems and networks in Japan. The issues raised have significance for other languages that require character codes that are not compatible with current international standards, and implications for global networks.

Chapter 16, by Lucio Teles, looks at learning through interaction with computer-mediated peers, mentors, and experts, using global networks and conferencing systems. Global networks introduce new opportunities and issues for learning on a global scale, which should be taken into account by instructional designers. Two approaches to cognitive apprenticeship on networks are illustrated and elaborated through case studies.

In chapter 17, Howard Frederick presents the case for the emergence of global civil society, accelerated by decentralized communication technologies such as computer networking. Global civil society as represented by the nongovernmental movement is now a force in international relations in the cause of peace, human rights, and the environmental movement. This chapter outlines the concepts of global civil society and the NGO Movement, describes the obstacles that they face, and sketches the emergence of the APC network as an illustration of this worldwide phenomenon.

Part 4: Visions for the Future

Based on experiences in communication networking, where are we headed, and what concepts, goals, and concerns should guide us? The final four chapters set out their visions of the next steps.

In chapter 18, Mitchell Kapor and Daniel Weitzner suggest that while our society has made a commitment to openness and free communication, if our legal and social institutions fail to adapt to new technology, basic access to the global electronic media could be seen as a privilege granted to those who play by the strictest rules, rather than a right for anyone who needs to communicate. The authors set out their vision for the development of the International Public Network (IPN), an interconnected confederation of numerous networks that will form the main channels for commerce, learning, education, and entertainment in a global society. This chapter looks at lessons from the Internet as a testbed for developing public policy to guide the development of the IPN as a ubiquitous global network for the future.

In chapter 19, Shumpei Kumon and Izumi Aizu present a case for co-emulation as a strategy for developing a global hypernetwork society of the future. Co-emulation is a response to the information age whereby nations learn from one another to produce a prototype socio-economic model that each country can mold to fit its unique history and culture. Global networks can enable the sharing of collective goals and relevant information among their members and making collective decisions by means of consensus formation. Co-emulation offers a strategy for nations to move beyond competitive relationships into more consensual and reciprocal relationships to meet the social, economic, and environmental challenges of the twenty-first century.

Chapter 20, by Robert Jacobson, considers life in cyberspace for the network traveler. A person's ability in the virtual world to transcend time and space, to be anywhere, anytime, with anyone, is the principal attraction of virtual worlds technology. But throughout human experience transcendence has been a tricky business, leading to greater awareness or insanity. This chapter considers the possibilities and challenges of virtual cyberspace, such as training and individual effort to enter and master this environment.

Chapter 21, by Linda Harasim and Jan Walls, concludes with a look at the role of global networking in creating this book and the lessons of this experience for future global networks.

2   *Networlds: Networks as Social Space*

Linda M. Harasim

The fusion of computers and telecommunications over the past twenty years has created a worldwide web of computer networks; these networks, initially established for transferring data, have been adopted by people who want to communicate with other people. Human communication has become the major use of computer networks and has transformed them into a social space where people connect with one another. Computer networks are not merely tools whereby we network; they have come to be experienced as *places* where we network: a networld.

The computer screen is a window to this world, "accessed through any computer linked into the system; a place, one place, limitless; entered equally from a basement in Vancouver, a boat in Port-au-Prince, a cab in New York, a garage in Texas City, an apartment in Rome, an office in Hong Kong . . ." (Benedikt, 1991, 1).

"It feels like walking into a room full of friends . . ."[1]

"You have electronic mail waiting." Every morning . . . networks deliver messages to me from all over the world. Sometimes they are news, sometimes season's greetings, and sometimes business contracts and scripts. You are connected to the entire world using networks.[2]

The range and speed of computer networks has increased at a phenomenal rate, reaching tens of millions of personal computer users at home and at work, across globally connected telephone lines. Tools such as electronic mail, bulletin boards, and computer conferencing facilitate group communication across time and space. Groups can now socialize and work together regardless of different locations or schedules.

Computer networking does not replace other forms of human communication; it increases our range of human connectedness and the number of ways in which we are able to make contact with others. Historically, changes in the means of communication—from speech to writing to the printing press—have transformed human development and society. Technological change, writes Zuboff (1988), defines the horizon of our material world as it shapes the limiting conditions of what is possible and what is barely imaginable. New opportunities are opened, others are closed, augmenting and changing our material world and our relation to and within it. As a technological innovation and a social construct, global networks impact the ways in which we communicate, with transformative implications for how we form community, how we work, and how we learn.

This chapter looks at the kinds of worlds opened up by computer networks and considers such issues as: What kinds of social spaces do networks offer? What happens to communication mediated by networking? What critical issues need to be addressed in socializing networks into new environments for human communication? The chapter describes the new social spaces for human interaction available in the networld and examines how these spaces affect communication. The chapter ends by discussing issues in socializing and democratizing communication in the networld.

Networks as Place

Computer networking is, for many, already an integral part of professional, business, intellectual, and social life. Millions of users around the world are linked by thousands of computer networks and the numbers are growing exponentially (see Quarterman, chap. 3). Increasingly, small local and national networks are linking with large international networks like the Internet to become nodes on a vast global web. Some networks are private, others are public; some charge a fee, others are free to users. Whatever the differences, users are beginning to have a common experience: networks are a social environment. They become a destination, a place to link with other people.

The network has become one of the places where people meet to do business, collaborate on a task, solve a problem, organize a project, engage in personal dialogue, or exchange social chitchat. We "go to work" on the network and "drop in" to an online conference. Comments such as "See you online!" or "Let's meet online" reflect the experience of the network as a place to conduct work or socialize. The phrase "I'm here" is common, expressing a sense of presence that links people on the network. Yet where is "here"? It is likely that the receiver of the message has no idea of the physical location of the sender: home, school, work, or on the road. "Here" has come to signify a virtual world on the network, shared with others, constituted by the group.

A world is defined as all that concerns or all who belong to a specified class, time, domain, or sphere of activity. What kind of "worlds" are available on global networks? Three main networlds are described: social networlds, networkplaces, and educational networlds.

Social Networlds

The social networlds that exist on *electronic mail networks* are vast and wide ranging. The Internet, for example, hosts thousands of distributed groups, linking universities, offices, schools, and homes on a diverse range of subjects. As one networker noted:

Internet is a sort of international cocktail party where you can talk to people from all over the world about all sorts of things that interest you.

It's informative. You need a piece of information? Post a question to the right group and you will get what you wanted and a dozen more related references. Also, sometimes information . . . just comes to you.

I've made very good friends on the nets. I've gotten friendship, inspiration, consolation in times of loss, support in times of self-doubt, information and just plain fun.

A second forum for social community occurs on *computer conferencing and bulletin board services*. These systems are often organized around metaphors that reflect human settlement and activities: townhalls, classrooms, villages, clubs, and shopping malls. Rheingold describes the networlds on the WELL as close-knit virtual communities with friendships, feuds, marriages, divorces, and funerals (see chap. 4). Conferences on the Japan-based TWICS system (discussed in chap. 17) are organized around geographic metaphors that evolved, according to Shapard (1992), from user input.

We . . . came up with this elaborate structure of three main structural topics— *mura* (village), *minato* (port), and *yama* (mountain)—from which other structural topics would branch, such as *yoriai* (public meeting hall) for topics of general interest to our members, *akihabara* (the name of the infamous Tokyo consumer electronics district) for techie topics, *sekai (*world) for ported topics and topics related to regions elsewhere, *onsen (*hot springs) for recreational topics, and *yakuba* (town office) for topics about system policy and so on. We used Japanese names for local flavor and to emphasize a sense of place, even though the community was and remains very multicultural, with Japanese and a range of other kinds of people.

A third form of social networlds is found on *commercial videotex systems,* which present information as a page of text-based message enhanced with simple graphics. The French government-owned videotex network, Teletel, has transformed France into a networked nation, providing a network gateway to over twelve thousand information services for about 20 percent of the households in France. Over five million users access information on theaters, movies, or restaurants; schedule airline and hotel reservations; order items from computerized catalogues; and chat with one another on the synchronous *messageries.* The Teletel network (also known as Minitel) is simple to use and has become integrated into the fabric of French life: holidays are planned and reservations booked online; the TV music channel solicits online input from viewers; and millions of users from all corners of France chat as neighbors on the network.

Commercial videotex networks exist in the United States as well. CompuServe is one of the oldest systems in the United States, first launched as an information service in 1979. By 1991, an estimated eight hundred thousand CompuServe users from over one hundred countries had access to fourteen hundred databases and services for shopping, travel, financial and news reports, games, and the most dynamic and popular part of the service—the group forums. Prodigy, GEnie, Delphi, America Online, and others offer similar online services and social meeting places.

Social communication accounts for a sizable portion of all network use. One recent survey among users of online (commercial) services found that of the respondents, primarily male professionals, two thirds used their computer and modem at home rather than in a conventional office (Rosenthal, 1992). Many of these also did work from home, since almost half (48 percent) utilized online business services. Over 80 percent, however, signed on to engage in social activities as well. The most popular online services were the bulletin boards or conferences. People talking with one another is the major use of all commercial service networks, and this survey reflected that reality. The survey showed that 79 percent used bulletin boards (or conferences) and 59 percent used email (email was used for business and personal uses). Other services were also popular: 48 percent of the respondents play online games; 32 percent shop electronically; 23 percent use airline reservations systems. Market research (23 percent) and media information (31 percent) were also widely used services. The respondents in this survey spent considerable time online: 42 percent spend six or more hours per week online, while 16 percent log more than fifteen hours online per week. For business uses, about $220 was spent per month, while the average personal user spent about $51 per month for services and transactions.

Networkplaces

The term "networkplace" is introduced here to describe the networld primarily devoted to work-related communication. For increasing numbers of business people and professionals, the networkplace is an integral part of how work is conducted. Networks make it possible for people to do information work effectively at locations remote from their managers, their coworkers, the people who report to them, and even from customers and clients with whom they must interact (Licklider and Vezza, 1988). For example, telework increasingly involves the use of networks to link the worker with the work; electronic cottage industries use networks to link producers with markets; networks are used by organizations to link employees with one another and with other sources of expertise and data resources. The network becomes a networkplace, enhancing and transforming how business and work are conducted.

Telework and telecommuting use networks to disperse assignments to workers in satellite and home offices. Teleworkers use networks to exchange work-related information with one another and employers, discuss and conduct joint tasks, interact with customers and clients, participate in meetings, and maintain social contact. Telework is increasingly attractive to companies struggling to reduce overhead, enhance productivity, and attract the best workers; to governments seeking ways to reduce overcrowding and pollution on highways and in urban centers; and to employees demanding alternatives to the stresses of commuting to distant centralized worksites and long absences from family and home. It can also enable gainful employment for people living in remote locations or who are housebound.

Global networks also facilitate new forms of entrepreneurship such as the "electronic cottage." A Japanese journalist describes working online:

> I decided to do some business online, because despite the extreme cost, the efficiency and information available online were worth more.
> You can live 'in the world' using CompuServe and other networks. I was born Japanese and I live in Japan. I can make many American and other global friends using online services. I am able to retrieve news and data from throughout the world. I am able to do business in America, online, without paying for air tickets. . . . You may easily understand that this globe is so small online. Friend after friend, business after business will visit you if you use networks. (Schepp and Schepp, 1990, 12)

Professionals such as academics, scientists, students, and researchers have adopted networking as an integral and in some cases principal work space. Knowledge workers use networks to collaborate with colleagues, access specific expertise, share information about current research, and generally sift, sort, and channel key information in the field (Hiltz, 1984; Greif, 1988; Galegher, Kraut, and Egido, 1990).

Businesses use networks to link employees and management in one or multiple sites, facilitating exchange of information and enabling teamwork among colleagues located in different parts of the country or the world. Manheim (chap. 7) describes how gains in productivity and competitive advantage are increasingly related to the use of global networks.

The new opportunities also bring new challenges. Ishii (chap. 8) notes that developing a global groupware tool is more a cultural than a technical task. The changing nature of work enabled by global network technologies raises organizational issues as well. Networking, as Sproull and Kiesler note in chapter 6, can change social relations: hierarchy and authority are shifted in favor of more decentralized, horizontal forms of organization. The design and implementation of a networkplace introduces issues such as whether networking brings increased monitoring over or increased control by the employees. The changes and opportunities for the organization of the future depend not only on the shape of the technology but also on how managers and users employ the opportunities that it offers for changing work structures.

Educational Networlds

As a result of over a decade of pioneering and visionary work by educators all over the planet, learners today can access virtual classrooms, online work groups, learning circles, peer networks, electronic campuses, and online libraries in a shared space, a networld, that connects people all over the globe (Harasim et al., 1994).

Educational networlds are a dynamic field of innovation and growth. In the United States alone, five million primary and secondary school students from about twenty thousand schools with as many as one hundred thousand teachers participate in local, national, and global network activities. Networks are used by educators in all parts of the world, and the number of users is growing rapidly, creating global classrooms and global campuses. Bellman, Tindimubona, and Arias, Jr. (chap. 14) describe the use of networks to link faculty, students, and researchers in American, Canadian, Latin American, and African universities for course delivery and collaborative projects.

Students in the networld engage in group learning projects with peers from other regions and countries; share ideas and resources; access information on current events or historical archives; and interact with experts, interviewing scientists or sending poems and short stories to peers and "electronic writers in residence." Techniques for teaching and learning are being reinvented and augmented through such approaches as cognitive apprenticeship (Teles, chap. 16) and learning circles (Riel, chap. 13). Networks amplify the range of learning experiences and solidify international linkages (Mason, chap. 12), expanding the range of resources that teachers and learners can access.

Teachers testify to the value of networlds for enhancing the learning options they can offer their students. And teachers find that they benefit as well from networking. The opportunity to interact with other teachers and to share ideas has resulted in teacher revitalization.

Educational networld applications are proliferating in universities, colleges, and distance education and training institutions as well. Adults can take credit courses at the college, university, or graduate school level, or participate in professional development, training, informal forums, or executive seminars that are offered entirely or partially online (see Feenberg, chap. 11).

Educational networlds introduce a new world of learning: the opportunity for interaction on any subject, with peers and experts from around the world; active participation in knowledge building and information sharing; and lifelong learning. Educational networlds promote the development of a learning society.

Human Communication in the Networld

Networlds are inhabited by a dynamic, diverse, and rapidly growing population, attracted by the new communication opportunities. Yet we know little about the nature of these opportunities and how the networking technology leads to specific advantages and disadvantages.

How does the mediation of computer networks affect human interaction and communication? What are the salient properties of the technology and how do they impact on the communication?

Networlds exist on many types of computer networks, and new ones based on high bandwidth multimedia systems are emerging. However, most networlds today use email, bulletin board, or computer conferencing systems that support communication that occurs by exchanging anyplace, anytime (asynchronous), text-based, computer-mediated messages between two or more people. These attributes provide a framework for understanding the nature of communication on the networld and the opportunities and constraints currently available to shape the network into a networld (Harasim, 1990). The framework below presents the most common attributes.

Anyplace Communication

Networlds are distinguished by place-independent communication, expanding the human neighborhood to global proportions. Networlds enable people to socialize, work, and learn based on who they are rather than where they are located. People have more choice.

Anyplace communication transcends geographic barriers to enable people to access the people and resources they need, regardless of where they are located. Global networking is made increasingly mobile and available anyplace with the advent of cellular and satellite technologies.

Networlds especially enhance access to those who might be hindered for reasons such as geographic remoteness, age, physical disability, or family or work responsibilities. Place-independence empowers otherwise isolated people by providing them with access to other people as well as to resources that they need to accomplish their goals. "Conventional media (particularly informal/unscheduled meetings) tend to disadvantage those physically distant from the central locus of work; by contrast, electronic media allow direct access to that locus irrespective of physical distance" (Bikson and Eveland, 1990, 286).

Global networks enable new social relationships such as global work groups. Networks are a fast, low-cost alternative to surface mail and overcome the expense and inconvenience of travel. In addition, employees in networked organizations report that the introduction of electronic mail gave them a new sense of the company as a whole and developed feelings of belonging to an organization that felt increasingly familiar and accessible (Zuboff, 1988).

Educational networks provide learners and educators with global access to expertise and learning resources beyond what is available in the local classroom, textbook, or library: students are able to link with teachers, experts and peers in all corners of the world to enhance regular classroom activities or for taking courses entirely online.

Global networks enrich our experience and knowledge options but also introduce new and complex issues. Cultural, linguistic, and political factors in global conversations can confound our ability to establish the meaningfulness of the discourse. Place-independence challenges many habits and customs of interpersonal and group communication.

Anytime Communication

Most networlds are based on asynchronous, not real-time, communication. The millions of messages that cross the globe each day testify to the power of overcoming time zones and personal schedules for enabling active communication.

Asynchronicity offers many advantages for conversations in the networld. The major benefit is the increased user control: the sender and the receiver don't have to be available at the same time. Networlds are always open, twenty-four hours a day, seven days a week. High-speed information exchange can reduce the time and work involved in distributing information among group members. Work can be discussed and the individuals can get on with their job, without the need for extensive coordination of personal schedules and delays in waiting for the next face-to-face meeting.

Active participation in decision making and knowledge building is facilitated by the fact that airtime is not limited and thus not as easily controlled by a few individuals. People who prefer or require more time to provide input find asynchronicity an advantage over real-time face-to-face situations. Analysis of interaction in educational networks (university courses) has shown that most students contribute actively and that the distribution of communication (the volume of input) is spread quite evenly among all the students (Harasim, 1987; 1989; 1991).

Participants can take time to formulate their ideas into a more composed and thoughtful response, contributing to improved quality of communication. This attribute is especially advantageous for educational and business networld activities, but, it is also important in the social networld, where the time to reflect before responding can enhance the exchange.

There are also constraints to asynchronous communication. Communication anxiety is reported by people who receive no response or at least no immediate reply to their message (see Feenberg, chap. 11). Moreover, the lack of immediate feedback makes it difficult to ascertain whether the receiver has understood the message; people find they are not as easily able to tailor their communication to be readily understandable (Finholt, Sproull, and Kiesler, 1991, 295).

Certain types of interactions, especially those associated with urgent or tight timelines, can be negatively affected. Asynchronous communication involves unpredictable and sometimes extensive lags in feedback. Real-time communication may be more appropriate to situations requiring immediate response. Processes of negotiation are extended within asynchronous environments. Research has found that the time required to achieve consensus is prolonged, but more people have provided input and minority views are voiced more often than in face-to-face situations (Rice, 1984).

Group Interactivity

Networlds provide new ways to meet people. Online, people can establish communication on the basis of shared interest, not merely shared geography. Posting a comment or question in the networld invites response and feedback, often generating consultation and multiple perspectives on a topic. We receive not only a response to our message, but in the process meet someone with similar interests. Global networks provide links to trusted sources and to new contacts.

The social and intellectual isolation that characterized human history has been reduced only with the advent of new communication technologies, from literacy and the printing press to the telegraph, newspapers, the telephone, and now increasingly, computer networking. Group interactivity distinguishes networks and creates the basis for networlds. Unlike broadcast media such as television, radio, or newspapers—which are noninteractive, one-way media involving passive receipt of information—in the networld people can act directly to question, probe, or elaborate on any piece of information that is posted. Different perspectives on an issue are generated and shared; the multilogue of the networld can provide a fuller picture. Moreover, group discussion and shared experience are powerful forces toward creating broad understanding.

Group interaction can be more evenly distributed in the networlds. Networlds do not eliminate domination by more vocal participants, but what is new is that dominance by a few doesn't exclude the ability of others to have their say. Yet, managing conversations within a global group can be daunting. Active participation and interaction can create information overload, and few information management tools are as yet available. While active participation in group activities offers important cognitive and social benefits for all participants, some tasks may become unwieldy without organization of the individual input.

Computer Mediation

Most networlds today are mediated by text-based messaging and the computer; multimedia telecommunication systems are not yet widely available. Nonetheless, text-based communication does offer important benefits for establishing meaningful and effective conversation.

Text-based messaging creates a new form of interpersonal interaction with advantages over postal mail, telephone calls, and even face-to-face encounters. It is at once direct while informal—enabling effective and efficient yet nonoffensive communication. Email messages have not become associated with the formality of letters; informality and imperfect typing are tolerated even in messages to an older person in a superior position or to a person one does not know well (Licklider and Vezza, 1988, 147).

Text-only communication can free people from the bonds of physical appearance and enable communication at the level of ideas. For example, in face-to-face situations physical and social status cues extend authority and influence over others. Cues such as dress, presentation, voice intonation, and seating arrangement denote power, leading to unequal communication between people. In the networld "status, power, and prestige are communicated neither contextually (the way secretaries and meeting rooms and clothes communicate) nor dynamically (the way gaze, touch, and facial paralinguistic behavior communicate)" (Kiesler, Siegel, and McGuire, 1991). Communication in the networld is "blind" to vertical hierarchy in social relationships (ibid.). Charisma, status, and other physical cues associated with appearance and presentation have less influence because they cannot be (easily) communicated electronically.

Text-based messaging benefits people who may not have a "voice" in face-to-face situations (i.e., due to discrimination based on cues associated with gender, ethnicity, race, age, socioeconomic status, or physical appearance). Bellman, Tindimubona, and Arias, Jr. (chap. 14) report that anonymity provided by the text-based interface of computer conferencing empowered Latin American female students to be active and to argue and debate with their classmates, whereas in the face-to-face classes they remained silent. For many people, the opportunity to formulate (and edit) their messages improves their confidence and communication skills.

Intellectual and social benefits are associated with text-based communication (Harasim, 1990). Traditional education is based on textbooks, lectures, and written assignments; interactive text-based messaging offers additional advantages to learners. Students can improve their writing, reading, and analytical skills online. The text-based nature of networlds requires that to be present students must "say something," send a message about the topic. Sending a message involves formulating and articulating an idea or comment, a cognitive act. Feedback to that message stimulates further consideration of the message. Discussion and interaction on the ideas often motivates the sender to either refine and expand the ideas or to correct or abandon them.

There is, moreover, a preservable record of the discussion: messages are stored on the computer and hence can be reread and reflected upon. A group memory is created. Asynchronous text-based conversation facilitates thoughtful consideration and review of messages and careful formulation of responses. The text-based nature of the communication enables users to observe each other's contributions, enhancing group learning and group maintenance.

People new to network communication may imagine a world of cold and impersonal messages, unable to convey emotion. Yet those in the networld point to the power of prose for expressing and releasing strong emotions (see Rheingold, chap. 4). Ingenuity in overcoming the mechanical constraints of the medium has also led to the creation of a range of symbols, called "smileys," such as the happy face :-) to express emotions. Nonetheless, difficulties in establishing intent do occur—attempts at irony or sarcasm can be misunderstood. The reduced cues in text-based messages make it difficult to resolve conflicts of ideology or interest (Finholt, Sproull, and Kiesler, 1990).

Establishing authenticity is also difficult online, especially in groups with little prior affiliation. There are many well-publicized stories and folklore about people who created entirely new persona online. The reaction to these cases is mixed: some people view them as impostors, others as explorers or seekers. Van Gelder (1991) reports the case of a man who used the network to play out assumptions about gender roles. In real life he was a psychiatrist; on the network he presented himself as a female neuropsychologist, "Joan," who had recently been severely disfigured in a car accident that had affected her speech and her ability to walk. Over the two years that Joan was online, she became a "monumental on-line presence who served both as a support for other disabled women and as an inspiring stereotype-smasher to the able-bodied. Through her many intense friendships and (in some cases) her online romances, she changed the lives of dozens of women" (ibid., 365).

Eventually it was revealed that Joan was not only not disabled, but that she was a he—"a prominent New York psychiatrist in his early fifties who was engaged in a bizarre, all-consuming experiment to see what it felt like to be female, and to experience the intimacy of female friendship" (ibid.). The response to this revelation was intense: many felt betrayed and outraged. Others wished to continue a friendship with the person, "to relate to the soul, not the sex of the person" (ibid.).

Computer cross-dressing and use of persona are condoned or even encouraged in certain networlds, such as those devoted to games and role plays. Anonymity or noms de plume have also been used in education and business to encourage frank response or unbiased exchange. Other networlds discourage anonymity or pen names. As Rheingold (chap. 4) notes, anonymity is not permitted on the WELL. The norms of the WELL are that "you own your own words."

The advent of video conferencing in networlds may help to alleviate identity problems, although a related medium—televirtuality—promises to further complicate how we establish authenticity and sincerity in networld conversations.

The mediation of the computer thus transforms communication options; the features discussed above combine to provide new and unprecedented forms of human interaction. The ability of the computer to store and process data augments our communication and intellectual skills and extends our reach and opportunities for human community. New tools such as word processing, spell checkers, spreadsheets, databases, intelligent agents (knowbots), hypertextual information managers, and supports for group decision making and knowledge building can enhance the quality of communication processes.

The mediation of the computer also promises more sophisticated networld environments, with increased bandwidth involving multimedia (see Kumon and Aizu, chap. 19) and televirtual systems (see Jacobson, chap. 20).

Socializing the Networld: Shaping Networks into Networlds

Technological features do not assure effective communication, and technical linkage alone does not create community. While the attributes of the networks enable significant advantages for human communication, they are not a guarantee. The creation of networlds requires human intervention in organizing the technology and in shaping the human interactions to make the promise a satisfying and effective reality.

Lessons gained over the past two decades of experience in network communication highlight the importance of designing the environment. Networlds are the intersection of social and technical systems; design involves both technical and social considerations. The networking technologies used to create networlds are, to use the classification of Galegher and Kraut (1990), permissive systems. These open spaces enable and require social shaping by users for the most effective and satisfying results.

As several authors in this volume describe, organizing group interactions online can make text-based messages feel and function like a meeting, a learning circle, or a cafe—transforming inhospitable message systems into a vibrant social community, a business team that functions effectively, a graduate seminar, or a group of people conducting a task. There is a purpose, a place, and a population.

Purpose: Task Structures

Tasks or activities in networlds are typically structured around a goal, an agenda, and a timeline. The purpose may be loosely formulated, as in an ongoing public conference for sharing jokes, or it may be tightly defined, as in accomplishing a specific task within a defined time period.

A networld involves organizing the activities so as to demarcate that group/task from others on the network. In this way, networlds suggest the experience of "doing something," with a certain population or group—be it shopping in an electronic mall open to the public or socializing with an intimate gathering.

Place: Spatial Structures

Definition of topics with specific purposes and memberships creates the sense of place on the network. An online classroom, for example, involves a structured environment, with different conferences for different activities: a seminar "room," a student "cafe," a resource "library," and a "help" line (Harasim et al., 1994). Group membership might be different in each space, as might the scheduling. Some spaces, such as the cafe, could be open to all students for the semester while others, such as a seminar room, would be open only to those students registered, and the seminar spaces would change weekly or according to some schedule for each new topic.

Early, satisfying, and productive adoption of networlds for work or play is related to familiarity. Metaphors provide familiarity and serve as navigational and cognitive aids, helping to organize the interactions and set participant expectations. To help us navigate around the maze more effectively, many networlds are organized around metaphors drawn from human settlements (offices, malls, campuses, cafes) and social structures (groups, meetings, seminars, parties). Choosing a particular topic takes the user to a virtual space filled with activities, information, or access to products and services.

Moreover metaphors convey what is socially appropriate: an online cafe or shopping mall carries the implicit convention of dropping in at one's own convenience or pleasure, whereas participants in an online graduate seminar or weekly business meeting recognize that a different code of behavior is expected.

Population: Group Roles

Group structure involves the definition of roles and responsibilities of the members of the group. Two roles are most common in the networld: the moderator and the participant. Moderators have rights and responsibilities distinct from the other participants. Moderators create the conference, establish membership, and may assist in maintaining the communication focus and flows.

The degree of moderator involvement varies, largely according to the nature of the activity. Social networks with loose affiliations such as mailing lists on recreational topics may involve little moderation beyond sponsoring the topic, administering the membership lists, and setting some social norms. Anyone can join, and participants can read or participate to the degree that they wish so long as they observe the social conventions and stay on topic. There are no formal expectations regarding quality, quantity, or timing of participation.

Moderated groups include large public forums or small closed gatherings in which one or more moderators actively organize the discussion: posing questions, maintaining the topic focus, synthesizing or weaving the themes that emerged in discussion, and encouraging participation.

Task-oriented groups involve significantly more organizational shaping. Additional roles may be identified: in addition to the moderating, roles associated with coordinating, with making presentations, with editing, or with synthesizing or assessing the discussions to date may be designated. Moderator responsibilities may be increased, shaping user interactions by such techniques as scheduling and sequencing the activities; providing an agenda; setting out roles, tasks, timelines, and responsibilities; providing spaces (such as subconferences) for small group activities or specialized topics; and setting an appropriate tone and normative behavior.

Networlds, like all social spaces, are shaped by social norms. Nonetheless, as a new form of social space they require a new set of social rules and etiquette to organize how we communicate online. In the networld these rules are often referred to as "netiquette"—the set of conventions that govern manners and conduct, the norms for behavior in that space. Each particular networld has its own culture and norms for acceptable and appropriate communication. Standards vary as to what is considered legal, tasteful, and manageable communication. It is typically the moderator or organizer of the specific group activity who sets the netiquette—whether by written guidelines or by modeling the appropriate behavior.

Democratizing the Networld

The shaping of the social interaction on the networld is a critical factor enabling effective and satisfying communication and community. Nonetheless, larger social forces need to be considered to ensure the democratic and democratizing potential of networlds.

Networks: Freedom or Control?

Computer networking today is largely the result of cooperation among self-reliant individuals and nodes. This notion of networking has connotations of increased self-organization and a conscious alternative to top-down organization (Zuboff, 1988; Feenberg, 1991). Zuboff (1988) discusses the potential for networking to enhance the horizontal dimensions of organizational life, in which management has reduced its needs for control and encourages nonhierarchical communication in which individuals are augmented by their participation in group life and in which work and play, productivity and learning, are ever more inseparable.

Yet, while networking can augment our communication potential, others worry that users of global networks will be caught in a Big Brother web of social control, in which all traffic and communication can be monitored and in which networks become nets to catch and confine prey. Zuboff (1988) has documented an example of a corporate research network transformed by management into a panopticon, a glass prison in which all actions are visible to supervisors.

As in the physical world, the networld is defined by social forces. Networks enable but do not guarantee democratic communication. Decisions related to access, cost, design, and control will determine the nature of the social system a networld can offer.

Globalization: Centralization or Decentralization?

The globalization of computer networking has generated a debate over whether networks will increase centralization of economic, cultural, and societal forces or offer new opportunities for reconfiguring economic and social development and facilitating new forms of settlement systems.

Given the flexible nature of systems such as computer networks, both centralization and decentralization are possible. The growth of multinational corporations as global entities is viewed as an indication of the potential of computer networking technologies to centralize market forces and create a homogeneous economy and culture.

However, scenarios of decentralization are also possible. The proliferation of computer networks has enabled new forms of work and education. Indeed, networking may lead to significant nonmetropolitan development, where place of residence is no longer determined by place of work. Economic and cultural forces may preserve some of their diversity and uniqueness while still participating in and contributing to a global network through strategies such as co-emulation, described by Kumon and Aizu in chapter 19. The development of global collaboration systems that acknowledge and support different cultural and linguistic codes is also important (see Shapard, chap. 15). Moreover, as Walls explains in chapter 9, support for cross-cultural communication can help facilitate global networking for local development.

Access: Different Networks, Different Citizens

Networks provide access to people, to services, and to information. The cost of networking tools is decreasing rapidly while telecommunication systems involving radio frequencies and satellites are able to reach people who have long been geographically and technically disenfranchised, promising new opportunities for collaboration, dialogue, and exchange on a global basis.

Yet there is no guarantee that wide dissemination of knowledge and information will actually occur and that vital information will be distributed equally to all. Will networks be used to facilitate a common sharing of knowledge, a pool of information accessible by rich and poor? Or will networks be used to segregate the "info-rich" from the "info-poor." While networks increase access to resources that many argue enhance our humanity and democracy, many of these services are expensive. If freedom of choice is important, what happens to those members of the planet who cannot afford the costs associated with access? Economic disenfranchisement may be the greatest challenge that looms for the global network (see Frederick, chap. 17). Will networking meet the dreams held by its proponents for equalizing access and enabling community on a global scale? Or will the best information be reserved for those who can afford it?

Awareness of the challenges together with efforts such as those described in the following chapters, and especially the vision of the International Public Network presented by Kapor and Weitzner in chapter 19, are part of the initiatives to democratize the networlds and make networks themselves a democratizing agent.

Policy: Role of the User

The history of computer networking has been characterized by user input and definition. From the transformation of electronic file transfer protocols into electronic mail networks to the appropriation and reformulation of online databases into dynamic, vast, global, human communication networks like Teletel, CompuServe, and the late Source, users have reshaped data networks into social networks.

User input has transformed cyberspace into social space characterized by open, lateral communication linkages. However, the future of these spaces is still to be determined, with tremendous implications. Commercial interests are seeking increased involvement and control. Policy (organizational and governmental) and technical constraints set by international standards, protocols, and economics are also consequential in shaping this social space (see Branscomb, chap. 5, and Kirby and Murray, chap. 10). What and who will determine the shape of tomorrow's networlds? There is a need to ensure the continuing role of user participation in the design and development of these spaces and in shaping policy regarding their use.

Conclusions

The need for human beings to communicate and develop new tools to do so forms the history of civilization and culture. Computer networks are recent developments and immediately were adopted by people for human communication and adapted into networlds—new spaces for social, work, and educational interaction. Networlds offer a new place for humans to meet and promise new forms of social discourse and community.

We are only at the threshold of understanding their promises and challenges. The way that network environments are shaped and designed influences the nature and quality of the social space that they offer. Social policy will also determine their role and implications. Social awareness of the need to shape networlds and to participate in that process will be essential to ensuring that networks enable humanity to express itself in new and hopefully better ways.

3   *The Global Matrix of Minds*

John S. Quarterman

Networks are not just technology. Faster networks lead to new services, then new uses, then communities. This chapter discusses aspects of the history and near future of a few networks to illustrate some patterns that have occurred on many networks. The network services mentioned here are intended to be typical of those also found on other networks. They are used as background to a sketch of the kinds of community and society that have been built from them. These communities cross national, organizational, and time boundaries. The most widespread use of the global Matrix of interconnected computer networks is communication among its users. This forms global matrices of minds.

The main historical example used in this chapter is the ARPANET (1969–1990, R.I.P.), which was the oldest of all computer networks before it succumbed to technological obsolescence. The main current example used here is the Internet, a global network of networks. The Internet permits interactive file transfer and remote login across all its parts. It also supports electronic mail, an asynchronous communications service.

Mail does not require direct interactive connectivity, and the Internet is just part of the worldwide Matrix of all computers that interchange electronic mail. Other parts of this global web of computers include UUCP (Unix-to-Unix CoPy), FidoNet, and BITNET, as well as many networks inside companies or other organizations, and many single-machine systems, some of them conferencing systems or BBSes (bulletin board systems). Many of these other networks use different kinds of network protocols (technological communication conventions). They are each webs of computers. Together they form the web of webs that is the

Matrix. Some parts of the Matrix, like USENET, are just services (in this case, news, or many-to-many asynchronous communication among people) overlaid on the other parts. Dewdrops on a forest of webs?

If you can send a file, using file transfer protocol (FTP), to nnsc.nsf.net, ftp.uu.net, or ftp.psi.com and transfer a file, you are on the Internet. If you can send electronic mail to any of those machines (or perhaps two million others), you are in the Matrix, whether you are on the Internet or not.

The relations of the networks in the Matrix have been described elsewhere (Quarterman, 1990; 1992). This chapter is about their uses and effects more than about the networks themselves. It builds from some technical information in its early sections to place, community, and society in its later sections. That the former leads to or enables or permits the latter is the subject of the chapter. It does not attempt to determine which of those verbs is appropriate. It attempts to raise more questions than it answers.

Speeds and Services

As shown in figure 3.1, available network speeds tend to grow in jumps. The ARPANET used 56Kbps (kilobytes per second) links for more than a decade. The Internet had 10Mbps Ethernet speeds commonly available from its inception in 1983, but used 56Kbps long-distance links until about 1987, when T1 at 1.544Mbps (megabytes per second) started to be used. Since then, network speeds have begun to climb. A T3 (45Mbps) test network is in place, and faster wide area network speeds are expected. FDDI local area network speeds of 100Mbps are now available. The speed increases shown for the years after 1990 are meant to be illustrative of a tendency for spurts every few years, with LAN speeds keeping somewhat ahead of WAN speeds. Such speed increases permit new services.

The ARPANET

The earliest multisite packet-switched network, the ARPANET, was intended for resource sharing. That is, the sponsoring agency, ARPA (now DARPA, the Defense Research Projects Agency), thought that a network to connect its sponsored organizations would be less expensive than

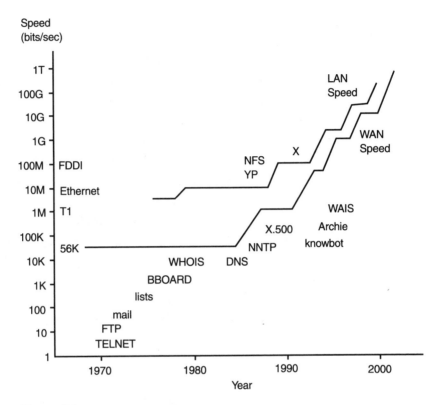

Figure 3.1
Network speeds and services

buying new large computers for each of them. The organizations could just use the network to log in on each others' computers and transfer files among them. This approach influenced the naming of network constituents: connected computers with users were called hosts, because people from elsewhere could log in to them as guests. It also influenced network protocol terminology, as processes or computers with resources to share were called servers, and processes or computers that used those resources were called clients. Services like FTP (File Transfer Protocol) and TELNET (remote login) were part of the original network plan, and were implemented soon after the first ARPANET nodes were in place in 1969. Host names were mapped to network addresses by a central file on each host, updated from a master copy at a centralized site.

Early ARPANET users quickly discovered they wanted to use the network to send messages to each other about the status of their projects. Electronic mail had been available on some time-sharing systems since the early 1970s (Carswell, 1988; Carl-Mitchell, 1992), but it had not previously been used on a network (since there had been no networks). The idea of networked electronic mail "was added to the File Transfer Protocol as an afterthought; it was an interim solution to be used only until a separate mail transmission protocol was specified" (Vittal, Crocker, and Henderson, 1977). This was done by 1971 (North, 1971) or 1973 (Bressler and Thomas, 1973). This seemed natural at the time, since mail was placed in a mailbox file per user, and the name of the mailbox file could be taken from the destination user's login name.

Mail was popular enough by September 1973 that headers were systematized in a de facto standard (Bhushan et al., 1973). This mail message format was based on that used on the TENEX operating system that ran on Digital's PDP-10 computers. The basic format was much the same as that of the current Internet mail message format, as defined in RFC-822 (Crocker, 1982), although To: and Cc: hadn't been invented yet. Conflicts with headers used on another operating system, Multics, soon led to more standard formats being developed (Vittal, Crocker, and Henderson, 1977). Mail was soon the most-used service on the network.

Users soon discovered that they often wanted to send mail not just to specific people but also to fixed groups of people, such as everybody participating in a particular implementation or planning task. These electronic mailing lists (or distribution lists) were implemented using aliases, that is, names that looked like mailbox names but that were expanded by mail agents to lists of addresses for delivery. This idea was formalized in 1977, along with a distinction between the envelope address (for delivery of a particular copy of a message) and mail headers (containing all relevant addresses) (Vittal, Crocker, and Henderson, 1977).

Mailing lists show that mail is something basically different from file transfer, since addresses in a mail alias may refer to users on any system reachable through the network; that is, they are not limited to the sending or receiving (or controlling) host, as in FTP. Thus, a mail transfer agent (MTA) distinct from FTP is useful. When the ARPANET mail specifications were rewritten in the late 1970s, they were separated from the FTP specifications, and implementations of the new Simple Mail Transfer Protocol (SMTP) server were separate from the FTP server (Postel, 1982).

The next step was made when system administrators noticed that mailing lists included a copy of the same message for each recipient on a host. This was a waste of disk space for large lists, since there were typically many users per host in those days. Many of those hosts were TOPS-20 or TWENEX systems. (These ran on Digital DEC-20 hardware; TWENEX was developed by BBN to run on Digital's DEC-20 computers and was descended from BBN's TENEX operating system for Digital's PDP-10 computers. Digital later revised TWENEX as TOPS-20.) On such systems, a mechanism called BBOARD became popular. Mailing lists could send one copy of a message to the BBOARD for each TOPS-20 host. Users would then use the BBOARD command to select a BBOARD and read the messages in the mailing list it corresponded to.

Eventually, there were enough users using mail, lists, and BBOARDS that they wanted ways to find each other's mail addresses and other contact information. The finger and WHOIS services were invented for this purpose. Finger shows information about users on a single system. WHOIS is a centralized database for a whole network, with access methods.

All this was on the ARPANET, before 1980, with links running at 56Kbps. This information is presented not only as a historical overview of a particular case—the protocols and services of the ARPANET were direct ancestors of those of some other networks, especially the Internet. There is, however, a pattern here of resource sharing, mail, lists, groups, and user information services that recurs on many other networks, even unrelated ones. We will return to this pattern later in the chapter.

Local Area Networks

While the ARPANET was spreading all over the country and sprouting links to Hawaii and Norway, local area networks were being invented. Here we concentrate on Ethernet. The original Ethernet, as invented at Xerox, had a theoretical maximum speed of 3Mbps and was designed to throw away bandwidth. The later version from Xerox, Intel, and Digital ran at 10Mbps, as did the protocol that was standardized as IEEE 802.3. Even though 10Mbps Ethernet was still designed to throw bandwidth away, 30 percent of 10Mbps is still 3Mbps, which is fifty-three times faster than 56Kbps. (It turns out that it really is possible to get

10Mbps transmission speeds out of 10Mbps Ethernet, but that is another story.)

A speed of 56Kbps wasn't really fast enough (at least when multiplexed) to handle distributed file systems. Ethernet was. Xerox implemented a shared file system and a distributed name service, as did others such as Apollo.

The Internet

Researchers involved with the ARPANET could see that one future of networking was interconnected sets of dissimilar networks, such as Ethernets, connected by slower wide area networks of ARPANET-like technology. The Internet Protocol (IP) was invented to permit this. IP permits building Internets, which are networks of networks that use IP, along with the Transmission Control Protocol (TCP), the User Datagram Protocol (UDP), and others in the TCP/IP protocol suite. (Other protocol suites, such as TCP/IP and ISO-OSI, can also support Internets.) In 1983, the ARPANET split into ARPANET (for network research) and MILNET (for operational use). Both ARPANET and MILNET became wide area backbone networks connecting local area networks into an Internet, then called the ARPA Internet, now called just the Internet. All the old ARPANET services were available on the Internet as part of the new TCP/IP protocol suite.

The growth of the Internet was spurred by the release of the 4.2BSD version of the UNIX operating system in 1983 and its revision as 4.3BSD in 1986. The 4.2BSD version contained an implementation of the complete TCP/IP protocol suite and was available for cost of distribution, since its development had been funded by public (U.S. Government and State of California) moneys (Leffler et al., 1989). Meanwhile, new hardware technology allowed faster, smaller, and cheaper computers to spread.

New companies, such as Sun Microsystems, were formed to take advantage of these developments. Sun invented a Network File System (NFS) that allowed relatively transparent remote access to files, unlike FTP, where the user has to explicitly transfer a file before using local native programs with it. NFS was written to be used on top of UDP (a TCP/IP transport protocol). It was made possible by the above developments plus the availability of fast network technology such as Ethernet.

Such networked file systems brought a need for quick and distributed access to information about users across at least a local area network. For this purpose Sun provided YP (Yellow Pages, now known as NIS, for Network Information Service). NIS was designed for fast networks and is almost solely used on them.

Fast local area network speeds also permitted new variations on remote login. The X Window System was invented by MIT Project Athena around 1984. It, unlike NFS and NIS, is also fairly widely used over even fairly slow wide area networks, but its development was clearly spurred by fast network speeds. Similarly, the Andrew File System (AFS) can be used over slow networks but was designed first on fast local area networks. Many other network applications developed on local area networks (Quarterman, 1991c).

NSFNET

About 1984, proposals were drafted for a national supercomputer access network, later called NSFNET, after the National Science Foundation (NSF). Deployed in 1986, this became the main backbone network in the Internet. The NSFNET backbone was implemented to use T1 (1.544Mbps) links about 1987. Experimental services such as packetized video and packetized voice became available (some of these had been under development on the old ARPANET but weren't practical until higher speeds were available).

The ARPANET was retired from service in 1988/89 because its link speeds were considered obsolete. Meanwhile, much of NSFNET runs over T3 (45Mbps) links.

Although the ARPANET and the Internet itself were started by the U.S. Department of Defense, the current Internet is much bigger and more diverse than its origins might indicate. Military organizations and users on the Internet are a small and shrinking minority. There are several national backbone networks in the Internet in the United States alone, including several, such as PSINet and AlterNet, that are privately owned and support themselves by charging for access. Even for NSFNET, only a small fraction of its funds come from the U.S. federal government, and those come from NSF, not DoD.

Elsewhere, Canada has its own national backbone in the Internet, as do many countries in Europe. There are several multinational IP backbone networks in Europe. Japan has three national IP backbone networks. Australia and New Zealand have their own. Many other countries, such as Argentina and South Africa, have international IP links, even though IP may not have spread far internally yet.

Other networks, often UUCP and FidoNet dialup networks, serve the rest of the United States. Sites connected that way do not have many basic Internet services, such as interactive file transfer (FTP) or remote login (TELNET). They are part of the Matrix, but they aren't part of the Internet—until they upgrade to IP.

Population

Higher network speeds are not the only cause of invention of new protocols. Increasing numbers of networks, hosts, and users also have effects. Figure 3.2 gives very rough estimates of the user population of the ARPANET and then of the Internet from the beginning (1969) to the near future (2000). The ARPANET (pre-1983) figures are outright

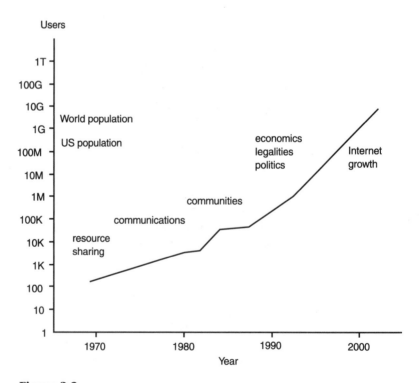

Figure 3.2
Internet growth and uses

guesses. The Internet (1983–1990) figures were computed by multiplying the number of networks in the Internet by an average of one hundred hosts per network and ten users per host, or one thousand users per network. That factor of one thousand users per network matches one arrived at by different means, which produced a conservative figure of 1.88 million users as of January 1991 (Partridge, 1991). In January 1992 the Internet had about four million users, and by August 1992 the Internet had about one million hosts and five to ten million users.

The growth rate from about 1987 has been exponential as the number of networks has doubled each year. This exponential growth rate is borne out not only by the figures for numbers of networks but also by recently published figures for numbers of hosts that were measured approximately every three months (Lottor, 1992). There are monthly measurements of numbers of hosts for Europe for 1991 that show the European growth rate is not only exponential, like the growth in the Internet worldwide, but is actually faster (Terpstra, 1992; Blokzijl, 1990). The Internet in Europe is actually increasing by a factor of four annually, instead of the worldwide growth annual factor of two (Quarterman, 1992).

The near future numbers (1991–2000) assume a simple continuation of the worldwide annual doubling. Obviously that exponential growth rate can't continue forever, since we run out of people on the planet before 2000. However, few who have tried to estimate Internet growth have shown any slacking in the exponential curve before the next five years or so. What is the real limit to Internet growth? Number of computer-literate people? Number of computers, including PCs and pen computers? There are by some estimates sixty million PCs in the world already, and that number is also growing rapidly.

Resource Naming

Meanwhile, Internet protocol developers had to contend with not just one or two networks but hundreds and anticipated thousands in a few years, together with tens or hundreds of thousands of hosts. The old centralized tables for mapping hosts to network addresses would no longer be adequate. A distributed host naming service, DNS (the Domain Name Service), was invented and deployed around 1984 to meet this need. This is one of the first examples of an Internet service that was clearly motivated by population pressures, not by higher available network speeds (e.g., DNS secondary servers just make a copy of the whole database). However, higher speeds later made the current very wide use of DNS practical.

Similarly, the old-style WHOIS service eventually proved to be inadequate for large user populations. New services such as X.500 (the ISO name and directory service) have been implemented and deployed for this reason. No service has adequately met this need yet, and this is an active topic of network research and policy discussions.

Increased numbers of networks and hosts have led to an alphabet soup of network routing and management protocols to deal with them, but those are peripheral to the main topic of this chapter because users do not see them directly; they merely support other protocols.

Resource Access

In a network of tens of thousands of hosts, it can be very difficult to find specific information. For example, FTP supports an access method called anonymous FTP, which allows anyone to connect to a host that supports it with FTP, log in as user *anonymous* with password *guest,* and retrieve files left there for general use. Source code for programs, binaries of programs, archives of mailing lists, protocol specifications, and a plethora of other information is available from anonymous FTP servers. But which anonymous FTP server host has the files you want? The traditional method of finding out is by polling or word of mouth—not very efficient.

A newer method is illustrated by the Archie service of McGill University in Montreal. The Archie server looks at a list of anonymous FTP servers, polls each one and retrieves an index from it, and keeps the indexes on a single host. Users may then connect to the Archie server and examine these indexes to determine which anonymous FTP servers have the files they want.

Similarly, the Knowbot Information Service (KIS), or knowbot for short, developed by the Corporation for the National Research Initiative (CNRI), automates searching servers that provide user directory information. A knowbot can be configured to use the WHOIS service, the X.500 service, the finger service on an appropriate host, and other services to fetch information about a user (or perhaps about a host, network, domain, or organization). Some formatting is done on the retrieved information to make it more legible, but no attempt is made to merge what comes from different servers, nor are relative values given.

Information Access

It would be even more useful if computers could be used to automate choosing information, not just finding it. A step in this direction has been made with the Wide Area Information Service (WAIS), recently operational on the Internet. WAIS not only assists in locating servers but also accepts rules from the user that help it determine what information to select. It can also be configured to keep looking and inform the user of new information.

Meanwhile, USENET news, which had developed independently on the UUCP dialup network at speeds of first 300bps, then 1200bps, 2400bps, and more recently 10Kbps and even 14.4Kbps, had grown very popular by about 1988. The USENET news network had about four hundred newsgroups at that time. Newsgroups are discussion forums somewhat similar to mailing lists, but kept by hosts like BBOARD, and different from both in being much more widely distributed geographically (worldwide) and somewhat more independent of underlying hardware or software platform (most USENET hosts run UNIX, but there are also MS-DOS, VMS, CMS, etc. hosts).

The amount of traffic became the main problem in keeping the network running. Successively faster modem speeds had permitted it to continue to grow, but even 10Kbps became too slow. Fortunately, many of the main USENET hosts were also on the Internet, and the new NSFNET T1 backbone allowed even more traffic. Since USENET news over UUCP over TCP over IP was not particularly efficient or convenient, the Network News Transfer Protocol (NNTP) was invented to allow convenient distribution of news over the Internet.

People

There is clearly a pattern of networks permitting services (e.g., FTP) that are then used to build other services (e.g., mail). Faster network speeds then allow more transparent relatives of the earlier services (e.g., NFS) and also new services (e.g., X, although some say it is just a spiffy kind of TELNET). Population pressures combine with available speeds to permit and demand more transparent and distributed services (DNS, X.500, NNTP). Eventually, increasing population requires development of services to find and access other services (Archie, knowbot). Finally, services are needed that not only find and retrieve information but that also actually interpret it for you (WAIS). But the more interesting aspect of this cumulative development of network services is what people do with them.

Resource Sharing

The original goal of the ARPANET was to share resources. This was also the goal that was used to justify funding of NSFNET and is one of the goals being used to justify the proposed NREN (National Research and Education Network) in the United States (Habegger, 1991).

Being able to access a computer located elsewhere is good and useful, as is being able to retrieve someone else's program or data. Resource sharing is essential to research and development or commerce. It is usually the first goal of R&D or enterprise networks. The first use of new network speeds is often more sophisticated resource sharing, for example, NFS, NIS, and X.

Even the USENET network developed from the UUCP mail network. UUCP stands for UNIX to UNIX CoPy, and the underlying protocol does file transfers and remote job execution. Mail is implemented as a combination of the two. News was added later by the same kind of combination. But resource sharing preceded communication on UUCP and USENET, just as it did on the ARPANET.

Communication

People want to talk to people, not just to machines. Computer networks rapidly become used for communication, thus known as computer-mediated communication (CMC). Mail was quickly invented on the ARPANET and UUCP. Even BITNET, whose underlying support mechanism emulates punch cards, has mail as its most widely used service. The X.400 Message Handling System (MHS) is another method of providing electronic mail and related services (Carl-Mitchell, 1991). However, let's avoid getting buried in network application protocol differences and talk about what happens when the protocols are used.

Places

People want to talk not only to individuals but also to groups. Mailing lists develop on every network that has mail. People begin to depend on them as places to get information or hear interesting news.

Travel

Given places, people begin to travel between them. Given enough places, navigation is necessary. Sophisticated management services like BBOARD, LISTSERV (on BITNET), and USENET news (with its many interfaces) develop.

At this level of sophistication, the appropriate metaphor for use of computer networks may not be communications—with its familiar analogies of telephones, paper post, fax, radio, and television—but travel, with its immediacy of experience and its tendency toward total immersion (rapture of the netways?).

Communities

Once you can go to other places and come back, you begin to notice there are some places where you feel more comfortable or get more work done. People begin to frequent these places, and some develop into communities. There is a sort of evolution from resource sharing through communication, places, and travel to community.

For example, communication serves as the basis of community but is not the same. I can communicate with a national politician by writing him a letter, but that doesn't mean I consider myself to be in a community with him. Even when communication does serve as the basis of a community, the community itself is something different. There is an analogy between the way community builds on communication and the way network protocols and services build on previous services and protocols. Mail is not just file transfer and remote job entry, even though it may be built out of them. Mailing lists differ from personal mail, even though they are built from it. And communities differ from mailing lists, even though they may be built from them.

Computer networks have never been used solely for work. One of the earliest online communities was probably the SF-LOVERS (Science Fiction Lovers) mailing list, which was widely distributed over the ARPANET as early as 1978, despite never being sanctioned by any network authority and after several attempts to suppress it. There are thousands of online communities today, many geographically distributed. These include the publicly advertised USENET newsgroups and Internet, BIT-NET, UUCP mailing lists, and others. Such communities can form whenever a group of people decide to start a mailing list.

Many networks have been justified on the basis of resource sharing, and many people say they use networks for communications. But some of those who pioneered networks such as NSFNET say that the real purpose was to form or facilitate communities. These goals are not necessarily contradictory. But it's easier to get resource sharing or communications funded by the federal government, at least if you're trying to get the money through DARPA (the military) or NSF, even though the specific resource sharing purpose of NSFNET, that is, supercomputer access, turns out to account for about 2 percent of the real usage of the NSFNET backbone.

These networked communities differ in some ways from other communities. By the nature of the services and networks that support most of them, they are distributed, asynchronous, and recorded. They are also diverse, and are described as egalitarian.

Some people worry that networked communities are "thin" communities in that they do not involve direct human interactions as in "thick" communities such as a baseball team, a musical group, or a neighborhood church. Probably more networked communities tend to be thin than, for example, work groups in businesses. However, many networked communities lead to interactions among their members by other means, such as traditional media like telephone and paper post, and especially by travel for personal meetings. Perhaps it would be better to say that the networks facilitate communities.

Politics

Wherever there are communities of people, politics follows. The battles over the creation or charter of a USENET newsgroup can make old-time Chicago ward politics look tame. On a larger scale, the existence, funding, and accessibility of the networks themselves have become political issues on local, national, and international levels.

Politics *in* networked communities (or using network communications) may be somewhat different than traditional politics, even *about* networks. Traditional communication media tend to fall into two groups. Paper press, radio, and TV reach mass audiences, convey information, and leave impressions. Paper post, telephone, and fax reach individuals, are interactive, and can be used for actions. Computer-mediated communications can do both. Could this lead to accountability of leaders? And perhaps empowerment of citizens?

Although power may come from the barrel of a gun, as Chairman Mao said, it is often preserved by secrecy. In networking, secrecy is not power and may not even be possible. Therefore, networking is subversive. That may or may not be the opposite of electronic democracy, but I will avoid that discussion here.

It is interesting to remember that all this was made possible by an early grant from the U.S. Department of Defense. But it has long since grown past the control of that department or of any government.

Economics

One of the reasons networks have become politicized is that some of them, such as the NSFNET backbone, are partly government funded and thus influenced by government-defined acceptable use policies. Government funding is provided by taxpayers, who often have differences of opinion over what their tax dollars should go for. One way out of that morass may be to privatize the networks (Kapor, 1991a), which would involve making them economically viable for commercial providers. This appears to be happening already (Quarterman, 1991d).

Legal Issues

Where there are differences over money or politics, we often find lawyers. And, in recent years, sometimes the FBI or the Secret Service. But those are other stories (Kapor, 1991b; Jackson, 1991; Sterling, 1992).

Society

I hope I have sketched the bumpy slope up from bits to barristers. Networks may start as solely technological tools, but they don't stay that way if they survive. They develop into places where people go, which turn into communities, which develop politics, economics, and legal issues. The sum of all these things is a society.

Radio and television produced a different society. Computer networks will, too. Perhaps this time we can avoid a few mistakes.

Boundaries

The basic function of computer networks is to transfer bits between computers, for use by humans. Computer network protocols are designed so that any pair of computers with the same protocols and a connection can transfer bits, regardless of where they are. This simplicity of abstraction makes it easy for computer networks to cross many kinds of boundaries. The utility of computer networks, partly derived from this ability, ensures that networks *do* cross boundaries.

The boundaries we discuss here are political, time, language, and specialties. We also discuss resource discovery and charging as two issues that are strongly affected by this boundary crossing.

Political

I have not been able to verify the rumor that in the early 1980s there was a trade of guns from Belgium for modems from the Netherlands, but the rumor nicely characterizes the importance and near-outlaw nature of networks to many people. European PTTs traditionally license modems. Yet people can get unlicensed modems and with them establish communications across national boundaries, bypassing PTT data carrier restrictions.

Ideas about freedom of speech vary per country, and what a government will do to its own citizens doesn't necessarily correspond to what it will do to foreigners. As John Perry Barlow of the Electronic Frontier Foundation (EFF) has pointed out, the First Amendment of the U. S. Constitution is a local ordinance. It does not apply, for instance, in the former Soviet Union, even though the KGB neglected to shut down RELCOM during the coup of August 1991, to their later chagrin but the satisfaction of those who resisted.

Time

Time zones can be a real problem for a medium such as the telephone. Tokyo is seven hours earlier than Vancouver. Actually, it is seventeen hours later, given that the world time zone system is centered in London, and the International Date Line is between Japan and Canada. So if it is 9 A.M. Thursday in Tokyo, it is 4 P.M. Wednesday in Vancouver. Even though Japanese often start work early, that still only gives about a one-hour window for someone in Tokyo (8:50–10 A.M.) to call someone in Vancouver (3–5 P.M.).

The problem is just as bad in the other direction. Paris is eight hours earlier than Tokyo, so when it is 5 P.M. in Tokyo it is 9 P.M. in Paris. Even though people in Tokyo tend to work late, there's still not much of a telephone window between Japan and Europe.

Paris to Vancouver is a nine-hour difference, so there's essentially no telephone window during regular working hours on either end.

Add to this time window problem the uncertainty of whether the other person is on daylight time (summer time in Europe) or not. This is telephone tag with a vengeance.

Tokyo
01 02 03 04 05 06 07 08<09+10+11+12+13+14+15+16+17>18 19 20 21 22 23 24

Vancouver
08<09+10+11+12+13+14+15+16+17>18 19 20 21 22 23 24|01 02 03 04 05 06 07

Paris
17>18 19 20 21 22 23 24|01 02 03 04 05 06 07 08<09+10+11+12+13+14+15+16+

Time zones are less of a problem for electronic mail or file transfer. When the sender posts electronic mail, it gets queued for transfer and will arrive whether the recipient is actually there at the time or not. A sender in Tokyo can queue mail at 5 P.M. Tokyo time, and it will probably be read in Vancouver the next morning (nine hours later). The recipient in Vancouver then has almost all day to respond in time to get mail back to Tokyo by the original sender's next working day. This tends to lead to a full day (from the viewpoint of either party) for turnaround on an exchange of messages. This delay may be increased if mail is being sent over a network (such as dialup long-distance telephone or X.25 PDN) that charges for connect time. Such networks often charge different rates at different times of the day, which leads system administrators to transfer mail at off-hours local time. However, dependable daily turnaround is usually better than chancy telephone tag that may result in no turnaround at all. And a mail transfer usually takes less time (and thus perhaps less cost) than a telephone conversation at any time of the day.

Worldwide mailing lists tend to show constant activity, because it is always the middle of the day (or the middle of the night, depending on the phase of the hacker) somewhere in the Matrix.

There have also been interesting collaborative software projects involving people in California working all day, followed by people in Melbourne, followed by people in Amsterdam, all using the same machine in time zone shifts by means of international interactive connectivity (e.g., 4.3BSD).

Language

Latin was once the lingua franca of the West ("plain speech," a language used between those with different native languages). Before that there was Greek. In the East, Chinese held a similar position, and in India, Sanskrit. In the House of Islam, Arabic is still such a language to some extent. Many of these languages were actually only widely used or intelligible across geographical or political distances in writing, and some were primarily liturgical languages, used almost solely for religion. But we are discussing a set of written computer media, so written languages are relevant.

The term lingua franca now usually refers to a family of pidgin or Creole languages, many originally based on Portuguese, that were used for trade in the Mediterranean and then elsewhere. Other trade pidgins were based on other languages, such as Arabic; Swahili started that way. These were primarily spoken languages (Dillard, 1975).

The rise of the vernaculars came around the same time as the spread of printing in the West. These had been primarily spoken tongues but became also written languages. Martin Luther, for example, was very influential not only in spreading his version of the Bible across Germany, but also in standardizing and making respectable the German he wrote it in. That language helped bind the Germany that had been a collection of hundreds of small to medium-sized states into a nation-state with achievements in the arts and especially the sciences that spread the language beyond its borders (Febvre and Martin, 1990).

As recently as a hundred years ago, German was the international (or at least Western) language of science and technology, French of culture, and English of trade. Today, English serves all three functions for much of the world. But many people read and write English better than they speak it.

Melbourne may be only an hour from Tokyo in time zones, but it is thousands of years distant in language history. A telephone conversation between Tokyo and Vancouver often encounters both time and language problems. The languages are still different with electronic mail, but those who do not have English as a native tongue can take time to organize and translate thoughts.

Most worldwide mailing lists are conducted in English. Some of them have large majorities of people with other native languages. Curiously enough, it is usually the nonnative English speakers who insist the most on the use of English, because they don't want to have to deal with somebody else's native tongue, which they almost surely won't know as well as English. Of course, many people don't know English as well as they think they do. An interesting custom that has developed on a few lists is to post a message in one's mother tongue, followed in the same message by one's translation into English. Thus those who know the original language can read it, and those who don't can read the English (and maybe correct it with what they know of the original language).

There is at least one electronic mail directory that was compiled in English entirely by people who have different mother tongues. Languages have been driven in the past by brute force (Latin), trade (the lingua francas), religion (Arabic and Sanskrit), and technology (the vernaculars and the printing press; English and movies and television), among other reasons, such as sheer number of people in a single nation (Chinese in its various forms). Will this new set of electronic media make English even more widespread? Or will it enable more use of national languages? Or even encourage some new Creole?

Thus far, one of the main reasons for the use of English internationally has been that the only really widespread character codeset, ASCII, is only capable of supporting American English and a very few other languages unaltered. That barrier fell in Japan some years ago for Japanese, and is starting to fall all over the world this year, with the release of new specifications and implementations of electronic mail formats (MIME) that extend the most widely used mail format (RFC-822) to handle most languages. Will the rest of the world, like Japan, prefer to use its national languages? Perhaps, even probably, since many countries already have found ways to do that. But will they use them for international communication?

Organizational

Networks tend to bypass some traditional communications mechanisms. You don't need to get everybody in the same place, as for a face-to-face meeting, or even at the same time, as for a telephone conference call. You don't need a secretary, a paper envelope, or a postage stamp. You usually don't have to wait days to weeks (or months, for sea mail) for delivery. The difference between local delivery and international delivery is often small. If you don't want a message, you can delete it and its bits get reused; there's no paper to destroy and no trees to worry about. At least one company (Sun Microsystems) has won an environmental award for shifting distribution of daily memos from paper to electronic mailing lists.

All these things lead to a tendency of people in the same organizations to use computer-mediated communication (CMC) and other network services heavily, both within the organization and with people outside of the organization.

In industry, there are numerous examples of companies as diverse as computer hardware and software manufacturers, oil companies, and banks, who say they simply could not do business without networks to organize their internal operations and to communicate with customers, as a recent survey shows (Quarterman et al., 1991; GAO, 1991).

In academia, networks permit researchers to communicate readily with a larger subset of the colleagues in their field than would otherwise be possible. They don't have to go to a conference or pay for long-distance telephone calls to exchange informal views. They don't have to wait months or years for a journal publication to see a formal write-up of research results. It doesn't take six months of waiting for paper post to compose a collaborative report with coauthors from different universities.

Networks can have interesting effects on education both of children, who can communicate with their peers worldwide, (Presno, 1991) and adults, who can avoid problems of timing and physical handicaps, and take advantage of the many-to-many features of CMC (Coombs, 1991).

Ready collaboration is of interest not only to capitalists and academics. Artists in growing numbers are using networks. Art is traditionally a relatively solitary activity, punctuated by occasional showings or performances, which are normally broadcast media. With networks, the audience talks back, and colleagues can be consulted. Art can become collaborative. One's colleagues and audience no longer have to be physically near by, nor have to all look or listen at the same time. They can be anywhere at any time: art can become global (Couey, 1991).

These advantages apply not only to the actual creation of art (which is often hampered by the lack of common visual and audio services on networks), but also to the facilitation of art, by allowing easier verbal criticism and scheduling of events. Networks also allow bypassing many of the hierarchies (funding, distribution, geographical) that get in the way of art.

In general, remember that CMC can be many-to-many. No traditional medium can do this. As we have already discussed, paper press, radio, and television are one-to-many, and paper post, telephone, and fax are one-to-one. A few variants, such as telephone conference calls, are many-to-many, but only on a small scale, and only in a limited manner, since only one person can really speak at once. With many-to-many CMC (mailing lists, news, bulletin boards, conferencing), *everyone* can speak at once, and everyone can decide what to pay attention to. Despite the potential (and often the actuality) of information overload, this basic capability of CMC promotes the globalization of any community that uses it and leads to the formation of communities where there may have formerly only been specialists (Quarterman, 1991e).

Networks can also make independent research more feasible. For the last hundred years or more, probably most respectable science and engineering has been done at large institutions, such as universities and government-sponsored research facilities. No doubt many people have and will continue to have good reasons for preferring such institutions. But this was not the way of Pythagoras or Socrates, nor of Charles Darwin. With networks, it doesn't have to be the way of all modern researchers.

Consider four reasons for large research institutions: physical plant for people and equipment; informal access to other researchers; access to libraries; and publication. Computers themselves used to be the pieces of equipment requiring the most maintenance, but you can now sit in a hammock in the sun and hack on one. CMC promotes informal access to researchers, and does so in such a way that it doesn't matter much where the researchers are. Libraries are still mostly on paper and in specific locations, but librarians and others are busily working on changing that (Barron, 1991). In the meantime, much current work is already available on the networks before it gets published on paper. More paper journals and book publishers are accepting online copy these days. Paper is usually still required for copy editing, but fast post services alleviate that problem. The independent researcher such as James Lovelock (who discovered the thinning of the ozone layer) may become no longer an anomaly, given networks.

Thus networks change and produce organizational structures in ways that promote both globalization and individualization (Asante and Gudykunst, 1989).

Size

Network size requires innovative solutions for resource discovery. However, that same size facilitates those innovative solutions. Consider Archie, which collects indexes of files available from anonymous FTP servers. It was written by a few people at McGill University in Montreal, and logged 120,000 uses in its first seven months. Also by the end of that period, most of its usage from 5 P.M. to midnight Eastern time was from Europe, prompting the installation of a European Archie server (Deutsch, 1991). Thus a few people in one country can affect usage patterns for the whole network by providing a service that people all over the world want.

Charging

Finally, the tendency of networks to cross boundaries of all kinds makes charging difficult, which makes supporting useful services and facilities difficult. This problem is exacerbated by the blurring by networks of boundaries between academia and industry, R&D and operations (Quarterman, 1991f).

This problem has to be solved, since far too much of current networks and networking technology is supported by volunteer or quasi-volunteer labor. As networks expand, they must be made to support their own weight, or, rather, their users must be persuaded to support them (Quarterman and Carl-Mitchell, 1991).

Conclusion

Networks lead to the formation of new communities and the global expansion of previous ones. Simultaneously, they may facilitate independence of individuals from large organizations. They cross political, time, language, and organizational boundaries. The large and exponentially growing sizes of current networks may produce problems for resource location and charging for services, but such sizes may also be part of the solutions to such problems.

Computers are means of communication at least as much as they are tools, and the global Matrix of interconnected computer networks facilitates the formation of global matrices of minds.

4   *A Slice of Life in My Virtual Community*

Howard Rheingold

I'm a writer, so I spend a lot of time alone in a room with my words and my thoughts. On occasion, I venture outside to interview people or to find information. After work, I reenter the human community, via my family, my neighborhood, my circle of acquaintances. But that regime left me feeling isolated and lonely during the working day, with few opportunities to expand my circle of friends. For the past seven years, however, I have participated in a wide-ranging, intellectually stimulating, professionally rewarding, sometimes painful, and often intensely emotional ongoing interchange with dozens of new friends, hundreds of colleagues, thousands of acquaintances. And I still spend many of my days in a room, physically isolated. My mind, however, is linked with a worldwide collection of like-minded (and not so like-minded) souls: my virtual community.

Virtual communities emerged from a surprising intersection of humanity and technology. When the ubiquity of the world telecommunications network is combined with the information-structuring and storing capabilities of computers, a new communication medium becomes possible. As we've learned from the history of the telephone, radio, and television, people can adopt new communication media and redesign their way of life with surprising rapidity. Computers, modems, and communication networks furnish the technological infrastructure of computer-mediated communication (CMC); cyberspace is the conceptual space where words and human relationships, data and wealth and power are manifested by people using CMC technology; virtual communities are cultural aggregations that emerge when enough people bump into each other often enough in cyberspace.

A virtual community is a group of people who may or may not meet one another face-to-face, and who exchange words and ideas through the mediation of computer bulletin boards and networks. In cyberspace, we chat and argue, engage in intellectual discourse, perform acts of commerce, exchange knowledge, share emotional support, make plans, brainstorm, gossip, feud, fall in love, find friends and lose them, play games and metagames, flirt, create a little high art and a lot of idle talk. We do everything people do when people get together, but we do it with words on computer screens, leaving our bodies behind. Millions of us have already built communities where our identities commingle and interact electronically, independent of local time or location. The way a few of us live now might be the way a larger population will live, decades hence.

The pioneers are still out there exploring the frontier, the borders of the domain have yet to be determined, or even the shape of it, or the best way to find one's way in it. But people are using the technology of computer-mediated communications to do things with each other that weren't possible before. Human behavior in cyberspace, as we can observe it and participate in it today, is going to be a crucially important factor. The ways in which people use CMC always will be rooted in human needs, not hardware or software.

If the use of virtual communities turns out to answer a deep and compelling need in people, and not just snag onto a human foible like pinball or pac-man, today's small online enclaves may grow into much larger networks over the next twenty years. The potential for social change is a side effect of the trajectory of telecommunications and computer industries, as it can be forecast for the next ten years. This odd social revolution—communities of people who may never or rarely meet face-to-face—might piggyback on the technologies that the biggest telecommunication companies already are planning to install over the next ten years.

It is possible that the hardware and software of a new global telecommunications infrastructure, orders of magnitude more powerful than today's state-of-the-art technology, now moving from the laboratories to the market, will expand the reach of this spaceless place throughout the 1990s to a much wider population than today's hackers, technologists, scholars, students, and enthusiasts. The age of the online pioneers will end soon, and the cyberspace settlers will come en masse. Telecommuters who might have thought they were just working from home and avoiding one day of gridlock on the freeway will find themselves drawn into a whole new society. Students and scientists are already there, artists have made significant inroads, librarians and educators have their own pioneers as well, and political activists of all stripes have just begun to discover the power of plugging a computer into a telephone. When today's millions become tens and hundreds of millions, perhaps billions, what kind of place, and what kind of model for human behavior will they find?

Today's bedroom electronic bulletin boards, regional computer conferencing systems, global computer networks offer clues to what might happen when more powerful enabling technology comes along. The hardware for amplifying the computing and communication capacity of every home on the world-grid is in the pipeline, although the ultimate applications are not yet clear. We'll be able to transfer the Library of Congress from any point on the globe to any other point in seconds, upload and download full-motion digital video at will. But is that really what people are likely to do with all that bandwidth and computing power? Some of the answers have to come from the behavioral rather than the technological part of the system. How will people actually use the desktop supercomputers and multimedia telephones that the engineers tell us we'll have in the near future?

People are likely to do what people always do with a new communication technology: use it in ways never intended or foreseen by its inventors to turn old social codes inside out and make new kinds of communities possible. CMC will change us, and change our culture, the way telephones and televisions and cheap video cameras changed us—by altering the way we perceive and communicate. Virtual communities transformed my life profoundly, years ago, and continue to do so.

A Cybernaut's Eye View

The most important clues to the shape of the future at this point might not be found in looking more closely at the properties of silicon but in paying attention to the ways people need to, fail to, and try to communicate with one another. Right now, some people are convinced that spending hours a day in front of a screen, typing on a keyboard, fulfills in some way our need for a community of peers. Whether we have discovered something wonderful or stumbled into something insidiously unwonderful, or both, the fact that people want to use CMC to meet other people and experiment with identity is a valuable signpost to a possible future. Human behavior in cyberspace, as we can observe it today on the nets and in the BBSs, gives rise to important questions about the effects of communication technology on human values. What kinds of humans are we becoming in an increasingly computer-mediated world, and do we have any control over that transformation? Have our definitions of "human" and "community" been under pressure to change to fit the specifications of a technology-guided civilization?

Fortunately, questions about the nature of virtual communities are not purely theoretical, for there is a readily accessible example of the phenomenon at hand to study. Millions of people inhabit the social spaces that have grown on the world's computer networks, and this previously invisible global subculture has been growing at a tremendous rate (e.g., the Internet is growing by 25 percent per month).

I've lived here myself for seven years; the WELL (Whole Earth 'Lectronic Link) and the net have been a regular part of my routine, like gardening on Sunday, for one sixth of my life thus far. My wife and daughter long ago grew accustomed to the fact that I sit in front of my computer early in the morning and late at night, chuckling and cursing, sometimes crying, about something I am reading on the computer screen. The questions I raise here are not those of a scientist, nor of a polemicist who has found an answer to something, but as a user—a nearly obsessive user—of CMC and a deep mucker-about in virtual communities. What kind of people are my friends and I becoming? What does that portend for others?

If CMC has a potential, it is in the way people in so many parts of the net fiercely defend the use of the term "community" to describe the relationships we have built online. But ferocity of belief is not sufficient evidence that the belief is sound. Is the aura of community an illusion? The question has not been answered and is worth asking. I've seen people hurt by interactions in virtual communities. Is telecommunication culture capable of becoming something more than what Scott Peck (1987) calls a "pseudo-community," where people lack the genuine personal commitments to one another that form the bedrock of genuine community? Or is our notion of "genuine" changing in an age where more people live their lives in increasingly artificial environments? New technologies tend to change old ways of doing things. Is the human need for community going to be the next technology commodity?

I can attest that I and thousands of other cybernauts know that what we are looking for, and finding in some surprising ways, is not just information but instant access to ongoing relationships with a large number of other people. Individuals find friends, and groups find shared identities online through the aggregated networks of relationships and commitments that make any community possible. But are relationships and commitments as we know them even possible in a place where identities are fluid? The physical world, known variously as "IRL" (In Real Life), or "offline," is a place where the identity and position of the people you communicate with are well known, fixed, and highly visual. In cyberspace, everybody is in the dark. We can only exchange words with each other—no glances or shrugs or ironic smiles. Even the nuances of voice and intonation are stripped away. On top of the technology-imposed constraints, we who populate cyberspaces deliberately experiment with fracturing traditional notions of identity by living as multiple simultaneous personae in different virtual neighborhoods.

We reduce and encode our identities as words on a screen, decode and unpack the identities of others. The way we use these words, the stories (true and false) we tell about ourselves (or about the identity we want people to believe us to be), is what determines our identities in cyberspace. The aggregation of personae, interacting with each other, determines the nature of the collective culture. Our personae, constructed from our stories of who we are, use the overt topics of discussion in a BBS or network for a more fundamental purpose, as means of interacting with each other. And all this takes place on both public and private levels, in many-to-many open discussions and one-to-one private electronic mail, front stage role-playing and backstage behavior.

When I'm online, I cruise through my conferences, reading and replying in topics that I've been following, starting my own topics when the inspiration or need strikes me. Every few minutes, I get a notice on my screen that I have incoming mail. I might decide to wait to read the mail until I'm finished doing something else or drop from the conference into the mailer, to see who it is from. At the same time that I am participating in open discussion in conferences and private discourse in electronic mail, people I know well use "sends"—a means of sending one or two quick sentences to my screen without the intervention of an electronic mail message. This can be irritating, since you are either reading or writing something else when it happens, but eventually it becomes a kind of rhythm: different degrees of thoughtfulness and formality happen simultaneously, along with the simultaneous multiple personae. Then there are public and private conferences that have partially overlapping memberships. CMC offers tools for facilitating all the various ways people have discovered to divide and communicate, group and subgroup and regroup, include and exclude, select and elect.

When a group of people remain in communication with one another for extended periods of time, the question of whether it is a community arises. Virtual communities might be real communities, they might be pseudocommunities, or they might be something entirely new in the realm of social contracts, but I believe they are in part a response to the hunger for community that has followed the disintegration of traditional communities around the world.

Social norms and shared mental models have not emerged yet, so everyone's sense of what kind of place cyberspace is can vary widely, which makes it hard to tell whether the person you are communicating with shares the same model of the system within which you are communicating. Indeed, the online acronym YMMV ("Your Mileage May Vary") has become shorthand for this kind of indeterminacy of shared context. For example, I know people who use vicious online verbal combat as a way of blowing off steam from the pressures of their real life—"sport hassling"—and others who use it voyeuristically, as a text-based form of real-life soap opera. To some people, it's a game. And I know people who feel as passionately committed to our virtual community and the people in it (or at least some of the people in it) as to our nation, occupation, or neighborhood. Whether we like it or not, the communitarians and the venters, the builders and the vandals, the egalitarians and the passive-aggressives are all in this place together. The diversity of the communicating population is one of the defining characteristics of the new medium, one of its chief attractions, the source of many of its most vexing problems.

Is the prospect of moving en masse into cyberspace in the near future, when the world's communication network undergoes explosive expansion of bandwidth, a beneficial thing for entire populations to do? In which ways might the growth of virtual communities promote alienation? How might virtual communities facilitate conviviality? Which social structures will dissolve, which political forces will arise, and which will lose power? These are questions worth asking now, while there is still time to shape the future of the medium. In the sense that we are traveling blind into a technology-shaped future that might be very different from today's culture, direct reports from life in different corners of the world's online cultures today might furnish valuable signposts to the territory ahead.

Since the summer of 1985, I've spent an average of two hours a day, seven days a week, often when I travel, plugged into the WELL via a computer and a telephone line, exchanging information and playing with attention, becoming entangled In Real Life, with a growing network of similarly wired-in strangers I met in cyberspace. I remember the first time I walked into a room full of people (IRL) whose faces were completely unknown to me, but who knew many intimate details of my history and whose own stories I knew very well. I had contended with these people, shot the breeze around the electronic water cooler, shared alliances and formed bonds, fallen off my chair laughing with them, become livid with anger at these people, but I had not before seen their faces.

I found this digital watering hole for information-age hunters and gatherers the same way most people find such places—I was lonely, hungry for intellectual and emotional companionship, although I didn't know it. While many commuters dream of working at home, telecommuting, I happen to know what it's like to work that way. I never could stand to commute or even get out of my pajamas if I didn't want to, so I've always worked at home. It has its advantages and its disadvantages. Others like myself also have been drawn into the online world because they shared with me the occupational hazard of the self-employed, home-based symbolic analyst of the 1990s—isolation. The kind of people that Robert Reich (1991) calls "symbolic analysts" are natural matches for online communities: programmers, writers, freelance artists and designers, independent radio and television producers, editors, researchers, librarians. People who know what to do with symbols, abstractions, and representations, but who sometimes find themselves spending more time with keyboards and screens than with human companions.

I've learned that virtual communities are very much like other communities in some ways, deceptively so to those who assume that people who communicate via words on a screen are in some way aberrant in their communication skills and human needs. And I've learned that virtual communities are very much not like communities in some other ways, deceptively so to those who assume that people who communicate via words on a screen necessarily share the same level of commitment to each other in real life as more traditional communities. Communities can emerge from and exist within computer-linked groups, but that technical linkage of electronic personae is not sufficient to create a community.

Social Contracts, Reciprocity, and Gift Economies in Cyberspace

The network of communications that constitutes a virtual community can include the exchange of information as a kind of commodity, and the economic implications of this phenomenon are significant; the ultimate social potential of the network, however, lies not solely in its utility as an information market but in the individual and group relationships that can happen over time. When such a group accumulates a sufficient number of friendships and rivalries and witnesses the births, marriages, and deaths that bond any other kind of community, it takes on a definite and profound sense of place in people's minds. Virtual communities usually have a geographically local focus and often have a connection to a much wider domain. The local focus of my virtual community, the WELL, is the San Francisco Bay Area; the wider locus consists of hundreds of thousands of other sites around the world, and millions of other communitarians, linked via exchanges of messages into a meta-community known as "the net."

The existence of computer-linked communities was predicted twenty years ago by J. C. R. Licklider and Robert Taylor who, as research directors for the Department of Defense, set in motion the research that resulted in the creation of the first such community, the ARPANET. "What will online interactive communities be like?" Licklider and Taylor wrote in 1968: "In most fields they will consist of geographically separated members, sometimes grouped in small clusters and some-times working individually. They will be communities not of common location, but of common interest. . . ."

My friends and I sometimes believe we are part of the future that Licklider dreamed about, and we often can attest to the truth of his prediction that "life will be happier for the online individual because the people with whom one interacts most strongly will be selected more by commonality of interests and goals than by accidents of prox-imity." I still believe that, but I also know that life also has turned out to be unhappy at times, intensely so in some circumstances, because of words on a screen. Events in cyberspace can have concrete effects in real life, of both the pleasant and less pleasant varieties. Participating in a virtual community has not solved all of life's problems for me, but it has served as an aid, a comfort, and an inspiration at times; at other times it has been like an endless, ugly, long-simmering family feud.

I've changed my mind about a lot of aspects of the WELL over the years, but the "sense of place" is still as strong as ever. As Ray Oldenburg (1991) revealed in *The Great Good Place,* there are three essential places in every person's life: the place they live, the place they work, and the place they gather for conviviality. Although the casual conversation that takes place in cafes, beauty shops, pubs, town squares is universally considered to be trivial, "idle talk," Oldenburg makes the case that these are the places where communities can arise and hold together. When the automobile-centric, suburban, high-rise, fast food, shopping mall way of life eliminated many of these "third places," the social fabric of existing communities shredded. It might not be the same kind of place that Oldenburg had in mind, but so many of his descriptions of "third places" could also describe the WELL.

The feeling of logging into the WELL for just a minute or two, dozens of times a day, is very similar to the feeling of peeking into the cafe, the pub, the common room, to see who's there, and whether you want to stay around for a chat. Indeed, in all the hundreds of thousands of computer systems around the world that use the UNIX operating sys-tem, as does the WELL, the most widely used command is the one that shows you who is online. Another widely used command is the one that shows you a particular user's biography.

I visit the WELL both for the sheer pleasure of communicating with my newfound friends, and for its value as a practical instrument for gathering information on subjects that are of momentary or enduring importance, from childcare to neuroscience, technical questions on telecommunications to arguments on philosophical, political, or spiritual subjects. It's a bit like a neighborhood pub or coffee shop. It's a little like a salon, where I can participate in a hundred ongoing conversations with people who don't care what I look like or sound like, but who do care how I think and communicate. There are seminars and wordfights in different corners. And it's all a little like a groupmind, where questions are answered, support is given, inspiration is provided, by people I may have never heard from before and whom I may never meet face-to-face.

Because we cannot see one another, we are unable to form prejudices about others before we read what they have to say: race, gender, age, national origin, and physical appearance are not apparent unless a person wants to make such characteristics public. People who are thoughtful but who are not quick to formulate a reply often do better in CMC than face-to-face or over the telephone. People whose physical handicaps make it difficult to form new friendships find that virtual communities treat them as they always wanted to be treated—as thinkers and transmitters of ideas and feeling beings, not carnal vessels with a certain appearance and way of walking and talking (or not walking and not talking). Don't mistake this filtration of appearances for dehumanization: words on a screen are quite capable of moving one to laughter or tears, of evoking anger or compassion, of creating a community from a collection of strangers.

From my informal research into virtual communities around the world, I have found that enthusiastic members of virtual communities in Japan, England, and the United States agree that "increasing the diversity of their circle of friends" was one of the most important advantages of computer conferencing. CMC is a way to meet people, whether or not you feel the need to affiliate with them on a community level, but the way you meet them has an interesting twist. In traditional kinds of communities, we are accustomed to meeting people, then getting to know them; in virtual communities, you can get to know people and then choose to meet them. In some cases, you can get to know people who you might never meet on the physical plane.

How does anybody find friends? In the traditional community, we search through our pool of neighbors and professional colleagues, of acquaintances and acquaintances of acquaintances, in order to find people who share our values and interests. We then exchange information about one another, disclose and discuss our mutual interests, and sometimes we become friends. In a virtual community we can go directly to the place where our favorite subjects are being discussed, then get acquainted with those who share our passions, or who use words in a way we find attractive. In this sense, the topic is the address: you can't simply pick up a phone and ask to be connected with someone who wants to talk about Islamic art or California wine, or someone with a three-year-old daughter or a thirty-year-old Hudson; you can, however, join a computer conference on any of those topics, then open a public or private correspondence with the previously unknown people you find in that conference. You will find that your chances of making friends are magnified by orders of magnitude over the old methods of finding a peer group.

You can be fooled about people in cyberspace, behind the cloak of words. But that can be said about telephones or face-to-face communications, as well; computer-mediated communications provide new ways to fool people, and the most obvious identity-swindles will die out only when enough people learn to use the medium critically. Sara Kiesler (1986) noted that the word "phony" is an artifact of the early years of the telephone, when media-naive people were conned by slick talkers in ways that wouldn't deceive an eight-year old with a cellular phone today.

There is both an intellectual and an emotional component to CMC. Since so many members of virtual communities are the kind of knowledge-based professionals whose professional standing can be enhanced by what they know, virtual communities can be practical instruments for information gathering. Virtual communities can also help their members cope with information overload. The problem with the information age, especially for students and knowledge workers who spend their time immersed in the info-flow, is that there is too much information available and no effective filters for sifting the key data that are useful and interesting to us as individuals. Programmers are trying to design better and better "software agents" that can seek and sift, filter and find, and save us from the awful feeling one gets when it turns out that the specific knowledge one needs is buried in fifteen thousand pages of related information.

The first software agents are now becoming available (e.g., WAIS, Rosebud), but we already have far more sophisticated, if informal, social contracts among groups of people that allow us to act as software agents for one another. If, in my wanderings through information space, I come across items that don't interest me but which I know one of my worldwide loose-knit affinity group of online friends would appreciate, I send the appropriate friend a pointer, or simply forward the entire text (one of the new powers of CMC is the ability to publish and converse with the same medium). In some cases, I can put the information in exactly the right place for ten thousand people I don't know, but who are intensely interested in that specific topic, to find it when they need it. And sometimes, ten thousand people I don't know do the same thing for me.

This unwritten, unspoken social contract, described by Walls in chapter 9 as a blend of strong-tie and weak-tie relationships among people who have a mixture of motives, requires one to give something and enables one to receive something. I have to keep my friends in mind and send them pointers instead of throwing my informational discards into the virtual scrap heap. It doesn't take a great deal of energy to do that, since I have to sift that information anyway in order to find the knowledge I seek for my own purposes; it takes two keystrokes to delete the information, three keystrokes to forward it to someone else. And with scores of other people who have an eye out for my interests while they explore sectors of the information space that I normally wouldn't frequent, I find that the help I receive far outweighs the energy I expend helping others: a marriage of altruism and self-interest.

The first time I learned about that particular cyberspace power was early in the history of the WELL, when I was invited to join a panel of experts who advise the U.S. Congress Office of Technology Assessment (OTA). The subject of the assessment was "Communication Systems for an Information Age." I'm not an expert in telecommunication technology or policy, but I do know where to find a group of such experts and how to get them to tell me what they know. Before I went to Washington for my first panel meeting, I opened a conference in the WELL and invited assorted information-freaks, technophiles, and communication experts to help me come up with something to say. An amazing collection of minds flocked to that topic, and some of them created whole new communities when they collided.

By the time I sat down with the captains of industry, government advisers, and academic experts at the panel table, I had over two hundred pages of expert advice from my own panel. I wouldn't have been able to integrate that much knowledge of my subject in an entire academic or industrial career, and it only took me (and my virtual community) a few minutes a day for six weeks. I have found the WELL to be an outright magical resource, professionally. An editor or producer or client can call and ask me if I know much about the Constitution, or fiber optics, or intellectual property. "Let me get back to you in twenty minutes," I say, reaching for the modem. In terms of the way I learned to use the WELL to get the right piece of information at the right time, I'd say that the hours I've spent putting information into the WELL turned out to be the most lucrative professional investments I've ever made.

The same strategy of nurturing and making use of loose information-sharing affiliations across the net can be applied to an infinite domain of problem areas, from literary criticism to software evaluation. It's a neat way for a sufficiently large, sufficiently diverse group of people to multiply their individual degree of expertise, and I think it could be done even if the people aren't involved in a community other than their company or their research specialty. I think it works better when the community's conceptual model of itself is more like barn-raising than horse-trading, though. Reciprocity is a key element of any market-based culture, but the arrangement I'm describing feels to me more like a kind of gift economy where people do things for one another out of a spirit of building something between them, rather than a spreadsheet-calculated quid pro quo. When that spirit exists, everybody gets a little extra something, a little sparkle, from their more practical transactions; different kinds of things become possible when this mindset pervades. Conversely, people who have valuable things to add to the mix tend to keep their heads down and their ideas to themselves when a mercenary or hostile zeitgeist dominates an online community.

I think one key difference between straightforward workaday reciprocity is that in the virtual community I know best, one valuable currency is knowledge, elegantly presented. Wit and use of language are rewarded in this medium, which is biased toward those who learn how to manipulate attention and emotion with the written word. Sometimes, you give one person more information than you would give another person in response to the same query, simply because you recognize one of them to be more generous or funny or to-the-point or agreeable to your political convictions than the other one.

If you give useful information freely, without demanding tightly-coupled reciprocity, your requests for information are met more swiftly, in greater detail, than they would have been otherwise. The person you help might never be in a position to help you, but someone else might be. That's why it is hard to distinguish idle talk from serious context-setting. In a virtual community, idle talk is context-setting. Idle talk is where people learn what kind of person you are, why you should be trusted or mistrusted, what interests you. An agora is more than the site of transactions; it is also a place where people meet and size up one another.

A market depends on the quality of knowledge held by the participants, the buyers and sellers, about price and availability and a thousand other things that influence business; a market that has a forum for informal and back-channel communications is a better-informed market. The London Stock Exchange grew out of the informal transactions in a coffee house; when it became the London International Stock Exchange a few years ago and abolished the trading-room floor, the enterprise lost something vital in the transition from an old room where all the old boys met and cut their deals to the screens of thousands of workstations scattered around the world.

The context of the informal community of knowledge sharers grew to include years of both professional and personal relationships. It is not news that the right network of people can serve as an inquiry research system: you throw out the question, and somebody on the net knows the answer. You can make a game out of it where you gain symbolic prestige among your virtual peers by knowing the answer. And you can make a game out of it among a group of people who have dropped out of their orthodox professional lives, where some of them sell these information services for exorbitant rates, in order to participate voluntarily in the virtual community game.

When the WELL was young and growing more slowly than it is now, such knowledge-potlatching had a kind of naively enthusiastic energy. When you extend the conversation—several dozen different characters, well-known to one another from four or five years of virtual hanging-out, several hours a day—it gets richer but not necessarily "happier."

Virtual communities have several drawbacks in comparison to face-to-face communication, disadvantages that must be kept in mind if you are to make use of the power of these computer-mediated discussion groups. The filtration factor that prevents one from knowing the race or age of another participant also prevents people from communicating the facial expressions, body language, and tone of voice that constitute the inaudible but vital component of most face-to-face communications. Irony, sarcasm, compassion, and other subtle but all-important nuances that aren't conveyed in words alone are lost when all you can see of a person are words on a screen.

It's amazing how the ambiguity of words in the absence of body language inevitably leads to online misunderstandings. And since the physical absence of other people also seems to loosen some of the social bonds that prevent people from insulting one another in person, misunderstandings can grow into truly nasty stuff before anybody has a chance to untangle the original miscommunication. Heated diatribes and interpersonal incivility that wouldn't crop up often in face-to-face or even telephone discourse seem to appear with relative frequency in computer conferences. The only presently available antidote to this flaw of CMC as a human communication medium is widespread knowledge of this flaw—AKA "netiquette."

Online civility and how to deal with breaches of it is a topic unto itself, and has been much-argued on the WELL. Jacobson, in chapter 20, discusses civility as one of the guiding principles in humanizing the net. Degrees of outright incivility constitute entire universes such as alt.flame, the USENET newsgroup where people go specifically to spend their days hurling vile imprecations at one another. I am beginning to suspect that the most powerful and effective defense an online community has in the face of those who are bent on disruption might be norms and agreements about withdrawing attention from those who can't abide by even loose rules of verbal behavior. "If you continue doing that," I remember someone saying to a particularly persistent would-be disrupter, "we will stop paying attention to you." This is technically easy to do on USENET, where putting the name of a person or topic header in a "kill file" (AKA "bozo filter") means you will never see future contributions from that person or about that topic. You can simply choose to not see any postings from John Doe, or that feature the word "abortion" in the title. An online community can be a society in which people can remove one another, or even entire topics of discussion, from visibility. The WELL does not have a bozo filter, although the need for one is a topic of frequent discussion.

Who Is the WELL?

One way to know what the WELL is like is to know something about the kind of people who use it. It has roots in the San Francisco Bay Area and in two separate cultural revolutions that took place there in past decades. The *Whole Earth Catalog* originally emerged from the counterculture as Stewart Brand's way of providing access to tools and ideas to all the communes who were exploring alternate ways of life in the forests of Mendocino or the high deserts outside Santa Fe. The *Whole Earth Catalogs* and the magazines they spawned, *Co-Evolution Quarterly* and *Whole Earth Review,* have outlived the counterculture itself since they are still alive and raising hell after nearly twenty-five years. For many years, the people who have been exploring alternatives and ideas not available in the mass media have found themselves in cities instead of rural communes, where their need for new tools and ideas didn't go away.

The *Whole Earth Catalog* crew received a large advance in the mid-1980s to produce an updated version, a project involving many geographically-separated authors and editors, many of whom were using computers. They bought a minicomputer and the license to Picospan, a computer conferencing program, leased an office next to the magazine's office, leased incoming telephone lines, set up modems, and the WELL was born in 1985. The idea from the beginning was that the founders weren't sure what the WELL would become, but they would provide tools for people to build it into something useful. It was consciously a cultural experiment, and the business was designed to succeed or fail on the basis of the results of the experiment. The person Stewart Brand chose to be the WELL's first director—technician, manager, innkeeper, and bouncer—was Matthew McClure, not coincidentally a computer-savvy veteran of The Farm, one of the most successful of the communes that started in the sixties. Brand and McClure started a low-rules, high-tone discussion, where savvy networkers, futurists, misfits who had learned how to make our outsiderness work for us, could take the technology of CMC to its cultural limits.

The Whole Earth network—the granola-eating utopians, the solar-power enthusiasts, serious ecologists and the space-station crowd, immortalists, Biospherians, environmentalists, social activists—was part of the core population from the beginning. But there were a couple of other key elements. One was the subculture that happened ten years after the counterculture era—the personal computer revolution. Personal computers and the PC industry were created by young iconoclasts who wanted to have whizzy tools and change the world. Whole Earth had honored them, including the outlaws among them, with the early hackers conferences. The young computer wizards, and the grizzled old hands who were still messing with mainframes, showed up early at the WELL because the guts of the system itself—the UNIX operating system and "C" language programming code—were available for tinkering by responsible craftspeople.

A third cultural element that made up the initial mix of the WELL, which has drifted from its counterculture origins in many ways, were the deadheads. Books and theses have been written about the subculture that has grown up around the band, the Grateful Dead. The deadheads have a strong feeling of community, but they can only manifest it en masse when the band has concerts. They were a community looking for a place to happen when several technology-savvy deadheads started a "Grateful Dead Conference" on the WELL. GD was so phenomenally successful that for the first several years deadheads were by far the single largest source of income for the enterprise.

Along with the other elements came the first marathon swimmers in the new currents of the information streams, the futurists and writers and journalists. The *New York Times, Business Week,* the *San Francisco Chronicle, Time, Rolling Stone, Byte,* the *Wall Street Journal*—all have journalists that I know personally who drop into the WELL as a listening post. People in Silicon Valley lurk to hear loose talk among the pros. Journalists tend to attract other journalists, and the goal of journalists is to attract everybody else: most people have to use an old medium to hear news about the arrival of a new medium.

Things changed, both rapidly and slowly, in the WELL. There were about six hundred members of the WELL when I joined in the summer of 1985. It seemed that then, as now, the usual 10 percent of the members did 80 percent of the talking. Now there are about six thousand people, with a net gain of about a hundred a month. There do seem to be more women than in other parts of cyberspace. Most of the people I meet seem to be white or Asian; African-Americans aren't missing, but they aren't conspicuous or even visible. If you can fake it, gender and age are invisible, too. I'd guess the WELL consists of about 80 percent men, 20 percent women. I don't know whether formal demographics would be the kind of thing that most WELL users would want to contribute to. It's certainly something we'd discuss, argue, debate, and joke about.

One important social rule was built into Picospan, the software that the WELL lives inside: Nobody is anonymous. Everybody is required to attach their real "userid" to their postings. It is possible to use pseudonyms to create alternate identities, or to carry metamessages, but the pseudonyms are always linked in every posting to the real userid. So individual personae—whether or not they correspond closely to the real person who owns the account—are responsible for the words they post. In fact, the first several years, the screen that you saw when you reached the WELL said "You own your own words." Stewart Brand, the WELL's cofounder likes epigrams: "Whole Earth," "Information wants to be free," "You own your own words." Like the best epigrams, "You own your own words" is open to multiple interpretations. The matter of responsibility and ownership of words is one of the topics WELLbeings argue about endlessly, so much that the phrase has been abbreviated to "YOYOW," as in, "Oh no, another YOYOW debate."

Who are the WELL members, and what do they talk about? I can tell you about the individuals I have come to know over six years, but the WELL has long since been something larger than the sum of everybody's friends. The characteristics of the pool of people who tune into this electronic listening post, whether or not they ever post a word in public, is a strong determinant of the flavor of the "place." There's a cross-sectional feeling of "who are we?" that transcends the intersecting and nonintersecting rings of friends and acquaintances each individual develops.

My Neighborhood on the WELL

Every CMC system gives users tools for creating their own sense of place, by customizing the way they navigate through the database of conferences, topics, and responses. A conference or newsgroup is like a place you go. If you go to several different places in a fixed order, it seems to reinforce the feeling of place by creating a customized neighborhood that is also shared by others. You see some of the same users in different parts of the same neighborhood. Some faces you see only in one context—the parents conference, the Grateful Dead tours conference, the politics or sex conference.

My home neighborhood on the WELL is reflected in my ".cflist," the file that records my preferences about the order of conferences I visit. It is always possible to go to any conference with a command, but with a .cflist you structure your online time by going from conference to specified conference at regular intervals, reading and perhaps responding in several ongoing threads in several different places. That's the part of the art of discourse where I have found that the computer adds value to the intellectual activity of discussing formally distinct subjects asynchronously, from different parts of the world, over extending periods, by enabling groups to structure conversations by topic, over time.

My .cflist starts, for sentimental reasons, with the Mind conference, the first one I hosted on the WELL, since 1985. I've changed my .cflist hundreds of times over the years, to add or delete conferences from my regular neighborhood, but I've always kept Mind at the beginning. The entry banner screen for the Mind conference used to display to each user the exact phase of the moon in numbers and ASCII graphics every time they logged in to the conference. But the volunteer programmer who had created the "phoon" (phases of the moon) program had decided to withdraw it, years later, in a dispute with WELL management. There is often a technological fix to a social problem within this particular universe. Because the WELL seems to be an intersection of many different cultures, there have been many experiments with software tools to ameliorate problems that seemed to crop up between people, whether because of the nature of the medium or the nature of the people. A frighteningly expensive pool of talent was donated by volunteer programmers to create tools and even weapons for WELL users to deal with each other. People keep giving things to the WELL and taking them away. Offline readers and online tools by volunteer programmers gave others increased power to communicate.

The News conference is what's next. This is the commons, the place where the most people visit the most often, where the most outrageous off-topic proliferation is least pernicious, where the important announcements about the system or social events or major disputes or new conferences are announced. When an earthquake or fire happens, News is where you want to go. Immediately after the 1989 earthquake and during the Oakland fire of 1991, the WELL was a place to check the damage to the local geographic community, lend help to those who need it, and get first-hand reports. During Tiananmen square, the Gulf War, the Soviet Coup, the WELL was a media-funnel, with snippets of email from Tel Aviv and entire newsgroups fed by fax machines in China, erupting in News conference topics that grew into fast-moving conferences of their own. During any major crisis in the real world, the routine at our house is to turn on CNN and log into the WELL.

After News is Hosts, where the hottest stuff usually happens. The hosts community is a story in itself. The success of the WELL in its first five years, all would agree, rested heavily on the efforts of the conference hosts—online characters who had created the character of the first neighborhoods and kept the juice flowing between one another all over the WELL, but most pointedly in the Hosts conference. Some spicy reading in the Archives conference originated from old hosts' disputes—and substantial arguments about the implications of CMC for civil rights, intellectual property, censorship, by a lot of people who know what they are talking about, mixed liberally with a lot of other people who don't know what they are talking about but love to talk anyway, via keyboard and screen, for years on end.

In this virtual place, the pillars of the community and the worst offenders of public sensibilities are in the same group—the hosts. At their best and their worst, this 10 percent of the online population put out the words that the other 90 percent keep paying to read. Like good hosts at any social gathering, they make newcomers welcome, keep the conversation flowing, mediate disputes, clean up messes, and throw out miscreants, if need be. A WELL host is part saloon keeper, part talk-show host, part publisher. The only power to censor or to ban a user is the hosts' power. Policy varies from host to host, and that's the only policy. The only justice for those who misuse that power is the forced participation in weeks of debilitating and vituperative postmortem.

The hosts community is part long-running soap opera, part town meeting, barroom brawl, anarchic debating society, creative group-mind, bloody arena, union hall, playpen, encounter group. The Hosts conference is extremely general, from technical questions to personal attacks. The Policy conference is supposed to be restricted to matters of what WELL policy is, or ought to be. The part-delusion, part-accurate perception that the hosts and other users have strong influence over WELL policy is part of what feeds debate here and is a strong element in the libertarian reputation of the stereotypical WELLite. After fighting my way through a day's or hour's worth of the hot new dispute in News, Hosts, and Policy, I check on the conferences I host—Info, Virtual Communities, Virtual Reality. After that my .cflist directs me, at the press of the return key, to the first new topic or response in the Parenting, Writers,' Grateful Dead tours, Telecommunication, Macintosh, Weird, Electronic Frontier Foundation, Whole Earth, Books, Media, Men on the WELL, Miscellaneous, and Unclear conferences.

The social dynamics of the WELL spawn new conferences in response to different kinds of pressures. Whenever a hot interpersonal or doctrinal issue breaks out, for example, people want to stage the brawl or make a dramatic farewell speech or shocking disclosure or serious accusation in the most heavily-visited area of the WELL, which is usually the place that others want to be a Commons—a place where people from different subcommunities can come to find out what is going on around the WELL, and outside the WELL, where they can pose questions to the committee of the whole. When too many discussions of what the WELL's official policy ought to be, about censorship or intellectual property or the way people treat each other, break out, they tended to clutter the place people went to to get a quick sense of what is happening outside their neighborhoods. So the Policy conference was born.

But then the WELL grew larger and it wasn't just policy but governance and social issues like political correctness or the right of users to determine the social rules of the system. Several years and six thousand more users after the fission of the News and Policy conferences, another conference split off News—"MetaWELL," a conference created strictly for discussions about the WELL itself, its nature, its situation (often dire), its future.

Grabbing attention in the Commons is a powerful act. Some people seem drawn to performing there; others burst out there in acts of desperation after one history of frustration or another. Dealing with people who are so consistently off-topic or apparently deeply grooved into incoherence, long-windedness, or scatology is one of the events that challenges a community to decide what its values really are, or ought to be.

Conclusion

Something is happening here. I'm not sure anybody understands it yet. I know that the WELL and the net is an important part of my life, and I have to decide for myself whether this is a new way to make genuine commitments to other human beings or a silicon-induced illusion of community. I urge others to help pursue that question in a variety of ways, while we have the time. The political dimensions of CMC might lead to situations that would preempt questions of other social effects; responses to the need for understanding the power relationships inherent in CMC are well represented by the Electronic Frontier Foundation and others (see Kapor and Weitzner, chap. 18). We need to learn a lot more, very quickly, about what kind of place our minds are homesteading.

The future of virtual communities is connected to the future of everything else, starting with the most precious thing people have to gain or lose—political freedom. The part played by communication technologies in the disintegration of communism, the way broadcast television preempted the American electoral process, the power of fax and CMC networks during times of political repression like Tiananmen Square and the Soviet Coup attempt, the power of citizen electronic journalism, the power-maneuvering of law enforcement and intelligence agencies to restrict rights of citizen access and expression in cyberspace—all point to the future of CMC as a close correlate of future political scenarios. More important than civilizing cyberspace is ensuring its freedom as a citizen-to-citizen communication and publication medium; laws that infringe equity of access to and freedom of expression in cyberspace could transform today's populist empowerment into yet another instrument of manipulation. Will "electronic democracy" be an accurate description of political empowerment that grows out of the screen of a computer? Or will it become a brilliant piece of disinfotainment, another means of manipulating emotions and manufacturing public opinion in the service of power?

Who controls what kinds of information are communicated in the international networks where virtual communities live? Who censors, and what is censored? Who safeguards the privacy of individuals in the face of technologies that make it possible to amass and retrieve detailed personal information about every member of a large population? The answers to these political questions might make moot any more abstract questions about cultures in cyberspace. Democracy itself depends on the relatively free flow of communications. The following words by James Madison are carved in marble at the U.S. Library of Congress: "A popular government without popular information, or the means of acquiring it, is but a prologue to a farce or a tragedy, or perhaps both. Knowledge will forever govern ignorance, and a people who mean to be their own governors must arm themselves with the power which knowledge gives." It is time for people to arm themselves with power about the future of CMC technology.

Who controls the market for relationships? Will the world's increasingly interlinked, increasingly powerful, decreasingly costly communications infrastructure be controlled by a small number of very large companies? Will cyberspace be privatized and parceled out to those who can afford to buy into the auction? If political forces do not seize the high ground and end today's freewheeling exchange of ideas, it is still possible for a more benevolent form of economic control to stunt the evolution of virtual communities if a small number of companies gain the power to put up toll-roads in the information networks and smaller companies are not able to compete with them.

Or will there be an open market in which newcomers like Apple or Microsoft can become industry leaders? The playing field in the global telecommunications industry will never be level, but the degree of individual freedom available through telecommunication technologies in the future may depend upon whether the market for goods and services in cyberspace remains open for new companies to create new uses for CMC.

I present these observations as a set of questions, not as answers. I believe that we need to try to understand the nature of CMC, cyberspace, and virtual communities in every important context—politically, economically, socially, culturally, cognitively. Each different perspective reveals something that the other perspectives do not reveal. Each different discipline fails to see something that another discipline sees very well. We need to think as teams here, across boundaries of academic discipline, industrial affiliation, nation to understand, and thus per-

haps regain control of, the way human communities are being transformed by communication technologies. We can't do this solely as
dispassionate observers, although there is certainly a huge need for the
detached assessment of social science. But community is a matter of the
heart and the gut as well as the head. Some of the most important
learning will always have to be done by jumping into one corner or
another of cyberspace, living there, and getting up to your elbows in
the problems that virtual communities face.

II Issues

5 Jurisdictional Quandaries for Global Networks

Anne Wells Branscomb

Global networks are offering new challenges to users, providers, and their lawyers as they produce new forms of information property, new concerns about access, new forms of miscreant behavior, new types of communications, and new kinds of communities. This chapter identifies some of the questions encountered in drawing proprietary boundaries within electronic spaces, establishing legal jurisdictions, applying existing laws, or promulgating new laws and regulatory schemes more appropriate for the new electronic frontiers.

Digital data transmitted by a computer network may easily cross national borders and be seen and modified by many users worldwide. Witness the speed with which the Christmas virus invaded the IBM intracorporate message system in December 1987 and the speed with which the worm designed by Robert T. Morris, Jr., circulated through and hindered access to the Internet in November 1988. The propagation rate of potential destruction demands instantaneous response and is, therefore, troublesome to a legal system that is slow and deliberative.

Networks using satellite technology inherently fail to recognize geographical jurisdictions. There are very few countries that lie within the entire footprint of a satellite. Signals intended for the United States spill over into Canada, Mexico, and the Caribbean. Signals to Europe cover the entire continent encompassing more than twenty nation-states, most of which have different laws concerning the use of information within their borders. The Internet, the world's largest system for interconnecting computer networks, now claims to reach millions of computer terminals in 107 nations (Landweber, 1992). Researchers cannot accurately determine the exploding number of users accessible through this global system.

Anyone who can purchase a small computer and a modem can network globally through existing telecommunications facilities. How can nation-states maintain sovereign control over information within their borders while employing the latest technology to enhance their economic development and to participate in world economy? A similar question also confronts institutional users who want to use the technology in increasingly novel and useful ways according to their own needs and capabilities. Thus large users (most often multinational companies) are successfully urging governments and public telecommunication monopolies to give them more and more freedom in configuring their own telecommunications networks for the exchange of information transnationally. This we might call corporate sovereignty.

There is also a serious concern about personal sovereignty over information. Many online information services that provide the opportunity to network can also monitor the content of the messages and/or package and sell the transaction-generated information to third parties who market that information for profit or bombard the individuals with junk mail offering retail merchandise or causes with which to become associated.

The primary concern in this chapter is how to exercise jurisdictional control over these new electronic information environments. The creation of global electronic villages of closed user groups or open public discussions has gone beyond the capacity of the law to keep up with these developments.

A political analyst at the Rand Corporation has offered a new lexicon for these jurisdictions. Adopting the use of the word "cyberspace" as the electronic environment that conquers, time, space, geography, and political organization,[1] Donald Ronstadt has also offered the word "cyberocracy" to describe something beyond bureaucracy that will rule cyberspace and "cyberology" as the study of the effects of information deployment as a major economic resource. The electronic communities and their social classes he calls "cybernets" and "cyberstrata." Whether or not one is attracted to these newly coined words, the reality exists that governance of global networks offers major challenges to the users, providers, and policymakers to define their boundaries and their system of governance.

What Ronstadt has recognized is the conflict between the jurisdictional boundaries of geopolitically organized nation-states and transnationally effective electronic communities knitted together by the technological marriage of the computer, the satellite, and optical fibers that weave a mesh of interconnectability for individuals and like-minded "others" distributed all over the globe.

> We are moving out of an era of global interdependence into an era of global interconnection. As these networks build, cutting across public and private sectors and national borders and interests, influential new sub- and supra national actors may increasingly compete for influence with national actors. As political and economic interests grow in protecting and expanding the networks, the networks themselves may increasingly take precedence over nation-states as the driving factor in domestic and foreign affairs.[2]

Extraterritoriality

This extraterritoriality within computer networks is terra incognita with no known territorial boundaries. Legal jurisdiction is largely territorial in nature involving the statutory reach of those persons residing within its boundaries.

Electronic communities abound, tied together through independent nodes operating cooperatively through various consortia of like-minded institutions, through dedicated corporate or institutional networks, through public switched virtual networks, through personal computer bulletin boards, and/or through computer conferences offered by information service providers such as CompuServe, Prodigy, or EIES (Electronic Information Exchange System). This multiplicity of communities suggests that electronic communities may choose to promulgate their own rules of the road on electronic highways and to enforce them with sanctions appropriate to their circumstances and codes of ethics. Indeed, as Eli Noam, an economist at Columbia University, has observed "Computer networks acquire quasi-governmental power."[3] Whether this power will be exercised in an authoritarian or democratic manner remains to be determined.

The earliest global networks, such as the electronic funds transfer system SWIFT (Society for Worldwide Interbank Financial Transfers), operate under very stringent rules to which member banks agree when joining the system. Network managers of university network services, which had been loosely organized and largely undisciplined, scurried to set up their own codes of conduct in the aftermath of disruption of services created by the Internet worm that Robert T. Morris, Jr., unleashed into this electronic environment in November 1988.

The process of meshing these codes of conduct with local, state and national laws will prove challenging. A dialogue held on the WELL, a computer bulletin board operating out of Marin County, California, and published in *Harper's* magazine, suggests that the "computer crackers" will push the outer limits of network security so long as there exists a barrier to the free flow of information.[4] And the recent revolt of Prodigy users protesting censorship of electronic messages suggests that users want more voice in determining the rules under which they will opt to participate.

What Constitutes Information Property?

Access to global networks facilitates the collection and sharing of personal data without regard to national borders and national laws concerning the collection and archiving of personal information. The following quotes indicate the nature of the concerns that are being raised by the ability of computers attached to global networks to gather and correlate data about network transactions.

The 'information revolution' has created new forms of property and made long familiar forms—from customer lists to telephone directories—valuable in new ways. (Walter, 1991)

Each of us dashes through dozens of private electronic intersections and turnstiles everyday when we phone, work, or shop till we drop. These data flows are easily monitored at many different points, and the rest is up to the electronic gatekeepers and tabulators. Buying broccoli by credit card is a serious undertaking. The profiles generated from electronic transactions of this kind are therefore detailed and reliable. (Peters, 1990)

The data swept up at a grocery checkout counter—your choice of toothpaste, breakfast cereal, deodorant, contraceptives, whether you smoke cigarettes or drink beer—is worth millions of dollars to stores and manufacturers. And its value soars when it is linked to the names of specific individuals, along with their lifestyles, shopping preferences and ability to pay.[5]

The telephone number is fast becoming at least as important an identifier as the social security card or the motor vehicle license number (which in many states are the same). Information obtained from use of the telephone has come to be known as transaction-generated information (TGI). Such TGI can be mixed and matched with census data, postal codes, and other publicly available information such as automobile and boat registrations, birth registrations, and death certificates to provide rather precise profiles of potential buyers of a variety of products.

This information has long been available (at a cost prohibitive to small marketers) from large corporate information gatherers such as Equifax Marketing Decision Systems. However, when Equifax joined forces with Lotus to offer a new product called "Lotus Marketplace: Households" that would make the same data available to smaller merchants at a fraction of the cost, thirty thousand people wrote in to have their names removed from the database. The product, a set of laser disks containing information about 80 million households and over 120 million individuals, could be ordered in small packages of five thousand names for $695 and would have been updated on a quarterly basis. The information contained was gleaned from forty different sources but carefully designed, according to Lotus executives, to protect privacy of individuals by not disclosing telephone numbers, credit history, actual income, age, or purchasing history.

Although this database was not available online, because the hard copy version was much cheaper, it is typical of the type of information that is available online when credit cards or any electronically readable media or "smart-card" are used to make a purchase. K-Mart, Sears, and Hudson collect point-of-sale data from credit card customers and either reward frequent buyers like the frequent flyers, or solicit to their tastes and buying habits. Williams-Sonoma, Inc. of California tracks one hundred fifty different characteristics of its customers. Quaker Oats, one of the most aggressive of the new "relationship marketers" has a database of 35 million households to whom it sends discount coupons and tracks their redemption. Citicorp has been experimenting with a database of two million consenting purchasers shopping at supermarket chains across the country to package clusters of coupons tailored to the individual purchasing habits and tastes. Suppliers can use this information to count their customers as well as to identify and market to those who purchase competitive products. Sharper Image maintains a list of 800,000 mail order customers along with 1.2 million shoppers at their mall stores. These names are correlated with information gleaned from returned product registration cards collected by National Demographics and Lifestyles, a Denver-based company specializing in the analysis of lifestyles of 30 million Americans.

Clearly the uproar over Lotus Marketplace, which was canceled along with another product designed to cover 7 million businesses, is merely the tip of the iceberg or more likely the smoldering fire from a volcano about to erupt. Citizens are becoming very apprehensive about the information collected and correlated about them and want to have a greater say about how the use of proliferating computer networks is affecting their mailboxes, their trash collection, and even their forests. More seriously they are concerned about the access to their credit ratings, medical histories, and personal lifestyles by third parties beyond their control. Information in the hands of the wrong people can be devastating.

Moreover, if this personal data is so valuable, why not share the value with the source? George Trubow, a professor specializing in privacy law, has suggested the quite ingenious but implausible possibility of crediting social security accounts each time personal data is purchased. Regulation of TGI is a legal nightmare waiting to happen. As computer networks expand, individuals, whether or not they are knowing users of data communications, will surely become more aware of the collection and correlation of information about themselves that is being exploited for some other entity's ulterior interest.

The treatment of personal data varies widely throughout the world.[6] In the United States there is no omnibus law. State as well as federal law applies, and the latter is primarily directed toward the collection of data by the federal government, although there are some restrictions on the collection of credit and financial information and electronic funds transfers.[7] In Europe there is a more concerted effort to harmonize laws related to data collection within the European Community. The Organization for Economic Cooperation and Development (OECD) promulgated voluntary guidelines to be used in the transfer of personal data from one country to another in 1980,[8] and the Council of Europe (consisting of twenty-six European nations) enacted its own convention for the protection of personal data the following year.[9] The twelve nations constituting the European Community have produced numerous recommendations concerning the treatment of personal information to which its member nations are expected to conform. Even so, the laws of the various European countries vary. Some apply only to individual personalized data and some apply to legal entities as well. However, as the EC becomes more unified after 1992, more conformity may be expected. Standards may be instituted to which other countries will have to comply if they expect to transfer data to and from these European countries. Indeed, the first prohibition against transfer of a mailing list took place in 1990, when the United Kingdom stopped an American direct mail organization from transferring information from the United Kingdom to the United States.[10]

Jurisdictional Barriers to Access

In an interdependent global economy, legal rights to access data stored in computers are critical to the normal operations of such an economy. The right to unencumbered transit across national boundaries is a fundamental aspect of the infrastructure of that global economy. Today no such right is guaranteed. National laws are just that, national in orientation and application. Telecommunications systems are also by and large national in scope, operation, and regulation. Only by consensus and treaty do nation-states give up their national sovereignty over information stored within and transiting across their boundaries.

There exists a long tradition that messages contained in diplomatic pouches are subject only to the laws and control of the national sovereign sending and receiving such messages[11] unless it is clear that they are acting in contravention of the laws or best interests of the host nation.[12] There is also a generally recognized principle that private messages sent through the telecommunications systems are to remain private.[13] Yet there are no generally recognized principles governing access to data stored or in transit across national boundaries. Indeed, until the enactment of the Electronic Communications Privacy Act of 1986,[14] there was no prohibition against electronic eavesdropping on data transmission in the United States.

Legal systems are nationally limited; jurisdiction can only be exercised by the national court system or by a cooperating jurisdiction that chooses to apply the laws of that nation state. Thus transnational application of national laws depends upon reciprocity, as in the case of extradition, or the strength of force whenever extraterritorial jurisdiction is claimed by virtue of nationality of citizens living or traveling abroad. In some cases, nations attempt to extend the force of their law beyond their borders by virtue of commercial activities of legal entities operating under the protection of their national laws.

As data resides outside the territorial boundaries of a nation state in that litigation occurs, we must consider how the courts obtain access to the evidence that is necessary to enforce domestic laws. Take, for example, the case of the Canadian law which prohibits circulation of racially offensive literature. A computer bulletin board operated by the Aryan Nations Liberty Net—based in Hayden Lake, Idaho; Fayetteville, North Carolina; and Dallas/Fort Worth, Texas—promoted white supremacy and was reported to contain a list of target names for extermination.[15] These messages, which contravened Canadian but not U.S. law, were readily available over the interconnected telephone carriers operating between the United States and Canada. Presumably, potential Canadian prosecutors could avail themselves (in this case) to the open lines to tap into the neo-Nazi bulletin board and download or print out the messages in the same way that the Canadian callers could. They could not however obtain jurisdiction over the bulletin board operators without obtaining an order of extradition, nor could they obtain an injunction against the bulletin board without the cooperation of the U.S. authorities, nor could they require the U.S. or Canadian telephone companies to deny access to that number without likely inhibiting the normal business use of such lines for other purposes. Perhaps they could obtain the cooperation of host country authorities to require bulletin board operators to post a message stating that accessing data from this bulletin board contravenes Canadian law.

Access to financial data stored in computers and available through networked lines has been explored in two cases involving the Bank of Nova Scotia, a multinational bank with over twelve hundred branches in forty-six countries.[16] A Miami branch of the Canadian bank was subpoenaed by a U.S. federal district court to produce financial data contained in subsidiary banks domiciled in the Bahamas, Cayman Islands, and Antigua. No documents were found in the Antigua branch, and both Bahamian and Cayman law prohibited disclosure of the data held by those branches. Nonetheless, the Miami Court mandated its production, with a fine of $25,000 a day for nondisclosure. Thus the cost of obeying two sovereigns may become very expensive (in this case the total levied was $1.8 million). However, as communication of data between nations with conflicting laws increases, some regularly established principles for the production of evidence seem timely and, indeed, necessary.

Another situation in which transnational access to data is critical was that of the Swiss banks in disclosing information about the bank accounts of ex-President Marcos to the Philippines government and of Duvalier (Baby Doc) to the Haitian government. The secrecy of the numbered Swiss accounts has been a prime attraction of the Swiss banking system. However, in the case of the Philippine and Haitian claims, national assets had been siphoned off by their national leaders for personal purposes and sequestered in these secret accounts. The disclosure of details was a matter of much controversy within the Swiss banking community. Ultimately, the decision was disclosure, but for the first time in the history of the system.[17]

Data residing outside the nation-state of its origin will be subject to political turmoil beyond the control of its owner. For example, Iranian assets were frozen by the U.S. government during the Iranian revolution and hostage crisis.[18] Panamanian assets have been frozen as a device for forcing Noriega to leave office, and U.S. companies were mandated by the U.S. government not to pay taxes lawfully assessed under Panamanian law.[19] When the Soviets invaded Afghanistan, the United States prohibited Dresser Industries from supplying data from a U.S.-situated computer to their French subsidiary, which was supplying pipeline equipment to the Soviet Union.[20]

In the case of national assets, it may be assumed that the political situation, in some cases, both requires and justifies the use of economic sanctions. However, it can also be argued that the stability of the world economy demands some rules of the road so that innocent bystanders will not be injured and critical industries can be permitted to continue operations.

Consequently, an excursion into the drafting of rights of access to transnational data must be entered with much caution, understanding the murky waters from which such rights must emerge, and comprehending the limited goals that can be attained.

Varying Definitions of Miscreant Behavior

Malicious and intentional destruction of data usually can be treated under the existing criminal statutes, although there is often a problem in interpreting the precise language to cover the new circumstances presented in the operation of computer networks. Definitions of criminal behavior do not necessarily conform in different countries. One of the reasons that the Hannover Hackers, convicted in Germany for unauthorized entry into U.S. data networks, were given lenient sentences was that the taking of U.S. data was not prohibited by German laws. Computer hackers operating in both Australia and the Netherlands have identified their activities roaming through U.S. networks, while thumbing their noses at U.S. authorities who had no jurisdiction over foreign nationals unless they have committed an extraditable crime. In order to obtain extradition the nature of the crime must be identical in both countries, and a nation can refuse extradition even if the nature of the crime is identical should they find it in their national interest to do so.

Reports of transnational transgressions abound. The OECD working party on transborder data flow gathered data on unauthorized access of Canadian computers by West Germans, Norwegians, and Americans. A West German perpetrator took control of a mainframe computer operated by a research facility in Vancouver, changed passwords and privilege levels and inflicted a cost of $20,000 to reconstruct and secure the system. In a dispute over a franchise, a Canadian company tampered with tapes stored in the U.S. firm, preventing their continued use.[21]

One of the major questions that is unresolved in an international context is whether information is property for the purpose of applying existing criminal statutes. In addition to the question of whether malicious destruction of data is an offense under the laws of the nation where the miscreant behavior is committed, there is a question of which country to seek redress of grievances, and whether or not one can identify and obtain jurisdiction over the miscreant culprit in any event.

In recent years computer networks have been invaded by "worms," "viruses," and other rogue programs that do not necessarily destroy, steal, or corrupt data but may merely overstuff mail boxes, use up space, or distract network managers attempting to identify and remove them.

This is what happened with the Internet worm inserted by Robert T. Morris, Jr., in November 1988. These are self-propelling programs that enter and reenter existing software and continue to cause disruption throughout the network despite cessation at the source. How to treat these intrusions presents new and unique challenges to the legal systems of the many nations that may experience a disruption of services caused by such miscreant behavior.

Although there is no assurance that terrorism can be contained, there is certainly a need for nations that expect to participate in the global information economy to band together to fight computer terrorists as any other kind of terrorism. Although there have been few instances of computer terrorism in the past, as terrorists become more computer literate the opportunities for them to take advantage of networks will become more apparent. Clearly, the cost of such terrorism is exorbitant in terms of lost time, lost business, and efforts to restore the systems to normal.

Hacking as compared with terrorism is not merely a matter of degree.[22] Terrorists are motivated by the desire to destroy data, whereas hackers are motivated by curiosity or determination to prove their computer skills. Indeed, many hackers think they are improving the state-of-the-art or identifying vulnerabilities. Contending with the hacker problem is more a matter of public relations, education, and an underlying social ethic that "cracking" is improper and should be punished. The criminal statute in the United Kingdom makes any unauthorized entry into an electronic network a misdemeanor and entries with malevolent intent a felony. The U.S. federal statute was interpreted to cover the unauthorized entry of the Internet worm by Robert T. Morris, Jr., into the network as punishable culpability[23] even though no malevolent intent could be established. Thus the law enforcement officials in the United States have shown a determination to crack down on miscreant behavior within the networks. In May 1990 the Secret Service executed Operation Sun Devil, the end ploy of a two-year investigation into the miscreant behavior of some computer hackers, and efforts to increase the curbing of miscreant behavior continues unabated.

Harmonization of the laws of most nations has not been achieved, although the laws in many countries are being changed to clarify that unauthorized entry and use, interference with, or destruction of computerized data is unacceptable behavior. Clearly a standardized and internationally harmonized definition of what is and what is not acceptable access to global networks and use of data found within is highly desirable.

There is also a question of vulnerability to distortion by negligence of the custodian. In most cases liability of the custodian of the data will be spelled out in contracts. However, such contracts can vary enormously and create uncertainties concerning the exposure to users and providers of the data. Clearly, there are cases in which negligence can be generally assumed to exist and others in which there can be agreement that no liability should accrue. Thus to the extent that clearly established norms of custodial behavior can be achieved, the efficiency of the information economy will be improved.

The Aldus virus, for example, was introduced to a large number of Macintosh users at a Mac conference in Toronto via a popular game program called Potato Head, allegedly to demonstrate how fast and how far software piracy can extend. As many attendees did copy the program for their own use, the perpetrators proved their point when a peace message popped up on the screens of thousands of Macintosh users on March 2, 1988, and wished them a happy anniversary of Macintosh use. However, the incident sent a shock of alarm through the computer software industry as several thousand disks of the Aldus Company were found to be contaminated. It was the first incident of commercially available software infected with a virus. Thus software providers became apprehensive that such occurrences could lead to a widespread concern about the integrity of the software sold, leading to warranties for fitness for use or the issuance of bug-free software—a requirement that many thought would lead to the detriment of the industry by overregulation and litigation.

The jurisdictional quandary represented by this incident is illuminating. The offending software was copied from a Macintosh machine residing in Canada. The transfer to commercial software occurred in a manufacturing facility in Ohio, but the injured party was the Aldus Company, a legal entity in Seattle, Washington. The district attorney has spent several years trying to decide whether or not to prosecute whom for what infringement of the law, and a great deal of the evidence has been gathered from electronic bulletin boards reporting comments about the effects of the offending software. However, a suit for damages for negligence would likely be appropriate if the situs of the negligence could be determined, whether in the United States or Canada, and the tortfeasor[24] were solvent and capable of paying damages assessed.

New Forms of Communication: Which Laws and Whose Laws Apply?

Problems keep arising because services like Prodigy don't neatly fit into any of the legal boxes we've developed over the past hundred years. Prodigy's online news services are a lot like those provided by newspapers, its conferences are like town meetings, and its Email like telephone service. All of these services are very different, but all are regulated in the same way—not at all.[25]

Digital signals do not differentiate between video, sound, image, text and data. All the bits traveling through electronic networks are similar electronic messages. Established laws governing communications transport apply specifically to mail, telephones, newspapers, cable, and radio and television broadcasting. In an electronic bitstream it may be impossible to distinguish into which of these legal categories they fall. Indeed, there may be categories of services such as computer bulletin boards or computer conferences that do not resemble any of the established legal regimes.

Already we are seeing the lines between cable and broadcasting becoming blurred as are the lines between what constitutes a common carrier and a content provider (e.g. newspapers, journals, and books). The large metropolitan newspaper (which is not traditionally regulated as a common carrier required to carry whatever is offered) has become a major distributor of printed advertising inserts of all kinds. The broadcaster has always been a hybrid of both carrier (though not regulated as common) and content provider with less first amendment insulation from mandated carriage of content (e.g., political announcements, fairness, and personal attack replies). Even the common carriers—the local telephone companies—are becoming information providers as well as providers of information transport. The Federal Communications Commission in the United States has recently authorized telephone companies to provide television services as a quid pro quo for installing the optical fiber to the home in the hope that the income from such service will facilitate access to a fully digital and networked environment for the future. Cable television companies also seek the opportunity to become competitive with the telephone companies by providing switched voice service to the home.

If the clarity of legal lines between what has constituted an unregulated newspaper from a highly regulated common carrier is becoming clouded, this is a modest problem compared with determining the legal status of the newer breeds of information services. In late 1990, there erupted a heated controversy precipitated when Prodigy, an online service co-owned by IBM and Sears, discontinued service to a number of its subscribers. The subscribers in question had mounted a protest against Prodigy's change in charges from a flat rate per month to additional charges for high-end users of electronic mail. According to Prodigy, 90 percent of the users were sending fewer than the thirty messages per month (or about 360,000 messages), which Prodigy strategists had predicted, but the other 10 percent were sending 3.6 million.

One user saturated the electronic mail services with twenty thousand messages in the month of August 1990, and average of forty-two messages per hour, a contingency Prodigy had not anticipated. When a group calling itself "The Cooperative Defense Committee," organized a revolt using the electronic mail service and urging that users boycott Prodigy's advertisers, Prodigy reacted precipitously by suspending thirteen organizers of the revolt, alleging harassment of other subscribers as the grounds, and prohibiting any discussion of the rate increase on the service.

At the time of the ejection, or excommunication, the protesters claimed to have garnered some nineteen thousand users to support their opposition to both the rate change as well as the presence of online merchants and advertisers on every videotex screen. However, the controversy involved far more than a mere dispute over rates. Indeed, the telephone companies are still trying to extricate themselves from the monthly flat rate for local service. More important, Prodigy was accused of censorship not merely for the curtailment of the discussion over the rates but for discontinuing several controversial computer conferences involving sexual preferences. Thus the public debate blossomed forth into a full-fledged airing of the nature of open discussion on electronic media.

Prodigy admitted to prescreening and editing public messages posted on bulletin boards and conferences on the basis that it was similar to the Disney Channel, a family service. The service agreement required members not to submit messages to the public forums that were "defamatory, inaccurate, abusive, obscene, profane, sexually explicit, threatening, ethnically offensive or illegal."

However, some of the consumers looked upon the electronic service as far more than delivery of advertisements, news, entertainment, and mail. What Prodigy failed to understand, according to William Zachmann writing in *PC Week,* was that:

> . . . a new medium such as an online service has a dynamic—even a life—of its own, quite independent of the intentions of its creators. They fail to see that online services like Prodigy are fundamentally neither electronic providers of information nor electronic substitutes for shopping or paying bills. These aspects are merely secondary. First and foremost, online services like Prodigy are a communications medium. They are a way for people to encounter other people electronically. They create a radically new social medium that will prove to be at least as important (and as revolutionary) as the telephone, radio, or television. (Zachmann, 1990)

The only case to confront some of these issues head on involved CompuServe, one of the earliest of the electronic mail and conferencing services. CompuServe was a computer time-sharing company looking for a way to sell unused time available on their equipment. For over a decade the company has developed a dedicated following of aficionados numbering 838,000 at the time of the litigation in 1991. CompuServe, now owned by H&R Block, offers a wide variety of conference topics that users may join to offer their own comments. In addition to electronic mail and conferences, the CompuServe Information Service (CIS) offers an electronic library of reference materials and many other information services. The open forums involving special topics number more than fifty. Users may also enter what is called a chat mode in which they encounter other users who are using the system, or online, at the same time that they are. This is an interactive discussion in real time rather than messages entered at asymmetrical time periods as in a computer conference or forum mode.

The forum that was the subject of the litigation was one called "Rumorville USA," a part of the Journalism Forum. Rumorville resembled, for most purposes, a daily newsletter and was operated by Don Fitzpatrick Associates of San Francisco, which assumed under its contract with CompuServe "total responsibility for the contents." CompuServe claimed that it had neither responsibility for the content nor an opportunity to prescreen the contents of Rumorville before it was entered into the CompuServe system. Thus it claimed no responsibility for alleged defamatory statements that appeared in Rumorville and for which the plaintiff was concerned.

The trial court agreed with the defendant that it was operating solely as a distributor and not as publisher and, therefore, could not be liable for the contents of the publishers placing material into the system:

CompuServe has no more editorial control over such a publication than does a public library, book store, or newsstand, and it would be no more feasible for CompuServe to examine every publication it carries for potentially defamatory statements than it would be for any other distributor to do so . . . Technology is rapidly transforming the information industry. A computerized database is the functional equivalent of a more traditional news vendor, and the inconsistent application of a lower standard of liability to an electronic news distributor such as CompuServe than that which is applied to a public library, book store, or newsstand would impose an undue burden on the free flow of information.[26]

This decision brought cheer to the providers of electronic mail and information services, since most, other than Prodigy, preferred not to assume responsibility for the content of the many forms of communication passing through their systems. However, the cheer may be short-lived as it pertains only to those messages that look more or less like publications and for which there is a responsible party upon whom liability can be placed. There is less certainty concerning the protection to be provided other forms of communications over electronic messaging systems. Providers of existing messaging and electronic information services have also been reluctant to assume the nomenclature of "information utility," which might insulate them from liability for content as a "common carrier" but would expose them to a right of access to anyone prepared to pay the price of admission, a hazard most are unwilling to assume. Thus the actual status remains in a legal limbo.

There are many proposals afoot including a full-fledged constitutional amendment guaranteeing first amendment rights to all electronic systems.[27] However, there are a myriad of legal issues to be resolved even if first amendment rights apply. First amendment rights can include both the right of a "publisher" to publish without government censorship as well as the right of privacy of the individual to control access to and issue of information coming into and out of the protected space called "home" or "persona." Moreover, it is not clear to what extent the right of anonymity will be preserved, as this has firm legal roots.[28]

It is not at all clear, however, that the law of the United States or other countries will recognize such individual responsibility in electronic media. Indeed, there is much danger that the law will attempt to cover all electronic media under the same rubric without recognizing the vast diversity of types of networks that are currently developing, some with unique cultures of their own.

New Kinds of Communities: Network Governance

More important than the substance of the legal rules that are likely to arise governing electronic communications is the question of what group will determine which laws or operating rules shall apply.

In 1990 a contributor to the WELL effected an electronic death by removing all of his contributions to the continuing electronic conversation. The WELL proclaims to its participants that each user is responsible for content entered into the system. However, there was an outcry of protest from the surviving participants when they discovered that Brian Newman had deleted his contributions from their collective memory. Many thought that the messages, once entered, became a part of the public domain. If not in the public domain, they considered their conference community property that should properly remain under their collective control or at least under the control of the operator of the WELL. A number were quite angry and recorded their complaints about Newman's unacceptable behavior. Certainly the integrity of the electronic conversation had been altered, but it is not clear whether or not any rights had been dishonored.

This incident demonstrates the ease with which "information products" can be authored by multiple contributors and the lack of clarity concerning who has a legal right to control the combined output. It also highlights a concern over the demarcation line between the private and public domain for information assets. How do we determine what can be protected as private speech? What has become part of the public domain or community property, and when does the transformation from private to public take place? Under the 1976 revision of the copyright law one must assume that any original work is protected by an unpublished copyright until published. Thus it is a matter of considerable legal interest when precisely a work is published and under what proviso it is released.

A computer bulletin board is a new breed—an electronic hybrid—that may be looked upon either as a public or a private place depending upon the desires of the participants. In normal circumstances this electronic environment might be considered to be more like a street corner or parlor where one is entitled to make informal remarks to one's intimate friends. Usually the material would not be archived, since the content is more of a transitory nature.

However, many bulletin boards are employed by more serious users, perhaps scientists pursuing common interests in a research project or environmentalists seeking a common solution to devastating effects of acid rain. The cooperative writing may, therefore, have substantial historical, political, or scientific value as a publishable research paper, journal article, treatise, or textbook.

These electronic pen pals have evolved into very cohesive electronic enclaves or "telecommunities," and they want to govern their own electronic environment. The Reverend Paul Milner, system operator for "Lutherlink," a computer network of the Lutheran church affiliated with EcuNet, has observed that the participants on his network want to do their own policing of behavior and they do not tolerate outside interference any more than they tolerate user behavior that is objectionable to the user group.[29]

What is the nature of the community in which this activity takes place? A community is usually governed by its duly enacted laws that represent the ethical values of the participants—for example, what is considered acceptable or unacceptable behavior? Should the laws of the community be those of the geographical locus or the electronic locus? If the latter, how should they be promulgated? By whom administered? Enforced by what sanctions?

New Forums for the Resolution of Disputes: Harmonization of Legal Systems

What institutions are responsible for resolving transnational disputes? The information marketplace is not national but global. Trade secrets are not recognized in most countries. For patents to be valid, they must be filed in each country. The same is true for trademarks. Not everybody recognizes the applicability of copyright to computer software nor indeed any obligation to compensate producers of information. Some nations permit copyrights only for nationals of the country or for artistic works "published" within the national boundaries.

In some societies, and some groups within our society, to plagiarize your teacher or mentor is the ultimate compliment and to withhold information that could be of value to society is sinful and to be derogated. Ethical values are not necessarily shared by different societies. Some are highly socialistic and others are highly individualistic. To live in the same networked world, each will have to accommodate to the other.

Efforts are underway to clarify the substance of intellectual property laws with respect to the new information technologies as well as to determine where and under what circumstances these laws can be enforced across national boundaries and what rights of access may be exercised by newly industrializing countries. Efforts are ongoing within the World Intellectual Property Organization (WIPO), the General Agreement on Tariffs and Trade (GATT), the European Economic Community (EEC), and the United Nations Conference on Trade and Development (UNCTAD) as well as through bilateral negotiations between interested governments and interest groups. The difficulties UNCTAD has experienced in attempting to reach an agreement on an international code of conduct for the transfer of technology to developing countries has presaged the complications that the General Agreement on Tariffs and Trade (GATT) encountered within the Uruguay Round to negotiate a General Agreement on Information Trade (GAIT).[30] The reliance upon the GATT, however, rather than the International Telecommunications Union (ITU) marks a significant change in the promulgation of global policies with respect to telecommunications services.

By placing services high on the agenda for the new trade round, trade ministers have, in effect, declared that telecommunications has become too important to the future prosperity of the world economy to be left in the hands of communication experts. (Aronson, 1987)

The efforts of the Organization for Economic Cooperation and Development (OECD) to issue a Declaration on Transborder Data Flows in April 1985 were designed to pursue a common interest of the developed economies to facilitate transborder data flows and harmonize policy objectives. The OECD has also been a leader in seeking harmonization of criminal laws with respect to curbing miscreant behavior in the use of computer networks.

The efforts of the European Community (EC) to harmonize the laws governing the deployment of computer communications within the twelve member nations constitutes a major multinational effort to seek accommodations among varying legal systems. The guidelines, which are numerous and complex, represent a major force in offering leadership to the world community and may in time become global norms, in the absence of strong objections of other regional groupings of nation-states (see Kirby and Murray, chap. 10).

There are numerous such groupings, however, most of which have initiatives directed toward the accommodation of their telecommunications systems to global interconnectivity. These include such regional entities as the Association of Southeast Asian Nations (ASEAN) and a consortium of South American Countries (ANDEAN). There are also many nongovernmental groups seeking to find new alternatives to the jurisdictional inadequacies. These include bar associations, law reform groups, user consortia such as the International Users Group (INTUG), and the International Chamber of Commerce. There are also a plethora of international conferences organized by policy institutes, management consulting firms, and think tanks of various ilk such as the Aspen Institute for Humanistic Studies, the Trilateral Commission, the Club of Rome, Tide 2000, the Atwater Institute, the International Management Institute, the Weizman Institute, the U.S. National Academy of Sciences, the Salzburg Seminar, Ditchley Park, Courcheval, as well as a number of policy-oriented institutes in universities and a large number of ad hoc efforts initiated by concerned citizens.

Conclusions

Global networks are the electronic highways of world commerce, culture, credit, scientific research, and literary productivity. They provide communications capability to both criminals as well as their captors. They are essential to our economic, social, and political survival. However, there are many conflicts of interest among user groups. Although encryption offers many attractions to privacy proponents, law enforcement officials claim that a completely secure system of encryption will inhibit their efforts to track down criminal behavior facilitated through the use of the networks.

Many nation-states fear loss of sovereignty over their territorial domains through the erosion of control over the private interconnections across national boundaries. Others fear a diminution of cultural identity and loss of ethnic integrity. Many fear a loss of control over their economic futures from the rapid proliferation of transnational data traffic that may reflect values that better serve the nationals originating the traffic than those on the receiving end. These concerns have been expressed most eloquently by the Swedes in their study of vulnerability, by the Canadians in their numerous policy studies, and by the Brazilians in the actions taken in pursuit of their informatics strategies for maintaining tight control over the development of the Brazilian computer market, and by the French in their massive investments in information technology. Nonetheless, the pressure for an integrated global economy are quite strong and many nation-states around the world, both large and small, developed and developing, are restructuring their national telecommunications systems to adapt to a more competitive international environment.

The global thrust of these new global communications highways is to serve people, not nations, as the geopolitical system of governance is currently formed. It is not apparent how the new information marketplaces and innovative political systems will be legitimized. It is clear, however, that the communications world is changing rapidly from one divided by national telecommunications entities to ones governed by a multiplicity of user groups who wish to promulgate their own rules of conduct. Currently the users, large and small, are pressuring governments for more leeway in organizing their own closed user groups and private networks, but groups of individual users are also organizing to lobby for more liberalization of the rules that govern their electronic environments. The new technologies offer a vast array of alternatives in connecting people, corporations, and institutions for business, entertainment, political, criminal, or cultural activities.

The next several decades will prove exciting for those engaged in working out the policy alternatives and forging the new institutional frameworks that will permit the many differing uses of such global networks to emerge in all of their diversity.

6   Computers, Networks, and Work

Lee Sproull and Sara Kiesler

Although the world may be evolving into a global village, most people still lead local lives at work. They spend the majority of their time in one physical location and talk predominantly to their immediate co-workers, clients, and customers. They participate in only a few work-place groups: their primary work group, perhaps a committee or task force, and possibly an informal social group.

Some people, however, already experience a far more cosmopolitan future because they work in organizations that have extensive computer networks. Such individuals can communicate with people around the world as easily as they talk with someone in the next office. They can hold involved group discussions about company policy, new product design, hiring plans, or last night's ball game without ever meeting other group members.

The networked organization differs from the conventional workplace with respect to both time and space. Computer-based communication is extremely fast in comparison with telephone or postal services, denigrated as "snail mail" by electronic mail converts. People can send a message to the other side of the globe in minutes; each message can be directed to one person or to many people. Networks can also essentially make time stand still. Electronic messages can be held indefinitely in computer memory. People can read or reread their messages at any time, copy them, change them, or forward them.

Managers are often attracted to networks by the promise of faster communication and greater efficiency. In our view, the real potential of network communication has less to do with such matters than with influencing the overall work environment and the capabilities of employees. Managers can use networks to foster new kinds of task structures and reporting relationships. They can use networks to change the conventional patterns of who talks to whom and who knows what.

The capabilities that accompany networks raise significant questions for managers and for social scientists studying work organizations. Can people really work closely with one another when their only contact is through a computer? If employees interact through telecommuting, teleconferencing, and electronic group discussions, what holds the organization together? Networking permits almost unlimited access to data and to other people. Where will management draw the line on freedom of access? What will the organization of the future look like?

We and various colleagues are working to understand how computer networks can affect the nature of work and relationships between managers and employees. What we are learning may help people to exploit better the opportunities that networks offer and to avoid or mitigate the potential pitfalls of networked organizations.

Our research relies on two approaches. Some questions can be studied through laboratory experiments. For instance, how do small groups respond emotionally to different forms of communication? Other questions, particularly those concerning organizational change, require field studies in actual organizations that have been routinely using computer networks. Data describing how hundreds of thousands of people currently use network communications can help predict how other people will work in the future as computer-based communications become more prevalent. Drawing on field studies and experiments, researchers gradually construct a body of evidence on how work and organizations are changing as network technology becomes more widely used. The process may sound straightforward, but in reality it is often full of exciting twists. People use technology in surprising ways, and effects often show up that contradict both theoretical predictions and managerial expectations.

One major surprise emerged as soon as the first large-scale computer network, known as the ARPANET, was begun in the late 1960s. The ARPANET was developed for the Advanced Research Projects Agency (ARPA), a part of the U.S. Department of Defense. ARPANET was intended to link computer scientists at universities and other research institutions to distant computers, thereby permitting efficient access to machines unavailable at the home institutions. A facility called electronic mail, which enabled researchers to communicate with one another, was considered a minor additional feature of the network.

Yet electronic mail rapidly became one of the most popular features of the ARPANET. Computer scientists around the country used AR-PANET to exchange ideas spontaneously and casually. Graduate students discussed problems and shared skills with professors and other students without regard to their physical location. Heads of research projects used electronic mail to coordinate activities with project members and to stay in touch with other research teams and funding agencies. A network community quickly formed, filled with friends and collaborators who rarely, if ever, met in person. Although some administrators objected to electronic mail because they did not consider it a legitimate use of computer time, demand grew sharply for more and better network connections.

Since then, many organizations have adopted internal networks that link anywhere from a few to a few thousand employees. Some of these organizational networks have also been connected to the Internet, the successor to ARPANET. Electronic mail has continued to be one of the most popular features of these computer networks.

Anyone who has a computer account on a networked system can use electronic mail software to communicate with other users on the network. Electronic mail transmits messages to a recipient's electronic "mailbox." The sender can send a message simultaneously to several mailboxes by sending the message to a group name or to a distribution list. Electronic bulletin boards and electronic conferences are common variants of group electronic mail; they too have names to identify their topic or audience. Bulletin boards post messages in chronological order as they are received. Computer conferences arrange messages by topic and display grouped messages together.

The computer communication technology in most networked organizations today is fairly similar, but there exist large differences in people's actual communication behavior that stem from policy choices made by management. In some networked organizations, electronic mail access is easy and open. Most employees have networked terminals or computers on their desks, and anyone can send mail to anyone else. Electronic mail costs are considered part of general overhead expenses and are not charged to employees or to their departments. In the open-network organizations we have studied, people typically send and receive between twenty-five and one hundred messages a day and belong to between ten and fifty electronic groups. These figures hold across job categories, hierarchical position, age, and even amount of computer experience.

In other networked organizations, managers have chosen to limit access or charge costs directly to users, leading to much lower usage rates. Paul Schreiber, a *Newsday* columnist, describes how his own organization changed from an open-access network to a limited-access one. Management apparently believed that reporters were spending too much time sending electronic mail; management therefore had the newspaper's electronic mail software modified so that reporters could still receive mail but could no longer send it. Editors, on the other hand, could still send electronic mail to everyone. Clearly, technology by itself does not impel change. Management choices and policies are equally influential.

But even in organizations that have open access, anticipating the effect of networks on communication has proved no easy task. Some of the first researchers to study computer network communications thought the technology would improve group decision making over face-to-face discussion because computer messages were plain text. They reasoned the electronic discussions would be more purely intellectual, and so decision making would be less affected by people's social skills and personal idiosyncrasies.

Research has revealed a more complicated picture. In an electronic exchange, the social and contextual cues that usually regulate and influence group dynamics are missing or attenuated. Electronic messages lack information regarding job titles, social importance, hierarchical position, race, age, and appearance. The context also is poorly defined because formal and casual exchanges look essentially the same. People may have outside information about senders, receivers, and situation, but few cues exist in the computer interaction itself to remind people of that knowledge.

In a series of experiments at Carnegie Mellon University, we compared how small groups make decisions using computer conferences, electronic mail, and face-to-face discussion. Using a network induced the participants to talk more frankly and more equally. Instead of one or two people doing most of the talking, as happens in many face-to-

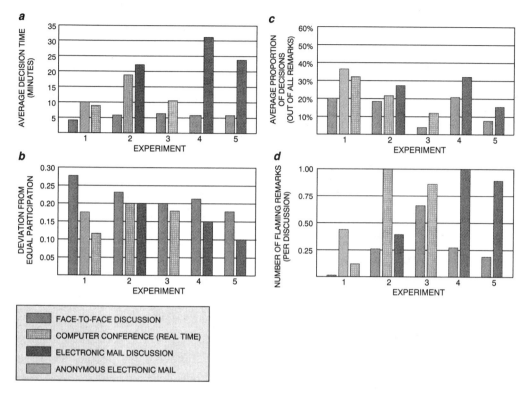

Figure 6.1

Laboratory studies reveal some ways in which networks affect how people work together. Ninety-four groups of subjects in five experiments were told to reach consensus decisions on several questions. Each group made some decisions electronically (through one or two network modes) and others face-to-face. When networked, all groups took longer to make a decision (*a*). On the other hand, they enjoyed more equal participation (*b*) and proposed more ideas (*c*). The electronic modes of discussion seemed to encourage "flaming," impassioned self-expression (*d*).

face groups, everyone had a more equal say. Furthermore, networked groups generated more proposals for action than did traditional ones.

Open, free-ranging discourse has a dark side. The increased democracy associated with electronic interactions in our experiments interfered with decision making. We observed the three-person groups took approximately four times as long to reach a decision electronically as they did face-to-face. In one case, a group never succeeded in reaching consensus, and we were ultimately forced to terminate the experiment. Making it impossible for people to interrupt one another slowed decision making and increased conflict as a few members tried to dominate control of the network. We also found that people tended to express extreme opinions and vented anger more openly in an electronic face-off than when they sat together and talked. Computer scientists using the ARPANET have called this phenomenon "flaming."

We discovered that electronic communication can influence the effects of people's status. Social or job position normally is a powerful regulator of group interaction. Group members typically defer to those who have higher status and tend to follow their direction. Members' speech and demeanor become more formal in the presence of people who have high status. Higher-status people, in turn, talk more and influence group discussion more than do lower-status people.

Given that electronic conversations attenuate contextual cues, we expected that the effect of status differences within a group should also be reduced. In an experiment conducted with Vitaly Dubrovsky of Clarkson University and Beheruz Sethna of Lamar University, we asked groups containing high- and low-status members to make decisions both by electronic mail and face-to-face. The results confirmed that the proportion of talk and influence of higher-status people decreased when group members communicated by electronic mail.

Is this a good state of affairs? When higher-status members have less expertise, more democracy could improve decision making. If higher-status members truly are better qualified to make decisions, however, the results of consensus decisions may be less good.

Shoshana Zuboff of Harvard Business School documented reduced effects of status on a computer conference system in one firm. People who regarded themselves as physically unattractive reported feeling more lively and confident when they expressed themselves over the network. Others who had soft voices or small stature reported that they no longer had to struggle to be taken seriously in a meeting.

Researchers have advanced alternative explanations for the openness and democracy of electronic talk. One hypothesis is that people who like to use computers are childish or unruly, but this hypothesis does not explain experimental results showing that the same people talk more openly on a computer than when they are face-to-face. Another hypothesis holds that text messages require strong language to get a point across; this hypothesis explains flaming but not the reduction of social and status differences. The most promising explanation of the behavior of networked individuals is that when cues about social context are absent or weak, people ignore their social situation and cease to worry about how others evaluate them. Hence, they devote less time and effort to posturing and social niceties, and they may be more honest.

Researchers have demonstrated decreased social posturing in studies that ask people to describe their own behavior. In one of our experiments, people were asked to complete a self-evaluation questionnaire either by pencil and paper or via electronic mail. Those randomly assigned to reply electronically reported significantly more undesirable social behaviors, such as illegal drug use or petty crimes. John Greist and his colleagues at the University of Wisconsin found similar decreases in posturing when taking medical histories from clinical patients. People who responded to a computerized patient history interview revealed more socially and physically undesirable behavior than did those who answered the same questions asked by a physician.

These studies show that people are willing to reveal more about undesirable symptoms and behavior to a computer, but are these reports more truthful? An investigation of alcohol consumption conducted by Jennifer J. Waterton and John C. Duffy of the University of Edinburgh suggests an affirmative answer. In traditional surveys, people report drinking only about one half as much alcohol as alcohol sales figures would suggest. Waterton and Duffy compared computer interviews with personal interviews in a survey of alcohol consumption. People who were randomly assigned to answer the computer survey reported higher alcohol consumption than those who talked to the human interviewer. The computer-derived reports of consumption extrapolated more accurately to actual alcohol sales than did the face-to-face reports.

These and other controlled studies of electronic talk suggest that such communication is relatively impersonal, yet paradoxically it can make people feel more comfortable about talking. People are less shy and more playful in electronic discussions; they also express more opinions and ideas and vent more emotion.

Because of these behavioral effects, organizations are discovering applications for electronic group activities that nobody had anticipated. Computers can be valuable for counseling and conducting surveys about sensitive topics, situations in which many people are anxious and cover their true feelings and opinions. Networks are now being used for applications ranging from electronic Alcoholics Anonymous support groups to electronic quality circles.

Just as the dynamics of electronic communications differ from those conducted orally or by letters, so electronic groups are not just traditional groups whose members use computers. People in a networked organization are likely to belong to a number of electronic groups that span time zones and job categories. Some of these groups serve as extensions of existing work groups, providing a convenient way for members to communicate between face-to-face meetings. Other electronic groups gather together people who do not know one another personally and who may in fact have never had the opportunity to meet in person.

For example, Hewlett-Packard employs human-factors engineers who work in widely scattered locations around the world. These engineers may meet one another in person only once a year. An electronic conference creates ongoing meetings in which they can frequently and routinely discuss professional and company issues.

In some ways, electronic groups resemble nonelectronic social groups. They support sustained interactions, develop their own norms of behavior, and generate peer pressure. Electronic groups often have more than one hundred members, however, and involve relationships among people who do not know one another personally.

Employees whose organization is connected to the Internet or to a commercial network can belong to electronic groups whose members come from many different organizations. For example, Brian K. Reid of Digital Equipment Corporation reports that some 37,000 organizations are connected to USENET, a loosely organized network that exchanges more than 1,500 electronic discussion groups, called newsgroups. Reid estimates that 1.4 million people worldwide read at least one newsgroup.

Networked communication is only beginning to affect the structure of the workplace. The form of most current organizations has been dictated by the constraints of the nonelectronic world. Interdependent jobs must be situated in physical proximity. Formal command structures specify who reports to whom, who assigns tasks to whom, and who has access to what information. These constraints reinforce the centralization of authority and shape the degree of information shar-

○ EMPLOYEE △ RETIREE

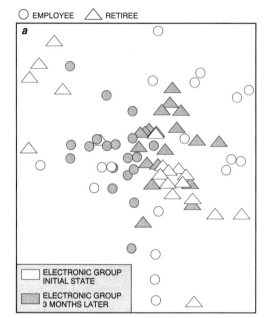

a

ELECTRONIC GROUP
INITIAL STATE

ELECTRONIC GROUP
3 MONTHS LATER

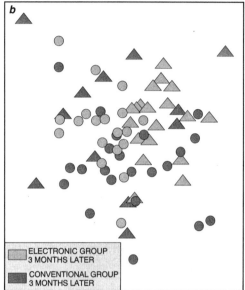

b

ELECTRONIC GROUP
3 MONTHS LATER

CONVENTIONAL GROUP
3 MONTHS LATER

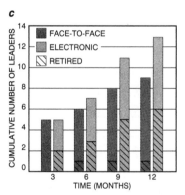

c

FACE-TO-FACE
ELECTRONIC
RETIRED

CUMULATIVE NUMBER OF LEADERS

TIME (MONTHS)

Figure 6.2
Dynamic group structures emerge when people converse electronically. These charts depict the behavior of two study groups, each containing a mix of employees and retired workers. One group worked in person, the other over a network. Members having the most information and social contacts appear near the center of the charts. Over time, the electronic group becomes more socially cohesive (*a*). Chart *b* compares the electronic group with the conventional group three months into the project and shows that retirees in particular become better integrated into the electronic group. Networks also encouraged more people to take on leadership roles (*c*).

ing, the number of organizational levels, the amount of interconnectivity, and the structure of social relationships.

Organizations that incorporate computer networks could become more flexible and less hierarchical in structure. A field experiment conducted by Tora K. Bikson of Rand Corporation and John D. Eveland of Claremont Colleges supports the point. They formed two task forces in a large utility firm, each assigned to analyze employee retirement issues. Both groups contained forty members, half of whom had recently retired from the company and half of whom were still employed but eligible for retirement. The only difference between the two groups was that one worked on networked computer facilities, whereas the other did not.

Both task forces created subcommittees, but the networked group created more of them and assigned people to more than one subcommittee. The networked group also organized its subcommittees in a complex, overlapping matrix structure, It added new subcommittees during the course of its work, and it decided to continue meeting even after its official one-year life span had ended. The networked task force also permitted greater input from the retirees, who were no longer located at the company. Although not every electronic group will be so flexible, eliminating the constraints of face-to-face meetings evidently facilitates trying out different forms of group organization.

Another effect of networking may be changed patterns of information sharing in organizations. Conventional organizations have formal systems of record keeping and of responsibilities for distributing information. Much of the information within an organization consists of personal experience that never appears in the formally authorized distribution system: the war stories told by service representatives (which do not appear in service manuals), the folklore about how the experimental apparatus really works (which does not appear in the journal articles) or the gossip about how workers should behave (which is not described in any personnel policy).

In the past, the spread of such personal information has been strongly determined by physical proximity and social acquaintance. As a result, distant or poorly connected employees have lacked access to local expertise; this untapped knowledge could represent an important informational resource in large organizations. Electronic groups pro-

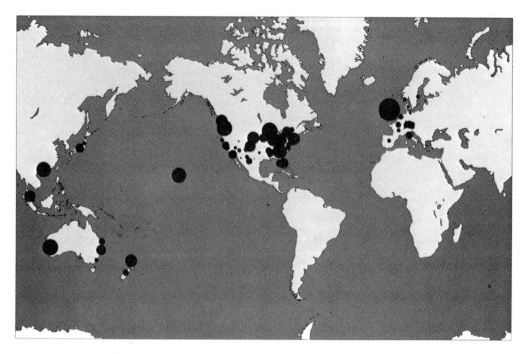

Figure 6.3
Electronic links have the greatest effect on workers located at outlying sites. Workers in field offices of Tandem Computers, Inc., whose headquarters are in Cupertino, CA, have access to data files via a network. Circles indicate how many times each office tapped into one file (consisting of employee-initiated questions and answers about company products and services) over a one-year period; the greater the usage, the larger the circle. Workers in distant or isolated offices, where local expertise is relatively limited, made the most use of the information provided through the network.

vide a forum for sharing such expertise independent of spatial and social constraints.

One significant kind of information flow begins with the "Does anybody know . . .?" message that appears frequently on computer networks. A sender might broadcast an electronic request for information to an entire organization, to a particular distribution list, or to a bulletin board. Anyone who sees the message can reply. We studied information inquiries in the network at Tandem Computers, Inc., in Cupertino, California, a computer company that employs 10,500 workers around the world. In a study we conducted with David Constant, we found an average of about six does-anybody-know messages broadcast every day to one company-wide distribution list.

Information requests typically come from field engineers or sales representatives who are soliciting personal experience or technical knowledge that they cannot find in formal documents or in their own workplace. At Tandem, about eight employees send electronic mail replies to the average question. Fewer than 15 percent of the people who answer a question are personally acquainted with the questioner or are even located in the same city.

Question askers can electronically redistribute the answers they receive by putting them in a public computer file on the network. About half of the Tandem questioners make their reply files publicly available over the company network to other employees. Tandem takes this sharing process one step further by maintaining an electronic archive of question-and-reply files that is also accessible over the company network. The firm has thereby created a repository of information and working expertise that is endlessly accessible through space and time (for example, the expertise remains available when an employee is out of the office or he or she leaves the organization). A study by Thomas Finholt in our research program found that this archive is accessed more than one thousand times a month by employees, especially those located in field offices away from the geographic center of the company.

The discretionary information sharing we discovered at Tandem and at other networked organizations seems to run contrary to nonelectronic behavior in organizations. The askers openly admit their ignorance to perhaps hundreds of even thousands of people. The repliers respond to requests for help from people they do not know with no expectations of any direct benefit to themselves.

One might wonder why people respond so readily to information requests made by strangers. Part of the explanation is that networks make the cost of responding extremely low in time and effort expended. Also, open-access networks favor the free flow of information. Respondents seem to believe that sharing information enhances the overall electronic community and leads to a richer information environment. The result is a kind of electronic altruism quite different from the fears that networks would weaken the social fabric of organizations.

The changes in communication made possible by networks may substantially alter the relationship between an employee and his or her organization, the structure of organizations, and the nature of management. Senior managers and key professionals usually have strong social and informational connections within their organizations and within their broader professional communities. Conversely, employees who reside on the organizational periphery by virtue of geographic location, job requirements, or personal attributes have relatively few opportunities to make contact with other employees and colleagues.

Reducing the impediments to communication across both physical and social distance is likely to affect peripheral employees more than central ones. We, along with Charles Huff of St. Olaf College, studied this possibility for city employees in Fort Collins, Colorado. Employees who used electronic mail extensively reported more commitment to their jobs and to their coworkers than did those who rarely used the network. This correlation was particularly strong for shift workers, who because of the nature of their work, had fewer opportunities to see their colleagues than did regular day workers. As one policewoman told us, "Working the night shift, it used to be that I would hear about promotions after they happened, though I had a right to be included in the discussion. Now I have a say in the decision making."

Organizations are traditionally built around two key concepts: hierarchical decomposition of goals and tasks and the stability of employee relationships over time. In the fully networked organization that may become increasingly common in the future, task structures may be much more flexible and dynamic. Hierarchy will not vanish, but it will be augmented by distributed lattices of interconnections.

In today's organizations, executives generally know whom they manage and manage whom they know. In the future, however, managers of some electronic project groups will face the challenge of working with people they have never met. Allocating resources to projects and assigning credit and blame for performance will become more complex. People will often belong to many different groups and will be able to reach out across the network to acquire resources without management intervention or perhaps even without management knowledge.

A recent case in mathematics research hints at the nature of what may lie ahead. Mathematicians at Bell Communications Research (Bellcore) and at Digital Equipment sought to factor a large, theoretically interesting number known as the ninth Fermat number. They broadcast a message on the Internet to recruit researchers from universities, government laboratories, and corporations to assist them in their project.

The several hundred researchers who volunteered to help received—via electronic mail—software and a piece of the problem to solve; they also returned their solutions through electronic mail.

After results from all the volunteers were combined, the message announcing the final results of the project contained a charming admission:

We'd like to thank everyone who contributed computing cycles to this project, but I can't: we only have records of the person at each site who installed and managed the code. If you helped us, we'd be delighted to hear from you; please send us your name as you would like it to appear in the final version of the paper. (Broadcast message from Mark S. Manasse, June 15, 1990)

Networking in most organizations today is limited to data communications, often for economic or financial applications such as electronic data interchange, electronic funds transfer, or remote transaction processing. Most organizations have not yet begun to confront the opportunities and challenges afforded by connecting their employees through networks.

Among those that have, managers have responded in a variety of ways to changes that affect their authority and control. Some managers have installed networks for efficiency reasons but ignored their potential for more profound changes. Some have restricted who can send mail or have shut down electronic discussion groups. Others have encouraged using the network for broadening participation and involving more people in the decision making process. The last actions push responsibility down and through the organization and also produce their own managerial issues.

A democratic organization requires competent, committed, responsible employees. It requires new ways of allocating credit. It increases unpredictability, both for creative ideas and for inappropriate behavior. Managers will have to come up with new kinds of worker incentives and organizational structures to handle these changes.

The technology of networks is changing rapidly. Electronic mail that includes graphics, pictures, sound, and video will eventually become widely available. These advances will make it possible to reintroduce some of the social context cues absent in current electronic communications. Even so, electronic interactions will never duplicate those conducted face-to-face.

As more people have ready access to network communications, the number and size of electronic groups will expand dramatically. It is up to management to make and shape connections. The organization of the future will depend significantly not just on how the technology of networking evolves but also on how managers seize the opportunity it presents for transforming the structure of work.

7 Integrating Global Organizations through Task/Team Support Systems

Marvin Manheim

How can an organization use information technology to gain competitive advantage in an era of globalization? By information technology, we mean all aspects of information systems and telecommunications (IST). Many organizations must address this issue today. For the private firm, competitive pressures are global in scope, even if the company itself is still focused largely or exclusively on local or regional markets. For the public sector organization, competition is also influenced by global forces; cities and regions face major competition because of the impacts of global competition on the firms located in the area or which the city or region wishes to attract to that area.

The objective of this chapter is to stimulate discussion about the critical directions that managers and researchers should pursue in developing and implementing effective information technology strategies in a globally competing organization (GCO). What IST strategies should a globally competing firm consider adopting? To answer this question, we first identify a number of critical issues facing globally competing organizations. Then, we establish a framework for screening candidate IST-based strategies. Third, we use this framework to assess possible strategies in terms of their effectiveness in meeting the critical issues. This assessment leads us to identify some promising IST-based strategies. Particularly promising are team-based strategies, using what we call "Task/Team Support Systems."

This analysis is based on interviews with more than eighty companies and organizations in the United States, Europe, and Japan (Manheim, 1992, 1990; Manheim, Elam, and Keen, 1989; Mitsubishi

Research, 1990. See also Biddle, 1990; Ives and Jarvenpaa, 1990, 1991; Sethi and Olsen, 1991).

Globalization and Its Implications

It is clear that almost every sector of business and many private and public activities are influenced by global forces. The nature of these forces are well documented (Bartlett, 1986; Bartlett, Doz and Hedlund, 1990; Porter, 1986; Manheim, Elam and Keen, 1989; Ives and Jarvenpaa, 1990, 1991; Lamont, 1991; Levitt, 1990):

- Tightly linked global financial markets
- Global sourcing of inputs, marketing and distribution of products, and manufacturing of components and final products
- Increased pressures for improved product quality and reduced product price
- Evolution of businesses toward more comprehensive and continuous global coordination and integration. For example, in some industries, such as computers and consumer electronics, "flexible manufacturing" means flexibility at the world scale: the ability to shift sourcing, production, assembly, and distribution flexibly as market conditions, relative currency rates, labor resources, and other factors change.

These changes are becoming especially important in the context of the creation of a single market in the European Community (EC) which is providing a major opportunity for firms to restructure their production, distribution, and marketing activities to achieve new competitive advantages. For example, Nissan consolidated all of its automotive parts distribution activities in Europe into a single distribution center located in Amsterdam. This center is coordinating production and distribution of vehicles throughout Europe, including assembly plants in Spain and England.

To compete successfully in this dynamically changing environment, firms need to be able to address effectively several key issues:

- Cost-quality improvement through coordinated manufacturing, including such coordination strategies as "just-in-time" and overall quality-improvement programs.

- Cost-quality improvement through simultaneous engineering, using integrated design teams, combining representatives from product design, engineering and manufacturing, and increasingly marketing and other functions.

- Integration of the order cycle, which begins when the customer places an order and ends with the delivery of the completed product to the customer, in order to shorten cycle time and reduce inventories, so as to be able to deliver the product to the customer as soon after order placement as possible.

- Provision of quality after-sale customer support, to provide customers with a high level of maintenance service, including spare parts availability and technically skilled in-service staff, and convenient access to add-on products and services, such as training, documentation, and product upgrades.

- Improving the product design process and shortening design cycle time—the time it takes to conceive of a new product, design it, put it into manufacturing, and deliver it to the market with a full support network.

- Globally coordinated flexible manufacturing, to coordinate effectively sourcing of components and subassemblies, distribution into multiple markets, and efficient use of a network of global manufacturing and assembly plants.

- Globally coordinated R&D, driven by the need for product development for global markets (Levitt, 1990), and by the recognition that unique research competencies exist in many different countries and cultures (for example, de Meyer and Mizushima, 1990).

Critical Strategic Issues: People and Organizations

These strategic issues around key business tasks raise serious questions about the formal and informal dimensions of the organizations in which these processes take place. We briefly highlight the key issues here and return to this topic in a later section.

Organization Structure and Coordination As globally competing organizations grow in scale, they search for the most effective form of organization structure and coordination mechanisms. The emergence of the European Single Market is a major factor in managerial thinking.

Clearly, to many managers, a unified market requires a single organization to manage production, distribution, and marketing for the EC as a whole. However, alternative forms are also being considered and no single form is now dominating the others.

Fluid Organizations—Teams   Increasingly, organizations are using informal or semiformal teams. For example, in a globally competing manufacturing organization, a design team may be constituted of ten to three hundred people, from functions ranging through engineering, manufacturing, packaging, distribution, marketing, R&D, and finance; from five to thirty different locations, on two to five continents and in two to twenty countries. Teams may be short-lived or may last for years, may be formally organized, semiformal, informal, or even loose networks. Teams are fluid; many teams come and go as issues arise and are resolved, or opportunities are perceived and seized (Mills, 1991).

Organizational Learning   The need for continued learning is acute in GCOs. As new teams are formed, individuals must be able to learn rapidly what is needed to deal with a new set of issues. As new knowledge is developed, it must be made available to other members of the team and to individuals in other parts of the larger organization. While responsibilities for maintaining formal assemblies of knowledge (e.g., libraries, databases) may lie in specific formal organization units, making that knowledge available on an as-needed basis throughout the larger organization is an important element of competitive advantage. Clearly, the ultimate objective is to make a piece of information available to individuals who don't even know they need it!

Information Technology as a Competitive Weapon

The possible uses of information technology as a competitive weapon are well known and continually debated (Benjamin et al., 1984; Business Week, 1985; Cash et al., 1988; Earl, 1988; Keen, 1988, 1991; Manheim, 1988; Manheim, Elam, and Keen, 1989; Strassman, 1985; Synnott, 1987; Wiseman, 1988; Hopper, 1990). We find it useful to assume that, under some circumstances, IST can help a firm achieve a competitive advantage and to apply a simple framework to stimulate development of candidate strategies and to assess strategy proposals.

Competitive Advantage or Competitive Necessity?

A *sustainable competitive advantage* means that an organization or a region is more effective than any competitor for a substantial period of time, say five to ten years. In the case of a firm, a sustainable competitive advantage can be defined as "producing profits that are significantly above the average for firms in the same industry."

A *competitive necessity* is some feature of an organization's strategy that must be adopted if an organization is to remain at least equally competitive with other leading organizations of the same type. (We draw on Clemons and Row, 1987, 1988.)

Based on these distinctions of competitive advantage and competitive necessity, we have hypothesized that an effective strategy requires four basic elements:

1. *Base:* elements to build a sound foundation—the technology, organization, and human resource base to survive as a viable organization and to lay a foundation for seeking competitive advantage.

2. *Parity:* elements to seek "parity," that is, to maintain competitive equality, based on an analysis of actions taking place in the industry and emerging competitive forces; those actions that are a "competitive necessity," to keep the organization at least comparable to its major competitors.

3. *Incremental initiatives:* focused actions, which, by targeting specific segments of the organization's markets, seek to achieve an incremental lead over competitors. The lead may be three years, two years, or six months. Competitors will likely respond and match these actions. Therefore, it is necessary to have a continual process of moving forward with next-step actions to keep ahead of competitors. Thus, a rolling, incremental lead is sought in focused areas.

4. *Breakthrough:* actions that seek to achieve a breakthrough and thereby a restructuring of the market and the firm's role in it such that a sustainable advantage is achieved.

In this model, from a normative perspective, we hypothesize that the conservative foundation of an organization's strategy should be developed by building upon a sound base and include those elements necessary to maintain parity as well as elements that form an effective program of rolling, incremental, focused initiatives. In addition, it is often desirable to include breakthrough elements that may have potential for achieving a sustainable competitive advantage.

From a perspective of evaluation of strategy proposals, we can also use this framework to classify candidate strategy elements in terms of their likely significance. Of course, this involves substantial, and substantive, judgments and assumptions.

In Manheim (1992) we apply this framework to analyze the strategic opportunities around the order cycle in globally competing organizations. In this area, presently, much management attention is devoted to building pipeline management systems (PLMS), which use electronic data interchange (EDI) and other techniques to integrate information flows among various trading partners in the supply chain. The need for such PLMS is widely recognized by manufacturing and merchandizing organizations, and many organizations are beginning to implement such systems. (OECD, in process; Roure, 1990, COMPAT 90, 1990; Bollo, Hanappe, and Stumm, 1991; Clemons and Row, 1988; Flaherty, 1986; Magad and Amos, 1989; Manheim and Mittman, 1988; Miyazawa and Koike, 1991; Sokol, 1989; Tanja, 1988). Progress is slow, and it is still difficult to implement such systems, nevertheless, the need is widely recognized, and the knowledge about how to do it is widespread. Therefore, we concluded that it is now a *competitive necessity* for a company to have a world-class capability to manage the order cycle. If a company fails to do this, it is likely that it will have higher inventory, order processing, and related costs than its competitors and will provide a lower level of service to its customers.

Where are the opportunities for competitive advantage if pipeline management systems are only a competitive necessity? We believe that the answer lies in thinking deeply about the organizational change dimensions around EC 92, global competition in general, and the business strategy issues identified earlier.

Earlier, we introduced the basic outline of our hypotheses: As a consequence of the changes in manufacturing, merchandising, and distribution, globally competing organizations (GCOs) in these sectors will be restructuring their formal organizations within the European region and on a worldwide basis. Regardless of the formal organization structure, however, the use of teams, both informal and formal ("committees") will be increasing substantially. We now explore these hypotheses in greater detail.

Organization Structure and Coordination

As companies wrestle with how to organize for increasing global competition, various organizational forms are emerging.

Major Organizational Forms
Bartlett and Ghoshal (1989) identify three major forces shaping GCOs: the need for efficiency drives a firm for global integration; the need for responsiveness to markets drives the firm to local differentiation; and the need to have continual and rapid learning throughout the organization drives an organization to seek innovation on a worldwide basis. This results in their identification of several types of company organizations.

Multinational   A multinational manages a portfolio of multiple national entities (Bartlett and Ghoshal, 1989, 14). Its key strategic capability is building a strong local presence through sensitivity and responsiveness to national differences

Global   A global company treats the world market as an integrated whole, and products and strategies are developed to exploit an integrated unitary market. The key strategic capability is the ability to build cost advantages through centralized global-scale operations.

International   In the international company, "the parent retains considerable influence and control, but less than in a classic global company; the national units can adapt products and ideas coming from the center, but have less independence and autonomy than multinational subsidiaries" (Bartlett and Ghoshal, 1989, 67ff).

Geographic versus Product Group
The influence of EC 92 has introduced additional complexities. On the one hand, we do see an evolution from multinational to global product groups. This is typified by Philips, Siemens, and others, which have been evolving away from national organizations (the multinational organization) to product groups on a worldwide basis: for example, consumer electronics. Thus, each product group is an example of the "global organization," as defined by Bartlett and Ghoshal (1989).

On the other hand, we also see examples of evolution to a geographic, regional structure, especially under the influence of EC 92. To many managers, a unified market requires a single organization to manage production, distribution, and marketing for the EC as a whole. Many Japanese companies—and some American and European companies as well—are putting into place a global structure with, typically, a four-region organization: Europe, North America, Japan, and the rest of the world. Each of these regions has significant authority and responsibility to act independently, to respond to its particular market and production conditions.

Tensions exist between these two forms. In the product group organization, there is still a need for some regional structures; after all, logistics issues within Europe do not require day-to-day management attention of the logistics managers in Asia. In the regional structures, there still is need for some product breakdown, and the regions must coordinate globally: development of new products, coordinated roll-out and marketing strategies, and coordination of R&D are all major issues in these new structures. As authority is being restructured and decentralized to the regional level, new coordination mechanisms must be established between regions.

In many companies, these two forces are not completely articulated. In our interviews with Japanese companies, they have indicated movement toward regional structures. However, in few cases have they moved significant responsibility for the integration functions out of Japan; of course, Honda is one major exception. Honda North America has independent design and manufacturing responsibility, as well as sales. In the case of Philips, it appears that in most product groups, the power has been taken away from the national (country) organizations and been placed in the global product groups, but the need for regional structures has not yet been resolved. In the case of Proctor and Gamble, a matrix structure was put in place, with strong power in the product groups but nearly as strong power in geographic regions.

Organization Structure—Multiple Power Centers
Given this tension among alternative organization structures, which will be dominant? Several researchers have observed that the organization structure that is emerging in some leading companies is different from any of these traditional organization forms. Bartlett and Ghoshal

argue that a new form of organization is emerging, which they call *transnational* (Bartlett and Ghoshal, 1989, 67 ff., 85 ff). Hedlund has called a similar form of organization a *hetarchical* organization. (Hedlund gives the Swedish firm, Ericcson, as an example; Hedlund and Rolander, 1990, 33.) This type of organization is based on their perception that

> One of the critical assets of a well-functioning MNC is its cadre of internationally experienced personnel, well versed also in the intricacies of intra-firm communication. This together with the hardware and software of information management, constitutes the nervous system of the firm—its perceptive apparatus, information processing systems, and activators for response to opportunities and problems. . . .
>
> It is obvious from the above that the most important part of structure is, not the formal organization, but the less easily describable management systems, communication processes, and the corporate culture. (Hedlund and Rolander, 1990, 33)

Drawing on the observations of both sets of researchers and our own interviews and observations, we extend and modify the arguments of these researchers to characterize the hetarchical organization as follows:

- Many centers, of different kinds, in different countries

- Different centers with different roles, many of which are specialized; both domestic and foreign subsidiaries may have particular strategic roles

- A formal hierarchical structure, for accountability, responsibility, and authority; especially for budgeting and finance, and for management of managers

- An informal power structure, in which multivalent power relationships are the bases of power. The formal hierarchical structure is balanced by a strong matrix thrust, where the matrix has more than two dimensions, so that the mechanisms of coordination and integration are primarily by persuasion, rather than by dictate.

- An environment in which firm culture is very important in establishing reference frames for negotiating agreements (Ohmae, 1989)

- Important power centers located outside the firm boundaries, in strategic partners of various types (customers, suppliers, distributors, etc.) (Johnston and Lawrence, 1988)

▪ An integrated network forming the basic structural framework of the transnational (Bartlett and Ghoshal, 1989, 89), with:

• Dispersed assets, managed by various centers
• Specialized operations, conducted at different centers
• Interdependent relationships among centers

In this type of organization, the critical assets are:

▪ The personal networks of relationships

▪ Human resource management processes and systems

▪ Information channels of all types

▪ Information technology systems

▪ Processes of change management that can be effective in this multi-valent decentralized environment

Hetarchic Organizations and EC 92

We hypothesize that, in the processes of putting in place new organization structures to deal with the single market, many GCOs will go through two phases. At first, some GCOs will organize hierarchically by regions while others will organize by product groups globally. Then, GCOs will discover that extensive, informal, lateral linkages are important to retain flexibility and responsiveness in global competition, and so they will transition, in a later stage, to explicit hetarchic organizations.

This hypothesis is at least partially verified by one example, the case of IBM in Europe (Hudson, 1991).

These days, it seems you need a computer to keep track of all the changes going on at the big, problem-plagued European operations of International Business Machines Corp. Take personal computers. Last July, with much publicity, an order whizzed out from IBM Europe's headquarters here to decentralize management of the European personal-computer business, moving key managers out of the Paris headquarters and into the field.

Then last month, with market conditions getting tougher, that strategy was revised. This time without publicity, the company ordered yet another reorganization, leaving some personal-computer management in Paris. "It's a correction; it's an evolution" from the original order, says Renato Riverso, IBM Europe's operations chief and second-ranking executive.

With the Armonk, N.Y., computer giant's worldwide profit unexpectedly tumbling in the first quarter, its top managers in Europe are back at the drawing board, hunting for ways to boost sales and save money. While change has become the norm at IBM around the globe since at least 1986, when John Akers became chairman, the latest round in Europe promises to be even more dramatic.

With the Italian-born Mr. Riverso and IBM Europe chairman David E. McKinney, an American, in command, the company's European operations are being reshaped into a novel structure that could become a model for how a multinational corporation should organize itself to do business in post-1992 Europe. The European plan will also guide financial performance in a region that last year supplied nearly half of the company's $6.02 billion net income and 37.5% of its $69.02 billion revenue.

The planning and implementation of the IBM Europe reorganization began more than a year ago. The blueprint was developed in a series of Paris management meetings and calls for IBM's European operations to become over the next five years or so more centralized in some respects and increasingly decentralized in others.

A key element of this plan is improvement of the pipeline management systems and other internal systems.

IBM's internal affairs—product warehouses, in-house computer systems, the planning of advertising—are being centralized to save money and boost efficiency.

For instance, the managers of IBM France, IBM Germany and other national organizations currently each run their own, slightly different but interconnected computer systems for billing, ordering and other company data. This arrangement, Mr. Riverso explains, means that across Europe IBM is paying 8,000 employees, out of a 108,000-worker European payroll, to tend a variegated, computerized management-information system with 150 to 170 data centers. Mr. Riverso wants to decrease the number of centers to between just three and five big ones over the next five years. (Hudson, 1991)

But, the approach being taken is not a uniform centralization strategy, but rather a decentralization strategy for some functions.

In contrast, external affairs, the marketing operations that deal directly with customers, are being decentralized so that sales decisions get made faster and better locally, rather than by a slow-moving headquarters bureaucracy.

As part of this effort, IBM, beset by customer complaints of red tape at Paris headquarters, is moving many key managers out of Paris and scattering them around the Continent. (Hudson, 1991)

The result is a strategy that looks somewhat like a hetarchical strategy.

The result, if the program is successful, will produce a structure that simultaneously takes advantage of possible savings from a unified European Community market and also avoids alienating local customers, who will still have parochial tastes. That is the hope, at least, and the plan is getting some flattering reviews even from a few IBM competitors.

If we want to come to a unified Europe after 1992, business has to go this way with decentralized marketing, observes Rolf Brillinger, chief executive of Germany's Comparex Informationssysteme G.m.b.H., which competes with IBM in selling mainframe computers. He adds, though, that he hasn't yet noticed any changes in IBM's behavior in the market place as a result of the gradually progressing reorganization. . . .

A glimpse of the planned new IBM Europe can be found in Richmond, England, where about 300 IBM employees in a local sales office are acting as guinea pigs for a Riverso-devised experiment in decentralized management. Under the old hierarchical marketing system, which still prevails in most other IBM sales offices around Europe, most of the contract bids that the Richmond sales force presented to its big corporate customers had to go first to IBM's British headquarters for clearance. Then, by aggregate value of the bids, 30% to 40% were kicked upstairs from there to Paris headquarters for approval.

The whole process, says Paul Aspin, manager of the office, often added days or weeks to a bidding process—and sometimes cost the company a sale.

Under the experiment, however, Mr. Aspin has authority to make many of his own decisions about structuring bids. He can hire consultants and software houses to help him. Within broad limits, he can modify the terms of a sales contract to please a customer. And his sales office is given a specific profit target to aim for, rather than focusing like other IBM sales offices primarily on a rigid revenue goal and an arbitrarily defined expense budget.

So far, the experiment has been a winner. Last year [when the trial began], while much of the rest of IBM U.K.'s business floundered, profits at Mr. Aspin's office were about 50% higher than the U.K. average—and about 20% better than they would have been under the old system. The office's revenue, of [pounds sterling] 100 million [$172 million], was about 10% higher than it otherwise would have been, he estimates. (Hudson, 1991)

Clearly, the processes of organization change to deal with EC 92 and globalization have only begun.

Teams

One hypothesis is that no formal organization structure can ever be right—neither the global, nor the multinational, nor the international, nor the product group, nor the regional structure. Rather, the hetarchical structure is the only one that can work in this dynamic environment. A key element in the hetarchical structure is the use of teams to achieve coordination around critical issues, tasks, or opportunities.

Teams cut across the formal functional lines of the organization (e.g., Mills, 1991). Teams may be short-lived or may last for years. Teams may be formally organized, or may be semiformal, informal, or even loose networks. Teams are fluid; many teams come and go as issues arise and are resolved, or opportunities are perceived and seized.

The working arrangements for teams and their members raise complex issues (Galegher, Kraut, and Egido, 1990; Gabarro, 1990; Hackman, 1990; Larson and LaFasto, 1989). Regardless, teams are being used very frequently and are major elements of an organization's strategy to deal with the critical strategic issues identified previously. Teams provide the capability to cut across formal barriers to communication and coordination and can offer an effective mechanism for rapid response. Teams also serve, often, to give individuals greater freedom and opportunity to be innovative and effective in dealing with the issue at hand.

Increasingly, teams are cutting across the boundaries of the firm (Johnston and Lawrence, 1988). Often, teams will involve members from other companies that are strategic partners: partners in a joint venture, in an R&D activity, suppliers of critical components, or important distribution partners.

The use of teams is found in all types of organizations, and especially in the hetarchical organization.

Strategic Opportunities: Overview

This discussion of the organizational forces sets the stage for an assessment of opportunities for using IST for competitive advantage. In Manheim (1992), we apply the conceptual framework of the multithrust strategy to assess IST opportunities in GCOs. The line of reasoning follows that of the pipeline management systems discussed previously. From this analysis, we conclude that there are several promising directions. Particularly promising is that of teamwork support.

Teams: Opportunity for Competitive Advantage

Because of the organizational forces affecting GCOs discussed earlier, team support systems are especially promising.

Example: Team Support Systems to Complement Pipeline Management Systems   We return to considering the order cycle. Managing the pipeline of materials flows illustrates the need for, and potential of, information systems that support teams.

Consider a product group in which components and subassemblies are sourced in eight countries on three continents, production takes place in five factories on two continents, and distribution of finished product is global. Further, assume that in this product group—which develops widgets, for example—there is some significant interchange of material across continents.

A production line for widgets goes down in Cupertino, which usually supplies widgets primarily for assembly in Ohio. This information is reported, on an "exception" basis, to a logistics team working closely with a production management team to coordinate the management of the pipeline supporting this particular product group. The team immediately goes into action: Where are widgets in transport anywhere in the world? What using plants are they being shipped to? What are the relative priorities of these shipments for different using plants? Are there inventories anywhere that could be diverted to meet the need? What are the opportunities for diversion of shipments in transit and the consequences of those diversions? Can other steps be taken to minimize the consequences of a proposed diversion?

This is a complex task: how can a production problem be overcome by a combination of production and/or logistics actions, possibly on a global basis? This is also a team problem: who needs to be involved in finding out critical information, in developing possible courses of action, in assessing their consequences, in making a decision where the decision will probably require a negotiated agreement among a number of individuals in several different countries and several different roles?

At present, this task is resolved using telephone, telex, fax, and possibly email. How could information technology support more rapid and effective accomplishment of this task in the future?

Task/Team Support Systems   We use the term *task/team support system* to designate a system designed to support the team working on a specific task.

A Task/Team Support System (T/TSS) is a system which provides full information system support, for individual and collaborative work, for the members of a team which shares a specific task or function, whether the individuals are working at the same or different places, and at the same or different times. A T/TSS in a globally competing organization is designed explicitly to support work by team members who are scattered geographically across different time zones and, often, different languages and cultures. (Manheim, 1992)

As illustrated by this hypothetical example, T/TSS are an important complement to pipeline systems:

- Pipeline management systems have as their goal the routinizing of operations of the order cycle. By themselves, they are not well suited to handle group problem solving of the nonroutine issues.

- Task/team support systems can be designed to support the handling of the nonroutine. They can be separate systems, or closely integrated with pipeline systems but their functionality is very different.

Example: A Task/Team Support System for Global Sales Task/team support systems are particularly promising for team support to specific tasks in a global company. Consider, for example, the problem of "team selling": managing a coordinated sales process in which a number of geographically scattered individuals participate.

The Rose Company (a fictitious name; the example is real) is a multinational logistics service provider with several hundred offices in more than twenty-five countries. Rose uses a mainframe computer and several regional minicomputers, integrated in a network, as the backbone of its pipeline management information system. A mixture of leased and public lines are used for telecommunications of data. Most offices are either online with the network or have dialup access over public-access networks. In addition to MIS capabilities, an email system is used widely throughout the company.

About a year ago, Rose senior management decided to have a more focused and more globally coordinated sales effort. The strategy that was implemented had these elements:

- Identification of a certain number (n) of target customers (actual or future)

- Designation of a senior manager as the sales coordinator for each customer

- Establishment of a bulletin board in the email system where company staff could post messages for each target customer

The operating process for team coordination included the following:

- Any time a Rose employee visits a target account, he/she is requested to post an email message summarizing information acquired.

- At least once a month, the sales coordinator for that account reviews the messages, prepares a summary, and sends out additional messages with comments, suggestions, and queries to all Rose employees, worldwide, concerned with marketing to that account.

- A global sales coordinator overviews the process, assists in preparing account summaries, and manages the various "conversations" from the perspective of a "facilitator." (The account coordinators are generally at high levels and have independent power bases, so they really can't be "directed" to do something.)

This T/TSS is credited with providing important assistance in Rose's recently gaining at least one major global account.

This use of an electronic bulletin board and messaging system is a simple example of a T/TSS. It shows what can be done with the basic technology widely available today, and appropriate management strategy. More advanced technologies, such as Lotus Development Corporation's NOTES system, provide power to do substantially more. (Manheim et al., 1992)

Task/Team Systems: An Opportunity for Competitive Advantage in Hetarchical Organizations As organizations become more hetarchical, there will be a greater and greater premium placed on the ability to coordinate laterally among individuals in multiple organizational units. This capability will be especially important in organizations with units scattered geographically across different time zones.

The T/TSS technology is new and emerging, and as yet few organizations have expertise in it. T/TSS leverages people skills; it is possible that an organization may be able to combine the technology with human resource development and management strategies that create together a unique and sustainable competitive advantage. T/TSS will have the potential of creating major opportunities for competitive advantage for globally competing organizations

As an example, consider the emerging structure of the worldwide air transportation industry. Major U.S. carriers such as United, American, Delta, Northwest, and USAir are focused on building their positions in the U.S. market and on extending from these positions into a global market. Major European carriers, such as British Airways, KLM, and others, are focused on extending their networks into North America and into other regions as well. KLM has a partial ownership in Northwest Airlines. As this chapter is being written, British Airways (BA) is buying a major stake (25 percent) in USAir.

The BA-USAir alliance is a good example of a hetarchical structure: BA's strong staff in London and USAir's strong staff in the Washington,

D.C. area will each remain strong, independent power centers. There are, and will continue to be, differences in expertise, responsibility, and authority, and neither center will be in position to dictate to the other, as in a traditional, hierarchical organization. Yet, to make this alliance work, it will be essential that key teams in both organizations work together very closely, in spite of the geographical distances separating them.

For example, schedule planning in a single airline is a very difficult task. Coordinating schedules in two very different airlines is even more difficult. Yet, the primary objective of the alliance is for USAir to feed domestic passengers to BA's global system, and vice-versa, so close and coordinated scheduling is a key strategic issue. To accomplish this, the schedule planning teams at both airlines, separated by the Atlantic Ocean and five-hour time differences, must be able to work collaboratively.

Designing A Task/Team Support System for a Specific Application

The BA-USAir example frames the problem: How can an organization design a T/TSS for a specific team and task? There are a number of software applications available from which a T/TSS could be built. (For a typical list of such products, see Coleman, 1992.) These products perform a wide range of functions, and few have the same mix of features. There are many products claiming to be "groupware," or "group decision support systems," or "workflow management systems," or "computer-supported cooperative work" systems, all widely used terms.

Which of these solutions is most promising from a management perspective? A clear concept of the needs in a specific situation is necessary in order to weed out those systems offerings that are irrelevant or inappropriate, and to determine what offerings, if any, will meet significant business needs.

In developing a strategy for using T/TSS, these issues need to be considered:

Need to Clearly Relate System Design to Strategic or Other Business Objectives
Because no single best system exists today, the strategic business purposes must clearly determine the selection of system support. That is, a T/TSS should be designed to achieve relevant and important business objectives. Clearly, there are situations in which

an organization may wish to implement a basic set of computer-supported cooperative work (CSCW) capabilities without specific objectives of a strategic or task-specific nature. We believe, however, that such efforts run a higher probability of failure than efforts that have clear business objectives and are focused, at least initially, on critical issues and processes.

Importance of Consideration of Social Processes Design   The strategic business objective involves the desire to create new team behaviors or change existing team behaviors (see Sproull and Kiesler, chap. 6). Therefore, careful consideration needs to be given to the social processes that exist in the target team and those that are desired. Where a team or approach to the subject task exists, that behavior needs to be studied and understood in order to understand the strengths and weaknesses of the processes of operation (Manheim, 1989; Gabarro, 1990; Galegher, Kraut, and Egido, 1990).

Importance of Implementation of Management Strategy   Where there is a proposed change in an organization, there is likely to be resistance. In the case of T/TSS, there is a significant likelihood that resistance to change takes the form of simply not bothering to use the T/TSS capabilities. Therefore, there is a need to anticipate and plan for potential resistance to the introduction of such new technologies.

Utilization of an Explicit Methodology for TTSS Development and Implementation   The basic platform for TTSS involves personal computers (or other terminals or workstations) and a networking infrastructure on a local area network (LAN) and wide area network (WAN) basis. At the most basic level, the network consists of the dialup public access network, but more elaborate networks are often appropriate (whether provided by the organization itself or outside vendors). The task of deciding what T/TSS applications to develop, and in what way, requires an explicit decision:

▪ In some organizations, the application developments are left up to the users and are done on a local, team-specific basis. However, it is still important to have initial, pilot applications developed by a core team to gain user attention and involvement in the process of developing specific T/TSS.

■ In other organizations, development of T/TSS is controlled centrally.

■ In many organizations, a mixed strategy is appropriate: users are free to develop their own T/TSS applications, but centralized support teams develop critical applications and integrated T/TSS that require substantial development efforts.

In many cases, an explicit methodology will be useful. Such a methodology should include steps such as the following:

1. Explicitly articulate strategic objectives. If the objectives are not clear, it may be necessary to initiate the process with a business strategy process (it is not unusual for major strategy questions to arise out of what appears, initially, to be a simple information systems project).

2. Examine the existing business processes. If appropriate, consider redesigning those processes to be more consistent with the strategy objectives.

3. Identify critical tasks to support those business processes. Assess how they are done now, and how it would be desirable for the team to perform them in the future.

4. Design specific T/TSS functions to implement support for the tasks as redesigned. In the process, it is likely that further redesign of tasks and of business processes will be perceived as desirable.

5. Assess the organizational issues around process, task, and T/TSS change implementation (Manheim, 1989); develop an implementation plan that includes managing change as well as implementing T/TSS software functionalities.

6. During and after implementation, periodically assess what has been done and its effects, in both technology and human dimensions. As needed, recycle, revising strategy, process, tasks, and/or T/TSS as appropriate.

Conclusions

What can an organization do to gain competitive advantage? Develop task/team support systems focused on strategically important, critical business tasks.

What can an organization do to implement T/TSS effectively?

- Focus on learning how to combine human resource and information technology strategies to provide coordinated support to task-specific teams, such as product design, customer service, logistics, or production coordination teams. In general, the direction for seeking competitive advantage will require exploiting information technology and human resources, including organization design, in new ways. Particular emphasis should be placed on T/TSS and related information technologies and on teams and network-building processes.

- Focus on developing expertise in T/TSS: experiment within your organization. Such T/TSS can be very valuable in internal operations. The best way to learn about T/TSS in order to develop services and marketing strategies is to use them.

Acknowledgments

Research support from the following is gratefully acknowledged: the Strategic Informatics Research Program and the companies supporting it—British Airways, Consolidated Freightways, Consolidated Railroad Corporation, Harper Group, IBM, Omron Co. Ltd., and Yellow Freight Co.; and the William A. Patterson chair at the Transportation Center, Northwestern University. Portions of the field work underlying this research were supported by the Japan Foreign Trade Council, Tokyo; by the Center for U.S.-Japan Relations, Northwestern University; by the International Center for Information Technologies, Washington, D.C., the City of Amsterdam, the Netherlands National Physical Planning Agency, the Province of North Holland, the Amsterdam Chamber of Commerce, Mitsubishi Research Institute, and Cambridge Systematics, Inc.

This chapter benefited from numerous conversations and joint activities with Louis Busuttil, British Airways; James Drogan, IBM; David Anderson, Andersen Consulting; Dirk Goedhart, Philips B.V.; Peter Keen, ICIT; Eric Clemons, Wharton School; Benjamin Mittman, Northwestern University; Joyce Elam, University of Texas; Shinroku Tsuji, Kobe City University of Commerce; Moriaki Tsuchiya, Tokyo University; John Robinson, Harper Group; Frank LeClercq, Amsterdam City Planning Department; Gary Biddle, American Standard Corporation;

Jacques Roure, SEMA Group; and Tatsuro Ichihara, Fumio Tateishi, and Nobuo Tateishi, Omron Corporation.

I gratefully acknowledge the benefits of the research support of the sponsors and the collaborations of colleagues, but I alone am responsible for any errors or biases presented here.

8 Cross-Cultural Communication and CSCW

Hiroshi Ishii

Culture has been likened to an iceberg: nine-tenths of it lies beneath the surface, out of our immediate awareness.
—Sharon Ruhly, "Orientations to Intercultural Communication" (in Fuji Xerox, 1984)

CSCW and Groupware

Computer-supported cooperative work (CSCW) emerged in the mid-1980s as an identifiable research field focused on the role of computer technology in group work[1]. CSCW examines how people work together in groups and how computer and communication technology can support them. CSCW attracts researchers, including myself, from a variety of fields—computer science, telecommunications, cognitive science, anthropology, ethnography, and management science (Greif, 1988; Galegher, Kraut, and Egido, 1990; Grudin, 1991; Greenberg, 1991).

"Groupware" was originally coined by Peter and Trudy Johnson-Lenz as the term for software intended to support and augment group work. Groupware became a buzzword in the computer industry, suggesting a technology breaking away from its original confinement to an individual task. Familiar groupware examples include electronic mail, bulletin boards, computer conferencing, group schedulers, group authoring tools, and window/screen-sharing software (Johansen, 1988; Schrage, 1990; Ellis, Gibbs, and Rein, 1991).

Although groupware was a software term, recently it has been used in a wider sense to describe multiuser systems including computer hardware and communication networks. Workstation-based desktop video conference systems such as TeamWorkStation (Ishii and Miyake, 1991) are an example of groupware in this wider sense.

Groupware is intended to create a shared workspace that supports dynamic collaboration in a work group over space and time constraints. To gain some collective benefits of groupware use, the groupware must be accepted by a majority of work group members as a common tool. Groupware must overcome this hurdle of critical mass at first. People do a lot of their work alone, without computers, or using different tools on different computer systems, and have developed their own work practices for these situations. In order to have new groupware accepted, continuity with existing individual work environments is the key issue because users work in either individual or collaborative modes and frequently move back and forth.

The Iceberg and Human Communication

Recently I have had the opportunity to work in Western academic societies such as ACM (Association for Computing Machinery), SIGCHI (Special Interest Group on Computer and Human Interaction), and the program committees of such conferences as CSCW, and ECSCW (European CSCW). Participating in these events has helped me to become aware of the importance of "culture" in the design of computer-supported communication media. These experiences can be compared to the sudden awakening from a deep sleep.

As I became personally aware of the differences between American and Japanese social protocols, I began to understand more deeply my own cultural background. I think of my re-awakening to the cultural component in my own thoughts and beliefs as a kind of counter-culture shock. I found that most communication difficulties come from cultural gaps among people. The same code can be interpreted in a variety of ways, depending on the under-sea part of the iceberg, the framework for interpreting words, gestures, and expressions that is part of membership in a culture (figure 8.1). Japanese and Americans and others have fundamentally different decoders at the cultural level, and communication difficulties may result when that fact isn't taken into account. I came to understand that the tools we are designing for CSCW are better seen as *cultural tools* than computer tools.

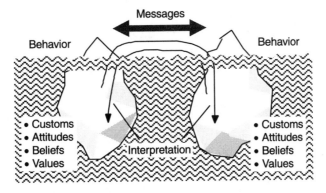

Figure 8.1
Human communication model (adapted from Fuji Xerox, 1984 with permission)

From HCI to HHI

Through many discussions, I, along with many foreign researchers, realized that the research into human interfaces, communication, and CSCW shares common goals—to understand the nature of cross-cultural communication and to design systems to facilitate the formulation and communication of ideas using computer technology. People who are trying to make computers easier to use are wrestling with one aspect of the same problem faced by groupware designers. We know a great deal about how our communication and computing technologies work, and we are beginning to learn how people use these tools in their intellectual work. We are also beginning to understand that questions about how people use tools together are cultural matters, and a few of us suspect that these technical issues might contribute to dealing with the broader human issues of cross-cultural communication. The ability of telecommunication and computer-based technologies to overcome time and space constraints seems to be an essential foundation for tools to promote international collaboration in a variety of fields. We are building on that foundation.

Human interface has long been interpreted as an interface between an individual user and a computer (so called human-computer interaction, or HCI). Research into ways to improve human-computer interaction had mainly focused on communication issues between the individual user and a single computer, such as screen layout, icon design, data visualization, pointing devices, and so forth (figure 8.2). However, the expansion of CSCW research and the spread of the groupware concept have had the effect of shifting our focus on human interface from HCI to "organizational interface" (Malone, 1988) or "human-human interaction (HHI)" (Ishii, 1990; Endo, 1992). "Multiuser interface" is a notion originating from this HHI view that subsumes the familiar concept of "user interface" (Ishii and Arita, 1991; Ishii, 1992). Multiuser interface stresses that the interface is for groups working together in a shared workspace. The new directions in designing CSCW tools for truly widespread adoption have had the effect of shifting our focus on human interfaces from HCI to human-human interaction mediated by computer and communication technologies (figure 8.3).

The telecommunications infrastructure for delivering powerful information tools to large numbers of people is being built today. Now that the technology has advanced this far, it is time to devote more effort to the human side of the system.

We do not interact *with* computers but *through* computers. Operating a computer is not a goal in itself for the vast majority of people; to most of the population, the greatest potential of computers lies in their capabilities as media for human-human interaction. For example, making a document using word processor software increases your ability to share the ideas with other people by sending the document to them through the mail or as an interoffice memo. If you can send the document electronically, instantly, anywhere, amplifying the power of the media again amplifies the power of the process. Word processing is just a microstep of higher cooperative workflow in an organizational context.

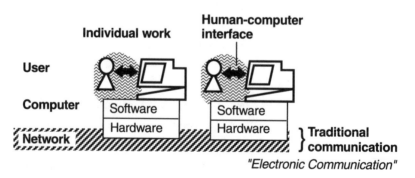

Figure 8.2
Traditional view of personal computing environment

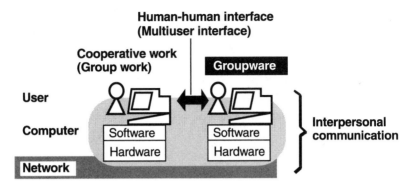

Figure 8.3
New view of interpersonal computing environment

Communication has also long been traditionally interpreted in terms of electronic communication based on the OSI (Open Systems Interconnect) seven-layers model, which is widely known by engineers in the telecommunication world, but doesn't make much sense to nonengineers. The OSI model deals with incompatibilities between different hardware and software by creating standard formats for exchanging data at different layers, each of which has a set of protocols for mediating between foreign systems. The way data is encoded for transmission is one layer, the way information is transported across a network is another layer, and the way information is presented on screens is yet another layer, and so forth. Engineers have worked to provide high-speed, broadband, reliable communication networks using a variety of hard technologies based on that layer model.

They have created the foundation for doing things with groups of people that haven't been possible before. In this OSI framework, however, the subjects of communication are not human beings but the computers or programs. This is not what I pursue. I much prefer to explore the notion of interpersonal communication because I believe the subjects of communication should be us, the people of the world. Designing CSCW tools shifts my focus of attention from the electronic communication level to the interpersonal communication level (figure 8.3).

Through the design of the TeamWorkStation, I realized that the notion of human interface is equivalent to the notion of communication at a higher level and that cultural gaps among people lead to communication difficulties. Therefore, I believe that international collaboration is required for human interface research and CSCW to investigate the nature of cross-cultural communication and the possibility of cross-cultural groupware. Specifically, how can we go about designing modern communication systems that will help people overcome the cultural barriers to communication?

Cross-Cultural Groupware?

Groupware consists of the computer and communication system that supports a group of people working together. In designing computer-based groupware it is important to capture the structure of social process in a group and embed it into the system. However, it is very difficult to build any general and standard model of human communication because protocols can be extremely different at a deep level from one community to another community. (Because of that, I designed Team-WorkStation as a *transparent* medium without embedding specific protocols.) The following two examples illustrate the difficulty of developing cross-cultural groupware.

The Decision-making Process and Nemawashi

As Walls also discusses (chap. 9), Japanese companies reach decisions in a way that is very different from most American decision-making processes. Decision making in Japan is a *collective process* involving many people. The person pushing a plan spends a lot of energy to gain consensus before the formal decision making. Before the proposal document is sent around, he or she explains the plan to everyone concerned at informal meetings and through personal contact. The originator of the plan tries to get the tacit agreement of others, and this effort decreases the possibility that the plan will not be supported. Getting a consensus beforehand is key to success. This kind of groundwork is called *nemawashi* in Japanese, which means that all the people who approve the plan at all levels have the feeling of participation in formulating it, and this makes it possible to implement the plan more smoothly (Nittetsu, 1987).

In American companies, responsibility and authority are clearly defined, and the person in charge usually can decide whatever comes within his or her immediate authority. Without moving into a discussion of which model is better, I simply wish to note that major differences exist between social processes associated with executive decision making in Japan and in the U.S. Decision making in these countries is based on different cultural principles and social processes. In the near future, we must begin to integrate deeper understanding of these principles and feed the results into CSCW system design.

For example, computer-mediated communication systems often include a public bulletin-board-like area where a group can discuss and debate an issue, along with a second, more private means of sending personal communications from any individual to any other individual or group of individuals (electronic mail, also known as email). Note how Japanese and American decision making teams might use the same system in somewhat different ways. Electronic nemawashi would mean that a lot of the communication would take place invisibly, in many email messages, behind the scenes of the public conferencing areas; American decision making might involve more or less similar behind-the-scenes communication, but a lot of the debating and decision making might take place on stage, in the public area.

GDSS (group decision support systems) is an active research field. There are a variety of theories of decision making, and the tools designed for GDSS are based on these theories. As always, the theories carry a lot of cultural assumptions and the tools impose constraints on the group of users. Therefore GDSS imported from another culture can easily fail. Understanding these social and cultural differences is a starting point toward the design of next generation groupware that can support cross-cultural collaboration. Of course, these brief examples are only generalizations. There are always exceptions, but I have found these generalizations to hold true to a significant extent. They require further study by social scientists and information system designers working together.

Face-to-Face Meetings

The style of meetings in America and Japan offers another illustration of the role of cultural differences in decision making (Fuji Xerox, 1984). Participants in American meetings try to contribute to the content of the meeting. American managers expect participants to take personal responsibility and make an active effort. People are often very assertive. On the other hand, participants in Japanese meetings try to achieve harmony with others. They defer to others and often wait for others to draw them out. Japanese may be satisfied with sharing information and getting a feel for others' views even if they can not get a concrete result such as a decision or solution to a problem. Japanese do not like to debate over issues and ideas. Direct attacks on the ideas of others, it is felt, may prevent the achievement of harmony and mutual understanding, a very deeply held cultural value. Japanese find it difficult to criticize the idea of another because it can be interpreted as an attack on the personality of the person whose idea was criticized.

Americans seem to place emphasis on the exchange of words and specific explanations of ideas. However, Japanese communication depends very strongly on the context of the discussion. Facial expressions, postures, and tacit understandings only hinted at in a few words are very important.

In my own experience in CHI and CSCW conferences, I found that turn taking is most difficult for me to learn to adapt to in discussions with Americans. Situation-oriented, nonverbal cues for turn taking in Japanese meetings are much clearer to me. In Japan it is very rude to interrupt someone who is speaking. We have been taught to be patient and to listen until the person is finished speaking. In America, however, people must interrupt others in order to take a turn. Otherwise, there is less a chance of being able to express one's ideas.

In face-to-face meetings, nonnative speakers of English always feel strong time pressure to understand and speak in real time. For me as a nonnative speaker, email is a more satisfactory medium of communication because email allows me to take time to read and compose the messages. Under the strong time pressure of face-to-face conversation, it is very difficult to concentrate on the discussion for hours.

Email is a narrow-band communication medium based on low technology compared to desktop video conference systems that are becoming available. Email uses flat text to express information. No multimedia. However, its asynchronous feature provides great benefits to nonnative speakers. I believe this is just one of many ways communication technology can play a positive role in encouraging cross-cultural communication.

Conclusion

Each community has its own style of communication, and the world is full of communities that differ in fundamental ways. However, we live together on the same planet and we must collaborate internationally to solve conflicts. I work in scientific research together with many friends with different cultural backgrounds. We cooperate and compete and discuss problems of mutual interest. Yet we know very little about the dynamics of cross-cultural communication and little about the unique cultural biases operant in the way that we communicate and make decisions. We need to understand each other better for that. We should use all the tools at our disposal to pay more attention to understanding the differences among us. And then we should start to think about how to overcome this gap with or without technology. Although I am not overly optimistic about what CSCW technology can do to overcome this gap, I expect the next generation of groupware will be designed to take these cross-cultural issues into consideration.

Acknowledgments

I thank Howard Rheingold for encouraging me to write an earlier version of this essay and for his valuable comments on the draft. I extend my appreciation to Linda Harasim, Robert Jacobson, Jan Walls, Bobbi Smith, Michael Hayward, Cyndia Pilkington, Andrew Feenberg, and many other participants of the GAN online discussion for their stimulating comments. Finally, I thank Yutaka Saeki, Shun Tutiya, Naomi Miyake, and Takaya Endo for the stimulating discussions on our common interests: socially distributed cognition and CSCW.

9 Global Networking for Local Development: Task Focus and Relationship Focus in Cross-Cultural Communication

Jan Walls

The general topic of this book is globalizing computer networks, but an effective understanding of the social and cultural dimensions of globalization presupposes an understanding of the nature of social networks. The hypothesis presented in this chapter is: for most people, online networks may be best suited for functioning as task-focused sociotechnical systems, which offer information, ideas, or other forms of enrichment to users whose stable relationship-focused affiliations are not online. Understanding the main issues of this discussion requires clarification of certain critical terms. We may want to begin, therefore, with an effort to clarify what we mean to mean (with apologies to Lewis Caroll) by such terms as *group, society, community, system, network, strong-tie* and *weak-tie* relationships. It will be necessary to give full consideration to the most fundamental notion common to all networks: *relationship.*

Groups, Tasks, and Relationships

It is usually safe to begin a serious study by quoting a Nobel prize winner. Nobel laureate Arno Penzias notes: "In the middle of a recent discussion of the future direction of Bell Labs' research, a friend remarked, 'The reason we are all here is to make money for the stockholders.'" Penzias was taken aback by that observation. "Is that really why my colleagues are so deeply involved in what they are doing? Clearly, the building we occupy, the equipment we use, and the salaries we earn all come to us from somebody who expects to make money—otherwise none of it would exist. But on further reflection I realized that 'the reason we are all here' doesn't tell the whole story" (1989, 219). He sensed the omission of an important ingredient in such a top-down view. For most of us, he observes, "the reason we choose to be here" turns out to be the opportunity to work with others, doing something we think is important.

In one breath Penzias touches upon the three primary aspects of human social activity: the task-focused aspect ("the reason"), the relationship aspect ("we"), and the space-sharing aspect ("are all here"). If we say "human relationships consist of individuals who share space, interests, or goals," we might imply any of the following assumptions:

1. Individuals are related primarily through shared space.
   Example: urban next-door neighbors

2. Individuals are related primarily through shared interests.
   Example: bridge club members

3. Individuals are related primarily through shared goals.
   Example: task force members

4. Individuals are related primarily through shared space and interests.
   Example: community center activity participants

5. Individuals are related primarily through shared space and goals.
   Example: condominium association members

6. Individuals are related primarily through shared interests and goals.
   Example: PeaceNet members

7. Individuals are related through shared space, interests, and goals.
   Example: agricultural co-op members

On first thought, we might assume that an online relationship does not involve assumptions 1, 4, 5, and 7, since there is no requirement for physical proximity, for face-to-face interaction. This argument is unconvincing for anyone who has been kept offline by a busy signal or has had to wait in line to get inside a busy host computing facility. So online networks are characterized by people who share time, space, interests and/or task focus—they do not necessarily share the same time or share body space, but online groups do share virtually the same elements that face-to-face groups share.

For analysis it is helpful to view groups as types of systems. A *system,* described most succinctly and abstractly, is any number of elements in some form of relationship with each other. A system may be primarily service oriented such as a telecommunications network; or production oriented such as a factory; or it may be biological such as a respiratory system; or it may be meteorological such as a weather system, or astronomical such as our solar system (cf. Boulding, 1985). A system whose members are linked together by technologies is called a *sociotechnical system* (cf. Pasmore and Sherwood, 1978).

An *online group,* then, is a sociotechnical system whose elements are related for a specific purpose or set of purposes, whether their own, or someone else's. A group may be a part of a larger group, as a work group or task force within a company or community. Its members are there sometimes only because the group contributes to their goals, sometimes only because they contribute to the group's; ideally, they should be there for both reasons, in which case we could describe their relationship as synergistic.

For sociologists, the term "community" usually refers to Ferdinand Toennies' famous ideal type called *gemeinschaft* in German, while "society" equates to his *gesellschaft* (Toennies, 1965). Toennies' *gemeinschaft* is a natural grouping of people based on kinship and neighborhood, shared culture, and folkways—a tribe or a peasant village would be a classic example. His *gesellschaft* refers to impersonal contractual and legal relationships, based more upon mutual need to achieve specific tasks or general goals than on blood relationships (kinship) or proxemic relationships (neighborhood). The modern city or state, therefore, is seen as a society rather than a community.

Community has also been defined by contrasting "a social relationship of solidarity between individuals based on affection, kinship, or membership of a community such as a family or group of friends" with one based upon the "division of labour and contractual relations between isolated individuals consulting only their own self-interest" (Bullock and Stallybrass, 1977, 256).

Daly and Cobb, Jr. (1989) suggest a very useful approach to understanding society and community by focusing on the relationship between them, rather than simply juxtaposing them in binary opposition. They view community as one form of society, although "a society should not be called a community unless (1) there is extensive participation by its members in the decisions by which its life is governed, (2) the society as a whole takes responsibility for the members, and (3) this responsibility includes respect for the diverse individuality of these members" (p. 172). Community, then, must be seen as emerging from the mutual commitment, mutual involvement, mutual responsibility, and mutual respect between a society and its individual members.

An interesting cross-cultural illustration of the above contrast is found in Ronald Dore's distinction between two types of business firm: the company law model, typified by Western capitalist corporations, and the community model commonly found in Japan. In the company law model, the firm is primarily defined as the property of the shareholders whose rights are paramount, where management is the trusted agent of the shareholders, and where management hires workers. In the community model, the firm is seen as a social unit made up of all the people who work full-time in it (not "for it"), whose shareholders are, like customers and suppliers and local authorities, one group of outsiders who have to be satisfied if the firm is to prosper, and whose management and workers see each others' long-term benefits as being interdependent (Dore, 1987, 53–55). So, in Tokyo, by any measure a "modern city or state," we see that a corporation is characterized by relationship patterns and stability of membership that characterize traditional communities.

Relationship-Focused Communities and Task-Focused Groups

Groups, then, may be seen as subsystems of larger social systems who come together for specific purposes. One may be "in a group, but not of it," while one is usually "in and of" one's community. One may participate in groups within one's own community, but the strategies of task achievement by that group, which we might call a *strong-tie* group, will be expected to make frequent reference to the common relationship pattern of the superordinate community, and may take longer to achieve a task than a *weak-tie* group of the same size. (For a thorough examination of the weak-tie concept, see Granovetter 1973.)

The functional difference between relationship-focused and task-focused group performance is well illustrated by the difference in time required for negotiation of a new contract by a typical Japanese negotiation team and a typical American negotiation team. The Japanese team will be expected to make frequent reference back to the superordinate community and its enduring relationship patterns prior to mak-

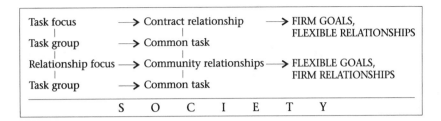

Figure 9.1
Goals and relationships in task groups and communities

ing any significant commitment. The American team, having been authorized to negotiate a deal, knows that its business relationships are defined and limited mostly by contracts and may be altered in order to respond to newly emergent opportunities. The Japanese, therefore, describe their own negotiation-to-delivery process as "slow-slow—>fast-fast," knowing that once agreement has been reached, action can proceed swiftly because everyone in the community will have been aware of, and probably will have agreed to, the approaching commitment before it has been signed. They describe the American process as "fast-fast—>slow-slow," implying that after the negotiators have signed the quick contract, they will then have to spend time engaging in retroactive *nemawashi* (preparatory consensus seeking). From a Japanese perspective, in other words, the American mode appears to regard relationships as a function of task achievement.

Figure 9.1 shows schematically how individuals may view their options for relating to other individuals for cooperative goal attainment in task-focused (contract-related) societies and in relationship-focused communities.

Communication may serve either as a means to achieve firm goals through flexible social relationships or as a means to maintain firm relationships by achieving flexible goals—that is, goals chosen or modified so as to contribute to the long-term relationships of the community. Therefore, we may say that the former is the dominant function of communication in *gesellschaft*, weak-tie groups, and the latter is the dominant function in strong-tie communities and their primary groups. Both functions, it must be stressed, exist simultaneously in societies as well as in communities, since it is axiomatic that any act of communication will have both content and relationship dimensions (Watzlawick, Bavelas, and Jackson, 1967, chap. 2). The difference between them can only be in relative emphasis on one aspect over the other. Thus in primary groups and communities, the relationship aspect of a communication act may be expected to play a more important role than it would in secondary groups. The interesting apparent exception, of course, is the urbanite secondary group whose primary purpose is to serve emotional or relationship-focused ends.

It has been argued that the goal-oriented function of task-focused groups, and by implication the content aspect of communication, has been overemphasized in industrial-commercial, *gesellschaft* societies. Leiss (1989) argues that "our society has split the process of caring that was united in traditional socialization networks. Caring for others outside the domain of the nuclear family, in terms of basic needs, has been relegated increasingly to public agencies. At the same time the formation of a sense of personal identity and well-being has been detached from the network of caring relationships and routed instead through the market-place—which . . . cannot successfully perform this function" (p. 123). Caring for someone, in other words, may refer either to a concern felt for their well-being or to a service performed on their behalf but not necessarily to both. This division of caring into concern felt and service performed is more characteristic of industrial-commercial *gesellschaft* societies than of community relationships in *gemeinschaft* societies. On the relationship between market-responsive dynamism and community-focused stability, the best argument for a multicentric society is perhaps found in Alberto Ramos (1981).

The Value of Having Both Task and Relationship Focuses

Relationship-focused groups are characterized by intimacy, long-term responsibility of members for each other, and stability of membership with holistic relationships. They are not easily entered into and not easily left behind under normal circumstances. But relationship-focused groups may also exhibit another characteristic—stagnation, unless their members and their internal relationships are invigorated by external linkages to other groups, involving the exchange of goods and technologies as well as information.

Task-focused groups, on the other hand, are characterized by respect for the individuality of their members, by task-oriented responsibility of members, and by mobility of membership with particularistic, rather than holistic, relationships. They are more easily entered into and are left behind with less remorse when better opportunities emerge outside the group. But task-focused groups also run the risk of disintegrating due to the lack of long-term commitment to internal relationships on the part of members.

The ideal society, therefore, will consist of an optimal blend of relationship-focused communities as well as numerous task-focused groups that exist primarily to serve the longer-term interests of stable communities. The diversity and mobility of task-focused groups, in other words, are useful primarily as sources of information, ideas, and other exchanges needed to energize and revitalize stable communities.

It would seem, then, that online groups (mediated by computer networks) are ideally suited to play the role of task-focused groups that supplement and enhance the performance of groups with broader mandates, including primary, relationship-focused communities, and by so doing they may also enhance the quality of the relationships within real communities. They can do this by allowing quick, easy access to the ideas, information, organizational strategies, technologies, and so forth, required to keep stable communities dynamic.

Intra-, Inter-, and Cross-Cultural Communication

What will happen when members of relationship-focused communities from different language-cultures come together to cooperate in task-focused groups online? Assuming that they share a common language, the major obstacles to effective online communication and cooperation will be described as "cultural," that is to say, different visions or expectations as to how elements should relate to one another (see also Ishii, chap. 8).

Intracultural Communication
Intracultural communication is the exchange of information between elements in the same language-culture system. I use language and culture as a single, hyphenated concept because one cannot be understood properly outside the context of the other. Linguistic knowledge without cultural knowledge may result in using perfect pronunciation and flawless grammar to say the wrong thing. For communication to be intracultural, people communicating within the same language-culture

system must not only use the same pronunciation (the face-to-face equivalent to spelling online) and grammar but also must reveal similar attitudes about the relationships between themselves—hierarchically between senior and junior positions, and between insiders and outsiders. In fact, it is quite possible to gain a better understanding of intracultural communication through making a cross-cultural study of interpersonal communication in different societies, comparing the differences between the two.

Within task-focused societies such as Canada and the United States, there may be great diversity among subcultures, including even subcultures characterized by relationship-focused communities. One would be ill-advised, for example, to generalize about Canadian culture without considering the diversity among Anglo-, Franco- and Aboriginal Canadians. Within relationship-focused societies, on the other hand, there may also be an abundance of task-focused groups whose sole purpose is to strengthen or enrich the primary relationship-focused community.

Intercultural Communication

Intercultural communication takes place when members of different language-culture systems exchange information, and each is aware of the expectations of the other concerning the relationships of the communicators. Intercultural communication, then, may be thought of as taking place through a "metacultural" mindset on the part of the participants. It may take place, for example, between French and English Canadians, at least one of whom is bilingual, and both of whom are knowledgeable about the culture of the other. One who is sensitive to and competent in intercultural communication may be seen as having achieved "intercultural personhood."

Cross-Cultural Communication

Cross-cultural communication takes place when at least one of the parties trying to exchange information is unaware of, or chooses to disregard, a significant difference in expectations concerning the relationships between the communicators. When a person from a task-focused society does not understand why a person from a relationship-focused society resists overtures to become less formal and more personal early in a new relationship, the communication may be described as cross-cultural rather than intercultural. As a result of recent advances in transportation and telecommunication technologies, cross-cultural communication has become a part of the lives of more people than ever before. Unfortunately, it also means that more people than ever before have the opportunity to engage in a dialogue that will amount to asking the wrong questions in anticipation of irrelevant answers. Education and practice are the only remedies.

Perspectival Enrichment: The Virtue of Cross-Cultural Networking for Intercultural Communication

Every dynamically stable community has one characteristic of a healthy investment portfolio: it maintains optimal diversity, resisting the urge to put all its eggs into one basket. Acquisition and retention of diverse alternatives for balancing dependence, independence, and interdependence among its members is one of the most important survival strategies for any society. Consider for a moment the case of Japan.

The Japanese have always been known as a group-focused people, even as a closed society. Yet the whole history of Japanese civilization has been one of continuous, if not continual, communication with foreign peoples, first Koreans and Chinese, later with more remote peoples. These foreign, cross-cultural relationships have almost always been task-focused relationships whose purpose has been to enrich their primary domestic community relationships. The result of practicing both *uchi* (inner) and *soto* (outer) modes of distinguishing-while-relating with others has often brought them the best of two worlds: stability and dynamism.

The specific benefits to Japan of international exchange for domestic enrichment (writing, watercolor painting, digital watches, automobiles, VCRs, computers, to name just a few) may be formulated into a syndrome, which I call the "Japan syndrome"—import, adopt, domesticate, improve. Japanese have been doing this for centuries, with an interesting result: they have not become any less Japanese, but have become more effectively Japanese. Through stable, enduring, affective, strong-tie *uchi* relationships, they enjoy relative stability; through flexible, effective, weak-tie *soto* relationships, they achieve dynamic renewal. The result comes close to the systemic ideal of dynamic stability.

At this point the moral argument may be raised that people linked in relationship-focused communities may tend to exploit those with whom they relate only through task-focused relationships. I do not deny that this happens. In fact there are abundant historical precedents for such exploitative relationships, even in the most egalitarian of societies. I wish only to suggest that simultaneous participation in relationship-focused and task-focused networks characterizes relationships within and between dynamically stable systems and does not require exploitative relations.

Task-Focused Networks for Relationship-Focused Communities: Cross-Cultural Applications for Intercultural Networks

This section introduces and discusses the notion that online networks probably are best thought of as "virtual groups" and "virtual communities," networked sources of information, ideas or other forms of enrichment for users who belong to "real" groups and communities for whom face-to-face relationships are primary.

Task Focus or Relationship Focus? Not Either/Or, but Both/And

As noted above, every act of communication simultaneously has both a content dimension and a relationship dimension. By way of analogy, it is also possible to hypothesize that every social group has both a goal dimension and a relationship dimension.

The chapter began by suggesting that human relationships consist of individuals who share space, interests, or goals, and that similar, or at least parallel, conditions prevail between face-to-face and online relationships. The seventh example of the various permutations was "Individuals . . . related through shared space, interests, and goals," and the example suggested was agricultural co-op members. This would be a classic instance of a stable community face-to-face relationship. If one or all the members of this face-to-face agricultural co-op community joined an international co-op online network, offering and receiving information and ideas with other co-op community members around the world for each other's benefit, this would constitute a good example of optimal networking across cultures. It would be a functional alliance of face-to-face communities linked through task-focused online networking across geographical, political, and cultural boundaries. The result would also be synergistic, since through the productive use of information and ideas, the whole would be greater than the mere sum of its parts. It could also be described as responding to a need to "link globally, act locally."

As is the case in most synergistic networks, the capacity to think and act independently, or in accordance with one's own community traditions, is not only not threatened but may in fact become enhanced if the newly accessed information or idea is imported, adopted, domesticated, and improved. The American jogger is allowed to enjoy doing her or his American thing even more by using the Japanese Walkman, which was originally accessed through international commercial distribution networks. The Chinese peasant's life is enriched through gaining advance knowledge of crop-threatening changes in weather through local broadcast of information that came from international meteorological information networks. In both cases, domestic intracultural goals are achieved through maintaining international, intercultural relationships. Through optimal association in task-focused networks, in other words, relationship-focused groups may become empowered to function more effectively as dynamically stable communities.

This is not to say that task-focused online networks cannot perform subversive functions—only that they need not. The facsimile transmission into and throughout China of foreign news coverage of the post-Tiananmen crackdown was perceived as subversive by the Chinese government, who claimed that the treasured relationship of unity between the Party and the people was being threatened. On the other hand, the same facsimile machines have allowed for the more effective transmission of graphics and handwritten Chinese language documents that enhance the attainment of goals that are shared at all levels of Chinese society.

Optimal Networking: Globalization without Homogenization

One theory that enjoys favor among communication scholars is called convergence theory, and states that if two or more individuals share information with one another, then over time they will tend to converge toward one another, leading to a state of greater uniformity (Kincaid, 1988). Empirical tests have supported the theory. Does this mean, then, that cross-cultural networking, through facilitating information exchange, will inevitably lead to homogenization of cultural diversity? Eventually, perhaps, but not necessarily in a headlong, careening rush toward entropic uniformity. Critical, conscientious choices are made by people who may wish to preserve relationship patterns that they find satisfying, while at the same time opting for access to the knowledge and information that circulates through communities around them.

With the globalized movement of factories, fishing fleets, and renewable and nonrenewable resources, it is in the interest of every relationship-focused local community to participate in task-focused international and intercultural networks.

Relationship-focused communities, characterized by a notion of stewardship over their shared physical space, can put goal-focused computer networks to good use by seeking manipulative knowledge (useful, action-oriented information, cf. Rifkin, 1987, 241–242) to be put to use in their relationship-focused communities. An online international network, therefore, may perform the valuable function of serving and preserving the interests of face-to-face communities.

There is no reason why local autonomy may not be respected along with global responsibility when it comes to "managing the global commons" (World Commission on Environment and Development, 1987). It is to everyone's advantage that humanity maintain a healthy diversity of sociocultural as well as economic, political, and technological strategies for managing their portion of the global commons. Acknowledging the virtue of diversity, however, implies and requires a healthy respect for divergent strategies of conceiving and expressing the nature of elements and relationships that characterize their part of the commons. It is therefore in our overall short- and long-term interest to participate in the globalization of communication networks, not instead of developing local ways, but precisely to gain a more enlightened, critical understanding of the virtue of "doing it our way." We may, in other words, commit ourselves to globalizing without necessarily homogenizing.

Sociologists in the West have observed that a new type of social relationship is emerging, generated by the electronic media. This has been referred to as "para-social interaction" (Goonasekera, 1990, 37). Through telecommunications, it becomes possible to interact within virtual communities of virtual networks that exist in a complementary relationship to one's own social networks in real communities.

The key term here is *complementary,* implying "not instead of, but in addition to." This is one of the beauties of using virtual networks to support the goals and relationships of real communities. To paraphrase the American sociologist W. I. Thomas (1966), "If people define communities as real, they may be real in their consequences." On the other hand, if we define community as virtual, it may also become real in its consequences.

10 Information Security: At Risk?

Michael Kirby and Catherine A. Murray

"We are at risk." The United States National Research Council began its report *Computers at Risk* (1991) with these words . The report goes on:

Increasingly, America depends on computers. They control power delivery, communications, aviation and financial services. They are used to store vital information, from medical records to business plans, to criminal records. Although we trust them, they are vulnerable—to the effects of poor design and insufficient quality control, to accident, and perhaps most alarmingly, to deliberate attack. The modern thief can steal more with a computer than with a gun. Tomorrow's terrorist may be able to do more damage with a keyboard than with a bomb. To date we have been remarkably lucky. . . . Unfortunately there is reason to believe that our luck will soon run out. . . . [1]

Across the Pacific, the Japan Information Processing Development Center (October 1991) has argued:

The development of network technology has enabled mutual connection of information systems across national borders, creating a borderless society in information processing. As a result, it is now possible to access any part of the world in the same amount of time, a social framework everyone acknowledges to be very efficient and convenient. On the other hand, the consequences of failures in information systems increase in proportion to the degree of network expansion. For this reason *unless all countries uniformly adopt the same level of minimum security measures, social stability cannot be maintained in an age of global information*. . . . The influence of security problems occurring in less protected systems can now extend even to sufficiently protected systems if they are connected via networks. This means that weak parts need to be eliminated from the whole. Today, actions taken locally can have only limited effectiveness in the field of information system security. (*We have now reached a junction when all countries must collaborate in the study of information security in the global age.*)[2] [emphasis added]

To all of that, many international observers would say amen. The need for an effective international regime of information security appears to be simple and self-evident. It is urgent and necessary. Indeed, the establishment of security measures is seriously overdue if one takes into account the enormous expansion of network technology that has already occurred.[3]

The thesis of this chapter is that we are at risk indeed. But the risk derives from something far more fundamental than the vulnerability of computer and information systems. The risk derives instead from the frequent incapacity of democratic policy processes in international and national institutions to keep pace with the social implications of technology.

Many political, institutional, and cultural obstacles can conspire against the achievement of international harmonization.[4] One need look no further than international airline travel for a case of melancholy failure.[5]

The need for a compatible international regime for security of information systems appears even more urgent than the search for an effective regime for air liability. The interactions of data communication are even more pervasive. The ramifications reach more directly into the lives of virtually every one of us. You do not have to travel to be caught up in the problem, although if you do, you are. The perils of loss and damage to life and property are even greater than in air mishaps. While we have survived all these years with a hodge-podge of improvizations in air liability rules, it is unlikely that we can get by for much longer without an appropriate agreement on international policy for the security of general information networks.

OECD Guidelines on Privacy

If there is any glimmer of hope, it arises from the comparative success of earlier international precedents in harmonizing informatics policy. The OECD Guidelines on Privacy were adopted and became effective in September 1980. The guidelines have proved most useful in the development of laws and policies in a number of OECD (Organization for Economic Cooperation and Development) countries, with legal traditions as diverse as those of Japan and Australia.

It is important to remember that the OECD's exercise on privacy did not commence in a vacuum. The Universal Declaration of Human Rights had included, in Article 12, a provision that:

No one shall be subjected to arbitrary interference with his privacy . . . Everyone has the right to the protection of law against such interference or attacks.[6]

This principle was picked up by the European Convention on Human Rights and by the International Covenant on Civil and Political Rights.[7]

The advent of computers presented a new problem for the privacy principle in Article 12 or (as it is now often called) data protection and data security. First, a number of the Scandinavian countries separately, then the Nordic Council and later the Council of Europe, produced drafts that sought to isolate the basic principles of privacy protection in the computer age. The principles were refined and reflected a largely chronological approach to the movement of data through a system. They governed the collection of the data, quality of the data once collected, the use of the data, the security applicable to the data, the rights of the individuals and others affected to have access to the data. The Council of Europe developed conventions that were open to its member countries. However, useful as the principles collected in those conventions were, they tended to be European in orientation and to reflect hardware provisions that were not always congenial to application outside of Europe.[8]

The choice then faced by the international community was a familiar one: fusion or fission. Fusion on the one hand would suggest sharpening the explicit legal obligations within the smaller subgroups of the communities principally affected, such as the European Community (EC). Indeed, directives are presently under consideration that, in explicit ways, will enlarge the obligations of member countries of the EC for the protection of privacy. The alternative path—fission—was to spread the basic, minimum principles to a wider world. UNESCO and the United Nations exhibited interest in privacy protection. Although some claimed that privacy was a luxury of developed societies, others pointed out that basic human rights were universal and as important to persons in Africa and Asia affected as to those in Europe and North America.

Distracted by other concerns and racked by institutional frictions, UNESCO and the UN system have proved less effective in pursuing this issue than the OECD. A body of intercontinental membership, the OECD connects the principal developed countries of the world, extending from Europe and North America to Japan, Australia, and New Zealand in the Pacific. Reaching consensus within the OECD on the value-loaded issue of privacy protection was a much greater challenge than achieving a similar objective within Europe, with its largely shared traditions and common economic interests.

Not surprisingly, various tensions emerged within the original OECD Group on Privacy. The Europeans, with fresh memories of the misuse of personal data by the secret police of totalitarian regimes, were perhaps more alert to the practical dangers against which safeguards were needed. The Anglophone countries, led by the United States, were more sympathetic to the importance of free expression and the free flow of ideas. The economic interests of the Americans reinforced their philosophical concerns that controls for privacy protection were actually disguised efforts of some European countries designed to protect local information technology industries rather than human values in privacy.

Notwithstanding these and other differences, agreement was finally struck. The Council of the OECD recommended to member countries that they should take into account in their domestic legislation the principles contained in the guidelines. It also recommended that they should endeavour to avoid creating, ". . . in the name of privacy protection, unjustified obstacles to transborder flows of personal data."[9]

The most influential section of the Guidelines on Privacy is part 2, "Basic Principles of National Application," which has affected a great deal of domestic policy-making and law-making. These basic principles were deliberately noncoercive in form. They did not envisage a binding treaty. The hope was that, by getting the basics right, we would lay down a system of voluntary compliance that, by good example, would permeate the laws and policies of member countries of the OECD. Has that hope been realized? In Australia and Japan, the OECD privacy guidelines have had noticeable, although gradual, effect on the development of national policies.

In Australia, the OECD guidelines were adopted, at the federal level, by the Privacy Act of 1989. That act applies to specified information systems under federal regulation, such as in the federal public service and credit reporting agencies. Australia was rather slow in acceding to the OECD Guidelines on Privacy because consultations with the states were thought to be necessary. Under the Australian Constitution, the states share certain law-making responsibilities with respect to privacy concerns. These consultations took some years.

The federal government's first effort to implement the guidelines in Australia was linked to a proposal to establish a universal identification card, with the engaging name of the "Australia Card." Defeat of that legislation in the Australian Senate actually caused a double dissolution[10] of the Australian Federal Parliament. When the government was returned, the legislation was represented. However, subsequently it was abandoned when huge public protests belatedly developed about the proposed universal identifier card. In Australia no one has to carry a passport or ID card. It was then that the government proceeded with the separate privacy legislation. The information privacy principles set out in the Australian Privacy Act follow very substantially the OECD guidelines.

A not dissimilar development occurred in Japan, although free of the federal complications that bedevil lawmaking in Australia and the United States. According to Professor Horibe, the word "privacy" was rarely used in Japan, at least before the latter half of the 1950s.[11] No precise translation of the concept, from its development in Anglo-American law and other Western law, could readily be achieved in the Japanese language. However, the idea gained attention after 1964 following a novel by Yukio Mishima concerning the private life of a political candidate.[12] By the 1970s, calls were being made for effective legal protection of privacy. A Personal Data Protection Bill was introduced into the Diet in March 1975 by the opposition. But no legislation was introduced by the government, and none was enacted. In August 1980, by which time the OECD guidelines were completed and awaiting approval by the Council of the OECD, Professor Horibe wrote a book, *The Contemporary Privacy.*[13] In it he proposed legislation, both nationally and locally, on the model of the OECD Guidelines. He has expressed the view that the recommendation of this international organization had "great impact" on the Japanese government.

In January 1981, the Administrative Management Agency set up a study committee that reported in July 1982. The agency proposed five fundamental principles for privacy protection, derived from the OECD guidelines.

There was no immediate legislative action at the national level, although some local governments enacted ordinances on the model of the report.[14] As in Australia, so in Japan. The national government, beset with many other problems, took a great deal of time to consider the proposal for privacy legislation. A further study group was established. Eventually, however, a bill was produced in April 1988 that was approved by both houses of the Diet. The Personal Data Protection Act of 1988 came into force on 1 October 1989. The act provided for a further delay in the introduction of the facility for disclosure and correction of personal data.

During Diet deliberations of the bill, attention was drawn to the neglect of the regulation of privacy in the private sector. The government gave a commitment that it would advance promptly its investigations in that regard. The Ministry for International Trade and Industry (MITI) in April 1989 issued a document setting out guidance on personal data, notably in consumer credit.[15] MITI adopted policies calling on industry associations to investigate the implications of guidelines on privacy in the private sector. Professor Horibe comments that:

The MITI policy will play a very important role . . . because MITI implemented the Report of the Personal Data Protection Subcommittee by issuing circular notices . . . and promulgating the 'Rule on the Register concerning the Measures etc. for the Protection of Computer Processed Personal Data' in the Official Gazette on July 7, 1989.[16]

In addition, guidelines have been subsequently published in Japan on personal data in financial institutions and on the protection of such data in local government. These are also based on the OECD guidelines.[17]

The result of the foregoing is a very clear demonstration of the ripple effect of the OECD privacy guidelines. The process of national adoption is, in fact, largely the same. Careful national deliberation and widespread consultation begins. Eventual legislation regulating the national public sector is passed. Later, specific provisions in relation to credit reference systems are incorporated. Now there are moves to extend the principles into the information systems of the private sector but to do so, at least at first, by guidelines rather than explicit, legal sanction.

This is exactly what the OECD Council and the Expert Group on Privacy had in mind. The intent was to give a common intellectual framework to the policymakers and lawmakers of member countries. Even without formal sanction attached either to adoption or to enforcement in domestic jurisdictions, the privacy guidelines have proved to be an important international statement of accepted standards. Within the OECD, only Turkey has yet to enact privacy laws. The guidelines have, moreover, bridged the different legal traditions between European and common-law countries. Legislative response to the concern of privacy protection in European countries has typically produced generalist data protection agencies, while those in the common-law tradition have typically established limited and specific remedies for particular problems pragmatically defined.[18] The machinery for enforcement varies. Inclusion of references to the privacy of legal persons or specific application to transborder data flow also varies. But what is common is a serious concern about the social aspects of the new technology and, particularly, adoption of the "golden rule"—the right of access—at the heart of the intent of the guidelines.

However beneficial an educative and persuasive force, the privacy guidelines have no self-executing authority in a court of law. Thus, no citizen in one community can protest in the courts of another that the protection of personal data had not been complied with by relying for proof on the guidelines. Conferring justiciable rights upon citizens of (and possibly citizens in) either member countries needs a future step in the development of law.

A significant contribution to harmonization of national laws, the OECD privacy guidelines may make the later adoption of enforceable international treaties easier and more likely. Concurrent moves in the United Nations and the European Community, among others, are proof of some ripple effect beyond the twenty-four members of the OECD. The fact that we are still a long way short of unilateral or mutually enforceable international law, let alone an international tribunal to which parties with a transborder dispute about personal data privacy can have access, is not a reason to underestimate the value of OECD guidelines. It is, however, an indication of the limitations of the guidelines in domestic forums, where there is an international element in a dispute; and the continuing risk that, pending the development of such international law, countries may be tempted to react in ways that might be considered inimical to the free flow of information. Such steps may be taken in order (a) to protect what they perceive as their legitimate interest in the privacy of their citizens and residents; (b) to retaliate against what is seen as foreign indifference to that interest; and (c) to ensure, at least in certain cases, that a loss of highly personal information will not occur, taking that information beyond effective local legislative control.

The privacy guidelines illustrate what can be done in the field of information security at the international level. But they also illustrate the relatively slow pace at which changes are introduced and the challenges remaining.

Information Security: New OECD Initiatives

Following the completion of the work on the privacy guidelines, the OECD's activities in informatics policy abated. But a major new problem was looming on the horizon: computer-related crime. Computer crime challenges the adequacy of the territorial principle and points up a need to achieve extraterritorial jurisdiction, a need to harmonize substantive criminal law; and the problem of direct penetration of information systems. Important changes in substantive and procedural law to cope with penetration into systems clearly call for harmonization on a wider scale beyond the frontiers of Western Europe.

The Equity Funding case, for example, illustrated the faith which citizens and business people blindly place in the product of information systems.[19] Directors of an insurance company stored 56,000 false life insurance policies with a sales value of $30 million in a computer. When the accounts were closed, these false policies were found to represent two-thirds of the value of the company's portfolio. The data from the computer printout of the Equity Funding Corporation had simply been accepted at face value by lenders dealing with the company.

Similarly, in 1981, a survey conducted by the Local Government Audit Commission in the United Kingdom showed that 21 percent of the 320 firms covered stated that they had been victims of computer fraud in the previous five years.[20] In Sweden, all cases of embezzlement between 1981 and 1983 were analyzed. More than 10 percent involved computer-related fraud.[21] A private study in the United Kingdom in

1984 found average losses of £31,000 in the field of computer fraud from manipulation of computers. Similar results were found in the Federal Republic of Germany.[22]

Under the stimulus of these and other developments, the OECD issued an analysis of legal policy on computer-related crime in 1986.[23] It contained guidelines for national legislatures and suggested common denominators for the approaches that should be taken in view of the international character of many computer-related offenses.

Similar steps were also under consideration in the Commission of the European Communities.[24] Eventually the Council of Europe's Committee on Crime Problems published the results of its research. A report issued in 1990, as guidelines for national legislatures laid out what it described as a "minimum list" and an "optional list" of data offences that should be covered by local law.[25] Most helpfully, the report contained a review of the initiatives of a number of national legislatures, including the United Kingdom, the United States, and Canada. It also contained an analysis of the particular problems presented by the international aspects of computer-related criminality involving transfrontier activities. The report concluded:

> Computer-related criminality involving a transfrontier situation is becoming increasingly important. Because of the nature of computers, there is an increasing potential for storing, moving, using and manipulating data by contact from long range, and the ability to communicate and to transmit rapidly large quantities of data between computer systems over a long distance. . . . The offence may be committed partly in one jurisdiction and partly in another, or even partly in a third one, initiated from practically any place in the world. Obstacles such as distance, border control or necessity of physical presence are no longer relevant.[26]

A forum on the vulnerability of international financial information held in Toronto, Canada in February 1990 triggered a newfound sense of urgency. Cases of serious harm caused by the manipulation of information systems "[s]ometimes with fraudulent intent, sometimes without intent to secure personal gain but with reckless indifference to the consequences of the conduct involved" were reported.[27]

The forum on financial information further recorded invasions of systems by viruses with arresting names such as "Internet worm," "world peace virus," "the Jerusalem virus," the "AIDS Trojan horse," the "Italian bouncing ball virus" and so forth.[28] Participants noted:

Already cases of damage to innocent users of information technology systems have been prosecuted in the courts. The possibility of significant increases in such cases must be faced squarely. Laws, security practices and investigative techniques must be improved to deter would-be offenders, to detect those who offend, to secure their conviction and punishment and to provide for fair apportionment of liability for the losses which occur from their actions and from error in the process. Whilst action on the level of individual jurisdictions is proceeding in all of the countries represented at the forum, at different levels of detail and different speeds, and whilst some international cooperation has been achieved (notably in UNCITRIAL . . . OECD, the Council of Europe, etc.) there is no international agency with a specific mission to examine and advise on the harmonization of laws and practices in all of the regions represented.

Because of its intercontinental membership and activities, its economic mission, and its proven track record in facilitating international consensus on principles relating to information technology and transborder data flows, the OECD seemed to forum participants to be a suitable venue for the further exploration of some of the computer offense-related concerns.[29]

Perhaps stimulated by this vote of confidence, the Committee for Information, Computer and Communications Policy (ICCP) of the OECD eventually established an ad hoc group of experts to prepare guidelines for the security of information systems. That group held its first meeting at OECD headquarters in Paris in January 1991 and elected the Honorable Michael Kirby as chairman. Despite a long tradition of strict confidentiality in its deliberations, the Expert Group on Information Security has involved intensive participation of industry representatives and a series of informal consultations within national administrations and other national experts. The guidelines were completed in June 1992 by the expert group and will be presented for adoption by the Council of the OECD in 1993.

Status Of The OECD Project on Information Security

The vision set out in successive OECD drafts of Information Security Principles follows the format of the successful Privacy Guidelines significantly. The guidelines are preceded by a review of the necessity for an international approach to this issue. They include recommendations that steps be taken *nationally* to reflect the principles promulgated in them and *internationally* to secure harmonization of the applicable rules.

The information security principles are grounded, as most earlier studies on the subject are, upon the need to ensure that the information system respects the three identified chief components of information security. These are:

1. Availability—the applicable data must be present, accessible, or attainable and immediately capable of use for a purpose by persons authorized to access it.

2. Confidentiality—the data should not be made available or disclosed to persons who are unauthorized to have access to such data.

3. Integrity—the data once accessed must not be altered or destroyed in any unauthorized manner.

This tripartite division of the concept of security in the context of information systems is very well established in the literature.[30] More recently, however, a number of writers have suggested that there are further aspects that must be incorporated into an effective information security system. Two such criteria are:

1. Authenticity—assuring the genuineness of the data

2. Utility—its usefulness once accessed[31]

Work to expand or redefine these essential concepts of data security is at the heart of the OECD group and has not yet been done by any international intergovernmental agency elsewhere. Four other core "principles" are under consideration.

1. Awareness—means should be readily available for those entitled to be informed about the existence and extent of the measures that have been put in place for the security of information systems. This is fundamental so that a person whose data is stored in the system can decide whether the protection of confidentiality and privacy (as well as intellectual property and other rights) are adequate.

2. Proportionality—the measures for security should be proportionate to the degree of reliance on the data and the magnitude, possibility, and implications of any breaches of security. No completely secure system can be devised. Even the best encryption codes can usually be broken.

The greatest perils are those of human error and failure. The measures put in place should be proportional to the needs for security. Such measures should keep in mind issues such as cost effectiveness. An undue obsession with security for its own sake should be avoided.

3. Balance—it is essential, in free societies, to realize that measures for secrecy, restriction and security are necessarily in competition with the free flow of information. The legitimate entitlement of the community and of other individuals to the benefits of the free flow of information must be balanced against the claims of the government, corporations, and individuals to the enforcement of data security.

4. Accountability—there should be an identifiable person who is responsible for the enforcement of the applicable security principles and accountable for derogations from them.

Several other key issues are under consideration by the group. These include:

- The desirability of promoting international harmonization of technical, administrative, and other standards

- The need to clearly allocate risks and liability

- The need to provide for jurisdictional competence in multijurisdictional cases

- The need to provide for mutual assistance and improvement of extradition laws for transborder crimes

- The need to provide penal measures for deliberate or reckless interference in information systems.

OECD's Mission

Both initiatives of the OECD to harmonize informatics policy must be judged in the context of the overall strategy and mission of that organization in the current world economic and political ferment. That mission was most recently expressed in the communiqué issued by the council of the OECD twenty-four member countries on June 5, 1991. The basic values of "pluralistic democracy, respect for human rights and market oriented economies" shared by the OECD countries were affirmed.[32]

To these ends, the ministers stressed the need for OECD and non-member countries alike "to formulate coherent policies in the fields of economics, environment, social affairs and technology that are mutually reinforcing in support of broadly based sustainable development." In addition, "close policy cooperation [to] help to provide a sound global economic environment" was identified as a top priority for strengthening international economic cooperation.

The ministers called on the OECD to further "develop and deepen its work on structural issues and, where appropriate . . . , in those issues which lie beyond the ambit of current international negotiations, consider the feasibility of elaborating operational arrangements."

Specifically, the ministers noted that technology is increasingly underpinning national economic performance and demonstrating "need for governments better to coordinate and ensure coherence amongst domestic policies in these fields." With a view "to reducing divergencies which cause frictions in these policy areas," the ministers asked the OECD to explore the need to improve existing "multilateral instruments and . . . to develop additional 'rules of the game'" in an appendix.

The work of the Expert Group on Security of Information Systems must be understood in this context. The group derives legitimacy not just from the delegation of the ICCP Committee that set it up but also from the overall strategy of the Ministerial Council of the OECD at a time of rapid economic and political change in the world.

Other Initiatives

The OECD is not alone in its endeavors on information security. In the field of data protection, the Council of the European Communities has established a working party. Their report (June 1991) was steering toward an EC strategic framework for the security of information systems.[33] Their object is to identify user requirements, the needs of suppliers and service providers, and to develop standardization, evaluation and certification, and technological and operational advances in the security of information systems.[34] The action plan is intended to complement "evolving European and international standardization activities in this field."[35]

Many of the participants in the EC exercise also took part in the work of the OECD group. That group was also aware of the activities within the government of the United States to secure common national standards for computer and communications security.[36] So far, work within governmental agencies has been related largely to the protection of national security or to meeting one major element of security: vital confidentiality. But the National Research Council report has acknowledged that U.S. programs ". . . have paid little attention to the other two major computer security requirements, integrity (guarding against improper data modification and/or destruction) and availability (enabling timely use of systems and the data they hold)." These requirements are important to government system users, and they are particularly and increasingly important to users of commercial systems. More wide-reaching and flexible guidance than that offered by the so-called Orange Book published by the National Security Agency is needed, according to the NRC, and it should be guidance that stimulates the production of more robust trustworthy systems at all levels of production."[37]

Several other initiatives of governmental agencies and academic scholars have been designed to isolate, in a theoretical and practical way, the basic objectives to be achieved for security and the means of securing them.

One of the most important of the practical analyses studied by OECD experts was that employed by Japan's MITI to develop computer systems security standards. The point made by the MITI analyses is that measures taken for the security of information systems have largely concentrated on protection against loss or damage caused by natural disasters and by systems structures to date. Yet the rate of computer-related crime in Japan is low. Perhaps for that reason, security awareness of Japanese systems managers is described as generally low. The object of the MITI standards is prevention—to improve knowledge, to encourage a proper conceptualization of the issue, and to meet new challenges, such as those presented by computer viruses.

Japan's first security standards were laid down by MITI in 1977. They have been revised in 1984 and again in 1991. These standards do not, as such, have legal force in Japan, but could serve as a basis for procurement of IT (Information Technology) product systems by government organs or corporations. As well as the general standards of MITI, there are particular standards laid down in Japan by the Ministry of Posts and Telecommunications, the National Police Agency, the Ministry of Autonomy, and other bodies.

The MITI standards are organized into facility, technical, and operating categories. They are put forward primarily to stimulate action that will prevent breaches of security. Obviously, prevention is preferable to the post facto provision of punishment of offenders or remedies for those who suffer loss. Ultimately, however, the law will have to provide avenues for criminal and civil redress. In Japan, criminal and other laws have been partly revised and enacted from June 1987 to provide for punishment in the case of illegal production and destruction of electromagnetic records, willful disruption of another party's business through electronic means, and property crimes.[38] Property crimes are defined to include the illegal acquisition of profit by providing false data or illegal commands to a computer to produce forged records regarding the acquisition of, or change of, property rights or by providing the described forged data for a third party's clerical use. Two proposed crimes excluded from this amendment to Japanese law and left for future study are illegal acquisition and/or transfer of data processed and stored by computers and unauthorized use of a computer.

Conclusions

The intent of the OECD Guidelines on Information Security is to provide a similar voluntary framework for harmonization of domestic policies as the remarkably successful privacy guidelines. Effective, compatible legislation to deter, detect, and redress illegitimate intrusions into data security is urgently needed throughout the international community.

The task for developing an international regime to respond to the vulnerability of information systems is complex and far from complete. We must keep the institutional and cultural impediments to achieving policy consensus clearly in our sights. We should learn from failures to achieve international consensus in analogous areas like airline regulation, where globalization of technology equally presents the international community of nation-states with an urgent need to find common rules. We must reflect the various concerns of national administrations and experts so that we produce the best policy possible given the state of the technological art.

The OECD has, in the past, provided an important contribution to the development of law and policy relevant to the age of informatics. Hopefully, the Guidelines on Information Security will enjoy similar success.

III *Applications*

11 Building a Global Network: The WBSI Experience

Andrew Feenberg

Human communication on computer networks is an evolving technology rich in possibilities. Computer companies have not always been leaders in exploring these possibilities, many of which were first identified by playful or curious users who came up with unexpected applications.

The French Minitel network is one of the most successful instances of such informal innovation. The designers of the network did not anticipate the popularity of messaging, which was introduced by hackers and grew explosively, at one point generating nearly half the revenues of the system.[1]

A similar story is told by Quarterman (chap. 3 of this volume) about the Internet, host to millions of scholars and researchers around the world. No one planned this development, which grew up more or less spontaneously around programs with a different mission.

Users thus played an unusually active role in the early development of computer-mediated communication, and their contribution is likely to be decisive for its future (see Harasim, chap. 2). They have shifted the emphasis from strictly utilitarian applications toward enhancing human contact and understanding on a planetary scale.

This chapter discusses one of the earliest educational experiments in international networking. In 1982 the La Jolla, California-based Western Behavioral Sciences Institute (WBSI) opened the first educational program employing the computer as its chief communications medium. During nearly ten years of activity, hundreds of highly placed executives from all over the world worked in its online courses with prominent university faculty. Together these users invented a new application of the computer that continues to influence our under-standing of its potential. The history of this remarkable experiment follows.

The WBSI Experience

Planning for The School of Management and Strategic Studies began in late 1981 under the leadership of Richard Farson, president of WBSI.[2] At the time, CMC was still an untested educational technology, with the exception of some informal experimentation on Control Data's Plato system and a course in writing offered on The Source, an online service, in 1981.

The school targeted high-level executives who could not afford long absences from their jobs. The electronic delivery system provided these executives with an exciting initiation to computers through a commu-nications application suited to their skills and interests.

Courses were focused on such issues as technology and development, the global economic and social environment, and systems thinking. These subjects were chosen because of their particular relevance to leadership in a rapidly changing and ever more complex world. Profes-sors from major universities were recruited, primarily in the "soft" social sciences. Most of them found computer conferencing to be an effective educational medium. Over the years many participants have testified to the value of what they learned at WBSI.

The initial format consisted of a two-year program: four six-month sessions online, each composed of thematically related month-long courses with a running commentary by a communications specialist. Each six-month session was introduced by a week of face-to-face semi-nars in La Jolla. During that week participants met the faculty for the coming term and learned to use the computer. The cost was set at nearly $25,000 for the two years.

The plans were ambitious and innovative, but the experiment got off to a rough start. The first session began in January 1982 with a stellar group of eight participants, including a Los Angeles City Councilman, a director of the Venezuelan national oil company, the presidents of several small high-tech companies, and vice presidents from some larger mainline firms. But all told, more faculty and staff than students attended the initial face-to-face seminar.

The real problems began when the participants returned home. Since no one had ever been taught on a computer network before, there were no models. The first courses consisted of either professorial monologues that made interesting reading but were unsatisfactory as computer conferences or telegraphic questions followed by days of inactivity while the teachers waited for responses. Meanwhile, various technical problems inhibited the participants from joining in the conversation, such as it was.

Recall that these were the early days of the personal computer. We used modified Apple IIE's with 48K of RAM and 300 baud Hayes modems—donated by Dennis Hayes who was himself a participant—to access the Electronic Information Exchange System (EIES) network at the New Jersey Institute of Technology. EIES offered an early experimental version of the sort of communication service later popularized by The Source and CompuServe. This setup was so complex, it took a full page of instructions just to sign on and many more pages to list the basic EIES commands.

Somehow, we got through that first term. We were fortunate in having sympathetic technical support staff who patiently instructed the participants online or over the phone whenever they needed help. Pedagogical questions were addressed in a closed faculty conference in intense and sometimes contentious discussions that finally yielded an innovative interactive teaching style appropriate to the medium.

By the second term, the group had more than doubled in size and there was hope of developing a viable program. Eventually over 150 participants from twenty-six countries were active, with a comparable number of faculty and staff at least nominally available online. WBSI was off and running.

The school quickly evolved in unexpected ways. Several clients—for example, Digital Equipment Corporation and the United States Army—sent many new participants each year in an attempt to broaden their intellectual reach. Where else could they hope to find professors from Harvard, Yale, and the University of California, a Jonas Salk, a Carl Rogers, and a Stewart Brand, all available in an information-age setting? WBSI became a kind of academic supplement to the training departments of these organizations.

As time went on, WBSI discovered that it was engaged not just in providing an educational program but more fundamentally in building a new type of virtual community. The bonds between participants were so strong that most continued on as alumni members at the end of the course and returned to La Jolla year after year.

What was the attraction? The WBSI network was composed of an odd mix of businesspeople, executives, military officers, research administrators, and scholarship participants from the public sector. They formed a new kind of international club with a high premium placed on frank, intelligent talk.

The members' offline activities, their politics, and their ideas about life were often very different, but all of them enjoyed exchanging ideas with each other and the faculty. CMC made it possible for them to stay together in spirit while separated by continents.

Using laptop computers, participants could even connect with the group while traveling, and enrich the discussion with reports from remote parts of the world. Members stationed abroad were sometimes among the most active, for example, our correspondent in a remote corner of the Arabian penninsula who had few companions in his desert station.

The common language was English; native speakers were forgiving of foreign participants' minor errors. The presence of these foreigners made an enormous difference. One cannot easily imagine the impact of Colombians and Japanese on discussions of drug policy or trade. Certain kinds of cliches became impossible. The usual rhetoric, inspired by television journalism, gave way to the authority of local experience. Serious reflection became possible as we gained insight into the meaning of events for participants.[3]

WBSI went through many crises as the years passed, but the participants themselves helped us to survive and grow. In the end, the loss of several important sources of support and the continuing recession were too much for the institute's fragile finances. It finally closed in November 1991.

In the remainder of this chapter, I discuss some of the things this experience taught us about community building, pedagogy, and software design. These lessons may perhaps help others attempting to build similar networks in the future.

Building a Community

Online groups need not form a community to work effectively together so long as the members have well-defined roles in performing a shared task. But both roles and tasks were unclear at WBSI. Although officially a non-degree-granting educational program, for many participants it was more of a club or a subscriber-written magazine than a school. In such a group, nothing short of personal loyalty could hold the participants together and sustain the educational activity in which they were nominally engaged. Thus WBSI had to become a vigorous community to survive at all.

How did a community emerge out of this diverse collection of strong personalities scattered over the globe? WBSI attempted to create a warm personal atmosphere at the face-to-face seminars; however, these efforts may have been less important than certain unintended consequences of the program design. In fact, without wanting to, we put the participants through a shared ordeal that brought them together more closely than anything we could have planned.

In most cases, the participants first encountered either computers or CMC through WBSI. Important people though they were, our training program placed them all in the embarrassing position of children on the first day of school. Soon they formed a brave band of technological adventurers with a whole new vocabulary to describe the complexities, frustrations, and excitement of communication by computer.

This frontier solidarity was amplified by our initial problems with delivering the courses. We had always bragged about the experimental character of the program; now the participants were finding out just how experimental it really was. But because they were prepared, they tried to help rather than withdraw in disappointment. And once they became deeply involved in saving the program, they naturally identified strongly with it and each other. It was really "their" program, a fact that constituted the group as such and assigned it a common mission.

To facilitate participant involvement, WBSI created a so-called meta-conference in which everyone was invited to offer suggestions and to communicate about anything that did not fit into the regular conferences. This type of free discussion conference has become commonplace in online educational programs. Often called the "cafe conference," it has a wide variety of uses, from debating current events to dealing with personal problems or complaining about the program itself. The cafe conference is an important transmission belt for an emerging online culture. Participants feel fully represented as human beings on a system that welcomes them in this way, rather than excluding all but their professional contributions.

In 1985, a group of WBSI participants formed a private conference for more intimate personal discussion and support, a sort of online encounter group. There they could talk freely about life events that affected them deeply. One participant, for example, lost his job as vice president of a large firm, and his situation was discussed for several weeks. Another died of cancer, joining his friends online till the end. Participants learned to understand better the dilemmas of foreign members of the group whose personal and national crises were often intertwined. This was particularly true of our Colombian participants whose lives were tragically altered by the civil strife in their country.

The "COM" or "community" group, as it was called, was led at first by a professional psychologist expert in working with encounter groups. He found that the participants were more supportive of each other but revealed less of themselves than was customary in a face-to-face setting. He concluded that this was because of their commitment to remaining together, unlike the casual acquaintances involved in a brief encounter. In a very real sense, WBSI had invented a new social form. The experiment was so successful that other COM groups were formed, and this feature was added to the program. It too became an important factor in WBSI's transformation into a community.

How far can we generalize from these experiences? Certain aspects of the WBSI community probably cannot easily be repeated by other institutions. Computers are no longer such romantic symbols of the technological frontier, and no one today has to begin an online program with the problems we had in 1982. Nevertheless, several features of the experiment are generalizable: the use of conferences for free discussion and personal interchange, and the excitement of international networking, a still unfamiliar and innovative computer application. Programs that engage their participants as persons rather than organizing them around specific tasks ought to be able to generate the sense of ownership necessary to community through similar means.

Inventing a Pedagogy

It is a well-established principle of psychology that people learn a dominant role, such as teaching, primarily through playing the correlated subordinate role, that is, learning. But since most online teachers have had no prior conferencing experience, they need preparation before facing what Roxanne Hiltz calls a "virtual classroom" (Hiltz, 1986).

Skilled teachers rely implicitly on a host of small social techniques that are unavailable on a computer network. The new online teacher feels like someone who has never been in a classroom before and is suddenly shoved into a room full of students and told to sink or swim. Where should I stand? Why are they waving their hands at me? How do I know if they understand what I am saying? How long do I wait for an answer to my questions? When does the class begin and end? Early public mistakes in such basic matters are bound to be embarrassing and diminish the teacher's authority.

WBSI's first attempts at online teaching were disastrous. Great teachers were helpless in front of a class of sympathetic but sceptical students scattered between Caracas, Philadelphia, and San Francisco. One teacher offered elaborate presentations that resembled written lectures. While interesting, these had the undesirable effect of reducing the participants to silence. In a face-to-face classroom, teachers can determine from subtle clues whether students' silence signifies fascination or daydreaming. But silence on a computer network is unfathomable; it is intensely disturbing to address the electronic void. Hence the "communication anxiety" of conferencing participants, especially those with leadership roles (Feenberg, 1989).

Those who experimented with nondirective techiques had even more disappointing results. No one seemed to understand their all too brief questions, and so they too faced a wall of silence. Later we understood that it takes far more nerve to admit confusion and ask for clarification in a written medium than face-to-face. Days passed as the students and faculty wondered, each in their respective corners, what was going on. The lack of tacit cues such as raised eyebrows or puzzled looks proved fatal to this teaching style in the online environment.

With the encouragement of our consultants, Peter and Trudy Johnson-Lenz, I experimented with introductory comments several screens in length designed to lay down explicit ground rules for discussion, and then posed problems and asked questions illustrated by specific examples. This approach brought in the participants. Once they were talking, the WBSI faculty made further discoveries.

Conferencing participants are uncomfortable unless they can act as if they were substituting writing for speech in some more familiar setting. They must treat the conference as a meeting, a discussion group, even a cocktail party in order to establish shared expectations. Without a reassuring communication model, they are fearful of writing the wrong thing and withdraw into the perfect silence of a blank screen (Feenberg, 1989). With this in mind, faculty imposed a framework of norms and expectations modeled on a college seminar.

To reproduce the seminar environment, one needs online equivalents for such things as opening the discussion with a short orientation session, calling on individuals to speak, assigning work to be delivered in class, getting a sense of the group's wishes, and distributing short readings for discussion and comment.

Just as students are discouraged when their comments are ignored in the classroom, so they react negatively when their online messages get no response. Most faculty accepted responsibility for replying to every otherwise unanswered message, as they would in a classroom.

CMC courses are necessarily based on classroom discussion since students quickly lose interest in lengthy online lectures that would be more appropriately printed and distributed by mail. Teachers and participants learned to input texts of medium length, no more than a page or two, asking questions, responding, commenting on the subject at hand. One hundred to two hundred such texts would compose a typical month-long seminar at WBSI.

As in a regular classroom, the teacher is responsible for provoking and leading discussion. Accordingly, he or she must design an agenda and supply a comment every few days to sustain the interaction. However, strict enforcement of the agenda discourages participation. This points to the central problem and opportunity of teaching in the virtual classroom.

Computer conferences tend to diverge toward multiple monologue unless an active moderator works to keep participants on the subject. But the subject may not be as focused as in a face-to-face setting. Often it consists of several loosely related matters brought up simultaneously in a multithreaded discussion. Each strand represents a participant's personal path into the conference. To arrest the free flow of such a conversation with frequent calls to order is likely to produce only vexed withdrawal.

Instead of trying to control conversation negatively, the teacher-moderator must periodically offer what are called "weaving comments" to identify the common threads holding the discussion together and giving it unity. Such comments enable participants to move beyond monologic personal viewpoints toward true dialogue and synthesis. Weaving comments also help the group to achieve a sense of accomplishment and direction and supply it with a code for framing its history by establishing a shared boundary between past, present, and future. In advanced courses, teachers may assign this task to the students themselves (Harasim, 1991), but, in any case, someone must perform it. Weaving, I believe, is the key to online pedagogy.

Once we had made these basic discoveries, we tried to share them with new teachers in a "moderating conference" where those who had already taught on the network could prepare the newcomers. For a while I led these conferences. Although we called it training, it actually consisted of giving faculty practice participating in a discussion led by someone else before they faced a virtual classroom.

Among the faculty I trained in this way were dozens of brilliant scholars, most of whom, I am convinced, had never had a serious pedagogical discussion before in their lives. No doubt they had never needed to discuss the theory of an activity that came to them as naturally as classroom teaching. But, confronted with the challenge of an entirely new setting, they enjoyed debating pedagogical issues.

Extensive experience and discussion yielded pedagogical lessons that formed the "lore" of the WBSI school, passed down from one group of teachers to the next. Although some of these lessons would be less relevant to online technical education than to our type of program, any institution that introduces educational CMC should develop a base of practical knowledge among its faculty and encourage its transmission.

Designing an Educational Interface

Computer conferencing was invented to overcome certain limitations of electronic mail (or email). Email substitutes electronic transmission for the delivery of pieces of paper, but it conserves the person-to-person communication model of ordinary postal service. The postal model depends in important respects on the use of paper as a medium. When information is delivered in the form of sealed printed matter, a personal addressee must break the seal and dispose of the information locally, for example, by filing or forwarding it.

In principle, CMC can dispense with this social structure. The sender transmits his or her message to a host computer where it is deposited in a virtual file shared by all the members of the group, whatever their location. Where users of the host computer all see the same files, one has a bulletin board useful primarily for information exchange on a relatively small scale. Private, topically designated discussion spaces are defined for those with a shared interest on larger systems handling a wider variety of participants and tasks. This structure supports continuous small-group communication over long periods. Hence the name, computer conferencing.

The change from email seems technically trivial, but one should not underestimate the originality of designers such as Murray Turoff and Jacques Vallee who first broke with the postal model and began finally to realize the computer's potential in group communication.

Despite abandoning the person-to-person structure of email, early conferencing systems shared many of its other features. Rationalistic assumptions blinded designers to the specificity of group needs. They believed that they could understand and organize communication logically, on a priori grounds, rather than sociologically, in terms of the realities of actual experience. They took it for granted that users would want to write on the computer equivalent of a blank page, a contextless void. Designers sought the one best way to organize a generic communication process and referred to all messages by such neutral names as topic, item, or comment. It is true that this was a plausible approach in the early days of CMC, given the limitations of the available equipment.

However, most online groups need a familiar framework adapted to their culture and tasks. They are repelled by what might be called contextual deprivation. This problem was masked at first by the fact that experienced computer users, who were the first to try out the new systems, recognized the computer itself as a sufficient context for their interactions. But decontextualization was invariably perceived as confusing and unfriendly by ordinary users, such as the participants in the WBSI school.

The radical difference in outlook between the computing professionals who design programs and the ordinary people who use them shows up in other ways as well. Under the influence of their engineering culture, software designers create powerful programs that are difficult for these users to master.[4] But outside engineering itself, simplicity, not power, is a sine qua non of successful communications software.

The WBSI experience foreshadowed the type of user resistance that has slowed the progress of educational CMC. Since most educational organizations cannot create their own conferencing system from scratch, they must either impose some engineer's conception of communication on their members or take the risks of trying to adapt an existing system to their own needs. The easier it is for participants to withdraw from the program, the more important it becomes to make the necessary adaptations.

WBSI's first technical director, Darrell Icenogle, addressed this problem by adding an extra layer of simplified commands tailored to our users and sheltering them from the engineering culture embodied in the underlying CMC program. This final command shell ran on the users' terminals. It served both as communications and word-processing software and as an interface to the conferencing system running on the host.

Our discoveries in this domain came in two stages.

In 1983, at the invitation of the Department of Commerce, WBSI organized a six-month computer conference on productivity in the American economy for fifty chief executive officers of Fortune 500 companies. Portable computers were donated by the Kaypro Corporation, a pioneer in that field, and modems by Dennis Hayes. We assumed, correctly, that if executives were difficult to get online, CEOs would represent a worst-case scenario.

To solve this problem we built a radically simplified terminal interface for EIES based on a software product called MIST developed by the Johnson-Lenzes. This program automated the sign-on procedure and included a local wordprocessor with prompted, single-key up- and downloading from the terminal. These features made it possible to abbreviate training without losing the audience. Most of the CEOs were actually able to participate in the program.

Soon the WBSI school had its own interface to EIES called, at first, the "Onion" and later "Passkey." This interface, designed to run on PCs donated by Digital Equipment Corporation (DEC), was in continuous use in one form or another throughout the later history of the school.

It proved extremely helpful in bringing international participants into the program as we could incorporate a wide choice of local sign-on procedures into the terminal program and spare our members some fairly complex technical labor.

In 1987, DEC asked WBSI to evaluate VAX Notes, its own recently released computer conferencing program. DEC also funded the development of a prototype terminal interface for VAX Notes based on Passkey. The result was the Social Factors Project which culminated in the transfer of the WBSI management school from EIES to computers running VAX Notes at the institute.

The aim of the project was to develop a framework for understanding the transformation of the computer from a *tool* for individual users into a *medium* of group activity. Computer conferencing, we argued, requires electronic social environments every bit as complex as the buildings in which face-to-face encounters take place. There is no generic answer to the question of where to put walls, doors, and corridors. Architects and interior designers must devise solutions corresponding to the anticipated needs of each type of user. So too, designers of CMC systems must anticipate the group requirements of the users of their products. The software's social architecture effects the success of online group communication just as the location of chairs, tables, blackboards, and podiums effects face-to-face interaction (Feenberg and Bellman, 1990).

We recommended that DEC develop an advanced conferencing system in which a common interface on the terminal and the host would replace the usual clumsy process of connecting two separate programs. Users would hardly be aware of where they were on this "client/server" system. An integrated hypertext or videotex program would archive incoming material for easy retrieval. Conference moderators such as teachers would enjoy special facilities for organizing their work and tracking participants. Network managers would be able to download programs, directories, and assignments to groups of users at remote locations, periodically retailoring their communications software as the conferencing schedule advanced (Feenberg, 1986).

The interface was to be tailorable to group-specific tasks and needs, such as project management, information exchange, and distance education. Given our expertise in the latter, we concretized these ideas with specifications for an educational version of VAX Notes. We identified features that would be particularly important for this task, such as a simplified form-making functionality for quickly composing tests, access to mathematical symbols, and so on. We contrasted such features with others that might prove more important for groups engaged in other activities, arguing that in each case the most important functionalities should be "foregrounded" in the menus of the terminal program while the rest would be available to sophisticated users in the background on the host.

DEC did eventually make an experimental in-house version of Passkey incorporating videotex but, surprisingly, their program was slow, clumsy and difficult to use (Blackburn and Mason, 1991). The old culture apparently overwhelmed the new.

Despite this disappointment, our ideas were not entirely stillborn. Whether inspired by Passkey or independent in conception, a number of similar interfaces have been developed over the last few years, and new versions of EIES and Portacom, two early conferencing systems, were recently released with built-in terminal interfaces. Lotus Notes, a new and very powerful business system, was designed from the start to have such an interface. It can fairly be said today that no conferencing system should be considered state-of-the-art without this component.

Conclusion

Traditionally, correspondence courses and night schools have been stepchildren of the academy, despised junior partners of undergraduate residential education. This situation is changing today as lifelong learning becomes a reality for many white collar employees. The effects are also felt by distance education, which has always served a large proportion of adults.

These social trends have improved the climate for networking experiments (Eurich, 1990). As WBSI demonstrated, CMC can create a new kind of planetary classroom in which students and teachers from all over the world will be able to meet and exchange ideas. Distance education need no longer languish in the shadow of conventional college teaching. Given imagination and support, the learning society will emerge as a global computer network.

12 Computer Conferencing and the New Europe

Robin Mason

The European Context

Powerful forces lie behind the current drive to unite, or at least integrate, various European countries into a single community. Although economic considerations are undoubtedly central, the growing awareness that nation-states are interdependent at levels far beyond the economic, is playing a significant part in the many initiatives drawing Europeans closer together. National political considerations may be the major factors in resisting unification, but undoubtedly a basic lack of understanding of the cultural differences among the various European countries is also a significant deterrent.

Technological advances in communications are directly related to the dynamics of this phenomenon of globalization.

A major factor is that telecommunications in particular, and information technologies in general, are no respecters of national political borders. An event in one country can have immediate impact in another, because of the speed with which information flows, and because of the dramatic form in which it can be presented. Events, issues and problems can no longer be contained within a country or a region; if significant, they become global events, global issues, or global problems. (Robinson, 1991)

The liberating power of communications was forcefully underlined by the recent dramatic events in Central and Eastern Europe—email messages describing events and emotions were available on the networks all over the world. It is no longer possible for governments to retain control over the dissemination of information. In fact, widespread dissemination of information, through education and training, is one of the cornerstones of the Commission of the European Communities program:

> We at the Commission are convinced that the combined activities of training, learning and education are probably the key factors for the future of Europe, both in economic growth as well as the improvement in the quality of life. (Majo, 1991)

Telecommunications technologies are seen by the commission as the key to increasing the amount of education and information dissemination while keeping the costs realistic. Both terrestrial and satellite communication systems that support electronic mail and computer conferencing, and host computer-based training programs, expert systems, and a vast range of databases, are providing the foundations for networking education, industry, and local communities. Three main needs can be met by the development on a European scale of a telecommunications network.

1. Development of intercultural understanding
2. Updating training facilities for small and medium-sized enterprises
3. Meeting the demand for lifelong education

The most obvious inhibiting factor to a European-wide education and training program is the extent of linguistic and cultural diversity among the participants. The search for pedagogical techniques, for technological solutions, and for program strategies to cope with this diversity is a major part of present research and development work. Providing real interaction between different cultures is just one of the strategic ways of using an electronic network.

Meeting the needs of small and medium-sized enterprises (SMEs)—for professional updating, for exchange of information, and for access to new technologies—is also paramount to the development of economic strength and competitiveness in Europe. A computer network can not only link small organizations together but also provide access to a central database of information and training facilities.

Finally, although distance education has for a long time been more accepted and legitimated in Europe than in North America, the call for lifelong education and the increasingly frequent need to update technical training have promoted telecommunications to the forefront of pan-European educational programs because of the convenience, flexibility, and cost benefit compared to traditional face-to-face training programs.

The purpose of this chapter is to examine the ways in which electronic networking applications have met the challenge of the European context and contributed to the development of a "European village." A wide range of networking examples are mentioned as they illuminate particular European issues; this general discussion is followed by a detailed case study of one project that shows these issues in context.

The Role of the Commission of the European Communities

The spread of electronic networks across Western Europe is very uneven, mainly due to the policies of individual governments in relation both to telecommunications and to education and training. France and the United Kingdom are undoubtedly the most advanced:

> French telecommunications policy has resulted in the most advanced infrastructure, based on the TRANSPAC packet switched system, whilst the UK's deregulation policy has increased the availability of terminal equipment (e.g., modems and fax) and hence access to commercial and educational networks. The other European nations are slowly catching up, but in most countries, access to networks is still rigidly controlled and hence too expensive for general education. (McLure and Heap, 1990)

However, the Commission of the European Communities (EC) has had a major impact on the growth of networks throughout Europe, not only through its support of economic harmonization and technical standardization but also through its funding of a variety of research and development programs involving electronic networking. Two of their many programs that have implications for the development of networks are COMETT and DELTA. COMETT is a program that fosters collaboration between universities and industry to improve the level of training and to give it a European dimension. DELTA focuses on the development of European learning through technological advance. It funds projects that aim to give tangible results for Europe as a whole, "as regards increased feelings of solidarity, the strengthening of cultural, social and intellectual diversity, reduction in the inequalities of opportunity and the removal of language barriers" (Rebel, 1990). In terms of networking, three environments are promoted for development: the corporate training situation, the institutional education setting, and the home environment.

The Added Value of Electronic Networks

The proliferation of network applications with a pan-European dimension demonstrates a certain acceptance that there is educational and European "added value," relative to the costs, in using telecommunications-based strategies. The benefits found from a wide range of projects can be summarized in five categories.

1. Promoting cultural awareness
2. Supporting language learning
3. Providing efficient and flexible education and training
4. Facilitating business partnerships and community projects
5. Enabling research and development on advanced technologies

Cultural Awareness

As with cross-national exchanges of all nonelectronic sorts, many networking applications have as a major objective the fostering of intercultural understanding and awareness. What telecommunications adds to other intercultural programs is speed of exchange:

The instant response that is possible when using Email makes it a motivating force for many students. Moreover, being able to write for a real audience is a powerful stimulus that can transform the attitude of a class and develop students' ability to write well . . . Furthermore, the value of the opportunity simply to make friends should not be underestimated, since in the process a great deal of information about social and cultural background can be exchanged. (Milligan, 1991)

Milligan is referring to an Anglo-Dutch email project for primary school children, sponsored by Shell and organized by the National Council for Educational Technology (NCET) in the United Kingdom.

Another provider of intercultural electronic services is Campus 2000, which offers the most extensive online facilities to educational institutions in the United Kingdom. In addition to a wide variety of databases, Campus 2000 provides group mailing facilities for schools as well as the conferencing system, Caucus. It has actively fostered links with European schools and teaching institutions and provides links to thousands of users with compatible email systems in Europe and other parts of the world. For example, it has been connected by a gateway link to Edutel, the teacher information service supplied by the French Education Ministry; thirty-six schools in both France and the United Kingdom took part in six curriculum-based projects during 1991. Similarly provision has been made for up to one hundred German schools to have direct access to Campus 2000 to take part in a program of collaborative communication projects. The aim of its European Studies Project is to provide an environment in which pupils can work together on joint projects with an international dimension and cooperate in research on contemporary European issues.

The system is used for pen pal exchanges between students wanting to practice their use of foreign languages, but group events also take place. For example, two schools in England and a school in Germany launched a new activity based on the Campus Satellite Education Project. Pupils aged thirteen simultaneously viewed a selection of news broadcasts on the ASTRA satellite in German and English. For two hours a rapid exchange of electronic mail took place from both sites in response to what was viewed. The organizer of the event from England commented that he believed communicating with Campus 2000 provided exciting new links across international borders and had the potential to provide genuine sources for foreign language material. He also felt its greatest contribution was in helping to establish more informed and more enlightened Europeans.

PLUTO is a loose cooperation of individuals and institutions involved with teaching and teacher training in Europe and engaging electronically in exchange of ideas, experiences, and educational material related to the classroom in many subjects. The participants are faculty members at teacher training colleges or universities, student teachers, classroom teachers and their students at general and special schools, and, trainers for in-service training institutions of private enterprises. At present they have email connections with participants from over fourteen European countries and are making many contacts into Eastern Europe. One of the goals of the project is the development of European cooperation:

It is clear that the future of the world depends more than ever upon global cooperation. It is also clear that the proper use of the technologies now available to us will do much to foster that cooperation. It seems vital, therefore, that we move as rapidly as possible to a situation in which pupils in any one country regard it as entirely normal that, as a part of their week-by-week classroom activity, they should be working alongside (in an electronic sense) their peers from other countries. Already, there are very few technical barriers to such cooperation; the barriers that exist are as much fiscal, political and perhaps psychological as anything. (Gwyn, 1991)

Although the project has only an email and file transfer capability, the aim has been to move beyond pen pal activity to create a setting in which classes could collaborate in joint European projects based on shared databases, spreadsheet, and desktop publishing activities.

One of the major problems faced by all pan-European networking projects at the primary and secondary school level is the difference in curricula among the various countries. Furthermore, there is a remarkably small window of "common time" in which schools in two or three countries are available for joint projects (due to different holiday, examination, and term times). Yet many evaluations of interschool networking projects conclude that the first criteria for success is that the networking element be fully integrated into the classroom activity; otherwise, it is soon perceived as a time-consuming, frustrating, additional extra.

CMC between two classrooms is a complex business—in effect team teaching at a distance—and requires extensive and detailed planning between the teachers concerned. (Somekh, 1989)

This issue is discussed in greater depth in the case study at the end of the chapter.

Language Learning

The benefits that electronic interaction brings to language learning are related to the opportunity to use the foreign language in context, often with native speakers. Experience shows that students using computer conferencing in second-language learning spend more time writing and are encouraged to be more creative than their traditional counterparts (Smith, 1990). The need for foreign language skills in the European context is of such importance that many computer language projects have been instituted both in the educational and business environments.

A report commissioned by the Dutch Ministry of Education on the use of telecommunications applications in secondary schools in Europe concludes:

> Of the more than 67 projects that we studied for our research, almost all involved computer-mediated communication, mostly for second-language practice or for improving cultural awareness. A few of the projects were associated with well-known U.S.-based projects and networks, but most are European in origin. (Collis, 1991b)

Collis goes on to describe the European Schools Project, originating from Amsterdam, which organizes "teletrips," each involving schools in more than one country, and based on local research projects generally organized around language and geography.

Campus 2000 facilitates many language-learning exchanges and provides access to the FELINE database's modern languages section which consists of carefully selected authentic texts taken from French, German, and Spanish satellite TV news broadcasts. Each text is accompanied by exercises at an appropriate level, and can be retrieved for printing out complete with all diacritics.

Berlitz has also begun using computer conferencing in its language teaching for the corporate market. On the basis of earlier trials, it is now planning a European Electronic Language School to continue the use of computer networking in European-wide language and personnel development programs.

Email, conferencing, and fax are the main tools in another European language project originating from Preston College in the United Kingdom and including five other countries. The networking facilities will be used not only for students to practice language skills but also for teachers to develop joint teaching material. One of the problems encountered in previous exchanges, where students actually visit the country of their second language, was the incompatibility of syllabuses and teaching methods. By using jointly written material and a communications medium to develop ideas and discuss differences, it is hoped to facilitate educational exchange programs across various European countries.

Efficient and Flexible Education and Training

It is now recognized in this "information age" that continuous training and updating of the workforce is a necessity and, therefore, that traditional face-to-face teaching solutions cannot meet this need either in quantity or quality. Many information technologies require telecommunications, and hence it makes pedagogical sense to use telecommunications for training in this field. Using computer conferencing and electronic mail in the training process brings still further benefits.

- Flexibility as to time and place of training, enabling remote or local access to training materials
- Active and interactive opportunities for the learner, so that distance learning can be as exciting and collaborative as face-to-face training
- Efficient use of specialized teachers and tutors, putting at the learners' disposal, the know-how and the expertise wherever they exist

JANUS is a DELTA project to develop an interactive satellite link with voice and data communications for European distance education and training. Site-to-site transmission will be handled by satellite, while local area networks and telephone systems will continue to deliver the data to the individual student's home. One of the goals of the project is to support joint authoring of courses by members of the European Association of Distance Teaching Universities (EADTU). However:

Another goal is for students and faculty members at universities belonging to JANUS to be able to access the network through ordinary CMC connections, even from their home PCs using ordinary modems and existing public data (terrestrial) networks. JANUS has as its task the planning of such a network, which could develop into a "European Electronic University Network." (Collis, 1991a)

The 1992 European regulations regarding higher education require teaching institutions to make their courses available to potential students from any EC country. The JANUS network will make it possible for distance teaching universities to support their courses across Europe via computer conferencing, synchronous voice transactions, and data transfer. Trials of the network will begin in 1992.

EPOS is another DELTA project involving a consortium of European national telephone and telecommunications utilities interested in developing an open learning service, initially for the in-service training of their employees. Their aim is to promote an online training system that is accepted by trainees and caters to the enormous differences in approach to education and training throughout European countries. In addition to looking at broadband technologies available with ISDN, the project has considered computer conferencing. The project leader from the Italian telephone company, SIP, says:

For several years now the scientific community has been making intensive use of electronic mailing and conferencing systems for its daily work. All that is required to apply this technology to the world of distance learning is some relatively simple development work to improve the user friendliness of existing academic systems. This means nothing more than achieving the quality of the best commercial products. (Walker, 1991)

A third European networking project, called COSYS, aims to design and implement a production and delivery system for open and flexible education and training materials. The rationale behind the project is that there is currently too much fragmentation among course producers, publishers, and course providers. None have the resources to invest in the production of high-quality multimedia courseware for a European market. Production solely for national markets is of limited commercial interest, and cooperation between public and private providers seems necessary to meet the diversified needs of the European training market. The advent of desktop publishing has meant that most course material is available on disk. However, the main impediment to the reuse, updating and repackaging of this material is the lack of standardization of the computer-based tools. This project, therefore, will use hypermedia systems to make available multimedia course material—articles, extracts, graphics, video, and other raw teaching material—electronically through email, computer conferencing, online databases, and high-speed connection through ISDN. Users of the system—trainers and other course providers—can browse through the system and get an overview of existing course material within a given learning domain and then pick and mix different modules and categories of course material according to the actual educational situation: in a classroom, on-the-job distance learning, self-study material, training of trainers, or in-house training.

All three of these projects are investigating in different ways the provision of networked training and education across European borders. All three are tackling the problem defined by Collis in her state-of-the-art report on telecommunications-based training in Europe:

In Europe, cross-national means not only cross-regulatory, but also cross-language and cross-cultural, involving layers of important considerations with respect to the cost-effectiveness of broad-scale training. (Collis, 1991a)

These particular projects have now moved beyond the pilot, experimental stage and on to implementation and validation.

Facilitating Business Partnerships and Community Projects

One of the most established uses of widespread electronic networks is undoubtedly the opportunity to coordinate joint projects with partners in various countries and time zones. Multinational corporations, such as Digital Equipment Corporation, have been using their in-house conferencing system for some time to manage projects both within the company and in some cases with clients and other experts. In the context of Europe, networks are also used to facilitate finding partners for joint projects, both in the commercial and noncommercial sectors.

EuroKom is a conferencing and file transfer service designed to support research teams, businesses, and government organizations in their communications requirements. The host for the system is situated in Dublin and is based on a version of PortaCom, one of the most commonly used conferencing systems in Europe. It was originally established by the EC to support the research participants of its various development programs, coordinating and managing projects that have multinational and multi-institutional users. Although the explosion of networking in Europe in the last two years has changed the balance, EuroKom was probably the most heavily used conferencing system operating in Europe.

In many ways, the most exciting and innovative uses of European networking spring from the community sector. Manchester, England, is the first of a growing number of "networked cities" being sponsored by local, national, and EC funding. By establishing a computer information and communications service, Manchester offers local businesses and community organizations cheap, easy access to powerful computer facilities as well as a gateway to European partnerships. Manchester is part of a consortium of nearly a dozen European cities aiming to set up similar facilities. Some have a definite community bias; others are primarily aimed at business, particularly SMEs. The one in Crete, for example, wants to facilitate small farmers' access to pricing fluctuations in the vegetable market in other European countries.

Many established nonelectronic networks have begun to put parts of their services online. One example is the IRIS network, set up in 1988 by the EC to facilitate the vocational training of women. Two years later a bulletin board was established for the service, allowing members of the network to post information announcing training programs, calling for cooperative partners and exchanges, or requesting further particulars of courses. Similarly, BC-Net is a business cooperation network set up to bring together potential partners for European businesses interested in transnational cooperation. BC-Net advisers analyze, with the aid of a coding system, the cooperation opportunities proposed by enterprises, forward them to the central unit in Brussels to carry out the matching operation, handle the replies from Brussels, and occasionally participate in the negotiations leading to business cooperation agreements. This network makes it possible to help SMEs participate more easily in EC-funded research programs while smoothing the difficulties standing in the way of cooperation between firms in different member states. This service is now being made available on the Manchester host.

GeoNet, with a truly international user base, originates in Germany. Its email and information system is one of the largest in Europe, although it is not run by a large corporation. Systems are operated by independent companies that collaborate through the GeoMail Association.

Using the GeoNet backbone is a consortium of Electronic Village Halls. This concept of "telecottages" was originally developed in Scandanavian countries to provide isolated village communities with access to data processing, telecommunications, and computer-based training. Instead of linking individual households to the network, advanced technology facilities are concentrated within a teleservice center, which is thus at the disposal of the entire local community to be used in a number of different business and community activities. As similar facilities are being set up in other European countries—Germany, Greece, the United Kingdom, and Ireland—the sites are linked through a gateway so that local groups have access to a much larger community. New sites get advice on how established sites overcame various problems, and ideas and experience are swapped through the mailbox facility.

Poptel, which operates on GeoNet from a London base, provides electronic networking for the noncommercial and nongovernmental community. One active group on its system includes the various members of the European trade union institutes. Another small but growing use is that by the cooperative movement, known as the Industrial Common Ownership Movement. Exchange of information and coordination of projects are the primary benefits, although communication with the former East Germany and Poland is also a benefit as it is presently easier through GeoNet than by telephone. Although the bulletin board facilities on GeoNet are theoretically comparable to those of a conferencing system (ability to comment on messages and divide topics into separate conference areas), it is interesting that the kind of interaction typical of most GeoNet messages is businesslike, practical, and hard-edged. The sort of chatty, discursive conversations characteristic of most conferencing interactions never developed on GeoNet.

Several aspects of the use of networking by the private, community-based sector are worthy of note. First of all, one of the main deterrents to further use of electronic networking in this area is the technology itself. Communications software is still too difficult for the naive and isolated user; the computer jargon of most manuals and support staff is off-putting, and the logging on procedures are considered tortuous. Second, leaders of these community-based projects are aware of the importance of influencing the development of telecommunciations policy on a European scale. The needs of the private, noncommercial sector are, in many respects, quite different from those of the business and education lobbies which tend to dominate policy making and funding allocations. Despite the rhetoric, business approaches are inherently competitive, not collaborative. They tend to judge computer networks on their ability to save money (on travel or fax), or to advertise their products, or to access information. The community uses of networks are fundamentally more collaborative, more interactive and hence more in line with the basic structure of networking. The uses that community-based projects make of networks are, perhaps, more imaginative and truly innovative (see Rheingold, chap. 4). The networking needs of the nonprofit sector must be given due weight by policymakers, as ultimately these applications could be the most enduring uses of electronic interactivity (see Kapor and Weitzner, chap. 18).

Research and Development on Advanced Technologies

Networked projects are the focus of considerable research and development work in Europe. How can networking be exploited for teaching advanced technology, while at the same time appealing to trainees from different cultures in SMEs? As computer and telecommunication technologies have penetrated both the manufacturing and service sector at a growing rate in Europe, certain high-tech sectors have begun to experience skill shortages that threaten Europe's economic competitiveness. Many of the DELTA and COMETT research projects have testing and validation phases, during which various advanced learning technologies are implemented in pilot settings. Several projects attempt to assess the adequateness of particular technologies for different market segments and include cross-cultural comparisons. By setting up experimental test-situations in which trainers and technologists can pilot new techniques, the EC will be able to participate in the evolution of telecommunications strategies for teaching and training.

EuroPACE, a consortium of industrial and university partners, offers a unique distance-learning environment in Europe by means of satellite transmission. Presenters, who are experts in state-of-the-art technologies, offer short courses that are delivered to nearly two hundred industrial and academic receiving sites and viewed asynchronously by groups of mainly European company professionals and managers as well as university staff and postgraduate students. Although all participants and lecturers have access to the computer conferencing system PACE-COM, the most extensive use of the system is for coordination among the managers of the various receiving sites. However, the conferencing system provides more successful support for the live events that EuroPACE also transmits on its satellite channel:

It has been argued that asynchronous and text-based computer-mediated interactivity fits better into a multi-lingual environment than audio-based interactivity . . . The use of PACECOM for teacher-learner communication during our monthly live programs has increased during the last year. Most users seem to prefer to address the teachers through PACECOM, rather than putting the questions by telephone, directly to the teachers in the studio. The choice is free. (Nipper, 1991)

Two projects from the DELTA exploratory phase (1989/90) also used computer conferencing along with other telecommunications media to carry out research on cross-national learning environments. The OLE project (Organizational Learning in Enterprises) set up a multimedia virtual classroom, using existing technology to simulate an ISDN network between workers in shoe production factories in Denmark and Portugal. The project combined slow-scan television image exchange through a picture telephone with a computer conferencing system and local PC support. The major findings of the project related to the problems of collaborative teaching in multisite settings. The second project, OLEW (Open Learning Experimental Workshop) aimed to test the main features of an open learning educational environment for the skilled and professional market, using computer and video conferencing to link various European sites.

The second phase of the DELTA program is under way. Partners in each project must represent at least two member states and usually include universities, SMEs, large industrial partners, and government agencies. "The stimulation of this sort of large-scale initiative is providing a substantial impetus to the investigation of telecomunications-based possibilities for learning and training" (Collis, 1991a).

Although many more European networking projects could be listed in this way, a more useful approach is to look in detail at one particular example and to draw out the lessons from a well-documented and evaluated application.

ELNET Case Study

The Centre for Electronic Communications and Open Support Systems in Education is based at the Southampton Institute in the United Kingdom. It was supported by the U.K. Department of Education and Science to research the educational application of electronic communications technologies and to support teachers in implementing new and emerging computer-based systems within their curriculum. The U.K. Department of Employment funded CECOMM to run a three-year project establishing an electronic network of educational establishments in the United Kingdom, France, and Germany. ELNET, the European Business and Languages Learning Network, was therefore set up among institutes of higher education in the three countries to carry out group activities within the principal curriculum areas of business and language studies. The aims of the project were:

- To develop strategies for learning in multicultural groups

and secondarily,

- To develop a low-cost, telecommunications-based European distributed communications infrastructure
- To investigate the organizational impact of cross-cultural learning groups
- To develop techniques and models for managing distributed learning systems

Fifteen colleges in the three countries were matched to engage in cross-institutional collaboration.

"Virtual College" Design

ELNET initially saw its role as obtaining agreements from the various colleges to work in learning partnerships where each of the pairs would design the curriculum strategies, lead the interaction, and provide the content and other resources. In short, the ELNET team would act as facilitators and network providers only. Although this approach worked well with some colleges, it broke down completely with others:

It became evident that the learning partnership approach restricted the use of the medium. This is because as students and tutors became familiar with the medium it became clear that anybody could talk to anybody. (Davies, Davies, and Jennings, 1992)

As the project progressed, this devolvement of responsibility for teaching to the colleges was seen as only one way of using ELNET. A clear demand for the centralized provision of learning experiences and resources emerged. One of the reasons involved the difficulties over partner availability during vacations, term times, work placements, national holidays and so forth. Another reason related to the limited view of single conferencing "classrooms"—in fact, students made valuable contacts across the partnerships, and even outside the ELNET network altogether (as Caucus has distributed nodes in the United States and Japan).

The ELNET team therefore reappraised its approach at the midpoint of the project and decided to take a more interventionist approach, offering content in addition to infrastructure. They set up a conference called Eurodesk, an intensive, mutilingual, competitive simulation game. Working in teams, students responded to a barrage of news items in three languages (some of it spurious), simulating a news wire service. They had to collate the information and write a report to an imagined American business partner. This required each group to collect the news items each day, translate them, work out the key emphasis of each one, combine and compare them with earlier items, prioritize according to significance, and produce recommendations and a summary of the items. ELNET also developed a teaching simulation called EcoEurope, which involved environmental issues, this time requiring teams from two countries.

Technological Infrastructure

Part of the ELNET project was the development of the conferencing system, Caucus, into an easily accessed, multilingual, distributed host. In fact, these technological goals of the project were much easier to achieve than its social and pedagogical ones. Caucus is now available in English, French, and German, with transmission of multilingual character sets across public data networks. Conferences are distributed between French and U.K. hosts (a German host proved impossible to set up within the time frame) with updating procedures at regular intervals. Local dialup facilities were established in all three countries, ensuring low-cost access.

One technical shortcoming remains to be resolved, although it is not specific to ELNET (see Shapard, chap. 15, for a discussion of the ASCII problem for Asian languages): the full sets of French and German characters cannot easily be generated and do not appear on all computer screens and printers:

It is appreciated that this is a thorny issue, dating back to the establishment of the ASCII norm, which has plagued IT specialists ever since they began to deal with language teachers. However, it is a problem which needs a solution, as language teachers can still argue against the use of technology because 'the students will never learn to spell correctly'. It is hoped that the introduction of the ISO norm and the use of a graphical interface will overcome this problem once and for all. (Davies, 1992)

Davies also highlights the difficulties involved in developing language interfaces for conferencing systems; namely, that it requires the right mix of skills bridging at least three disciplines (languages, information technology, and communications) to find appropriate translations for a host of unfamiliar lexical terms.

Organizational Issues

Integrating networking technology into existing educational institutions was identified as a major challenge by the ELNET team from the start. The implications for each institution in taking part in the ELNET project consisted of at least four distinct activities:

1. Designation of tutors and technology

2. Identification of multilingual student groups in the curriculum area

3. Negotiation of curricula, topics, and teaching methods with partners abroad

4. Allocation of time to learn to use and teach via the technology

With little or no special funding to the institutions for hardware, tutors' additional time, or telephone costs, the project was founded almost entirely upon good will. In the case of the U.K., decisions about resource allocation are made at the institutional level. Furthermore, U.K. tutors adopt a fairly flexible attitude to demands of their work, such that additional duties are generally undertaken without expectation of extra payment. In France, these decisions are taken at a regional level. Conditions of employment are such that tutors' duties are clearly laid out, and any additional work must be handled by additional funding. Thus, despite wholehearted commitment of the institution to the project, progress was dependent on different elements within the educational system.

Nevertheless, learning groups were established across the fifteen sites, although the time taken to work through institutional differences meant that less was achieved by the groups than was originally envisaged.

Access to machines by the various students in the project brings out another aspect of the cultural difficulties facing international electronic networking. The attitude toward the provision of IT resources in U.K. schools has moved beyond the idea of an exclusive preserve of IT teachers to one of open access. Consequently, U.K. students used ELNET at their convenience in open access rooms. Female students in particular were enthusiastic users, developing networks with other users on the system. The situation in France is completely opposite: IT is seen as a specialty to be strictly controlled by IT experts. Equipment is kept locked up, access is difficult to arrange and is always mediated by a tutor. Messages were not input by students, therefore, but by tutors or occasionally by IT specialists. The situation in German colleges lies somewhere between these extremes. IT equipment is located in specialized rooms and is controlled, but not as strictly as in French schools. German messages were input by individual students or by a student leader of the team. However, the enthusiasm, dedication, and focus of the Germans resulted in their overall input equalling that of the U.K. students—despite the fact that they joined the system nearly one year after the students of the other two countries! The French input amounted to only about 15 percent overall, while the Germans deluged the system when entry for them was finally arranged, and they overwhelmed the others with questions, information, and enthusiastic interactions.

Curriculum Integration

Integrating conferencing activities into the ongoing curriculum of the classroom is the sine qua non of successful educational networking (see also Riel, chap. 13 and Teles, chap. 16). This integration proved fraught with difficulties in the European context where not only are curricula very different but teaching methods are as well. French colleges were unable to make any changes to the strict and stringent studies curriculum laid down by the Ministry of Education. They managed to participate in the multidisciplinary approach of ELNET only by each separate tutor (of physics, geography, economics, and languages) dealing with a common subject (for example, nuclear energy). The two simulation games run by ELNET were impossible for the French to partake in, as they simply did not fit into the rigid categories of French timetables and subject areas. German schools also have a fairly controlled curriculum but are not nearly so inflexible as their French counterparts. One German school managed most of their participation in ELNET after normal school hours, for example. Fortunately, the U.K. colleges had much greater flexibility regarding curriculum covered, methods of teaching, and scheduling in the school year. Consequently the U.K. colleges could bend to the stricter demands of the other two countries.

Finally, both German and French attitudes toward the social chat conference were uniformly hostile; their orientation was entirely toward work-based conferences. The cafe conference was therefore inhabited primarily by U.K. students.

Despite this lack of compatibility, or perhaps because of it, one of the positive outcomes noted by tutors in the project was the impact of ELNET on curriculum integration. For instance, French teachers gathered together for the first time to discuss common curricula and discovered areas of overlap in their teaching. Opening up discussion about teaching methods across national borders was also stimulating for tutors.

Language Learning

The major advantage of the computer conferencing system as a tool for language learning is the opportunity it provides for communication in a natural context with native language speakers. ELNET aimed to foster cross-cultural group learning through a student-centered approach.

> Some of the best examples of authentic communication took place within the less tightly structured conferences—those where the students were allowed to respond in their own way once the theme had been introduced. (Davies, 1992)

However, it was also apparent that only students with adequate language skills benefited from this approach. Consequently a number of teacher-directed activities were initiated, such as the Eurodesk simulation. Where teachers accompanied this by a tightly managed series of classroom activities taking place simultaneously offline, it was highly successful.

The project identified a major obstacle to further cross-cultural language learning projects, whether online or not: the lack of good second language learning among most U.K. students.

> It is quite clear from my observations of the conferences taking place within ELNET that most UK students are at an enormous linguistic disadvantage compared to their French and German partners, especially the latter. This was underlined by comments and observations by teachers in all three countries. Only those UK students who are studying languages at A-level appear to be deriving the maximum benefit from ELNET. All other UK students appear to be floundering in waters that are far too deep for them. (Davies, 1992)

Most U.K. students required a structured, teacher-directed approach; otherwise all partners resorted to English as the lingua franca. German students of the equivalent U.K. level spend three to four times as many hours learning English as U.K. students spend in foreign language learning. Additionally both French and German students are exposed to considerably more English through films, music, and other aspects of popular culture, and their need to learn English is more motivating than the reverse is for U.K. students. Nevertheless, computer networking was shown to be a valuable tool in foreign language learning; its application to the European context merely needs refining in light of the ELNET experience.

Summary of ELNET Outcomes

An obvious but nonetheless interesting outcome of the ELNET evaluation was that the technology was perceived by the users to be a non-issue. Students' experience of computer networking was positive and easily acquired. Another finding common to many networking applications was that the length of time needed to implement conferencing and produce a working, educational system far exceeded the expectations of the planners. Many of the tutors commented that after two years of use, they were only just beginning to get a feel for how to exploit it. Although users were generally positive about the ELNET experience, the organizational and pedagogical problems are major areas of concern for future projects of this kind. Face-to-face teaching institutions are not organized to work laterally across other institutions nor, for that matter, to work asynchronously. Furthermore, the time overlap, when all the ELNET colleges were available for online work throughout the school year, was only six weeks (from January to mid-February). At all other times, only subsets of groupings were interacting. Finally, the time, effort, and energy required on the part of tutors to devise and sustain an intercultural online program was so significant that it really cannot be contemplated without solid institutional support and funding. At the end of the three-year project, the funds for sustaining the program at these schools had not been found. The lack of resources at this level of educational provision in all three countries led the ELNET team to conclude that, on the whole, this was the right technology in the wrong market. The development of computer conferencing at a technical level is ahead of the curriculum and institutional implications of its use.

Conclusions

The sheer number of networking applications that span European borders denotes success at one level. Electronic networking is clearly meeting some of the communications needs of Europeans as they attempt to integrate in corporate, educational, and community sectors. The ELNET case study sets in a particular context both the positive aspects of European networking—the opportunity to bridge linguistic, cultural and educational differences—as well as the negative aspects—the practical, financial, and pedagogical problems.

Despite all this apparent activity, the present use of computer networking in Europe is not a runaway success story. The technical side of the process—setting up suitable equipment, logging on, and acquiring familiarity with online commands and procedures—is still a significant hurdle for most users and a major deterrent to those who are isolated without technical support. Second, the network infrastructure is still far from adequate outside universities and large corporations and is very expensive, even in Western Europe. An online course offered today across Europe in which students were expected to log on from their homes over telephone lines would probably have a very small market. Finally, and most significantly, the actual take-up, sustained use, and quality of interaction in many of the interactive online systems falls considerably short of the potential of the medium. The evaluation report on a computer conferencing network for graduate students and tutors across the five Nordic countries concluded:

To learn how to use a new media [sic] is one matter. To learn how to integrate it into day-to-day practices, is quite another. (Rasmussen, Bang, and Lundby, 1991)

Do all these examples amount to the development of a "European village"? The fact that people are communicating across European borders does not constitute a new community. The European village is still a long way off, and given the rise of nationalism and ethnic differences elsewhere in the world, the efforts to promote such a vision are working

against the tide. Nevertheless, these networking activities are significant in themselves, representing a will to understand and communicate and a desire to think beyond national borders. A fair conclusion,
then, is that individual projects are positive steps on the long march
toward a new, integrated Europe.

13   *Global Education through Learning Circles*

Margaret Riel

The goal of global education is to promote multicultural sensitivity and understanding of interdependent systems that operate in today's world (Tye, 1991). Global education helps students to see that social problems, cultural issues, or economic relationships aren't constrained by national boundaries.

Global education is not a new curriculum topic but a new approach to interdisciplinary study across the curriculum. This process of education requires a vision that comes from other domains. The aims of global education are to help students see the complexity of the world through the eyes and minds of people whose viewpoint is very different than their own; to help students and teachers employ a systems approach to thinking about cause and effect in an international arena; and to encourage learning and teaching about the history and culture of all people. This approach seeks to promote a sense of global history, an awareness of common human aspirations in a diverse world, and the will and ability to tackle the great problems and issues facing all the inhabitants of our planet.

Change in the Role of Teaching and Learning

A call for global education is a response to the changes in society and requires an accompanying change in the classroom. But change in the classroom will not occur unless teachers act as agents rather than as objects of change. The global approach to education requires a change in the role of the teacher and the learner. Most notably it involves increased opportunities for collaborative problem solving, both for teachers and students.

Teachers are currently isolated from their peers and from learning opportunities because they spend most of their working time alone in classrooms. The isolation of the teacher becomes reflected in a view of learning as a process that takes place in the minds of students working quietly at their desks. It is difficult to imagine how teachers working alone in their classrooms are going to be able to provide students with a worldwide perspective in a rapidly changing world.

Efforts to restructure schools address change in the role of the teachers. They frequently recommend the development of school-site management teams or restructuring teams composed of teachers, administrators, parents, and community leaders. These efforts provide teachers the experience of working in teams. These school-based teams are playing an important part in changing schools, but their effectiveness can be extended by increasing ties beyond the school setting. If we want teachers to provide students with a global perspective, then it is critically important to find ways to strengthen teachers' links to world events and to global issues. Participation in a Networld (see Harasim, chap. 2) is one way to accomplish this.

The Use of Communication Technology in the Classroom

Communication technology offers tools for promoting the global education of students and teachers. Through international collaboration on educational tasks, students can begin to appreciate the complexity of issues and the consequences of actions. Teachers, working with their peers in other countries, have a very wide range of instructional resources to draw on for designing learning environments. With good educational planning, communication technology can serve both as a way to educate students and provide an ongoing learning context for teachers that accomplishes the goals of global education.

When teachers and students engage in cooperative learning activities mediated by computer networking, the power and speed of human learning is extended by their collective knowledge and rich set of experiences. Computer telecommunication provides a human context for learning. These human networks—the connections established between people who are distant in time and space—can extend learning in a social and global world.

The social skills needed to work in groups with distant partners do not develop with the same speed as communication technology. Most networks are arranged around a conference or party model (see Rhein-gold, chap. 4) where individuals enter a shared electronic space that is rich with possibilities. But it remains a difficult task to find or create a project that meets the needs of a particular group of students. Student and teacher time are valuable but limited resources that constrain the search for educational activities on free-accesss networks.

Knowing how to plan, organize, and complete projects with distant partners is far from trivial. Studies of network projects have found an extremely low success rate (1–2 percent) among projects that are intro-duced by individuals on open structure, free-access networks (Staple-ton, 1992). Open computer access to people in distant locations does not, in itself, stimulate creative thinking or integration of ideas. Infor-mal or unfocused discussions on networks are time consuming and offer little in terms of lasting educational change. But careful planning has lead to some success in constructing new learning environments for students (see also Mason, chap. 12 and Teles, chap. 16).

Global Education through Learning Circles

Learning circles are small electronic communities that form to accom-plish specific goals (Riel, 1992). Students and teachers from a small number of classrooms located around the world form a learning circle to work together for a specified period of time to accomplish a common goal. The AT&T Learning Network is organized into learning circles because this task-oriented grouping provides an effective way to inte-grate communication technology, classroom curriculum, and the aims of global education. Teachers and students who share academic inter-ests but represent different geographic or cultural perspectives are grouped together.

Six to nine classes form a learning circle. Students in these classes design and organize curriculum-based activities using computer tele-communications. Learning circles on the Learning Network help stu-dents share written information with distant peers in much the same way as "circle time" or "sharing days" are used in primary grades to help young students share verbal information with local peers. Students conduct research on society's problems and global issues; compare historical, geographic, and environmental concerns; and share local news, events, and opinions with their peers.

Learning circles in the educational community, like "quality circles" in the business community, involve participatory management by teachers. No one teacher controls a learning circle. It is a collective construction by the participants.

Curriculum-based educational projects are the central focus of learning circles with technology playing an essential but not highly visible role. Instead the emphasis is on community-based research shared with global partners as a way to make the impersonal and complex global issues concrete and personal. Research that takes students into the community looking for local clues of global patterns encourages cross-curricular study, involves community members in school learning, and helps students learn more about their own local community through contrast with others.

Each classroom group in a learning circle helps create the circle publication at the end of the session that summarizes the completed work. This publication process helps students review and evaluate the exchanges they had with students in other locations. The choices they make about what to include in their final report and how to organize the information helps them to organize what they learned.

Phases of a Learning Circle

Learning Circle interaction is structured by phases with goals and tasks facilitating cooperative planning among the participants. Six phases guide the interaction from the time the circle begins to the time it ends.

1. Getting ready: The first phase involves receiving and reviewing the materials, and testing the communication software. A 24-hour help line is available to assist in solving any connection problems.

2. Opening the circle: The second phase begins with a circle news message welcoming participants to their learning circle and introducing the circle participants. Introductory activities are organized to help teachers and students learn more about each other and the schools and communities represented. Some introductory activities involve sending materials through the postal mail as well as online.

3. Planning circle projects: Each class in a learning circle has the opportunity to sponsor a learning circle project centered on their curriculum or interests. Sponsoring a project requires planning, requesting, collecting, and analyzing information from other students, focused on a topic or issue chosen to fit with the classroom curriculum.

4. Exchanging student work: Students send their work on each of the projects sponsored by the other classes in a reciprocal teacher and learner relationship. Students become reporters, authors, poets, or researchers responding to the requests of other schools. Often a class is divided into several small groups, and each group is responsible for responding to one of the other class projects.

5. Organizing the circle publication: Students review and evaluate the learning experience and organize the information received from their peers into a summary that becomes part of the circle publication. Each school distributes their summaries either online or through postal mail to all the other classes. The circle coordinator also sends a cover page, opening letter, list of schools, and table of contents.

6. Closing the circle: In the final week of the circle, students assemble their circle publication. The project summaries received from each of the schools are combined with material provided by the circle coordinator and then published at each school. Students and teachers say goodbye to their online partners and the session ends.

Global Education in the Local Context

Hanvey (1977) established five interdisciplinary goals for global education. Using examples of student work drawn from learning circle interactions, I illustrate how these goals are being accomplished through collaborative work via computer telecommunications.

1. Perspective consciousness: An awareness of and appreciation for other images of the world.

2. State of the planet awareness: An in-depth understanding of global issues and events.

3. Cross-cultural awareness: A general understanding of the defining characteristics of world cultures and an emphasis on understanding similarities and differences.

4. Systemic awareness: A familiarity with the nature of systems and an introduction to the complex and international system in which governmental and nongovernmental actors are linked in patterns of interdependence and dependence in a variety of issue areas.

5. Options for participation: A review of strategies for participation in issue areas in local, national, and international settings.

Perspective Consciousness

Definitions of self come from understanding the self in relationship to others. Learning circles on the AT&T Learning Network challenge students to find ways to define themselves for others who live in distant regions, often with very different social and cultural characteristics. In "Classroom Surveys," with questions about themselves, their school, their community, in the preparation of "welcome packs" sent by postal mail students, and in circle projects, students are asked to reflect on what sets them apart as special and what they share in common with their peers in distant locations. These activities help students think about symbolic representations and their meanings. Statues, flags, music, natural formations, clothing styles, foods, preferences, and images are used to represent what one group holds as important about themselves and their world.

These comparisons expose students to variable patterns of everyday life resulting from different cultural adaptations to geographic and climatic conditions. Both similarities and differences encourage students to be more conscious of who they are and why they live the way they do. For example:

Students discovered that their peers in the desert terrain of Coober Pedy, Australia, live in underground homes to escape the heat of the sun. These dugout homes are neither heated nor cooled as the earth provides a constant pleasant living temperature. Living in the ground, rather than on top of it, creates different types of harmony with the environment. For example, underground creatures, like snakes, sometimes block air passageways.

As students considered these differences, they gained a richer understanding of the choices that are involved in their own life patterns.

▪ Alaskan students described the "setting" of the sun in the fall and attending school in the everyday of night.

- Students in the southern hemisphere sent revisions of Christmas carols that describe holidays in the bright summer season sun.

- Messages arrive from Japan written on a day that has not yet arrived.

These experiences help students locate themselves in a global environment and develop an understanding of how their unique location on the earth is related to their experiences of day, night, seasons, and time.

Learning circle interaction also makes it possible for students who need more time to express their ideas or have language handicaps to interact in a way that does not emphasize their difficulties. Students from a lock-up juvenile detention center worked on projects with students from a private college-preparatory school. The quality of the finished work from these different groups was comparable, but the social supports for those creating the work were very different. The presentation of self can be very strong in this different format as is evident in these two examples, one from a deaf student and the other from a student in a school where all of the students are on probation. These students challenge others to think about identity in different ways.

To my circle friends,

MY FEELINGS ABOUT BEING DEAF IN THE HEARING WORLD

It's not easy being deaf in the hearing world because there are many problems that you may confront. For example, some deaf people are treated as if they were different or not normal. Sometimes a hearing person who doesn't know about deafness acts as if we, as deaf people, are not very intelligent. For example, some hearing people expect us to be mute and only use sign language. They may think that we are very helpless and are not able to lead good lives when we become adults.

I sometimes am confronted by others who never saw a deaf person speaking. They would crowd around me and ask me a lot of questions. I've been asked if I knew how to swim or ride a bicycle! It is kind of weird when I am asked if I do things that most kids do. Especially if I think of myself as a normal, ordinary kid who does everything but hear.

Most deaf kids can tell if a hearing person likes them or is pretending to like them out of pity. We don't need pity if we are normal. It won't work

---

if you try to pretend to like a deaf person out of pity because they soon won't want to be friends with you. We are somebody! A lot of deaf people have gone on to become teachers, lawyers, actors, actresses, authors, professors and so forth. We are human just like hearing people because we make mistakes and learn from them. There are deaf people who prefer to sign; there are deaf people who prefer to talk just like me. I am a hearing person who cannot hear. I don't think of myself as a deaf person.

In fact I never did.

April

Desperate

Willy Ridgley
Thomas E. Mathews Community School
Marysville, CA

Starved for destination,
A beggar man by trade.
A desperate man needs more
Than someone else to blame.
Friendless,
It appears he hides behind his tears.
The things he's lost,
The things he will never have at all.
The forgotten man wanders
Misplaced in the world.
Obscurity is all that he sees and can recall.
He's all alone.
The destitute find meaning
In a different way of life.
The doorways that they dwell in
Are shelter for in the night
The shining crystal possessions
Are set out for his display.
His only purpose is to find food
To get him through the day.

All these contrasts challenge the unexamined assumptions that students hold about their world. This exchange of images and symbols helps students and teachers begin to understand both the similarities and differences among people in different places.

State-of-the-Planet Awareness

Teaching is creating an environment that enables students to teach themselves (Bredo, 1989). Research on peer tutoring suggests that teaching something to someone else is a very good learning strategy. In the reciprocal teaching and learning design of learning circles, each class of students and their teacher sponsors, or teaches, one of the projects in a learning circle. The other classes participate in, and learn from, their involvement in these sponsored projects.

Many of these projects are organized to help students learn more about the state of our planet. In fact, student-designed surveys of the most important social problems of our time almost always place environmental problems at the top of the list. For example:

- Students in British Columbia sponsored the "Environmental Investigator" as their section of their collective newspaper, *The Global Grapevine*. They asked the eight schools in their learning circle for essays or poetry centered on local environmental issues. They sent out and published the results of their survey on the environment and invited students in other locations to send questions related to the environment to a column called "Ask Dr. Enviro." For the answers to some questions, these elementary students took a trip to the nearby middle school to get help from the science teacher.

- A discussion of the whaling industry among classrooms in several American schools proved to be more complex since some of the discussants depend on whales as their primary source of food. Eskimo children's description of the excitement of the village and their cooperation in the sharing of the food after a successful harpooning expedition contrasted sharply with California children's descriptions of the show tricks of Shamu, at Seaworld, and those who call for an end to the killing of whales.

- Students in one elementary class in Canada sponsored a project called "Weather Patterns and the Greenhouse Effect." Their teacher worked with them to integrate weather and pollution data they requested and received from across the United States and in Australia. The teacher reported that her students realized the importance of their work when they had completed the summary and shared it with their peers in their circle publication.

■ Students in Belgium sponsored a research project on waste caused by excessive packaging of goods. Students collected and compared the packaging of many different types of products and assessed the best and worst examples in different countries.

Working across classrooms gave students who do not live near an ocean or mountains or rivers or plains an opportunity to find out from peers in these locations the nature or scale of environmental problems. As demonstrated in these examples, communication can provide multiple perspectives not often found within a single classroom.

Cross-Cultural Awareness

Students develop ethnocentric positions when they are not exposed to differences. They also assume that other people should be like themselves. To achieve cross-cultural awareness, they need to learn how people who may look very similar are different and how people who look very different are similar. Local communities and neighborhoods offer a limited range of variability. Interaction in learning circles offers additional experiences. Consider these examples:

When students in Louisiana received the class photo from their partners in New York, the students turned to the computer and wrote, "Great to see the pictures of you all, but where are the brothers?????"

The teacher reported that the students were very surprised to see that the students they were working with in that school were all white. The students' surprise indicates a fairly common event in computer communication—people assume similarity of the other until evidence to the contrary is received. Developing contrasting examples can make it easier for groups that normally avoid one another to learn about the other.

There is also a sharing of information on how to solve problems that arise from cultural clash, as illustrated in this next example.

The students from a German classroom described an increasing number of students from different ethnic backgrounds who were entering their schools with resulting cultural conflicts. The relationships among students were becoming a serious problem in their schools. These German students, relying on American television as their source of knowledge, asked their circle partners to tell them how schools in the United States managed to achieve such a high degree of successful integration of minorities.

They found that schools located in different states had very different responses. Each class shared very different views on the amount of racism that existed in their community. Some accepted the characterization and described the importance of valuing the unique contribution of everyone. Most of the schools indicated that the problem was very difficult and far from solved but offered some advice on how to work together.

Students in Alaska were surprised by the active interest that members of their learning circle expressed about all aspects of their lives. They had initially felt isolated and timid about participating, but their teacher reported that with each question they answered, the students developed a stronger identity and pride in their own cultural background.

The Alaskan students invited the elders of the community to come to their class and help them answer questions about their Eskimo way of life. In this way, the interest of others helped the students define themselves.

Elementary students in Puerto Rico sponsored a writing project on health with a global focus. They asked students in other locations to interview school nurses about health problems that were a concern in their school. They wanted to know if students in other schools shared some of the same health problems.

The information exchanged provided students with a way to compare problems that face different groups of students.

Obvious visual markers of race, ethnicity, gender, age, or physical appearance are not initially available in computer messages. The absence of these markers reduces the tendency to form stereotypes. Instead, the "voice" created in the text creates an impression of the writer. Well-dressed students in a suburban neighborhood school and students with purple spiked hair, tattoos, or torn clothes who are unlikely to be able to work together comfortably in the same physical space have worked closely together on the Learning Network. Helping students to share their ideas across cultural boundaries while physically remaining in a comfortable space may increase their sensitivity to common human conditions.

Systemic Awareness

Gaining an understanding about the systemic relationships in our world is a challenge we all face. Dramatic events, like the invasion of a small country in the Persian Gulf or race riots in South Central Los Angeles, create worldwide focus on actions within larger systems of meaning. What is the meaning of these events for people in different locations, and how are shared meanings constructed? Distant and international links do not, in and of themselves, create deeper or more insightful understanding, but the thoughts and ideas of those in other places can provide valuable clues as we try to piece together the meaning of events. This awareness is more likely to develop among high school students who are being encouraged to see past scud missiles, gas masks, or beatings.

In 1989 when East Germans began to flee their country through Poland to relocate in West Germany, students in the United States were sending surveys to their German peers in their learning circle to better understand their views of this new development. These students were exchanging information on the problem when the course of history began moving so fast that it was difficult to follow. The students in West Berlin sent daily messages to their circle trying to make sense of each new development and the consequence it would have for world democracy. In this circle, the work on projects was suspended as the participants in all classes tried to deal with events that were taking place and what the fall of the Berlin Wall would mean for a new world order.

The complexity of society's problems and their specific relationship to social and cultural systems becomes an object for study as students try to understand one another's surveys or responses. Consider this example from Japan.

Students in Japan wanted to know more about parent-child relationships in different locations. They constructed a parent-child survey with many questions about activities in the family and attitudes of children and parents.

This project led to discussions of the meaning that the notions of dependent and independent have in different cultural systems. Japanese students described themselves as highly dependent on their mothers for all their daily needs making it possible for them to devote maximum time to their studies. Independence in this frame was to be without this level of support and traditionally in Japan had negative connotations. For students in the United States, to be overly dependent on parents was understood as immaturity, and independence or self-reliance was a more highly valued characteristic. In Japan, dependence was related in a positive way to the cultural value of group consciousness, whereas in the United States, independence was related to individuality and self-sufficiency. But both systems are changing, and the students in the different locations were actively trying to understand the differences.

Systemic change can also be the result of new technology and different social organizations.

A school in West Germany located in a farming district sponsored a project on the plight of small farmers. They were surprised to find that students who lived on small farms in Illinois were facing many of the same extreme conditions that faced German farmers.

By comparing the state of the small farms in both countries they were able to understand some of the economic and political forces that were related to the change in farming practices.

During the war in the Persian Gulf, elementary students from Saudi Arabia were trying to explain to their peers that while they did not agree with what Sadam Hussein did, they did not think he was a "bad man." They also related the fear that comes from the sound of missile attacks and the fear of being separated from their parents.

Either by looking at a world event from different perspectives or by examining parallel causes for local events, the students in these examples gained an understanding of the interrelationships among different systems. The network provides one way to extend learning beyond our short history to a better understanding of our place in a world system and a search for answers within complex economic, political, environmental, cultural, and social systems.

Options for Participation

Schools are in a very sensitive position with respect to political activism. Teachers are responsible for educating, not indoctrinating, children. Teachers need to present students with strategies for participating in issues in local, national, and international settings without promoting particular political positions. The purpose of global education is to promote certain attitudes in students: an awareness of the world around them, a certain openness to alternative perspectives, a pride in self that isn't dependent on putting down others. When students become involved in real problems, they begin to realize that even the actions of one person can have consequences for the whole social system. Many issues that students discuss in school are political, but the development of plans for social action will be determined by the school community. For example, a logging community may be intolerant of a school-sponsored writing campaign to save the spotted owl, while another community may accept this as a valuable learning experience.

Students have become involved in beginning school-based recycling programs, in joining environmental organizations and programs for cleaning up oceans, lakes, and parks, and in promoting issues of health and safety. For example:

Secondary level students in Germany sponsored a project on nuclear energy and nuclear accidents. They sent a survey asking students to find the answers to questions about the location of the nearest nuclear power plants, and if students knew how safe they were from plane accidents, bombs, or earthquakes. They also wanted to know what agencies organized protests against the use of the nuclear energy.

While this project did not suggest that students take a particular political action, it did make students aware of worldwide concern over the risks of nuclear energy.

Students in a New York school chose to explore drug abuse by teenagers. Student opinion in this New York school was against serving alcohol at parties. Their Australian peers wanted to know "How do you have fun at a party without alcohol?" The New York students responded by citing the high risks associated with alcohol, particularly the number of accidents that involved drinking teenagers. Their own survey of the high school students at each of their learning circle schools showed that between 80 percent and 100 percent have driven or ridden in cars with drivers under the influence of alcohol.

The finding that so many students, even those who were discussing the problems of drinking and driving, find themselves in cars without sober drivers is frightening. Involving student teams in the design of better transportation systems for teenagers is one way that students might be able to participate in changing our society.

Learning circles provide teachers with the necessary direction and support to explore creative ways of integrating communication technology with school curriculum and community programs. The project approach to exploring and solving real problems that characterizes learning circle activities encourages the integration of different subjects helping to place knowledge and skill in the context of their use in the adult community. Knowledge that is constructed as a consequence of interaction with the community leaders, teachers, and classmates is likely to be retained long after information memorized from books is forgotten.

The Learning Network and the Professional Development of Teachers

The projects and learning circle publications document student learning. But what effect does this participation have on teachers? Teachers often work in a vacuum. With little opportunity to share good teaching ideas, they can neither demonstrate their skill nor learn from others. When a class sponsors an activity, the classroom project has a new audience. Teachers and students in other places are not only invited to look into the classroom to see what takes place, but also to walk in, sit down, and become the learners. The teacher also receives similar invitations from other classes to step out of the role of teacher and join with students from all over the world as a learner.

When teachers involved in learning circles were asked to list the most important educational benefit of their participation, they placed their own professional development as more significant than the enhancement of student learning. This finding validates the critical role of teachers as the source of any educational change (Cuban, 1986; Bredo, 1989; Winn and Coleman, 1989; LaFrenz and Friedman, 1989). As Cuban (1986) describes, teachers stand at the threshold of classrooms, making decisions about what innovations enter the classroom and how they are used with students. His research on the influence of past technological innovations (radio, television, and films) leads him to question the role technology plays in changing education. Change does not lie with communication technology itself. It is the teachers and the strategies they use to incorporate collaborative learning into their educational practices that make a difference. Students involved in computer network projects do not need to be tied to the computer. Students creating new inventions, canvassing the environment, or completing surveys at their desks may all be involved in learning activities that are linked by computers but are not dominated by them.

There are no forms of technology that can revolutionize the classroom while bypassing the teacher. If there is change, it will be in the way teachers and students create the context of a classroom and the interaction that takes place among the people who make up the life of a classroom. Global education will have to address teacher education as well as student education before it will be an important component in classroom instruction.

LaFrenz and Freidman (1989), responding to the visions proposed by educational leaders, call for more programs that will affect teacher training and support. Computer networking provides a multipurpose tool. What makes computer networking unique is that it provides a way for teachers to gain a global perspective at the same time as they create learning contexts for their students. In this way teachers and students are involved in a global learning experience.

Global Networking

Our experiences with learning circles show that computer networking offers a strategy for joining teachers and students where everyone is simultaneously teacher and learner. Education is not a spontaneous activity. It must be carefully designed, planned, and executed. If computer communication services promise schools the technology without any resources for educational activities, then the institutional and social circumstances that keep teachers operating in a professional vacuum will not be changed. One of the reasons that Dewey's progressive ideas failed to take hold is they were costly in terms of teacher time and energy. How can teachers working alone be expected to recreate, year after year, an exciting new environment for students' learning?

Computer networking offers the possibility of developing a stimulating, cooperative context for teachers and students. But it is the quality of the dialogue on the network and not the speed of the technology that will be the crucial factor.

14 Technology Transfer in Global Networking: Capacity Building in Africa and Latin America

Beryl Bellman, Alex Tindimubona, and Armando Arias, Jr.

Computer communication networks are rapidly extending to most areas of the world. These involve a combination of networks ranging from public, academic, governmental, and military data packet switching systems to Fido PC-based networks. Scientists and other scholars, within and outside of academia, communicate with colleagues internationally to both network with each other and to conduct computer-supported collaborative work. Such projects range from the sharing of information to actual coordination of research efforts establishing "virtual laboratories." The use of electronic mail and computer conferencing is an accepted delivery system for various academic programs in postsecondary and continuing education at universities in the United States, Canada, Latin America, Europe, and Asia. Recently several networking projects have been advocated for Africa, Eastern Europe, and Russia. In this chapter we discuss the formation of an academic computer communications network between several institutions in the United States and Latin America and how this model is being used to help develop a network for Africa with which it will interface.

In the educational environment these technologies are useful in a variety of ways, ranging from methods to augment and supplement regular coursework to distance education applications. The use of computer conferencing and electronic mail introduces writing across the curriculum and teaches essential computer concepts as an integral part of every course. Students engage each other and the faculty in discussion group-like conferences, which improve critical thinking and promote learning. When used in distance education, conferencing lessens the distance of the student from the professor and other students in the course.

Students log on to a host computer either at their own university or by accessing a data packet switching network. Students read or download all waiting items in one or more computer conferences for the class. They then respond by writing their comments on what was read, very often after having taken time to reflect and do research for their electronic class contributions. These mediated or "virtual" classrooms differ from face-to-face classes in that students are required to be much more active and to interact not only with the faculty member teaching the class but also with the other students enrolled. In this way, online education is less competitive than traditional methods and is more of a collaborative learning experience (Hiltz, 1990; Harasim, 1990).

In 1985, Arias, Jr. and Bellman established the Binational English and Spanish Telecommunications Network (BESTNET). At that time, they used computer conferencing and electronic mail as an interactive component to bilingual video lectures or telecourses. Arias, Jr. and Bellman were initially concerned with how to improve student feedback to instructional television courses that were microwaved to a satellite campus of San Diego State University about 125 miles away, adjacent to the Mexican border. Students were greatly dissatisfied with the video courses, often feeling like second-class students compared with those taking the same course on the main campus.

The study *Ivory Towers and Silicon Basements* (FIPSE, 1986) made three recommendations in regard to equity for nontraditional learners: (1) careful consideration of issues related to equity should be part of any plan for introducing computing into the curriculum; (2) access to computing means recognizing that different students have different needs and that some programs should be tailored accordingly; and (3) programs that enable students to overcome isolation and passivity in their learning experiences do the most to promote equal educational opportunities and experiences. The BESTNET project addressed each of these recommendations in its focus on providing new interactive technologies to nontraditional and minority learners. The project was unique in its focus on tailoring both the program and the software to meet the particular needs and requirements of students. By fostering electronic discussions within course conferences and in tutorials, study groups, and electronic office hours, the project helped students overcome the isolation and passivity that hinders academic performance. The university attempted to provide student feedback by allowing students to telephone the instructor during class to ask questions. However, only a few students took advantage of asking questions in this manner, and the majority of students continued to feel alienated. We also determined that questions asked in lecture classes were often more relevant to course management than to content. We introduced computer conferencing as a method for holding student discussion groups or lab sessions, and electronic mail was a means for the faculty member to answer personal questions in the form of online office hours. In this manner, all students were required to interact with the professor and with each other about the content of the lectures and text.

Our project originally involved production of a series of Spanish language/English translation distance-education video courses in the sciences, mathematics, and computer/information fields. In our evaluation of the project, we learned that students were particularly responsive to the computer conferencing interactions and did not need as much formal presentation of lecture materials by video as we had originally believed. As a result, we began to rely more heavily on computer conferencing interactions for both the presentation and discussion of materials and used video and other materials to supplement or present information for those discussions. Because we found conferencing to be as effective as the dominant or stand-alone form of course delivery, we explored applications of computer conferencing in different kinds of courses.

We are now involved with three kinds of courses delivered by computer. The first form is one in which students do not see the instructor but communicate with him or her in computer conferences or virtual classrooms, during synchronous online office hours utilizing the computer phone or chat utility, and with private electronic mail messages. In the second format, faculty make formal video lecture presentations to complement the discussions in computer conferences. In the third course format, faculty members conduct part of the course online and also have face-to-face interaction with the students. These courses are team-taught among several institutions. Students participate online with faculty and students at other campuses, with the elected option of a local faculty member offering a section of the course on his or her campus.

The virtual classroom studies of Hiltz (Kerr and Hiltz, 1982; Hiltz, 1990, 1993), our BESTNET studies (Arias, Jr. and Bellman, 1990a, 1990b,

1987; Bellman, 1988) and reports on educational conferencing in Europe (Adrianson, 1985; and Adrianson and Hjelmquist, 1985) report no significant difference in performance among students taught in face-to-face and computer conferencing based courses, which supports the viability of this method for distance learning programs. These studies also found that computer conferencing worked particularly well in minority student education. This is a consequence of the self-paced timing of instruction, the ability of students to receive immediate feedback about their errors, and the ability to ask questions in a more anonymous communicative setting.

Hiltz and Turoff (1978) described how computer conferencing is especially viable for the handicapped. In addition to the obvious benefit of having students interact from more available and manageable physical environments, the students do not suffer from prejudices experienced in regular classrooms. Students are evaluated solely on the basis of their academic performance. All physical handicaps are invisible to the medium, and students are treated as full members of the class without having to experience discrimination because of physical appearance, speech impairments, or other factors that often inhibit their participation in face-to-face classroom situations.

The same studies also demonstrated that female learners do very well with the medium. In face-to-face interactions, women are often forced into a facilitation role and many times lose turns to speak in conversation with men because of implicit sexism in interactions (Lakoff, 1975). In computer-mediated discourse, women are able to express themselves much more easily and fully without being interrupted or ignored (Harasim, 1986).

This ability of the medium to encourage more assertive involvement in the education process among traditionally more apprehensive and passive learners was demonstrated in a BESTNET course taught at a rural satellite campus of San Diego State University, situated in a community on the U.S./Mexico border and serving mostly adult Latino students. The instructor wanted to determine if the use of anonymous pen names for students in the conferences would elicit more candid comments about the poems and essays required in his course on modern American literature. He conducted the course via a host computer at the Western Behavioral Sciences Institute, which provided both topics and reply branches in the conferences.

Each student was assigned a topic with its own reply branch. In this way, students commented upon the class assignments and also upon what each other had written. The computer conference was used to supplement to face-to-face lectures and class discussions. The class elicited several hundred comments, which ranged from detailed commentaries on the assigned texts to debates among the students over the interpretations. One of the male students was particularly outspoken about the homosexual references of several of the authors. The majority of those in the class were adult Hispanic women, who, in the context of the anonymity provided both through the medium and their pen names, engaged him in heated debate. By the end of the course, several of the women students had become very assertive and had no inhibitions against openly debating his ideas. When the students met in class face-to-face they did not engage in heated debate, nor was any attempt made to criticize the ideas and comments of anyone in the class, yet the debate and active discussion flowed on the computer conference. Although the class began with no one knowing anyone else's identity, the students soon began to share their computer pen names with friends. Within the first two weeks, either through direct revelation or secondhand gossip, all computer identities became known. Consequently, the use of anonymous identities was a valuable pedagogical resource for initiating the discussion, but it was the anonymity provided by the text-based medium that sustained it and promoted the strong assertive remarks.

In 1992 the BESTNET project involved over three thousand students and faculty accounts from over a dozen institutions in the United States and Mexico. BESTNET faculty, using a combination of user interviews and content analyses of conferences for various types of courses and collaborative research projects, have reported the following findings:

1. The technology greatly augments regular classroom instruction and is a viable technology for off-campus or distance education.

2. Computer conferencing is a viable interactive component of videotaped or live instructional television courses providing individualized attention to student needs and requirements that cannot be obtained using traditional methods of audio and video feedback.

3. Computer conferencing supports a socratic method of instruction whereby students are active in the learning process rather than being

passive recipients. The anonymity of the technology promotes discussion that is often inhibited by concern for negative faculty and/or student face-to-face feedback.

4. Computer conferencing promotes participation and learning in traditionally apprehensive learners. In traditional classroom situations, many students are often reluctant to interact with anyone other than their instructors, whereas computer communications promotes student-to-student interaction. The technology is particularly useful for facilitating group discussion and criticism in virtually all areas of the curriculum.

5. The technology facilitates writing across the curriculum and greatly improves editorial and logical skills. It is particularly viable for reaching linguistically and culturally diverse learners.

6. Computer-naive students learned with equal facility as those more sophisticated with the technology. Social science and humanities students having no more than basic word-processing skills learned and accepted the technology at an equivalent level with students taking advanced computer science courses.

7. Computer communications tends to improve literacy even when a liberal attitude is taken toward grammar, syntax, and spelling. Writing skills improve with active participation in computer conferences.

8. The medium promotes more critical than hostile competitive discussion.

The Internationalization of BESTNET

Recently, BESTNET was extended to include students and faculty at several sites in Latin America and Canada, and is in the process of involving universities in Kenya and Zimbabwe, working in conjunction with Southern African FidoNets. This was accomplished by developing the distributed computer conferencing and videotex network over the Internet/NSF-NET, which interconnects over 700,000 host computers at university campuses in the United States, Canada, Europe, and Asia. At the present time, there are no Internet nodes in sub-Saharan Africa and only a few in Latin America. However, to implement the project immediately, the network was developed by utilizing public or government-owned data networks currently operating in Africa and Latin America.

These networks permit the networking of computers in the selected countries in both Africa and Latin America, which then transmit to the California State University systemwide computer communications network (CSU-NET), which operates a public data network gateway into its system. CSU-NET is the largest internal, academic, regional network on the Internet. Once connected, international users are able to access a variety of databases and other services available both on BESTNET and elsewhere on the Internet, including the National Science Foundation supercomputer network.

BESTNET involves a distributed set of mini and mainframe computers that are interconnected using the Internet and national X.25 networks. In this manner each of the countries involved has a mainframe in their local area for electronic mail, conferencing, and database access. This is significant as it facilitates both the transfer of technology to the countries involved and local capacity building in technical and programmatic areas.

The Need for Networking in the Developing World

The relationship between information processing and communication on the one hand and modern economic and social development on the other is widely recognized among the African countries. The efficient and effective exchange of information among researchers, educators, administrators, industrialists, and policymakers is crucial for the conversion of research results into useful products of economic and social value.

At the research level, interaction and communication with peers and potential users of research results are necessary for the stimulation, self-confidence, relevance, and effectiveness of scientists. Modern scientific research relies heavily on the ability to communicate; gather reliable data; have access to widely dispersed data and information (including analysis); collaborate on projects; hold discussions, meetings, seminars, and conferences; and repackage and disseminate the results. The pace and complexity of modern research have greatly increased the communication needs of researchers, scientists, educators, and their institutions. Scientists isolated are scientists unable to articulate their purposes and needs; such scientists soon become obsolete.

The provision of appropriate information systems and services for this group of information generators therefore becomes apparent.

The dissemination of information to other user groups has to be designed and implemented carefully. Sometimes the information has to be repackaged or consolidated before delivery to specific target audiences. For example, published results of scientific and technological research in fields such as agriculture, health, the environment, and economics must be repackaged to be understood by administrators, policymakers, extension workers, and other intermediaries as well as by the such final users as farmers and the community at large. This calls for innovative and appropriate methods, media, and techniques, such as print and nonprint forms, audiovisual, or even oral according to the prevailing conditions and/or traditions.

The phenomenal improvements in information processing and communication capability brought about by rapid, convergent developments in computer and telecommunication technologies are well recognized in Africa. This enhanced awareness of potential opportunities is indicated by visible efforts in many African countries to create and sustain the enabling institutional and human environment for utilizing these new capabilities. A recent study group of the Board of Science and Technology in Development of the National Academy of Sciences was impressed to find virtually all the modern information technologies already in use in some African institutions. These technologies encompass desktop publishing, CD-ROM and other databases, electronic mail and computer conferencing, as well as telefax. The population of microcomputers is significant and growing rapidly. In Kenya we estimate that from about two hundred computers in 1980, there were close to ten thousand units in 1990 in educational, business, NGO (nongovernmental organizations), and governmental environments. There are numerous international projects and systems, especially in international business, banking, and transportation, located on the continent as well as relevant rural and grassroots projects.

A growing number of X.25 networks are being established in Africa. Where these networks do not exist, there is another system that still permits computer communications interaction between African faculty and students among themselves and with faculty and students in the United States and Latin America. This system is called FidoNet, a micro-to-micro based store-and-forward system. It permits users to call up a distant computer using a telephone and modem or packet radio and modem to a computer that is attached to a telephone and/or packet radio receiver. The user is able to send information to the computer, which is then forwarded to other microcomputers during low-cost non-prime time telephone rates. The information is then transmitted to other microcomputers in the same fashion until it reaches a computer networked to an X.25 network or the Internet. At that point the information is directly transmitted to the targeted host. In this manner electronic mail can be transmitted to all sites within a few hours. FidoNets are viable only for electronic mail, not for computer conferencing. However, they do permit interaction to take place, and there are currently a number of FidoNet electronic mail conference/group mail discussions occurring in Southern Africa and in Latin America.

The Problem of the Last Mile

Despite strong interest in Africa for computer networking, there is a serious problem often referred to as "the last mile." This is a combination of national governmental policies that restrict transborder flows of information and local level politics within and between institutions that restrict usage either by refusing access to the technology or by making access too difficult for easy use.

Over the last few years several African countries have initiated national X.25 packet data networks (PDN) and require all data transmission to utilize the service by making direct dialup illegal. These national PDNs require a large initial payment and then charge for each packet sent and received. In 1991 Kenya officially instituted its PDN, KENPAC, with nodes in Kisumu, Mombasa, Nairobi, Nakuru, and Nyeri. Both dedicated and dialup access is available. The availability of this service marks a significant change in governmental policy from ten years ago when computers were treated in several agencies with some suspicion and concern that they would inhibit employment in several sectors.

The PDN charges are still prohibitive for many organizations in Kenya. They include a large initial deposit, a monthly fee, and charges for packets sent and received. The costs of international connections are so expensive that they are restrictive except for banks and a few other private, for-profit enterprises. Nevertheless, there is a growing demand in the nonprofit, academic and research communities for computer networks. Recently a group of Kenyan expatriates in the United States, Canada, and Britain organized an international chapter of the Kenya Computer Institute to develop plans for a trans-Kenya computer network. They created a listserve or electronic mail distribution list on the Internet and BITNET and opened several conferences on BESTNET (called KCI-NET).

Initially this group wanted to develop a network in concert with efforts to strengthen NGO information management and communications in Africa. The purpose of the Kenya-based network includes (1) information sharing among NGOs in cooperation with African governments to network both urban and rural organizations; (2) improving the quality of communication lines in Africa, which includes efforts such as Panaftel (the Pan African Telecommunications Network) that is attempting to develop microwave links throughout the continent as modeled on links established between Kenya and Ethiopia in the early 1980s; and (3) developing the role of government and public institutions in networking. This involves integrating universities as well as other governmental groups into a network. The group is also addressing various governments' concerns that information flow across national boundaries is a national security issue.

In an effort to test both the political and technical feasibility of African networking, a FidoNet-based project called EASANET was developed with nodes in Nairobi, Kampala, Dar es Salaam, Lusaka, and Harare. EASANET is an experimental project to practice and experience issues involved in networking. The project is more concerned with making traffic possible than with the content of what is transmitted. The transmissions are either by direct dialup on the Fido network or by data packet radio, as is the case in Harare. The most developed Fido network in Africa is run out of South Africa and is known as UNINET, which networks to institutions inside South Africa, Botswana, Swaziland, Lesotho, and Zimbabwe. Both UNINET and EASANET connect to GreenNet in England and to the Internet for international electronic mail access.

In the late 1980s PADIS, the Pan African Documentation and Information System of the United Nations, set up a series of nodes in selected countries that had dialup access to a central node in Ethopia. The latter has a dedicated 24-hour lease line to the United States. The network was used only infrequently, however, and only the Ethiopian node has been operational. In 1991 the American Association for the Advancement of Sciences in conjunction with PADIS sponsored a workshop on the need for a trans-African network. The recommendations were to establish subregional networks and especially to address the necessity of "getting out of the African region" and not just communicating within Africa. The workshop also stressed the importance of links that are not just lease lines to the United States. Some argue that such connections are simply extensions of neo-colonial policies as they do not build local capacity nor lead to the transfer of technologies.

The AFRINET Project

The BESTNET project is now being extended to Africa to establish a distributed educational, scientific, and social development research network that networks a number of African universities and scientific research organizations with each other and with international academic and scientific institutions. The BESTNET model is to develop a series of interconnected widely distributed nodes on a global basis. These nodes are connected using a combination of PDNs that have gateways into each other. In this manner, the entire distributed network of computers is essentially transparent to the user. The user need only log onto his or her own local node, and interconnections are automatically made to distant nodes to access conferences and databases. Each participating node is a central part of the network. Thus, in a distributed system it is something of an oxymoron to talk about "distance education" or "distance collaborative work," as there is no real center. This system promotes both the transfer of technology and local capacity building. Rather than serving as a neo-colonial link to any developed country, the network is diffuse and belongs to all members. There is a shared sense of responsibility and a genuine attitude of mutual benefit.

The creation of AFRINET as a distributed African link to BESTNET networks international scientists in a series of conferences dealing with issues ranging from biotechnology, food systems, cooperative development, business and public administration management, biomedical research, to the social sciences and humanities, while concomitantly developing a virtual exchange of students and faculty for academic programs.[1] Although these conferences may supplement some of the online courses, they are independent of them and promote collaborative and conjoint research efforts among the international participants. Using videotex, we are establishing a number of scientific databases of African research materials that are distributed among several African nodes as well as developing others on international nodes that pertain to African scientific research and academic interests. We also network social and community development groups online and organize both academic and commercial uses of the network. In this manner we are building a sustainable network combining academic, social development, and commercial interests and support.

Networking the AAS and BESTNET in AFRINET

At the present there are no Internet nodes in sub-Saharan Africa. Thus, to immediately implement the project, we are developing the network by encapsulating DECNET for X.25 networks currently operating in Africa. These public data networks permit the networking of computers in the selected Latin American and African countries, which then transmit to the California State University systemwide computer communications network—CSUNET and permits interconnection into the distributed BESTNET network with gateways into the Internet with its array of network libraries, databases, and services.

It is thus possible to interconnect VAX computers, for example, at the University of Zimbabwe in Harare with those at the African Academy of Sciences in conjunction with the University of Kenya in Nairobi. We also are working to provide nodes to university and related scientific laboratories in other African countries where local telephone capabilities and national policies allow. This permits much needed computer-mediated interactions between African scientists in such areas as pest research, marine biology and fisheries research, biomedical sciences, natural products development, agronomy, community development, and science/social science policy.

Using the international X.25 connection into CSUNET, these scientists also interact with colleagues in the United States, Latin America, and Europe who are involved in the BESTNET network, and have a direct gateway into international scientific and library databases. Concomitantly, international scholars can have access to African and Latin American researchers and their respective databases stored as distributed nodes on host systems in those countries. BESTNET thus promotes computer-communications-supported collaborative work and research among scientists and with international scholars outside of each continent.

In addition, students and faculty from Latin American and African universities interact with their counterparts in the United States, Canada, and Europe who are already taking part in BESTNET. There is an ongoing virtual exchange of faculty and students in different countries as preliminary to onsite exchanges already being developed by the California State University and the other university systems in BEST-NET. In addition, other courses are cotaught by faculty across international boundaries, and students are in continual contact with colleagues and research issues in otherwise impossible ways. Students take courses in biological, natural, social, and communications sciences at their local nodes. These course conferences are open to students enrolled at all institutions. They do so by signing on to their local university hosts that are connected to the Internet or, initially in Africa, by computers connected to it through the CSUNET gateways. The lists of conferences that appear on their computer screens are distributed among the international universities. However, students enter any given conference from their local node and interconnect to the distant node where it is housed. Thus, from the user's point of view the distributed network appears seamless.

Distributed Global Nets

Our project is a fully distributed computer communications network, which is encapsulated as an independent system over the NSF-NET/Internet with gateways to KENPAC, ZIMPAK (in Zimbabwe), and other African X.25 networks. The ease of functionality in our distributed conferencing, videotex, mail, and computer phone greatly facilitates the use of computer communications for both scientific research and international distant education programs between African and international institutions.

Developing South-South Communications with Latin America

The situation in Latin America is more advanced, as there are X.25 systems in most countries and also a growing number of Internet nodes. Initially we are building international south-to-south networks of universities and research institutes using whatever modes of communication are currently available. This involves the use of X.25 DPNs in Africa and Latin America connecting as distributed nodes in the BEST-NET TCP/IP Internet-based network through gateways in the California State University CSUNET network. In the case of countries that do not have either Internet, X.25, or other DPNs, we are using FidoNet micro-to-micro store-and-forward connections. Fidos are being successfully used in East and Southern Africa for conference-based discussions using email distribution lists similar in structure to listserves on the Internet and BITNET. We are currently developing in concert with the California State University statewide nursing program a series of distance education programs in the allied health fields with Southern African universities in Botswana, Lesotho, Swaziland, Zimbabwe, and South Africa, which are to be delivered using FidoNet interactions with conferences in our BESTNET network. These courses involve interactions with a number of Latin America universities that are using computer conferencing on distributed nodes in BESTNET. In conjunction with projects sponsored at the Latin American Scholarship Program at American Universities (LASPAU) at Harvard, BESTNET nodes are being established at universities in Chile, Brazil, Uruguay, and Argentina. Comments in the conferences will be ported to Africa as email on the FidoNet, and concomitantly the latter mail is entered as batch comments into relevant conferences. This promotes interactive dialogue across international boundaries. In addition we are involving scientists in Africa and Mexico conducting research in insect sciences in a series of conferences and joint databases called PESTNET. This involves the insect physiology research database at the University of California at Davis working in collaboration with the Mayan sustainability project of UC-Riverside in Merida and the Universidad Autonoma de Yucatan.

In addition, BESTNET is being used to coordinate efforts between oceanographic research institutes in Mexico at the Universidad Autonoma de Baja California with researchers in Africa in RECOSCIX, Regional Committee on Scientific Information Exchange. This project is associated with the UNESCO International Oceanographic Council. It provides computer communications database access and email discussions for marine science and fisheries in the Western Indian Ocean. It has twelve collaborating institutions in Eastern Africa and islands from Somalia to Mozambique. The project currently operates a user dialup node into Belgium from the Kenya Marine and Fisheries Institute (KEMFRI) in Mombasa, Kenya and then distributes information on paper. The project has been accessing BESTNET for over a year, and is to be a distributed node in Kenya.

Addressing Information Needs in Development

BESTNET is organized according to priorities specifically outlined in the IDRC (International Development Research Council) manual *Sharing Knowledge for Development,* which contains objectives identified as critical for successful communications programs in the African context. We have taken these into account in the development of our larger global project. The objectives include the following:

1. To improve the effective utilization and sharing of existing knowledge and resources at the local, national, and regional levels. In our project we are working directly with universities and research institutes in Latin America and Africa, designing a large distributed network to link them together. The design requires that where possible each institution have its own node or direct access to one at the regional or national level. This permits participating countries to have a direct role in the network rather than having to rely on outside donors for support.

2. To design and implement information systems and services that are relevant to the local environment and that address specific needs and problems. In our network we assist in the development of local computer conferences and databases on each node that pertain to the immediate needs of the area and region. These conferences and databases are then distributed to be accessible from any one of the other nodes in the network. In this manner, we are developing computer conferences and databases that are both national and international (Latin America, United States, and Africa) dealing with such conjoint interests as oceanographic and fisheries research, agriculture and pest research, and more.

3. To improve sharing and data transfer at the national and regional levels by promoting standards, compatibility and use of methodologies, technologies, and tools adapted to the environment. We have designed a system that can handle multiple standards. Where possible the network runs on the Internet, and where the Internet does not exist we

utilize X.25, X.28 and X.400 standards that are interfaced to the Internet by gateways in the United States. This permits a global distributed network of interconnected nodes over a variety of standards. In addition, although the network runs on a DECNET platform, we have developed a multilingual front end to the system that permits connection to and from the network and other services on different kinds of vendor hosts.

4. To improve the indigenous capacity to plan, develop, and implement national and regional information policy. By organizing a distributed global network we promote the indigenous local-level capacities in these areas. We are promoting the development of Internet nodes in both Africa and Latin America where possible and working in collaboration with public packet data networks by providing gateways into the Internet. Our network works in a distributed manner, which interconnects nodes in a number of institutions in the countries involved. The distribution of nodes leads to the transfer of technology to those countries and building of local capacity in both technical and programmatic areas.

5. To secure long-term commitment for sustainable information programs. The implementation of the project involves local level support and design in concert with indigenous information policies. Consequently, the project is organized in accord with a developmental model that incorporates local information needs and perceived goals. This promotes local long-term commitment by both the institutions and governments involved.

6. To stimulate greater use of local technical expertise in information handling by promoting South-South cooperation within Africa and also Latin America. The transfer of technology and the technical and programmatic capacity building in both Latin America and Africa in the project is a major step in the formation of such South-South cooperation, including both exchanges of educational programs and collaborative research.

7. To build human resources in information sciences through needs-based training at all levels and, particularly, training of managers and trainers to strengthen the multiplier effect. The promotion of the "virtual exchange of students and faculty" among participating institutions includes courses in information sciences, telecommunications, and related disciplines. The courses involve an exchange in which faculty

collaborate in the instruction and students engage each other across institutions.

8. To improve the capacity of people involved in the provision of information to act as agents of change. By building local-level capacity in information technologies in conjunction with programs involved with agricultural, health, education, and economic development, the information technologists and communication specialists in Africa and Latin America are directly involved as change agents.

9. To promote a two-way flow of communication so that rural and urban poor people participate in an interactive dialogue on issues affecting them. The formation of a global communication network directly involves the development of programs in each country that are targeted throughout the society. These programs are designed to reach both urban and rural sectors by providing new educational opportunities in allied and primary health care, agriculture, pest control, and courses across a range of academic disciplines. These courses and projects are fully interactive and provide as part of their design the means for an interactive dialogue on issues affecting the participants. This includes the delivery of the baccalaureate, masters, and certificate programs in allied health to six Latin American and five southern African countries, to programs ranging from public administration to social sciences and humanities.

10. To improve the capacity of local scientists and technologists to obtain relevant information and bring about a more effective transfer of technology at the grass roots level. The project directly involves the formation of "virtual labs" for computer-communications-supported collaborative work. These include not only the use of electronic mail and computer conferencing to improve communication between scientists but also the use of a variety of computer communication technologies to promote conjoint research. Videotex-structured distributed databases, electronic libraries and reserves permit the transfer of articles and papers to international sites, and access to the range of Internet services including the supercomputer backbone.

The Future of Global Networks

New networks are being established in the emerging nations of Eastern and Central Europe and the former Soviet Union. By 1994 EARN and

Internet nodes will be available in Hungary, Rumania, Czechoslovakia, and Poland in Europe, and there are plans to establish Internet nodes throughout Russia, including a trans-Siberian research network from St. Petersburg. On June 18, 1992, the first Joint Russian Research Network Workshop was held at the P. N. Lebedev Physical Institute of the Russian Academy of Sciences in Moscow. The objectives of the meeting included the sharing of information, experiences, and research network proposals; the formalization of a "Russian Research Networks Organizing Team"; and the preparation of the basis for a business plan for Russian research networks for 1993. The BESTNET model has been selected for the plan, involving the use of networks for the global virtual exchange of students and faculty between universities, the establishment of virtual labs for collaborative and coordinated research among dispersed scholars in both academic and research institute settings and efforts to network the economic development experiments and projects for the sharing of information and collaborative work.

15 Islands in the (Data)Stream: Language, Character Codes, and Electronic Isolation in Japan

Jeffrey Shapard

Once upon a time long ago, Japan was naturally secluded from most of the world by vast distances of land and sea. The only way in, or out, was to sail treacherous seas. The flow of trade and ideas and information and communication, what there was of it, was a difficult process. Then came the Portuguese and the Dutch in the early seventeenth century with their missionaries and their merchants. So destabilizing was their influence that the powers that were, the Tokugawa Shogunate, limited the access of these westerners by allowing them to sail only into the port of Nagasaki and to reside only on a small artificial island called Dejima, constructed for this purpose and linked to the rest of Japan by a narrow bridge. From 1641 until 1856, when Admiral Perry and his fleet of warships put an end to this policy of national seclusion in a chain of events that toppled the Tokugawa Shogunate, opened Japan to the world, and opened the world to Japan, tiny Dejima was the only window between Japan and the world. Its residents could not wander off the island to mingle with the rest of Japan, and only a small handful of Japanese were able to go to Dejima (Kodansha, 1983).

In a way that resonates strangely with history, the Japanese language and the prevalence of character codes incompatible with international standards results in a new kind of natural seclusion today for the individuals on the *pasocom tsuushin* (personal computer communications) islands of Japan, as well as for the researchers on the JUNET/WIDE archipelago. This chapter gives an overview of language and character codes in electronic networking in Japan, discusses a case illustrating problems faced and solutions taken, and proposes directions for further research and development. The Dejima Syndrome in the Japan context is used as an example.

Differences in languages and the character codes needed to support them are important issues of global scope that must be addressed more widely, and which must result in broader thinking throughout the field of computer networking. Narrow vision, one-byte seven-bit ASCII biases, the assumptions about character coding that arise from them, inadequate international standards, and local solutions that disregard what international standards there are and that pay no heed to the ramifications for others—all these are serious related problems that inhibit, rather than enhance, increased connectivity and communications.

Setting Sail: The Japanese Writing System

The origins of modern Japanese remain a matter of some academic controversy, pulled between linguistic reconstruction through analysis (Miller, 1972) and desires for mystical uniqueness as an isolate (Kindaichi, 1979). Whatever the real story of its origins, the Japanese language does not come from China, although its writing system does.

The anthropological linguist Edward Sapir (Sapir, 1921; Mandelbaum, 1970) noted that language and culture are two sides of the same coin. The Japanese language illustrates the dynamic borrowing by Japanese of useful aspects of foreign cultures, from the Chinese *han* ideograph character writing system itself, which came to Japan with wandering Chinese and Korean traders and Buddhist priests a couple millennia ago, and the new lexical items (words) it allowed to be created, to the variety of localized lexical items from other languages borrowed along with the concepts and things they describe. *Kanji* (the Japanese form of han ideographs) and the supplemental scripts derived from them have become an integral aspect of Japanese culture.

Modern Japanese writing typically involves a combination of the following:

- Kanji (Japanese form of han ideographs) for most of the core lexical items, with several readings possible for many of them, *on-yomi* if based on original Chinese readings, of which there may be several, and *kun-yomi* if based on native Japanese lexicon

- *Hiragana* (cursive syllabic characters) for grammatical functions and inflections, and for native Japanese words done more easily than in kanji

- *Katakana* (block syllabic characters) for sounds and for words borrowed from other languages
- Little hiragana and katakana as *furigana* alongide kanji to help the reader figure out which readings are being used
- *Romaji* (roman characters) sprinkled about for effect
- Arabic numerals (0–9) and various other symbols for punctuation, footnoting, listing, currency symbols, and so on

Despite the "Nihongo boom" (an increased interest in the Japanese language) over the last ten years, most likely as a result of Japan's emergence as a world economic power, perhaps no more than a million people outside Japan speak or, especially, read and write Japanese, and fewer than 1 percent of these are Japanese expatriates or emigrants. At the end of 1991, there were 620,000 Japanese living abroad, most of them in North America (258,300), South America (130,600), Western Europe (109,700), Asia (83,900), and sparsely populated Oceania (21,400) (KKC, 1991). Japanese is, therefore, a very big local language.

Treacherous Waters: Platforms, Standards, and Other Characters

Kanji and the complex nature of the Japanese writing system have been a major challenge in Japanese computing and computer networking and have slowed down development in ways not faced by those who can get by just fine with the smaller set of 94 printable characters of the total 128 characters defined as part of the seven bits of the one-byte American Standard Code for Information Interchange (ASCII) (Lung and Nakamura, 1991). Even by using the full eight bits of a one-byte character code, the resulting 256 possible combinations still fall far short of the 7,000 or so needed for modern Japanese. But ASCII seven-bit biases, especially in English-speaking countries where so much research and development in computers and networking have come from, are in the very kernel of most computer operating system environments.

By 1983, the Japanese Industrial Standards bureau (JIS) had defined a Japanese character set that contained 6,877 two-byte characters: 6,353 kanji in two levels (2,965 kanji arranged by pronunciation in level one and 3,388 kanji arranged by radical in level two), 86 katakana, 83 hiragana, 10 numerals, 52 English characters, 147 symbols, 66 Russian characters, 48 Greek characters, and 32 line elements (Lunde, 1990). Each byte contains seven bits, with the high bit undefined. The original JIS C6226 code was expanded in 1985 as JIS X0208 and JIS X0202 (equivalent to ISO2022) to include more kanji and to be closer to the ISO (International Standards Organization) standard. Since ASCII is often used along with kanji, JIS X0202 defines escape sequences used for shifting between one-byte seven-bit ASCII and two-byte seven-bit JIS X0208 kanji characters. As a result of some of the problems faced by mainframe operating systems where two-byte codes were too difficult to implement, there is also JIS X0201, which defines one-byte codes for katakana (Murai and Kato, 1987). In late 1990, JIS defined a supplemental character set called JIS X0212 to include another 5,801 kanji, 21 symbols and diacritics, and 245 diacritic-marked roman characters, bringing the total defined kanji character codes to 12,156, although computer manufacturers have yet to implement them (Lunde, 1992).

However, while the JIS character codes gave a useful common reference, computer makers and software developers in Japan had their own needs and created their own variations. For example, Nihon DEC (Digital Equipment Corporation Japan) developed DEC kanji code, based on JIS C6226 in organization but using two-byte, eight-bit codes rather than two-byte seven-bit codes. Later, a group of UNIX systems developers got together in a task force and advisory committee convened by AT&T International (now UNIX Systems Laboratories) to develop an enhanced UNIX code (EUC) for kanji. They ended up accepting a proposal based on DEC kanji code, that is, a two-byte, eight-bit approach rather than the JIS two-byte, seven-bit standard (Burkley, 1989a). Meanwhile, as the *pasocom* (personal computer) revolution hit, ASCII Corporation in collaboration with Microsoft developed yet another kanji code: Shift-JIS or MS-Kanji, with a combination of a one-byte 8-bit code compatible with JIS X0201 and a two-byte 8-bit kanji code compatible with nothing else, differing in basic organization from both JIS and EUC. Kanji character code development for personal computers was influenced by processing speed considerations, and it seems to have been overlooked that these underpowered little toys would ever need to be connected and have to talk to real computers either as "intelligent terminals" or as peers on a network. To top it all off, Shift-JIS is also the system kanji code on the millions of inexpensive portable Japanese language *waapuro* (word processors) that have flooded the market in recent years, combining with personal computers to make the most incompatible character code also the most widespread in Japan.

So, today, in addition to the two-byte, seven-bit JIS C6226 and JIS X0208/X0202 kanji codes, various two-byte, eight-bit proprietary variants in the mainframe and minicomputer environment, and the two-byte, eight-bit EUC in the UNIX environment, there is also the mixed-byte, eight-bit Shift-JIS on millions of pasocom and waapuro.

And these are treacherous waters for network sailors.

Archipelagos and Islands: Isolation and Parallel Realms

There is a contrast between the significant international connectivity of the Japanese academic network realm of the JUNET/WIDE archipelago and the nearly absolute isolationism of the islands in the pasocom tsuushin realm. They are in parallel, but each seems to have little interest in or awareness of the other. While JUNET/WIDE researchers continue to pioneer the application of international standards in the Japanese context, pasocom tsuushin system developers continue to reinvent the wheel in nonstandard ways and develop local solutions incompatible with international standards.

The most significant networks in Japan in terms of size, connectivity, and global networking are JUNET (Japan UNIX Network) and WIDE. They are closely related. JUNET, which began in 1984 with dialup UUCP (UNIX-to-UNIX Copy) test links between two public universities and one private university (Murai, 1990), now connects over three thousand computers in more than three hundred organizations (Frey and Adams, 1990) and is growing rapidly. The WIDE (Widely Integrated Distributed Network) Internet is an infrastructure network that provides IP (Internet Protocol) connections to sites at member organizations, operates the JUNET backbone, and provides Japan's primary IP connectivity with the rest of the research world. WIDE evolved out of a project team assembled in late 1986 "to design the future JUNET," and is oriented toward internetworking, open systems, and global connectivity (Murai, 1989; 1990).

The main function of JUNET is communications. Member organizations connect to backbone sites to exchange electronic mail and Net-News. Electronic mail addresses and headers strictly follow de facto international Internet standards. JUNET NetNews includes over 120 Japanese language newsgroups in the fj.* category (Lunde, 1992), as well as over a thousand of the worldwide USENET newsgroups in English. The official kanji code of JUNET is JIS X0202 (equivalent to ISO2022), which is based on JIS X0208. As a two-byte, seven-bit character code it can pass through the narrow straits of the seven-bit ASCII world most of the time. Although the total number of people outside Japan who read and write Japanese may be minuscule in comparison to the domestic population, the designers of JUNET wanted connectivity both in Japanese as well as in English and other languages. Global connectivity is a basic operating principle of JUNET/WIDE.

When JUNET began, international communications had to be in English or romanized Japanese. This played a role in Japan's reputation as a "black hole" of information, with so much flowing in and so little flowing out. Jun Murai has described how network design and development are not just a matter of link protocols and addressing but an approach to the "total computing environment," which in the case of JUNET also involved kanji support in a windowed user interface to the messaging systems. Once Japanese researchers could communicate easily with each other in Japanese through JUNET, then the amount of public traffic, as well as JUNET membership, also increased dramatically and has continued to grow. A non-Japanese participant complained at a conference that the increased public NetNews traffic in the fj.* category was all in Japanese. Jun Murai replied, "Ah, but we have done our part in making it accessible. Learning Japanese is still up to you" (Murai, 1989). Fair enough.

Until 1984, individuals who wanted to use their personal computers for telecommunications had to go to systems abroad, such as the information utilities CompuServe and The Source (now defunct) in the United States. The only way to get to these systems, other than direct international dialup, was through KDD's (Kokusai Denshin Denwa, an international telecommunications monopoly in Japan) Venus-P public X.25 data network. Nevertheless, despite the high costs for individuals, and despite the fact that telecommunicating with others through U.S. systems meant telecommunicating in English rather than in Japanese, pasocom tsuushin had captured the imagination and enthusiasm of a segment of the growing market of personal computer users, and it began to take off.

By the end of 1984, there were more than a half dozen bulletin board services (BBSs) operated by individuals and hobbyist clubs. All but a couple were in English (Shapard, 1991). In the years since, grass-roots BBSs in Japan have boomed. Today there are well over a thousand public access personal computer BBSs in Japan, and all but a dozen or so are in Japanese (MBM, 1991). Most personal BBSs in Japan are isolated islands in the datastream, where the only access is direct access, but a few networked exceptions exist, such as the small but active FidoNet-Japan group (Yamada, 1990) and other efforts based on unique locally developed automatic "porting" mechanisms (e.g., Electronic Networking Forum, 1991). The kanji character code of the little islands dotting the seas of the Japan BBS realm is Shift-JIS, the kanji character code of Japanese personal computers.

From 1985, multiuser commercial subscription or usage fee systems began to emerge in the electronic seas of the large Tokyo and Kanto plain market, where 30 percent of the total population of Japan lives. Some of the earliest, largest, and still active, are ASCIInet (1985), operated by the people who brought us Nihongo MS-DOS and Shift-JIS kanji, JALNET (1985) of Japan Air Lines, EYE-Net (1985) of the Fujimic media group, PC-VAN (1986) of NEC, and Nifty-Serve (1987) of Fujitsu. PC-VAN and Nifty-Serve each claim user memberships in excess of 300,000 and compete for market dominance. Meanwhile, outside of Tokyo and in collaboration with local government and local business, regional online systems such as COARA (1985) in Oita Prefecture (Kyushu) have emerged to serve local communities. All of these larger systems have active online communities and extensive public data network connections, with members coming in from other parts of Japan and the world. But the only access is direct access, and even this can be a problem as a result of the seven-bit biases of not just a few so-called international public data networks in the world beyond Japan.

Off in the research lab, with a high-resolution graphics terminal on your desk, a powerful UNIX workstation nearby, and the rest of the world just a TELNET command away (for direct access) through high-speed IP links, it is easy to lose track of the very different context and environment of users of personal computers and 2400bps modems. Likewise, people who are just learning how to turn their machines on and off (and are in near total befuddlement with the "techno-esoterotica" of modem commands and serial parameters that confront them before they can even get to a local BBS or commercial information utility) are busier looking for something simple that works than taking much interest in solutions that adhere to international standards for greater connectivity. They are still trying to get their oars in the water and get that most basic connectivity of direct access.

Isolation in Tokyo Bay: The Case of TWICS

TWICS started as one of the first half-dozen pioneer BBSs in Japan in 1984, evolved into one of the first public multiuser systems in 1985, and became one of the first commercial operations in 1986 as an electronic mail and conferencing service (Shapard, 1986; Shapard, 1990; Quarterman, 1990). TWICS has been a settled island in the electronic seas of Japan for a long time, globally accessible through international public data networks since 1986, and networked through intersystem mail since 1987. But despite a certain international notoriety as one of the few systems in Japan so accessible, TWICS still has only a small population of a little over 700 members who remain isolated from most of their Japanese neighbors while at the same time enjoying connectivity with much of the rest of the world online. Language and character codes have played a role.

The Nature of the Community and Its Communication Needs

Most of the early members of TWICS were also active members of systems abroad, which they accessed directly through international public data networks. So, while they lived and worked in Japan, they were also members of what was then a fairly small community of people using pasocom tsuushin internationally. TWICS has always had a multicultural population, from the system operators to the members who used the system. There is no cultural majority, although the largest segment of the population is Japanese (Shapard, 1990).

The early TWICS members perceived themselves as part of a larger international community of those people who had to spend much time going out through international public data networks to various systems abroad. Eventually, this changed into a perception more like that of the JUNET members, where they were able to share information and ideas with people elsewhere in the world from the convenience of a local "home" system as part of the world of electronic mail networks.

JUNET originally served researchers in the same field but in different organizations in Japan and gave them a channel to professional colleagues elsewhere. The initial focus was international as much as it was domestic.

However, like other pasocom tsuushin system users in Japan, TWICS members primarily come online as individuals, rather than as part of a site or organizational membership. Unlike JUNET, the host computer functioning as the community or "home" mailbox server was not located within the domain of an organization that most of the members shared while not online.

The first domestic applications of pasocom tsuushin in Japan were to provide locally that which had only been available overseas, that is, communications facilities and databases. And, having this locally meant having it in Japanese, the local language. Since almost everyone who could read and write Japanese, and who had personal computers and software that supported kanji, were Japanese living in Japan, the initial focus was absolutely local and domestic. TWICS, with its use of English and its multicultural community, has been a notable exception.

The social and communications needs of the TWICS community members are as various as the membership is eclectic. Some members use the system primarily for professional purposes, especially for communications with people abroad. In this they are like the users of JUNET, of which TWICS (twics.co.jp) is also a member. The researchers on JUNET are members of the larger world academic and research community, and their communications are basically professional in nature, transcending national boundaries. Some members of TWICS join primarily as a result of personal social needs, like those of other pasocom tsuushin systems in Japan. Their purpose is to pursue personal interests and meet new people. Public access BBSs and commercial online services provide them with a wider scope and new ways to meet people they would otherwise not have the chance to meet.

In the middle are the open community areas, the public topics and conferences open to all TWICS members. A lot of crossover happens as those with primarily professional needs benefit as well from the local relationships they develop and those who came online for personal social needs benefit from increased professional relationships as the world online opens up to them.

Attempts to get Japanese language communications started in public areas on TWICS have largely failed, mainly because the Japanese members prefer to use English, or, rather, prefer not to be "segregated" according to language. The most extensive Japanese language communications on TWICS have been through the use of romaji, which can be done with ASCII characters and therefore supported by any terminal. Writing and reading Japanese through romaji, however, is "unnatural" to Japanese speakers, something akin to English speakers writing and reading in phonetic script. One TWICS member, a mathematician, told me about some statistics he had run during his graduate school days for a linguist doing a study (unpublished) on the readability of Japanese with different scripts (Yoneda, 1986). The use of only kana or romaji, rather than the usual kanji/kana combination, resulted in readability rates not all that much different from those of Japanese reading English, a foreign language.

Language segmentation leads to isolation, and communities require a shared common language. In the case of TWICS, with its multicultural community and their international communication needs, this shared common language has been English. TWICS is at the same time a part of the larger global community of people interconnected through the matrix, as well as a tiny English language island isolated from the communities of the nearby islands of the Japanese language pasocom tsuushin seas.

The Influences of Language, Character Codes, and Environment

JUNET researchers required international connectivity from the beginning. While they may be using English internationally and kanji domestically, it all has to travel through the same channels. Japanese researchers and others abroad need kanji as well, even if they are located in some seven-bit ASCII environment. So, JUNET adopted kanji character code standards compatible with international standards. The developers of JUNET had the need as well as the means to get past the original limitations of their computing environment and the local-solution directions of their domestic computer industry.

Personal computer users, on the other hand, also wanted kanji in their interfaces and online communications, but they were stuck with Shift-JIS. As with so much else in the personal computer field, Japanese

BBSs and then larger commercial systems evolved without paying much attention to developments for other kinds of machines and environments. When the host systems were home-rolled BBSs running on personal computers, the total Japanese language environment was based on Shift-JIS, the only game in town as far as they were concerned. This has caused more than a few problems along the way, as the larger commercial and regional systems run not on MS-DOS personal computers but on larger multiuser systems. So, while their own internal system kanji codes were EUC or other JIS variations, their interfaces had to be Shift-JIS. And they have often continued this right down into the heart of their messaging systems and databases, thereby rendering themselves into character code isolation.

Although TWICS has from the beginning supported Japanese in various forms, global access requires the lowest common denominator in terms of assumptions about the kinds of character codes supported by the personal computers and terminal software of the member users, and this means one-byte, seven-bit ASCII and the use of English, the most widespread global language, as the system default language. An early design principle was "global access with local flavor." Global access meant access with no assumptions about the user equipment, and therefore a reliance on international standards such as English and ASCII. Local flavor meant Japanese place names and style. The paradox is that, despite the names, if things are in ASCII or English, then they are not Japanese.

The computing environment, and the influence on kanji character codes resulting from the design philosophies of their makers, has also had a strong influence on the use of kanji on TWICS, or the lack thereof, as the system evolved through several platforms. Short of getting all the Japanese computer makers and software developers to agree on a single, common, kanji character code, and one that is compatible with international standards, which in turn must be designed to recognize the needs of languages like Japanese, the short-term solutions involve filters between the different kanji codes. There are three ways to go about doing this.

Kanji Filter Solution 1—on the Personal Computer One approach to the filter solution is to use terminal software on personal computers that handles the interactive filtering at that end of the connection.

This is the most efficient solution, as most personal computers are underutilized in the first place when used as mere terminals. However, it makes assumptions about the terminal equipment on the user side and introduces unfair biases for Japanese language users. Many of the more popular Japanese terminal programs, especially those for the ubiquitous NEC PC-9801 series, only support a limited number of kanji character filters, and for some reason, EUC/DEC Kanji and JIS X0208/X0202 are often not supported. Also, a lot of people use convenient and low-cost Japanese language waapuro for telecommunications, which have even fewer options.

Kanji Filter Solution 2—on the Host Computer   The second solution is to put interactive filter mechanisms on the host side, generally in the terminal drivers or some other interactive filter.

This can be done fairly easily with UNIX terminal drivers, and most UNIX systems in Japan now support interactive kanji filtering in their terminal drivers, although the manufacturers do it in different ways. It is a different story with operating systems like VMS.

The first time TWICS went to Nihon DEC with this problem in 1986, their reply was to offer the source code and a license to change it. In 1988, TWICS went back to Nihon DEC again to argue that their support of interactive kanji character code filtering in the VMS terminal driver would help increase their market share in business use and to propose a solution (Rikitake, 1988). The reply was that such solutions did not fit into DEC's own global strategies, regardless of how big the lucrative Japanese market was with all those people sailing Japanese pasocom and waapuro in their local and incompatible seas of Shift-JIS.

Kanji Filter Solution 3—File-to-File   The third solution is to forget about interactive kanji filtering altogether and use kanji file filters instead. In addition to the kanji character code file filters provided by Nihon DEC for Nihon VMS, for example, there are several others available as shareware to solve this problem (Lunde, 1992). They are generally written in such a way that they can be compiled and run on various platforms, including those that do not have other Japanese language support, and thereby allow any host system to handle kanji messages and file exchange.

If someone with a personal computer wants to send a message in Japanese and their own machine and software only support Shift-JIS, they use an editor or word-processing program to write the message and save it in a file. Then, they connect it to the host system or server and transfer the file through a file transfer protocol like Kermit or XMODEM or ZMODEM. After that, they run it through the filter utility on the host system to convert it to a kanji code that will work. For example, they convert it to JIS X0208/X0202 if it is going through a seven-bit data path, or to someone on JUNET, or in a Japanese language newsgroup on USENET. Finally, they send it or post it. It can be a little bit easier to display kanji messages, as the filters can direct their output to the terminal screen, but it still requires a couple extra steps.

In addition to the "native" EUC/DEC Kanji code of the VMS system, TWICS also has EUC/DEC and Shift-JIS in jCaucus, over 120 Japanese language USENET newsgroups with JIS X0208/X0202, and links with others systems where either EUC/DEC or JIS X0208/X0202 must be used, depending on the site. It is small wonder the networkers in Japan stick to the most familiar kanji codes of their own favorite electronic island. The more is not the merrier.

Global Directions: Building Bridges for the Future

The issues raised in this chapter regarding multibyte character codes are not unique to Japan, but are shared by other people in East Asia who have writing systems derived from Chinese han ideographs. Chinese speakers use *hanzi* (Chinese form of han ideographs) of various sorts in the People's Republic of China (PRC), Taiwan, Hong Kong, and elsewhere. Korean speakers use a combination of some *hanja* (Korean form of han ideographs) along with their own phonetic alphabet *hangul,* derived from hanja in shape but similar to Arabic or Hebrew in the method of indicating syllables. And Japanese speakers use a combination of kanji (Japanese form of han ideographs) along with their own syllabic kana scripts, katakana and hiragana (described earlier), as well as some romaji (roman characters like the English alphabet) and Arabic numbers.

The classical Chinese han character set, with is origins over 4,000 years ago and its often complicated fonts for up to 50,000 ideographs, has evolved into several variations today for writing and computing (Burkley, 1989b):

People's Republic of China

- Up to 7,500 hanzi (with simplified 6,763 hanzi)
- GB 2312 two-byte code
- Input through phonetic conversion and radical composition

Taiwan

- Up to 15,000 hanzi (PRC simplification not recognized)
- Proposed three-byte code
- Input through phonetic conversion and radical composition

Korea

- Up to 4,000 hanja (for formal writing)
- Up to 40 hangul
- Ministry of Education two-byte code
- Input through hangul composition and hangul to hanja conversion

Japan

- Up to 7,500 kanji (with 1,945 taught in school)
- Up to 100 kana in addition to romaji and Arabic numbers
- Various two-byte codes
- Input through kana to kanji conversion or romaji tokana/kanji conversion

One-byte character codes are clearly inadequate to accommodate the needs of the speakers of East Asian and most other languages with writing systems derived from origins other than those of European languages today. The 128 basic one-byte, seven-bit ASCII codes are only useful for English and languages that use the same character set, with no additional diacritics such as accent marks and so on (see Mason, chap. 12, regarding problems in networking with French and German character sets). Enhancements that add support for another 128 characters through the use of the full eight-bits of a one-byte code remain local, not international, solutions, as they will display differently in other contexts.

Two-byte character code solutions, such as those proposed by ANSI (Unicode), ISO (ISO2022), and various computers makers like DEC, are also the subject of great controversy and debate (Burkley, 1989b; Sheldon, 1991), even with their potential room for 65,536 character codes. The problems are both technical as well as political.

The primary technical problem with two-byte character codes is that up to 40 percent of the 65,536 possible spaces are lost by setting aside all codes that include C0 and C1 sequences that could result in a character being interpreted as a control code (Sheldon, 1991), a problem illustrated by Japanese Shift-JIS. There is just not enough space then left to include all the various hanji of Chinese, the hanja and hangul of Korean, and the kanji and kana of Japanese as separate language character code areas. People trying to use these languages together would need to switch in and out of different language character code modes, and additional codes would be needed to indicate the language mode of a series of text. One proposed solution to this problem is to unify the han characters into one basic set where they overlap, and then support the local variations in separate areas. Other solutions involve using more bytes in the basic character code, such as the three-byte code proposed in Taiwan, or a four-byte code such as ISO10646, which would support over four billion spaces. And this is where the politics come in.

The Chinese agree to a two-byte international standard with a unified set of han characters, but the Koreans and the Japanese have problems with it (Sheldon, 1991). Language and culture are closely related, and writing systems that have been in use for nearly two thousand years can take on a rather mystical quality regardless of the origin. Despite the ancient Chinese origins of Japanese kanji, the Japanese consider their kanji to be Japanese, and not just a subset of han characters. And they resent the assumption that they should continue to work with compromises forced onto them for compatibility with the short-sighted vision and narrow assumptions of a field that is only now beginning to recognize that ASCII is not enough for the world.

Conclusion

In conclusion, as we sail the electronic seas and explore, settle, and develop the virtual world online, we face many of the same issues that our ancestors have faced in the past as their cultures collided with those of others, and as they discovered whole civilizations built upon vastly different assumptions. We can learn from parallels in history and lessons gained through research in various fields and disciplines as we design the new environments in which we work and communicate. Or else we can stumble along in the blindness of our own narrow biases and wonder why this technology leaves us isolated from others rather than living up to its promise of greater connectivity.

16 Cognitive Apprenticeship on Global Networks

Lucio Teles

Apprenticeship is a time-honored way for novices to learn various skills ranging from carpentry to medicine and law (Rogoff, 1984). When the skills to be learned are cognitive in nature, the process is called cognitive apprenticeship (Collins, Brown, and Newman, 1989).

Cognitive apprenticeship has, throughout history, benefited from "learning technologies." The printing press, for example, allowed apprentices to access knowledge contained in books instead of relying exclusively on masters and peers for oral transmission of knowledge (Ong, 1982). More recently, computer-mediated communication has introduced new opportunities for cognitive apprenticeship in online environments (Levin, 1990; Harasim et al., 1994).

Online apprenticeship, also called *teleapprenticeship* (Levin, 1990), refers to apprenticeship mediated by access to masters and peers on computer networks. The learner accesses the online learning environment, which is characterized by five attributes: one-to-many and many-to-many communication; asynchronicity or time independence; place independence; text-based presentation, and computer mediation (Harasim, 1990, see also Harasim, chap. 3). In this environment, online apprentices can build and share knowledge through goal-oriented learning interactions with peers, experts, and mentors, and through full-time access to specialized sources of information. Adoption of computer networks by educational institutions has led to the development of online environments to support science, English, history, geography, and many other subject areas.

This chapter focuses on apprenticeship techniques in global network environments. Two approaches to online apprenticeship are illustrated: online *mentorship* and *peer collaboration* in global networks, which are supported by various apprenticeship techniques, such as scaffolding, fading, and exploration, which will be discussed.

When conducted over global networks, the process of apprenticeship raises operational as well as content issues. *Operational issues* refer to the logistics of setting up the learning interaction, that is, learner's access to the network, the coordination of different school terms, holidays, and so forth. *Content issues* refer to cross-cultural communication matters such as interaction between people with different cultures, habits, and history. In global networks subject areas such as history, geography, languages, and others are permeated by cultural views. It is the work of the educational designer and moderator of online environments to make the best use of these differences for learning purposes. Designers of learning environments have to take into account issues of cross-cultural communication for learning to be enabled on a global scale.

Cognitive Apprenticeship and Learning Environments

Much current educational research is concerned with how learning takes place and which factors can enhance cognition, in order to understand how this process can be facilitated. The sociohistorical school, an approach which influences much of the work on this area, postulates that learning is both an individual, self-directed activity as well as a social endeavor (Brown and Palincsar, 1989). The implication for educational practice is that collaboration and group interaction should be actively supported to promote learning. Individual learning can be combined with coaching, peer interaction, and collaborative work to encourage social learning interactions with instructors, peers, mentors, and experts.

The "places" where learners and their instructors, mentors, or peers interact are called learning environments (Collins, Brown, and Newman, 1989). These environments are shaped by participants according to various approaches to instructional design, moderating, and self-paced learning. When designing or evaluating learning environments, four dimensions and their respective characteristics should be considered: content, methods, sequence, and sociology. If careful attention is given to these dimensions, an "ideal learning environment" can be attained (ibid.).

For learners, the social component of the learning activity is developed through the coaching or help offered by people who know the target skill (masters or experts) or are in the process of learning (peers). Individual learning combined with the support of knowledgeable others through the processess of modeling, observation, and successive approximations is called apprenticeship.

Collins, Brown, & Newman (1989) identify the dimensions and characteristics of ideal learning environments to support cognitive apprenticeship (table 16.1). Learning environments may combine these characteristics in different ways, based on various assumptions, needs, and teaching approaches. All combinations and designs aim at facilitating mastery of cognitive skills.

These characteristics are important design factors supporting knowledge building in online learning environments. Although learning is mediated by the computer, the process itself is composed of human interactions that must be detailed and provide collaborative instances. A carefully designed environment that provides instances of collaboration, coaching, scaffolding, reflection, and exploration is essential to supporting online apprenticeship.

Online apprenticeship provides a variety of learning tools to individuals willing to work within the constraints and the potentials of computer-mediated communication. When combined with a carefully designed environment, global networks can offer new learning options. Two frequently used approaches to online apprenticeship are: mentorship and peer collaboration.

Online Mentorship and Peer Collaboration

In apprenticeship through mentorship, a professional or a knowledgeable person shares knowledge with apprentices of the trade. Appren-

Table 16.1
Characteristics of ideal learning environments

Content	Methods	Sequence	Sociology
Domain knowledge	Modeling	Increasing complexity	Situated learning
Heuristics strategies	Coaching	Increasing diversity	Culture of expert practice
Control strategies	Scaffolding	Global before local skills	Intrinsic motivation
Learning strategies	Fading		Exploiting cooperation
	Articulation		Exploiting competition
	Reflection		
	Exploration		

Source: Collins, Brown, and Newman, 1989, 476

ticeship can also be facilitated through a process of peer collaboration. Peer collaboration can occur in various formats: one-to-one, structured group collaboration, or unstructured group collaboration. In the one-to-one collaboration format, two peers support each other's learning needs. In structured group collaboration, learners are given a task to perform online and have to collaborate to achieve the final results. Finally, in unstructured peer collaboration, apprentices raise issues in online environments and obtain valuable feedback from people knowledgeable in the subject area.

Domain Knowledge and Knowledge-Building Strategies

Domain knowledge refers to the content area that the learner is addressing. The conceptual and factual knowledge as well as the procedures for problem solving in the target area are part of the domain knowledge. Learners use a variety of heuristics, control, and learning strategies to master domain knowledge (Collins, Brown and Newman, 1989). Many subject areas such as writing, history, languages, and geography can be successfully taught online.

In the domain knowledge of poetry, the apprentice needs to know words, syntax, and grammar as a prerequisite for poetry writing. Knowing these required skills, the apprentice can then learn how to write short stories and poems. The development of skills for creative writing implies learning how to successively construct effective and correct sentences, paragraphs, and verses and how to revise to achieve clarity. At the same time apprentices model other poets.

Many literature and creative writing classrooms in Canada are networked to provide students with access to online mentors (writers, poets, English professors). Using the computers and modems in the school lab, students submit their poems or stories on the network to obtain feedback from the mentor.

In one case the online mentor for creative writing is based in Vancouver, Canada, and the students are located in different cities and towns in North America. The mentor is a professional writer, newspaper columnist, and English professor. A student submitted a poem, written for a class assignment, seeking stylistic improvements. The mentor responded with suggestions for changes. A learning interaction was initiated with the initial submission and posterior feedback given by the mentor.

The complete revision/rewriting process to obtain the final copy (submission, feedback, individual work; resubmission, new feedback, individual work, and so forth) took place over one month. The result is a poem improved in its rhythm, prose, and images. Through transcripts of the online interaction, the successive stages of improvement can be tracked. Supported by the mentor's coaching (comments) and scaffolding (feedback or concrete suggestions for improvements), the student revises and rewrites the poem. The two versions are reproduced below. The parts changed by the student are in boldface:

Original Version of the Poem (December 14, 1991)	Final Revised Version (January 21, 1992)
Red is the colour of sunsets,	Red is the colour of sunsets,
and of glittering garnets	and of glittering garnets
as they fall through slender fingers	**slipping through slender fingers**
with scarlet nails, to land	with scarlet nails, to land
on to the snow-covered ground.	on snow-covered ground.
It is the sound	It is the sound
of slow, quiet blues	of slow, quiet blues
in a smoke-filled room;	in a smoke-filled room,
the intense beat of the bass	the intense beat of the bass
reflected in a woman's sultry face,	**mirrored in a sultry woman's face,**
red lipstick against pale skin.	red lipstick against pale skin.
A volcano's eruption,	**A man's distraction;**
fire, destruction.	**his heart's frustration.**
The birth of a passion	The birth of a passion
hatred or love	hatred or love
the rush of hot blood	the rush of hot blood
through a young poet's head.	through a young poet's head.
A velvet dress is red	A velvet dress is red
against a lover's cheek	against a lover's cheek
the desire to speak	the desire to speak
of things forbidden.	of things forbidden.

In a final message to the learner, the mentor writes:

I think the poem is much improved and much more powerful. The rhymes and near-rhymes (distraction/frustration/passion) work well. The tone is more controlled, so the impact of the last four lines is all the greater. Over all the poem has grown and strengthened through your revision. Good stuff!

The apprentice had access to various techniques to master the domain knowledge of creative writing, including scaffolding, reflection, and exploration.

Scaffolding

Scaffolding refers to the intellectual support provided to the learner in the form of comments, suggestions, feedback, and observations. As the learner progresses, the mentor fades until mastery is achieved by the apprentice:

> This idea [of scaffolding] can be illustrated in diverse domains of informal learning, where individual skills originate in cooperative activity through a scaffolding process. Inititally in the learning of language or other skills, the teacher carries the greatest responsibility in the activity, erecting a scaffold for the child's limited skills. As the child's learning and development progress in a given domain, the scaffold gradually diminishes, the roles of learner and teacher become increasingly equal, and the point is finally reached where the child or learner is able to do alone what formerly could be done only in collaboration with the teacher. (Greenfield, 1984)

The creative writing student received feedback to improve the poem. Part of a mentor's message to the student is reproduced below as an example of scaffolding:

> . . . you've chosen an irregular rhyme scheme and meter, and I'm not sure why. You have some straightforward rhymes like "bass/face" but also some near-rhymes like eruption/destruction, love/blood. I can accept an inconsistent rhyme scheme, even if it's arbitrary, but here I feel a little lost. Similarly, your lines scan unevenly—which is fine, except that sometimes your meter is quite regular and we expect to stay with its rhythms.
> . . . Look again at the whole poem, and see what you might change in the early part that would enhance the impact of the last 4 lines.

Scaffolding can come in a variety of formats, depending on the subject area, apprentice's needs, and types of resources one has access to. It aims at providing the learner with the necessary support to master a particular learning task.

Reflection

Asynchronous communication, that is, the opportunity to interact with others on one's own time, gives the learner the flexibility to research or to use metacognitive strategies to address issues raised by peers or mentors and to have the time to research and to reflect before responding. This is different from a face-to-face learning interaction when an immediate response is expected. Asynchronicity facilitates reflection, an important cognitive skill in apprenticeship.

The learner reflects on the feedback received from the mentor and successively shapes and reshapes the poem. The mentor critically reads each revised version and gives support in the form of comments and suggestions. This continuous support facilitates the learner's reflection to achieve mastery of a skill. A question asked by the apprentice illustrates the reflective character of the interaction:

I think I'm going to make "mirrored in a woman's seductive face" into "mirrored in a sultry woman's face" because seductive and sultry just aren't the same thing to me, and in this case I really mean sultry. What do you think?

Exploration

Exploration involves getting students into a problem-solving situation where they might have to play the role of an expert (Collins, Brown and Newman, 1989). Exploration occurs in many ways. In the example that follows, schools set up a program called "Writers' Link" whereby grade 4 students write short stories and submit them to online peers for revisions. A group of three to five students in the same classroom work together to review the submitted story and to give feedback to the writer. Three "editors" read a short story and sent the following message to the writer:

Dear Chris:
We really liked your ending because it expressed your feeling's about your rabbit. We also think that you shouldn't use floppy so much and instead you could use words like soft, droopy, bendable, etc. We also think you should try changing the opening sentence and try not to list things so much. Next time try making your paragraph a little longer. When my group read about your rabbit we felt your rabbit was very special to you.
From your editors: Kelly, Lindsay, and Brad

In performing the role of editor, the students must carefully read the story to assess its merits and weaknesses. With the support of the teacher, the editors identify a number of aspects of the story that should be improved and others that deserve praise. Through this process they, too, learn about revisions and sentence structure.

Sequencing Instruction

Well-designed and sequenced learning tasks are important components in the mastering of a particular skill. In online courses taught at Simon Fraser University, undergraduate and graduate students take on tasks relating to mastery of the content, including skills in presentation and analysis. In the sequencing of instruction, students first read the required texts and then are asked to discuss and analyze the underlying concepts. Once students learn the concepts under the moderation of the instructor, they take on the role of instructor and each moderates one online course session. The instructor monitors the discussion and exchanges personal messages with the moderator to clarify issues and to help in the moderation of the course session. In this way students first observe the instructor's performance as an online instructor and then assume responsibility for teaching a particular course topic online, and in this process, learn about the theme itself.

By moving from less to more complex learning tasks, the student increasingly assumes the responsibilities and tasks of a practicing researcher. The learner is also exposed to an increased diversity (Collins, Brown, and Newman, 1989) as she or he interacts with peers. In this way, the apprentice learns about conceptual issues in research methodologies and then applies them to the discussion of various research projects developed by colleagues in the final course sessions. Such sequencing allows for mastering of research skills and gives the learner the step-by-step support needed for knowledge building.

Peer Collaboration for Expert Practice

Peer collaboration refers to the process of cooperatively sharing knowledge with colleagues. Harasim (1990) describes the many-to-many communication attribute of computer conferencing as a feature that facilitates group work and peer interaction:

Collaborative or group learning in the face-to-face classroom refers to instructional methods whereby students are encouraged or required to work together on academic tasks . . . Educational research identifies peer interaction among students as a critical variable in learning and cognitive development at all educational levels. (p. 43)

Curriculum design and implementation consititutes an important part of the time and the resources schools allocate to teacher professional development. Peer collaboration on global networks can be used to support curriculum design and implementation. The following case focuses on a teacher who used peer discussion on global networks for professional development in course design.

Cross-Cultural Awareness Case Study

A social studies teacher in British Columbia, Canada, designed a new curriculum for his grade 9 class. In the design of the new curriculum, the teacher wanted to emphasize cultural awareness through direct contact and used global networks to provide his students with the opportunity to interact with peers in Japanese schools. He contacted a teacher in Japan on a computer network who was interested in participating and whose students could communicate in English. Global networks facilitated the teaching of cross-cultural awareness through peer communication between the two cultures: teacher/students in Canada and teacher/students in Japan. (While the common language was English, some messages were in Japanese; Canadian counterparts also learned a few words and sentences in Japanese.)

The peer cross-cultural communication program for curriculum development between Japan and Canada lasted five weeks. During that period eighty-four messages were exchanged, including eleven messages between the two teachers.

Several operational issues had to be considered. These included finding an international peer, preparing/negotiating the program with the partner or peer, becoming aware of different school deadlines and holidays, and identifying areas of mutual interest. As a result of the program both the teachers and the students benefited. The Canadian teacher learned how to design and implement a cultural awareness program for grade 9 social studies curriculum via global networks. Three major ways were identified in which the cross-cultural experience enriched teacher development for curriculum design:

1. I learned how to set up a peer cross-cultural communication program via electronic mail;
2. I learned about the Japanese culture through direct exposure to people in Japan; and,

3. I improved my knowledge of the Japanese language in the process of teaching my students basic Japanese words and in translating some of the messages sent by the Japanese.

Students experienced an innovative learning experience that motivated them to actively participate.

Another example of the use of networking for professional development is the model of the Ask-an-Expert conference, a meeting place for teachers to exchange ideas for classroom teaching (Teles and Duxbury, 1991). Teachers enter questions or comments about a topic and an "expert" in that area quickly replies. For example, one teacher posted this message:

I am teaching a unit on buoyancy to a Gr. 6/7 class. So far we have compared the buoyancy of objects in salt water and fresh water. Could anyone recommend any other safer, readily available solutions which would make interesting comparisons with fresh water? Is there anything which makes objects in fresh water even less buoyant? Just exactly how does one explain density to kids at this age?

This teacher received two responses to the question. The first was:

Well, you might try Vodka. It is less buoyant than water, and its buoyancy is the standard measure of its alcohol content.

And a second, lengthier one:

May I add to previous suggestion. An old chestnut was to take a jar or beaker of methanol (spirit duplicating fluid) and put an ice cube in it. It sinks! I suppose you could do some interesting things by using a solution of alcohol and water that would change the behaviour of objects very nearly at neutral buoyancy. The other suggestion I would have would be to place an eyedropper that has enough water in it to barely float in a tall bottle. Cover the bottle with some rubber dam or a balloon fragment that leaves a little air space. When you hold the balloon on with an elastic band or some tape you can now push down on the balloon to increase the pressure on the surface of the water and this pressure increase is transmitted through the water to the bit of water in the eyedropper and it pushes upward and compresses the air in the dropper. The dropper is now not buoyant and it sinks to the bottom.

This support for knowledge building in teacher professional development for classroom teaching shows a "culture of expert practice" among teachers who share knowledge with their peers. The Ask-an-Expert conference exemplifies the kind of peer interaction and collaboration that takes place in network environments.

Conclusions

Online apprenticeship is a new learning option. Apprentices access global network environments to learn a variety of skills and to share knowledge through access to mentors, peers, and experts.

The design of the environment is an important consideration that can affect apprenticeship in different ways. When apprentices interact and learn online, they develop cognitive processes such as exploration, reflection, and knowledge sharing. In the process of learning they benefit from various techniques such as coaching, scaffolding, and accessing to peers and experts.

Various apprenticeship techniques that have been used traditionally are now being used in network environments. Apprenticeship techniques, when applied in network environments, are to a great degree the product of well-designed learning interactions to support the learning of particular skills. In the active interaction (Harasim, 1990) between the learner and a peer, mentor, expert, or instructors lies the key to the success of these techniques in network environments.

Global networks introduce new opportunities and issues for learning on a global scale that have to be addressed by designers of online environments. There is a need for a pedagogy of global networks and research on the many issues raised by learning in cross-cultural environments. A body of knowledge is being built in this area of apprenticeship and online learning environments. The best teaching strategies and learning options are still being explored. This new knowledge will add valuable information to learning in network environments on a global scale.

17 Computer Networks and the Emergence of Global Civil Society

Howard Frederick

WHEN IN THE COURSE OF HUMAN EVENTS it becomes possible to dissolve the communication frontiers that have divided peoples one from another and to assume among the Powers of the Earth the interdependent and balanced communication relations to which the Development of Technology has entitled them.

WE HOLD THESE TRUTHS TO BE SELF-EVIDENT, that all human communicators are created equally, endowed with certain Unalienable Rights, among them the right to hold opinions without interference and to seek, receive, and impart information and ideas through any media and regardless of frontiers. This Right to Communicate includes the right to be informed as well as to inform, the right to reply as well as to listen, the right to listen or to ignore, the right to be addressed as well as to speak, and the right to use communication resources to satisfy human social, economic, and cultural needs.

THAT TO SECURE THESE RIGHTS, a global computer communications network has now arisen benefitting the Common Good of Humankind by loosing the bonds of the marketplace and the strictures of government on the media of communications and allowing that part of human endeavor known as global civil society to communicate outside the barriers imposed by commercial or governmental interests.

These are possible opening lines of what might be called a *Charter of Communication Interdependence* of the global nongovernmental movements for peace, human rights, and environmental preservation. The growth of such global interdependent communication relations has been greatly accelerated by the advent of decentralizing communication technologies such as computer networking. Global civil society as represented by the "NGO movement" (nongovernmental organizations) now represents a force in international relations, one that circumvents hegemony of markets and of governments. This chapter outlines the concepts of global civil society and the NGO movement, describes the obstacles that they face from governments and transnational corporations, and sketches the emergence of the Association for Progressive Communications network as an illustration of this worldwide phenomenon.

"Community" used to be limited to face-to-face dialogue among people in the same physical space, a dialogue that reflected mutual concerns and a common culture. For thousands of years, people had little need for long-distance communication because they lived very close to one another. The medieval peasant's entire life was spent within a radius of no more twenty-five miles from the place of birth. Even at the beginning of our century, the average person still lived in the countryside and knew of the world only through travelers' tales.

Today, of course, communications technologies have woven parts of the world together into an electronic web. No longer is community or dialogue restricted to a geographical place. With the advent of the fax machine, telephones, international publications, and computers, personal and professional relationships can be maintained irrespective of time and place. Communication relationships are no longer restricted to place, but are distributed through space. Today we are all members of many global "nonplace" communities (see Harasim's discussion of Networlds in chap. 2 and Rheingold's portrayal of virtual communities in chap. 4).

In the last decade there has emerged a new kind of global community, one that has increasingly become a force in international relations. We speak of the emergence of *global civil society,* that part of our collective lives that is neither market nor government but is so often inundated by them. Still somewhat inarticulate and flexing its muscles, global civil society is best seen in the worldwide NGO movement, nongovernmental organizations, and citizens advocacy groups uniting to fight planetary problems whose scale confound local or even national solutions. Previously isolated from one another, NGOs are flexing their muscles at the United Nations and other world forums as their power and capacity to communicate increase.

The concept of *civil society* arose with John Locke, the English philosopher and political theorist. It implied a defense of human society at the national level against the power of the state and the inequalities of the marketplace. For Locke, civil society was that part of civilization—from the family and the church to cultural life and education—that was outside of the control of government or market but was increasingly marginalized by them. Locke saw the importance of social movements to protect the public sphere from these commercial and governmental interests.

From the industrial age to the present, mercantilist and power-political interests have pushed civil society to the edge. In most countries, civil society even lacked its own channels of communication. It was speechless and powerless, isolated behind the artifice of national boundaries, rarely able to reach out and gain strength in contact with counterparts around the world. What we now call the NGO movement began in the middle of the last century with a trickle of organizations and has now become a flood of activity. NGOs today encompass private citizens and national interest groups from all spheres of human endeavor. Their huge increase in number and power is due in no small measure to the development of globe-girdling communications technologies.

Dutch social theorist Cees J. Hamelink (1991a, 5–8; 1991b) sees a new phenomenon emerging on the scene—*global civil society,* best articulated by the NGO movement. New communications technologies now facilitate communication among and between national civil societies, especially within the fields of human rights, consumer protection, peace, gender equality, racial justice, and environmental protection. From Earth Summit to GATT, from the United Nations General Assembly to the Commission on Human Rights, NGOs have become the most important embodiment of this new force in international relations.

The development of communications technologies has vastly transformed the capacity of global civil society to build coalitions and networks. In times past, communication transaction clusters formed among nation-states, colonial empires, regional economies and alliances—for example, medieval Europe, the Arab world, China and Japan, West African kingdoms, the Caribbean slave and sugar economies.

Today, new and equally powerful forces have emerged on the world stage—the rain forest protection movement, the human rights movement, the campaign against the arms trade, alternative news agencies, and planetary computer networks.

These decentralizing and democratizing qualities of new computer technologies are also benefiting a growing global movement for the common good. The promise of democracy is fulfilled when citizens can rise above personal, even national, self-interest and aspire to common good solutions to problems that plague the entire planet. The global commons is not just those parts of the planet outside national jurisdictions, such as the air, oceans, outer space, and Antarctica (International Journalism Institute, 1987, 18). It is also a common striving to reach certain transcendent goals. In times past, those goals included abolition of slavery, laws against child labor, and universal suffrage. Today's planetary challenge is environmentally, socially and economically sustainable development. People must reduce sharply the burden they impose on the carrying capacity of the Earth's ecosystems.

The continued growth and influence of this global civil society faces two fundamental problems: increasing monopolization of global information and communication by transnational corporations and the increasing disparities between the world's info-rich and info-poor populations. Global computer networking makes an electronic end run around the first problem and provides an appropriate technological solution to overcome the second.

Hamelink observed that the very powers that obstructed civil society at the national level—markets and governments—also controlled most of the communication flows at the global level. Government monopolies still control a huge share of the world's air waves and telecommunications flows. Even worse, a handful of immense corporations now dominate the world's mass media. If present trends continue, Bagdikian predicts that by the turn of the century "five to ten corporate giants will control most of the world's important newspapers, magazines, books, broadcast stations, movies, recordings and videocassettes" (1989, 805). Telecommunications infrastructures and data networks must also be included in this gloomy account.

Why is this happening? The most fundamental reason is that fully integrated corporate control of media production and distribution reaps vast profits and creates huge corporate empires. Already more than two-thirds of the U.S. work force is now engaged in information-related jobs (U.S. Department of State, 1988, 1.). Almost half the gross national product of the fourteen most industrialized countries, and one-quarter of all international trade, comes from services (Jussawalla, 1985, 11). Telecommunications services grew by 800 percent worldwide in the 1980s. According to UNESCO, the total world information and communication economy in 1986 was $1,185 billion, about 8 to 9 percent of total world output, of which $515 billion was in the United States (UNESCO, 1990, 83). Growth in this sector is accelerating, and it is no surprise that a few large corporations now predominate in the world's information flow. While there are more than one hundred news agencies around the world, only five—Associated Press, United Press International, Reuters, Agence France Presse, and TASS—control about 96 percent of the world's news flows (Mowlana, 1986, 28).[1] Corporations such as Sears, IBM, H&R Block, and Lockheed control the bulk of the videotex information markets in the United States.

In addition to transnational control of information, global civil society and the NGO movements confront the increasing gap between the world's info-rich and info-poor populations. In virtually every medium, the disparities are dramatic.

- An estimated 95 percent of all computers are in the developed countries.

- While developing countries have three-quarters of the world's population, they can manage only 30 percent of the world's newspaper output.

- About 65 percent of the world's population experiences an acute book shortage.

- Readers of the *New York Times* consume more newsprint each Sunday than the average African does in one year.

- The only third world country to meet UNESCO's basic media standards for per capita numbers of newspapers, radio, and cinema is Cuba.

- Only seventeen countries in the world had a gross national product larger than total U. S. advertising expenditures.

- The United States and the Commonwealth of Independent States, with only 15 percent of the world's population, use more than 50 percent of the geostationary orbit. The third world uses less than 10 percent.

- Ten developed countries, with 20 percent of the world's population, accounted for almost three-quarters of all telephone lines. The United States had as many telephone lines as all of Asia; the Netherlands, as many as all of Africa; Italy, as many as all of Latin America; Tokyo as many as all of Africa (Frederick, 1993, 75).

Even within the United States we have the info-rich and the info-poor. From the streets of Manhattan to the barrios of Los Angeles, from the homeless to the immigrant populations, from Appalachia to the inner cities, there are millions upon millions of our fellow Americans who cannot read or type, do not consume newsprint, cannot afford a book. For example, white children are 2.5 times as likely to have home computers as African-American and Hispanic children (Information Rich vs. Poor, 4).

To counter these twin trends that threaten to engulf civil society with commercialization and control, there has arisen a worldwide metanetwork of highly decentralized technologies—computers, fax machines, amateur radio, packet data satellites, VCRs, video cameras, and the like. They are decentralized in the sense that they democratize information flow, break down hierarchies of power, and make communication from top and bottom just as easy as from horizon to horizon. For the first time in history, the forces of peace and environmental preservation have acquired the communication tools and intelligence-gathering technologies previously the province of the military, government, and transnational corporations. Many people, organizations, and technologies are responsible for this development, but one organization has distinguished itself by specializing in the communication needs of the global NGO movement.

The history of the Association for Progressive Communications (APC) dates back to 1984, when Ark Communications Institute, the Center for Innovative Diplomacy, Community Data Processing, and the Foundation for the Arts of Peace—all located in the San Francisco Bay Area near Silicon Valley, California—joined forces to create what was then called PeaceNet, the world's first computer network dedicated exclusively to serving the needs of the movements for peace, human rights, and social justice. In 1987, PeaceNet became a division of the San Francisco-based Tides Foundation, and the Institute for Global Communications (IGC) was formed to direct and support its activities.

Parallel to this, with seed money from Apple Computer and the San Francisco Foundation, in 1984 the Farallones Institute created EcoNet to advance the cause of planetary environmental protection and sustainability. Farallones transferred EcoNet to the newly formed Institute for Global Communications in 1987. ConflictNet, dedicated to serving nonviolent conflict resolution, dispute mediation, and arbitration, joined IGC in 1990. Together, these three networks—PeaceNet, EcoNet, and ConflictNet—make up what we now refer to as the IGC networks, the largest computer system in the world dedicated to peace, human rights, and environmental preservation.

Inspired by the technological success of establishing these networks in the United States, the Institute for Global Communications began collaborating with a similar network in England, GreenNet. To raise funds, rock stars Little Steven and Peter Gabriel performed two "Hurricane Irene" concerts in Tokyo in December 1986. Thus it can be said that the idea of a global network for peace, human rights, and the environment was born in Peter Gabriel's New York hotel room in 1987 when the money was distributed and the original charter was drafted on a laptop computer.

With this impetus, in 1987 GreenNet and the IGC Networks joined together seamlessly, demonstrating that transnational electronic communications could serve these communities. This transatlantic link was so successful that, with the support of the MacArthur, Ford, and General Service foundations and the United Nations Development Program, IGC helped to establish five more networks in Sweden, Canada, Brazil, Nicaragua, and Australia. This led in 1990 to the founding of the Association for Progressive Communications (APC) to coordinate this global operation. Today, more than 15,000 subscribers in ninety countries are fully interconnected through low-cost personal computers. These groups constitute a veritable honor roll of nongovernmental organizations working in these fields.

APC members are fond of saying that they "dial locally and act globally." Today there are APC partner networks in the United States, Nicaragua, Brazil, Russia, Australia, the United Kingdom, Canada, Sweden,

Map of the Association for Progressive Communications (APC)

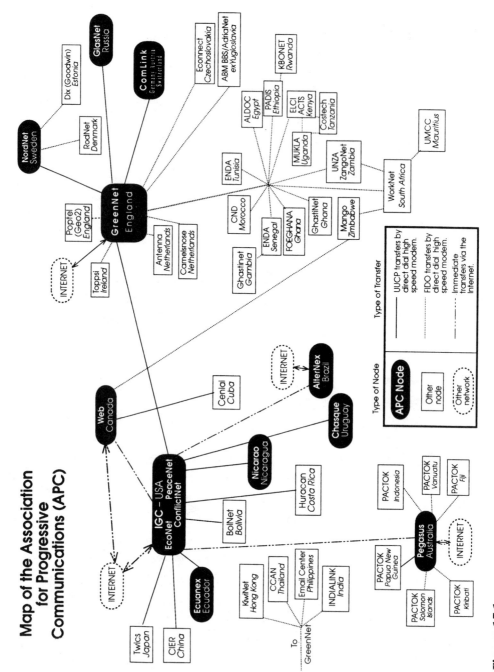

Figure 17.1

and Germany and affiliated systems in Uruguay, Costa Rica, Czechoslovakia, Bolivia, Kenya, and many other countries (see figure 17.1 APC Network Topology). The APC even has an affiliated network in Cuba and can boast of providing the first free flow of information between the United States and Cuba in thirty years. Dozens of FidoNet systems connect with the APC through gateways located at the main nodes. APC's largest computer, known as "cdp" or Community Data Processing, is located in Silicon Valley, California.

The APC networks can now set up complete electronic mail and conferencing systems on small, inexpensive microcomputers for between $5,000 and $15,000 with software developed since 1984 and available to partner systems at no charge. Individual users typically make a local phone call to connect to their host machine, which stores up mail and conference postings until contacted by a partner computer in the network, typically about every two hours. Aside from its low cost, this technological configuration is appropriate for countries whose telecommunications infrastructure is still poor. The file transfer protocols used between the computers have a high level of resiliency to line noise and satellite delays, and, if an interruption does occur, they are able to resume a transfer right at the point it was interrupted. This is particularly important for transporting large binary files, when the chances of losing the connection over poor quality telephone lines is significant.

Within the APC, main nodes at London (GreenNet), Stockholm (NordNet), Toronto (Web), and San Francisco (IGC networks) bring the communication flow in from regional nodes. Messages are then exchanged and distributed around the world so that a message from Australia can end up on a screen in Estonia in two to four hours. Messages can be sent through these machines to outbound fax and telex machines, to commercial hosts such as Dialcom and GeoNet, and to academic networks such as Janet, BITNET, EARN, and USENET/UUCP. The entire APC system is funneled on to the Internet through the IGC networks, which are a full Internet host (igc.org). The price is low by any standard; in the United States hourly connect charges range as low as $3 per hour.

Simply put, electronic mail (or email) connects two correspondents through a computer and a modem to a host computer. One user, let's say a peace researcher in Finland, uses her computer to dial into a local data network (analogous to the telephone network but for data traffic instead of voice). She either types in a message or uploads a prepared text into her host computer—in this case, NordNet in Stockholm. Within a short time that message is transferred via high-speed modems through the telephone lines to the host system of her correspondent, a university peace studies professor in Hawaii. His host system is the PeaceNet computer in California. At his convenience, he connects to his host and downloads the message. This miraculous feat, near instantaneous communication across half the globe, costs each user only the price of a local phone call plus a small transmission charge.

Unlike systems used by the large commercial services, the APC networks are highly decentralized and preserve local autonomy. One microcomputer serves a geographical region and is in turn connected with other nodes. The local node collects the international mail, bundles and compresses it, then sends it to the appropriate partner system for distribution using a special high-speed connection.

In addition to email, the APC networks also oversee about nine hundred electronic conferences—basically a collective mailbox open to all users—on subjects from AIDS to Zimbabwe. It is here that people can publicize events, prepare joint proposals, disseminate vital information, and find the latest data. APC conferences carry a number of important alternative news sources, including Inter Press Service (the third world's largest news agency); Environmental News Service (Vancouver), the United Nations Information Centre news service; Agencia Latinoamericana de Información (Ecuador, in Spanish); Alternet (Washington, D. C.); New Liberation News Service (Cambridge, Massachusetts); Pacific News Service (San Francisco, California); and World Perspectives Shortwave Monitoring Service (Madison, Wisconsin).

The first large-scale impact of these decentralizing technologies on international politics occurred in 1989. When the Chinese government massacred its citizens near Tiananmen Square, Chinese students transmitted detailed, vivid reports instantly by fax, telephone, and computer networks to activists throughout the world. They organized protest meetings, fundraising, speaking tours, and political appeals. Their impact was so immense and immediate that the Chinese government tried to cut telephone links to the exterior and started to monitor the USENET computer conferences where much of this was taking place (Quarterman, 1990, xxiii–xxiv).

During the attempted coup in the Soviet Union in August 1990, the APC partners used telephone circuits to circumvent official control. While the usual link with Moscow is over international phone lines, APC technicians also rigged a link over a more tortuous route. Soviet news dispatches gathered in Moscow and Leningrad were sent by local phone calls to the Baltic states, then to NordNet Sweden, and then to the London-based GreenNet, which maintains an open link with the rest of the APC.

Another example is the 1991 Gulf War, when computer networks such as PeaceNet and its partner networks in the APC exploded with activity. While mainstream channels of communication were blocked by Pentagon censorship, the APC networks were carrying accurate reports of the effects of the Gulf War on the third world, Israel, and the Arab countries, and news of the worldwide antiwar movement. For a movement caught off guard, amazingly smooth coordination took place rapidly across the country and the world. Competing groups agreed on common platforms, set synchronized action dates, and planned large-scale events across vast distances. Computer users seized the technology and made it work.

In 1992, the Association for Progressive Communications, through its Brazilian partner network Alternex, played a major role in providing communications services for environmentalists, nongovernmental organizations, and citizen activists before, during, and after the 1992 United Nations Conference on Environment and Development (UNCED) in Rio de Janeiro. The largest United Nations conference in history, UNCED was the first global gathering on the environment since 1972. It was also the first global summit to take place fully within the age of the NGO and computer technologies. APC maintained over thirty electronic conferences on UNCED documents, agendas, reports, discussion and debate, and even distributed *da zi bao,* or "electronic wall newspapers," from the conference. APC's information sharing allowed the United Nations process to be accessible to citizens around the world, thus providing broader citizen participation in a heads-of-state summit than was ever possible before.

Around the globe, other APC networks are working on issues of peace, social justice, and environmental protection. In Australia, the members of the Pegasus network are working to hook up the affluent 18 percent of the electorate that votes Green. In the United States,

EcoNet is helping high school students monitor water quality in local rivers. One such experiment involved fifty students along the Rouge River in Michigan. When in 1991 neo-Nazi skinheads ransacked a Dresden neighborhood populated by foreigners, users of the German partner network ComLink posted news of the event. Soon Dresden newspapers were flooded with faxes from APC users around the world deploring the action. All in all, tens of thousands of messages a day pass back and forth within the "APC village," and the number grows every day.

The partner networks of the Association for Progressive Communications have built a truly global network dedicated to the free and balanced flow of information. The APC charter mandates its partners to serve people working toward "peace, the prevention of warfare, elimination of militarism, protection of the environment, furtherance of human rights and the rights of peoples, achievement of social and economic justice, elimination of poverty, promotion of sustainable and equitable development, advancement of participatory democracy, and nonviolent conflict resolution."

The APC networks are trying to circumvent the information monopolies to construct a truly alternative information infrastructure for the challenges that lie ahead. By providing a low-cost, appropriate solution for nongovernmental organizations and poor countries, they are attempting to civilize and democratize cyberspace. They also provide an appropriate way to bridge the gap between the info-rich and the info-poor.

The world is truly moving into a "new order." The age of democracy may have had its beginnings in the French and the American revolutions, but only today is it finally reaching the hearts and minds of sympathetic populations around the world. This "preferred" world order of democratic change depends heavily on the efficiency of communication systems.

Perhaps the most durable impact of the APC networks is their promotion of that illusive phenomenon known as "world public opinion." One way that we can confirm the ascendance of global civil society is to examine the accumulating evidence for world public opinion, a cosmopolitan convergence of interactively communicating national civil societies. The 1980 MacBride Report observed that world public

opinion was "still in the process of formation, and thus fragile, heterogeneous, easily abused" (International Commission for the Study of
Communication Problems, 1980, 198). As we approach the third mil-
lennium, communications technologies such as the APC networks are
transforming international relations. They have greatly accelerated the
rise of global civil society and the NGO movement. Not only do they
report violations and victories of human rights but they are also demonstrating that *communication and information are central to human rights*
and to the emergence of democratic, decentralized, planet-loving
movements.

IV *Visions for the Future*

18 Social and Industrial Policy for Public Networks: Visions for the Future

Mitchell Kapor and Daniel Weitzner

Utopian dreams and dystopian nightmares about the "wired world" surround us in the popular, academic, and commercial media. We believe that new computer-infused communications technologies and the digital media that ride atop them hold tremendous potential to enrich our collective cultural, political, and social lives and to enhance democratic values in our society. However, policymakers face major challenges in the articulation, development, and implementation of public policies that ensure that the potential of digital media is realized.

The benefits of new electronic media will remain accessible only to a limited community of users until steps are taken to realize the promise of what we call the International Public Network. The IPN is not a single network but an interconnected confederation of numerous networks, all of which serve different needs and are optimized for their own particular uses. Since it is unlikely that any single network design could meet the needs of all users, standards must be developed that enable these diverse networks to interconnect and interoperate seamlessly from a user's perspective. The proper balance between diversity and homogeneity, global access, and local character must be sought.

The IPN is the vision of the Electronic Frontier Foundation (EFF), which was founded on a shared conviction that a new public interest advocacy organization was needed to educate the public about the democratic potential of new computer and communications technologies.[1] As a political advocacy organization, we work to develop and implement public policies to maximize civil liberties and competitiveness in the electronic social environments being created by new computer and communications technologies. Our primary mission is to

ensure that the new electronic highways emerging from the convergence of telephone, cable, broadcast, and other communications technologies enhance First and Fourth Amendment rights and other laws
that protect freedom of speech and limit the scope of searches and
seizures, encourage new entrepreneurial activity, and are open and
accessible to all segments of society.

As an organization that is also concerned with the culture that develops around new communications media, we hope to encourage and
publicize creative and community-building uses of computer-based
communications. In our quest to "civilize cyberspace," we hope to
become an organized voice for the burgeoning community of nationally and internationally networked computer users. It is our aim to be
a forum and, where possible, serve as a "testbed" for innovative electronic communications activities. In order to help realize the potential
of these new media, we are bringing the early adopters of these technologies into the political process, because we believe that those who
take the first steps in using the technology have a unique perspective
to offer to policymakers.

Framing a Policy Approach to the International Public Network

While we are convinced that the future holds tremendous promise for
new communications media, the public policy strategy we have
adopted proceeds in small, incremental steps. What we call the International Public Network will not be created in a single step: neither by
a massive infusion of public funds, nor with the private capital of a few
tycoons, such as those who built the railroads or the great shipping
empires. Rather it will emerge from the process of the convergence of
diverse networks reaching all over the world. Over time, the International Public Network will form the main channels for commerce,
learning, education, and entertainment in our global society. Other
media, such as the global postal system, broadcast TV and radio, and
telephone service are ubiquitously available in many parts of the world.
Our aim should be to ensure the same level of ubiquity for new electronic media.

The public policy and research agenda outlined here is a series of
practical, incremental steps that should help to create an environment
conducive to innovation and expanded access to networking applica-

tions. These are platform-building steps, which will not yield applications directly but will open up the Net and promote the development of services that meet the needs of an increasingly diverse community of users. Much attention has been devoted to the need for technical standards that enable interconnection and interoperability of heterogeneous networks. Though there is still much work to be done in this area, we will not address it here. Rather, our intention is to explore some of the legal, economic, and organizational infrastructure arrangements required to create an international public networking environment suitable for a diversity of uses and users.

In particular, we will use changes in the Internet as case studies for solving problems likely to occur in other public networking environments around the world. The Internet is a worldwide network of networks that reaches dozens of countries, includes nearly a million distinct computers, and serves many millions of users (see Quarterman, chap. 3). Conceived twenty years ago in the United States, and sponsored originally by the Advanced Research Projects Agency (ARPA) of the U.S. Department of Defense, the Internet (originally, ARPANET) has grown exponentially and now serves not only the research and education community but substantial sectors of industry and growing sectors of the public as well.

The Internet is a heterogeneous computing and communications environment tied together by common technical protocols. It offers a type of "thick" connectivity in which users are linked by full-time, high-speed connections. Because of its thickness, the Internet can serve as a kind of petri dish of technological and social experimentation and innovation. Popular applications on the Internet include electronic mail, computer conferencing, access to online information repositories, remote login to distant computers, and a host of emerging applications in the area of personal communications and information retrieval. The Internet is thick compared to the thin, intermittent, low-speed capabilities of the public, switched, voice telephone network when used by personal computer users with their modems reaching out to commercial online services and bulletin boards.

From the recent history of public data networking, we have gleaned some basic lessons, several of which we will discuss here. First, in order to promote free expression and the open exchange of ideas, public data networks should be operated under a policy of common carriage. That is to say, all messages will be carried regardless of content. Any harm that results from the message is the responsibility of the author, not the carrier. Second, government funding of and policies toward public networks can be used to promote a healthy competitive marketplace for networking services. Third, networks should be designed and operated to accommodate traffic off all kinds, commercial and noncommercial. Mixed-use networks provide more value to all users.

Protect Free Expression by Promoting Common-Carriage Regimes

Computer networks can only fulfill their promise as innovative communications media in an environment that encourages free and open expression. In some countries, legal principles of free speech protect freedom of expression in traditional media such as the printed word, and radio and television. But once communication moves to new electronic media or crosses international boarders, the legal mechanisms for safeguarding free speech fall away. There is no international legal authority that will protect free expression on transnational networks, nor do most domestic free speech protections fully extend to electronic media.

Common carriage is a centuries-old Anglo-American legal doctrine that has been evolved to promote open, efficient operation of earlier communications and transportation infrastructures such as turnpike, ferries, railroads, telephones, and telegraphs. A common carrier—the railroad operator, telephone company, or telegraph facility—has the duty to carry all traffic without regard to the content. So a railroad company cannot refuse to carry a package because it happens to be an odd color, nor can a telegraph operator refuse to transmit a message because it contains statements that the company finds politically objectionable.

Discrimination as to content is a violation of the common carrier's legal duty to the customer. Extension of such a duty to network operators is vital to ensure that all messages, without regard to content or identity of the sender, are delivered to their destination. Absent this protection, the communications carrier can become a private censor of all communications across its network.

Common carriers also have a duty to interconnect with other carriers. To promote economic efficiency and guard against the development of monopolies, carriers such as railroads, telegraphs, and telephone companies have been required to interchange traffic with competing carriers to provide customers with the most efficient routing of their packages (whether they be box cars or digital messages). Many network providers have interconnected on a voluntary basis without waiting for government regulatory fiat. These kinds of voluntary interconnection arrangements are to be encouraged. But in any case, interconnection is vital to the development of a networking environment that is easily accessible and serves the needs of a growing number of users.

The need for common carriage arises because, in the United States, the constitutional right of free speech can only be claimed when government action infringes on speech rights. Private communication carriers, therefore, are free to restrict the content of—censor—any messages that they carry, unless there is some statutory or contractual protection for the sender. (There is some legal authority that publicly regulated communication carriers, such as the Regional Bell Operating Companies, are subject to the First Amendment. However, the foundations of this position are uncertain even for basic voice telephone service and have been found inapplicable for advanced data communication services.)

So, in the United States, common carriage is a critical legal tool for ensuring open access to electronic media.[2] Internationally, many countries used to rely on state-owned PTTs (Post Telegraph and Telephone) for telecommunication services, where the principles of common carriage would be inapplicable. But as many PTTs are privatized and deregulated, some new policy framework will be necessary to ensure unimpeded access to media. As is a legal device drawn from the Anglo-American legal system, common carriage may not be appropriate to the legal systems of other countries. However, it does provide important guidance as to the goals of open communications policy.

Encourage the Growth of Interconnected, Market-Based, Network Communications Services

The tremendous popularity of the Internet has already demonstrated the value of public data networks in the higher education and research community. The success and ever growing use of the WELL, CompuServe, PeaceNet, EcoNet, and Prodigy combined with the 40,000 plus bulletin board services and the worldwide FidoNet system show the popularity of networking in other communities. However, the socio-economic profile of users of these services is still relatively narrow and elite. The majority of Internet users still come from highly educated backgrounds, and the members of CompuServe and Prodigy are over-whelmingly white, upper-middle-class men.

Despite current usage patterns, network-based communication serv-ices could have value beyond the currently limited universe of users. As these services become more useful, less expensive, and more accessible, the community of users may well grow. Just as other communications tools—the printed book, the written word, telephones, and televi-sions—were adopted only slowly, from the top down, the same pattern can be expected with networking. We can and should adopt policies and promote technologies that help make networked information re-sources accessible to an ever-broadening community of users.

The ongoing growth and change of the Internet offers many valuable lessons for access-expanding strategies. Started as a network that was only intended to serve the specialized needs of a small community of researchers in the late 1960s, the Internet has grown into global elec-tronic environment that supports millions of active users. In the 1960s, the average fifth grader, for example, had no need to use the ARPANET to access remote computing power. But in the 1990s, students at the elementary school level can benefit from having access to libraries and other online educational resources around the country.

Commercial Network Service Providers Expand Access

In the Internet world, and in the case of other network communities such as the Well and the IGC networks (PeaceNet, EcoNet, and Conflict-Net), commercial communications providers have played a key role in extending the reach of networked resources. Commercial Internet providers have become a critical means by which more and more indi-viduals and small organizations gain Internet access. For very low fees, various providers offer full dialup access to a full range of Internet resources. Similarly, networks such as the WELL are built up from com-mercially provided public packet networks that are accessible from local dialup sites all over the world. So to enable broader network access, we should seek to implement policies and technologies that support com-mercial, interconnected network services.

In the early history of the Internet, organizations that needed network access relied exclusively on connections offered by the federal sponsors of the Internet. At its birth, when it was known as ARPANET, little was known about how to build large public data networks. Federal research support played a critical role providing network access and in the development of public networking technologies. Since network technology was still in a precompetitive stage, direct government provision of Internet services was a reasonable and productive means by which to supply connectivity to institutions that needed it.

However, as current networking technology has stabilized, many private sector sources—including members of the Commercial Internet Exchange—are now able to offer Internet access as well. By offering low-cost connections and individualized service, private network service providers have made Internet access available to many who do not receive direct government sponsorship. Therefore, active government involvement in providing network access services can be ended.

As in the long-distance telephone market or the rail service, carriers will have to enter into cooperative agreements to be sure that an Internet customer on one carrier's service can send and receive data from customers on other services. Even with the backbone in existence, a significant amount of interregional traffic bypasses the backbone as part of bilateral arrangements between various regional networks. The Internet community has a long-established tradition of promoting interconnection and developing and adhering to international standards. There is every reason to believe that this pattern of cooperation will continue in the Internet community and in other network environments

The Commercial Internet Exchange, a trade association of commercial Internet providers, has shown that interconnection arrangements can be created, even between otherwise competing providers. Internet connectivity is now a commodity service that can be purchased on the open market just like other carriage services such as long-distance telephone service, shipping, air freight, or overnight mail.

In addition to funding patterns, architectural growing pains also hindered the development of a decentralized, commercially based Internet. When the upgraded National Science Foundation Network (NSFNET) of the mid-1980s was experiencing growing pains and performance degradation, building a high-speed backbone was a reasonable response on the part of the NSF. The data transmission technology at the heart of the backbone was in experimental stages; so, a government-funded backbone was appropriate to help develop this technology. But now, five years later, the building blocks of the backbone are available off the shelf and can easily be interconnected without direct government intervention.

Target Government Support Directly to Users, Not Government-Selected Carriers

One concrete step that can be taken to encourage the growth and development of commercial Internet services is to change the current pattern of network funding. Government agencies that have responsibility to connect institutions to the Internet should give the subsidy directly to the target institution, rather than making payments to backbone and regional network providers. The target institution can then take this money and purchase Internet connectivity from a variety of service providers.

Unlike several years ago, the time is now ripe for this kind of funding strategy because Internet services have become commodity services. Just like long-distance telephone service, or trucking, or overnight mail, an institution or individual that needs such services can find a variety of service options available in the market. This strategy will have the dual effect of promoting the development and diversification of Internet service offerings and giving consumers an expanded choice of service offerings.

Research Agenda: Standard Financial Settlement Practices for Interconnecting Networks

For interconnected, commercial networking services to flourish, settlement mechanisms will have to be developed that enable interconnected networks to share the cost of carrying each others traffic fairly. Early interconnections between various public data networks have been based on flat-fee or no-fee arrangements, but these are not lasting solutions. Commercial network providers can only be expected to interconnect with other networks if they are assured that uneven traffic flows between networks will not financially disadvantage one party. Such arrangements are commonplace in the international postal system and the international voice telecommunications infrastructure. All countries that participate in international post and telecommunications conventions agree to certain settlement arrangements that facilitate international participation in these communications networks while insulating individual participants from undue financial burdens.

Allow Mixed Commercial and Noncommercial Use of Networks

The NREN Implementation Plan

Growth in the U.S. portion of the Internet has encouraged the U. S. government to implement the new National Research and Education Network (NREN) with policies and technologies that support both commercial and research and education traffic.[3] The more information that is accessible over the Internet, the greater its value to its users. But the potential of the Internet as an information dissemination medium for both public and private institutions has only just begun to be explored.

As part of legislation that created the NREN, the U.S. Congress mandated that network services should be provided in a "manner which fosters and maintains competition within the telecommunications industry and promotes the development of interconnected high-speed data networks by the private sector."[4]

Under the NSF's management, the use of the Internet by commercial organizations has been wildly successful. Nearly 60 percent of all registered computing sites on the Internet are commercial organizations. Within two years this number is expected to grow to nearly 90 percent. It is not surprising, in light of this rapid change in the Internet environment, that even with the best intentions on the part of NSF, some problems occurred along the way. New policies based on a careful look at the market today can create a thriving commercial environment on the Internet.

Millions of scientists, students, government workers, and even the occasional Congressional staffer rely on the Internet as a primary computer and communications tool. Researchers exchange scientific information, students further their education, government workers communicate with others working on publicly funded projects. Some of us even use the Internet to stay in touch with political developments (see Frederick, chap. 17).

Eliminate "Acceptable Use Policies" that Restrict the Flow of Information on Public Networks

As part of its current management of the NSFNET backbone (one part of the Internet), the National Science Foundation has set a series of "acceptable use policies" (AUP) that define the type of traffic that can be carried over the NSFNET backbone. The major AUP restriction requires that all data carried over the NSF backbone be "in support of research and education."

This restriction frustrates two important NREN goals by precluding widespread offering of commercial electronic information services and discouraging commercial organizations from making full use of the Internet.

Public policies that allow both noncommercial and commercial information providers to offer their services over the NREN will enhance the productivity and creativity of researchers, educators, students, and other NREN users. This lesson can be applied fruitfully to other networks as well.

The Need for Service Classifications

Allowing public networks to support both commercial and noncommercial traffic is a necessary step toward realizing the potential of such networks as popular communications media, but this alone is not enough. In order to promote diversity of communications, older public infrastructures have developed techniques to support a variety of financial arrangements for their users. Postal services allow senders the choice of first class mail or overnight service in the case of urgent messages. Postcards are cheap but offer less privacy and diminished communication content. Parcel post is available for heavy loads that are sent in less of a rush. When acknowledgment of receipt of a message is required, certified mail is available. Telecommunications users also have a variety of options available when they use voice telephone service. Collect calls, person-to-person calls, and 800 and 900 numbers all represent a variety of financial arrangements available to meet different needs.

Some mail services are subsidized, or cross-subsidized, for public policy reasons. Nonprofit institutions benefit from special rates in recognition of the public service they perform. Libraries get low rates, as does anyone who mails books and is willing to wait a while for delivery.

Finally, members of the U.S. Congress get free mail to their constituents. In sum, service classifications are vital policy tools to promote infrastructure access for a wide variety of users.

All of these different classes of services make their respective communications infrastructures accessible to a wider number of users and meet a diversity of communications needs. Stranded travellers would find the telephone network useless and frustrating if the collect call or telephone credit card system was not in place. Charitable and political organizations would have a harder time communicating their message in print without special bulk-rate privileges. Market forces can be relied on to deliver some amount of service flexibility. But there will always be a need for direct or indirect subsidy to ensure that the communications infrastructure serves the needs of all segments of society.

The next stage of the development of the Internet can be used as a test-bed for these service classification schemes. In order to introduce service classifications on packet-based networks such as the Internet, new routing technology is required to sort out traffic of different classes. Current high-speed networks are based on data communications architectures that originated in the private networking world. For TCP/IP and other data networking technologies, the main concern was fast, efficient routing, not billing. The next generation of network routers must have the ability to expedite packets (or frames or cells) tagged with higher-priority classifications and defer delivery of lower-class messages until excess bandwidth is available.

Conclusion

The bulk of this discussion has centered around issues raised in U.S. policy arenas, but we believe that the lessons learned may well have broader application. Of necessity each country will have to retain significant local control over its own electronic communications environment. Furthermore, we do not believe that the policies of any one country should come to dominate the field. Yet, we must recognize that with respect to the International Public Network, the policies made by one local jurisdiction—whether it is a city, country, or regional grouping—may affect all who use the network.

Many of us have dramatic visions of the future of networking around the globe. Yet no set of policies will achieve those visions in one giant step. In this chapter we have outlined a series of incremental steps that can be taken toward our longer-term goals. Government policy has a continued role to play as networks grow nationally and internationally. We should all work toward policies that promote free expression, ensure access to a wide range of users, and take full advantage of competitive market forces to bring innovative, affordable services to users.

19 Co-Emulation: The Case for a Global Hypernetwork Society

Shumpei Kumon and Izumi Aizu

As we enter a new phase of modernization, the information age, many of the ways in which we live, work, and interact will undergo profound change. Increasingly the problems facing global society demand that we begin to act in ways that are more harmonious and sustainable with regard to the environment in which we live. The best way for Japan and other nations of the world to deal with this new phase in our collective history is to mutually emulate, that is, to co-emulate, those civilizational components that each lacks and that best respond to the demands that we will jointly face.

A new form of organization that we propose to call "intelprises" will engage, collaboratively and competitively, in the "wisdom game," a new type of social game[1] that aims to enhance the intellectual influence of its players. Intelprises will also act as agents for co-emulation between the individualism-based Western branches and the contextualism-based Eastern branches of modern civilization. In other words, co-emulation will be the main content of the wisdom game. Co-emulation offers a strategy for the transition to post-modern civilization that will take place in the twenty-first century.

We propose to call the next generation of networks "hypernetworks." In the technological context hypernetworks will provide more bandwidth and capability to handle a wide range of media, forming the information infrastructure to support the global activities of not only industrial enterprises in the wealth game but also intelprises in the wisdom game. In the sociological context they present a new social system that people join in order to share useful information, knowledge, and even wisdom and in which the dominant form of social interaction is persuasion/inducement. Global hypernetworks in this sociological sense will be the arena for the wisdom game.

From Networks Today to Hypernetworks Tomorrow

The term hypernetwork was first coined by Toru Ono, the voluntary "general manager" of COARA (Communication of Oita Amateur Research Association), one of the most active PC. networks in Japan, in the fall of 1989. Foreseeing the convergence of text-based communication and multi- and hypermedia computer technology, Ono and other COARA members used hypernetwork as a keyword to describe this near-future network technology and its social, economic, and cultural implications (Rheingold, 1992).

COARA evolved in 1985 in Oita (Kyushu) to develop the region into an economically autonomous area that does not have to rely on centralized Tokyo and the national government for guidance, leadership, or economic opportunities (Hiramatsu, 1990). In 1989, the local government installed the world's first free X.25 public packet network. Its goal was to provide uniform low-cost access to COARA and gateways to national and international information systems from throughout Oita prefecture.

Discussion during early online debates about hypernetworks centered on technology. Using text-based systems as a starting point, COARA members looked at trends in the development of computer and communication technology and proposed that hypernetworks be computer-mediated communication networks able to carry hypermedia, that is, nonsequentially structured text with multimedia handling capabilities (Nielsen, 1990).

In subsequent online discussions and two face-to-face conferences (March, 1990 and February, 1992), Kumon proposed to broaden the original technology-based definition to include wider sociological concepts. In earlier joint U. S.-Japan research efforts, Kumon had defined modern Japanese and East Asian society as a "network society." He used the term network to emphasize the complex web of human-to-human relationships that typify Japanese and other East Asian societies and referred to interaction between people, especially that emphasizing persuasion and inducement, as "human networking." He also attempted to define the next stage in the development of modern industrial society in a generic sense as "network society" (Kumon, 1992). In this usage, the term network refers to telecommunications and computer systems as well as to persuasion-oriented ways of human interaction.

The two different connotations of network society, sociological and technical/economic, needed to be defined, and the interrelationship between the two needed to be analyzed. The concept of the hypernetwork does this by representing a new type of society, based on the conventional Japanese or East Asian type of interaction, but significantly transformed as a result of the highly advanced technological innovations. Just as the term network is widely used to represent both technological and sociological concepts, this chapter uses the concept of hypernetwork in a way that has both technological and sociological connotations.

Informatization in Historical Perspective

Since the late 1970s, the massive penetration of information technology in general societal activities has heightened the awareness of change. We propose that the concept of hypernetworks can provide a new analytical framework to help understand this change.

The key word in this context is "informatization." This term is often used in a narrow sense to refer to the new wave of innovation in industrial technology. But there are two other waves that are rising at the same time: a wave of social evolution that is carrying us beyond industrialization and a wave of integrative change that is carrying us beyond modern civilization. It is thus possible to categorize the changes now in progress into at least three types: economic, sociological, and civilizational. We suggest using informatization in a broader sense encompassing all of these changes.

Informatization as an Economic Transition

Modern industrial society, which has passed through the age of light industry (the nineteenth-century system) and the age of heavy industry (the twentieth-century system) is now entering its third development stage with the advent of the age of the information industry—the twenty-first-century system (figure 19.1). This is the first meaning of informatization.

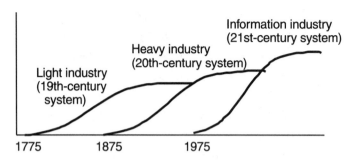

Figure 19.1

Three economic systems in modern industrial society

The nineteenth-century system began in the late 1770s, when it first became possible to produce iron in large quantities. Iron was used to build machines for production and transportation of consumer goods. Operating under the principle of free competition, small capitalists used hired labor and machines in their factories to produce consumer goods for sale as market commodities. Trade in these commodities involved the exchange of ownership rights.

The twentieth-century system began to evolve in the late 1870s when it became possible to utilize oil and electrical energy in large quantities. The development of internal combustion engines and electric motors that could be used in automobiles and electrical appliances brought machinery to households in the form of consumer durables. The new industries of this age were operated by large organizations that used huge amounts of capital. The competition between large enterprises took an oligopolistic form. These enterprises tended increasingly to lease or rent production equipment rather than purchase them outright. Trade was based increasingly on the right of use rather than the right of ownership.

We are now entering the third stage of industrial development, the twenty-first-century system of industrialization. The main driving force in this new period of industrialization is neither matter nor energy but information and knowledge. Information and knowledge have been recognized as vital factors of production, and they are increasingly being used as products in trade. The principle focus of trade in the twenty-first-century marketplace will not be the right to own or use goods but rather the services, especially information-processing services, that are produced using goods, especially machinery. Just as the twentieth-century system was characterized by the paradigm of mass production and consumption, the twenty-first-century system will be characterized by a new production/consumption paradigm in which products are customized or rapidly modified to cater to small groups of consumers. Just as steamships, railways, and other transportation systems enabled the rapid growth of markets in the 19th and twentieth-century systems, telecommunications networks and the media that they carry—hypernetworks—will allow the effective transfer of information essential to the functioning of the twenty-first-century system.

Instead of large bureaucratic organizations in the twentieth-century, network-type systems in which large numbers of small teams can cooperate and compete on the basis of loose and flexible bonds may be most effective in this context. Several authors have noticed this change and have attempted to clarify its nature. Malone, Yates, and Benjamin (1988) point out that, as information technology prevails, existing social systems such as markets and hierarchies will be replaced by what might be called electronic markets and electronic hierarchies. They predict that, in the information age, the proportion of economic activity coordinated by markets will increase vis-a-vis activity coordinated by hierarchies. Ken-ichi Imai (1992), upon examining the future of Japan's industrial organizations, concluded that today's keiretsu-type organizations[2] will be replaced by "network industrial organizations." These are neither markets nor hierarchies but social systems that stand between market and hierarchy. Bressand (1989) describes a "Networld" vision that electronic networks (infrastructure) and a common set of social/human networks (infostructure) will be combined to help create an interconnected global society that will bring people and organizations into closer contact beyond mere economy.

Informatization as a Sociological Transition

The second meaning of informatization is sociological and we use the concept of "games" to identify social behaviors. Having passed through phases of militarization and industrialization, modern civilization itself is about to enter the third phase of modernization (see figure 19.2). Here, a new social "game" will be developed that will in part or entirely displace the "prestige game" played by states and will complement the "wealth game" played by industrial enterprises.

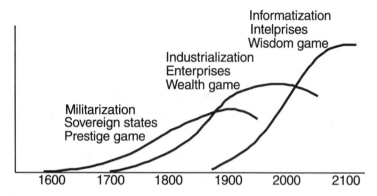

Figure 19.2
Three phases of modern civilization

The starting point for the first phase of modernization, militarization, can be traced to the collapse of the world empires that had created premodern civilization and the consequent emergence of autonomous territorial powers, or feudal lords, who achieved independence on the periphery of those empires. This was later followed by a revolution in military and maritime technology, which paved the way for the formation of the modern sovereign states in which the concept of sovereignty is held sacred. These sovereign states together formed a global societal system known as the international society in which they have competitively pursued the capability to dominate other actors (other states or their own people) by means of threat and coercion. One may say that these modern sovereign states are players in the prestige game.

The second phase of modernization can be described as the process of industrialization that resulted from the technological innovations of the industrial revolution. The modern industrial enterprises that formed the nucleus of the industrialization process held the concept of private ownership sacred. Together, these enterprises formed a global societal system known as the world market in which they have competitively pursued maximization of their wealth, that is, the capability to control other actors by means of exchange and exploitation. These enterprises are players in the wealth game. Although the social legitimacy of private ownership and wealth creation through free competition in the marketplace has not been lost, people are expressing doubts about the social inequalities and environmental damage that they cause.

Today a new social game is emerging on a global scale based on still another form of social interaction: persuasion and inducement through information and knowledge sharing. We can see the rise of a third type of mutually competitive social organization that attempts to enhance its intellectual power based on the concept of what we call information rights. Such new organizations, which we call intelprises, are engaged in a new social game, the wisdom game, in a new global societal system that might be called the global network.

In short, based on the waves of informatization, the process of modernization is about to move from the nationalist pursuit of prestige and the capitalist pursuit of wealth to a new phase based on competition to acquire wisdom or intellectual power of influence. The wisdom game, however, will not completely replace the other two games, especially the wealth game. In its early stage of development the wisdom game will be played together with the wealth game in a complementary and collaborative way. That is to say, we are living in an age of transition which has profound consequences for industrialized countries: the transition from the era of the prestige-and-wealth game to the era of the wealth-and-wisdom game.

Informatization as a Civilizational Transition

We have described the flow of social evolution within the context of modern civilization, but ultimately it is possible that this process will lead to the creation of post-modern civilization that transcends modern civilization. Given ever increasing concerns about the state of the global environment as well as about population and starvation problems, people are beginning to realize that the operationalization of industrial society should be transformed into new, more sustainable ways.

Post-modern civilization is likely to place a high value on inclusiveness and collaboration and on harmony with and adaptation to the external environment. It is also likely to be oriented toward continuity and stability rather than progress and development. In addition to competition in the free market, collaboration within groups of people or over networks will also play a major role in the social interaction. As discussed by Sproull and Kiesler in chapter 6, and Manheim in chapter 7, technological innovations, particularly in the field of information and communication, can support these collaborative activities on a local, national, and global scale. As the value system of modern civilization, based on the beliefs of development and growth, confronts ever increasing global problems, the need to find a new set of values oriented toward sustainability and harmonious symbiosis with the environment becomes apparent. The wisdom game will work as an agent of such a civilizational change.

How the Hypernetwork Society Will Be Shaped

To illustrate how hypernetwork society will be shaped, we outline some of the core elements and processes that we foresee: information rights, the social framework; intelprise, the new organizational structure; and groupmedia, the enabling technology.

Information Rights

To borrow from Albert Bressand's terminology (1989), the emergence of hypernetwork society will require not only physical/technical infrastructure but also a wide range of new social agreements binding the infostructure that is the social/human network. We propose that the core of such infostructure will be "information rights," a new concept of human rights that will supplement, and in part replace, property rights that have been widely accepted in modern industrial society.

People have three basic types of rights related to information processing and transmission. First, both as individuals and as members of a group, people need the right of information-processing autonomy. In other words, individuals should be acknowledged as having the right to reject the attempts of others to intervene in or influence, without permission, their own decision making process. This includes acts of interference such as censorship, being sent "junk" email, or being affected by the actions of a computer virus or system "cracker." We call this the "information autonomy/security right." Second, individuals and groups should be assured that any new information that they create or discover in the process of information handling naturally belongs to them. They should be acknowledged as the "instigators" of that new information and as having the right to demand that others give due credit or ask for their permission when they want to transmit that information to a third party. This we name the "information title/priority right." Third, individuals and groups should be acknowledged as having certain control rights over the gathering, processing, and use of information concerning oneself (or one's group) and hence the right to demand that others tell them what information they have about them and to prevent others from using it in ways that they do not like. For this, we want to use the term "information control/privacy right."

In the information society, not only intellectual property rights but also these more fundamental information rights must be firmly and globally established. At the same time, these rights need to be properly limited, since no social right can be absolute (and many of them stand in conflict with one another). It is particularly important to define and limit these information rights if we want to facilitate dissemination of the newly acquired technologies for information processing and telecommunication.

In modern society, property rights have been duly established as well as limited so that the ownership of most types of assets, both tangible and intangible, can be transferred to others. This social convention is embodied in the concept of the commodity, an asset that its owner promises is ready to be sold to others when a certain set of conditions (usually conditions of price) are met. Such arrangements have facilitated and accelerated the worldwide process of market exchanges. Similarly, to accelerate the global process of information and knowledge sharing, we must delineate information rights as soon as possible. A new concept of information, comparable to commodities in the case of goods and services, will emerge: information ready to be shared with others when a certain condition is met. One might call the kind of information that belongs to this category "the sharables."

Sharables in the wisdom game are given away or disseminated. They have value but not in the traditional economic sense. It is the wisdom content of the sharable that gives it value, and this value is realized when it is shared and understood. This compares to commodities that realize their value when they are sold.

Intelprise as the Main Actor in the Wisdom Game

As we described in the context of social systems and game theory, we are entering the age of the wisdom game from the age of the wealth game. Hypernetworks represent the basic information infrastructure of this new social structure, substantively changing the way people live, work, learn, and interact.

A new form of collaborative organization called the intelprise will emerge in this context, physically supported by groupmedia, in part supplementing and in part replacing the labor and capital-based organization called enterprise. The activities of the intelprise will be based on the notion of information rights. Just as industrial enterprises operate under the principle of property rights, thereby securing the free flow of the exchange of goods and services that these enterprises manufacture or provide, intelprises in the hypernetwork society will operate under the guiding principle of information rights to secure the free flow and sharing of information that these intelprises create and disseminate over advanced communications networks or hypernetworks.

Intelprises are neither enterprises nor states; they are a new type of network organization, one that uses persuasion and inducement rather than the methods of threat and coercion typified by sovereign states or exchange and exploitation typified by enterprises. Just as industrial firms accumulate wealth first by producing specific commodities and then selling them in the marketplace to make profits, the intelprises, as players of the wisdom game, will accumulate wisdom first by creating specific information and knowledge, or sharables, such as new theories, ideologies, policies, works of art, or alternative lifestyles, and then by disseminating them in the global network thereby gaining and increasing their supporting cast of believers.

Just as freedom of production and sales is of critical importance to industrial firms, freedom of research and dissemination will be of vital importance to intelprises. In the industrial society, the place where exchange of goods and services takes place is the world market. What is the proper name for the place where sharing of information occurs in the hypernetwork society? As a type of social system, we would like to call it the "global intelprise."

It is shortsighted, of course, to expect that the enterprises and competition of the wealth game will vanish in the hypernetwork society. Rather, just as cooperative operations exist between states and enterprises, various forms of cooperation between enterprises and intelprises may be developed. National governments, for example, secured the military stability of nations so that enterprises inside could concentrate on production and marketing of goods without worrying about the outside forces. Likewise, enterprises in the early hypernetwork society may support intelprises financially so that intelprises can concentrate on creation and dissemination of sharables without worrying about their financial stability. Intelprises, in turn, may support research and development activities as well as the marketing efforts of enterprises.

Furthermore, just as state activities or relationships between states may be shifting from those of military nature to an economic nature, it is possible to predict that industrial activities by enterprises to produce and sell goods and services may be less mediated by the marketplace, and facilitated more by global networks. Instead of open free markets, persuasion-based networks, then, will become the major field of information sharing.

Groupmedia as Enabling Technology

The core technologies for the hypernetwork society are those of information processing and transmission. More specifically, a convergence of CMC (computer-mediated communication), and groupware, or CSCW (computer-supported cooperative work), that together form "groupmedia" (Institute for Networking Design, 1992), will be necessary to enable the emergence of the hypernetwork society. Groupmedia will allow individuals to form new groups that share mutual interests, not necessarily within the same organization or the same geographic locale but in the scope of a larger communication network. The empowering nature of this technology has been well covered in other chapters in this book, particularly Frederick (chap. 17), Bellman, Tindimubona, and Arias, Jr. (chap. 14), and Ishii (chap. 8). Howard Frederick's discussion of the emerging global civil society is not only a good example of how groupmedia empowers small groups and individuals, but it also illustrates how it does so in ways that are oriented more toward sustainability and environmental protection than development and growth.

Groupmedia will become the major means in the formation of networks, supporting intelprises and promoting the wisdom game in the hypernetwork society. We and others foresee conventional text-based communication evolving into an integrated hypermedia communication system, incorporating image transmission and sharing capabilities without sacrificing its interactive nature. This will allow people to exchange values and emotions in addition to knowledge and information, thereby enriching the content and context of communications.

The heart of group communication exists in the quality of interaction. Thanks to its interactive nature, group communication will create new social groups that would otherwise never be possible. (For a detailed discussion of the characteristics and potential of these new groups, see Harasim, chap. 2 and Rheingold, chap. 4). We expect these new social groups and communities to provide the key structure for intelprises in the hypernetwork society.

Second, by providing powerful means for joint research, coauthoring, scheduling, project management, conferencing, decision making, and so on, groupware will become an essential tool in organizations, both in enterprises and intelprises. It may also provide the kind of highly creative environment that allows interactive sharing of knowledge and the thinking process. In order for groupware or CSCW to be widely accepted, as Hiroshi Ishii explains in chapter 8, we must understand more about the CW side, that is, how people cooperate to work, particularly among people with different behavioral or cultural patterns. This is particularly important as groupmedia will be used in a global context within the hypernetwork society.

The third area of groupmedia is a new mode of information processing that is currently evolving. As John Quarterman describes in chapter 3, the Wide Area Information Server (WAIS) already provides a massive information index stored across the vast computer resources over the Internet. The vision of the future that Apple Corporation exhibited with "Knowledge Navigator"[3] (Sculley, 1987), involves the use of the computer to determine where the information you need is located, as well as to access this information and rapidly manipulate, reorganize, and display it as you wish. The "Knowledge Navigator" is just one of many examples of how information may be processed in the near future. Thus in the hypernetwork society, new forms of network configuration like Internet and WAIS are expected to emerge. That is, rather than requiring that individual users initiate each communication activity, an autonomous network system over a wide range of networks can be established to facilitate easier exchange of information and messages. Networks thus become a major means of communication in the society.

Once the International Public Network that Mitchell Kapor and Daniel Weitzner refer to in chapter 18, Personal ISDN (Barlow, 1992), or other high-bandwidth transmission media become a reality, these kinds of services should be widely available.

Co-Emulation in the Global Hypernetwork Society

This chapter has thus far proposed that in the global hypernetwork society, new network technologies represented by groupmedia will help create intelprises. These intelprises will promote the wealth/wisdom game to make a new era of civilization, postmodern civilization, possible. What, then, is the strategy or principle to guide the participation of these players in the new game? We call it "co-emulation."

New Guiding Principles for the Global Network Society

Policy debates about U.S.-Japan relations on both sides of the Pacific are actually questions about the way the whole world will operate in the future.

Japan appears to be considerably behind the United States in various fields of information technology. Will Japan be able to fill the gap so that it can provide the technological basis for the new production/consumption paradigm that is emerging ? Or will the United States develop its own paradigm based on its lead in information technology? A third possibility, one explored in this chapter, is that the new paradigm will best be realized by the cooperation and convergence of the two industrial systems typified by the United States and Japan. We call this process "co-emulation" among civilizations (or among different branches of a civilization).

At this juncture it is useful to distinguish "civilization" from "culture." Biologists distinguish phenotypes, namely, forms and behaviors of living systems from their genotypes. The latter plays the role of a blueprint for the formation and development of the former. With respect to social systems, culture and civilization can be similarly defined.

We define culture as a subconsciously shared mindset of assumptions and values that guides choice among available civilizational features; the term civilization is understood to refer to a consciously shared apparatus of ideas (ideology/religion), knowledge (science and technology), rules and institutions, and goods and services.

Thus there is no way to directly observe culture. Culture can only be inferred from civilizational features as phenotypes of social systems. We can neither change existing culture nor introduce new cultural elements in any direct way. This implies that there is no way to co-emulate culture. Co-emulation can take place only at the civilizational level.

Chances are, however, that a specific civilizational feature, say, a new form of management transplanted from another society, might stand in conflict with existing culture and be eventually rejected. Nevertheless, we believe that some degree of freedom exists in the congruence between culture and civilization and that that is why co-emulation of civilization can work, at least to a significant extent.

"Japanese" Ways to Contribute to Global Problems

A convenient, though simplified, view of Japanese society involves a three-level structure of sub-, mid-, and supra strata (in other words, people, basic organizations, and interorganizational relations). Depending on which stratum one focuses on, Japan can be characterized as either "a contextualistic society," "an *Ie* society,"[4] or "a network society" (Kumon, 1992). At each level, Japanese society is very much oriented in a manner that closely reflects the networks that we see emerging with the information age. While most Japanese have a sense of an individual psychological self, and they are capable of behaving as actors, this self is strongly conditioned by a contextualist culture firmly embedded in group-oriented social relations.

How well or badly do these traits of Japanese society fit with the processes of informatization? Let us emphasize that the traits of Japan's social systems, especially of networks, are not necessarily unique to Japan. There are Americans who argue that most of the traits of Japanese management were widely shared by American business corporations at least until the early 1960s. Joyce Rothschild-Whitt talks of "collectivist organizations," such as cooperatives and communes that mushroomed in the United States during the 1970s, as displaying traits that most Japanese believe to be unique to Japanese organizations (Rothschild-Whitt, 1984).

The ever-increasing importance of groups of people, linked by technology, acting as the prime movers in the development of modern society and civilization, indicates that networks as social systems will play increasingly significant roles all over the world and acquire enhanced social legitimacy. This also suggests that at least some of the social systemic principles underlying Japanese society can not only be better understood in a positive sense but also be accepted and even emulated. It is not so difficult to imagine a universal applicability for Japanese-style consensus making, based more on shared emotion—that is, warm sympathy—than on allegedly cool, rational reason, and for Japanese-style management of a network organization based on collectively shared goals, decentralized mutual acts, and spontaneous coordination.

However, there are negative aspects that hinder Japanese in their attempts to be more acceptable and responsible members of the global community. For example, as Walls noted in chapter 9, human networks in Japan tend to be closed and selfish in the sense that they select "homogeneous" members who share their basic world outlook and values; their goals are often defined narrowly in terms of their members' welfare only. Computer networking in Japan—one of the base technologies of the hypernetwork society—also tend to be closed in isolated "islands" as Jeffrey Shapard has analyzed in detail in chapter 15.

Conclusion: Global Co-Emulation

How can these deficiencies be overcome? On Japan's part, one possible direction is through a serious and active introduction of the institutions and even cultures of the developed Western nations, to make Japan more westernized so that Japan and the West can more readily interact. However, opinion in Japan is divided about how far such homogenization is possible (or desirable).

Another course would be to go in the opposite direction and, having reevaluated the merits of Japan's traditional institutions and culture, make the best efforts to have non-Japanese understand these characteristics and to try to persuade them to accept and coexist with diversity or even actively propagating things Japanese abroad. However, here too, there is no agreement among Japanese themselves on what is typically Japanese or what is especially valuable about things Japanese for Western countries to "Japanize."

These two courses do not necessarily stand in contradiction to one another. To provide a socioeconomic model for the information age, we believe it is very important that all of us make serious attempts to emulate others and to help others to emulate us so that we can eventually meld socioeconomic arrangements typified by the United States, or the West in general, and those found in Japan, or the East in general.

The information age is inevitably leading to more and more networks in the West. The West, then, can surely gain from studying the positive and negative aspects of the network society in Japan. At the same time, Japan must become aware of the impact that its socioeconomic structure and behaviors now have on the world as a whole. It must realize that it can no longer confine the boundaries of its social networks to its own national or cultural borders. Instead it must draw examples from the more open societies of the West.

As we approach the end of the period of the prestige-wealth game, and a decline in the nationalistic confrontations that arose from their pursuit, the next danger comes from international rivalry and division. For intelprises to function on the global stage members must understand the culture and civilization of other peoples more fully than before. It is desirable in this situation that the world system of the next century be the era of co-emulation between the individualism-based culture/civilization of the West and the contextualism-based culture/civilization of the East.

20 Sailing through Cyberspace: Counting the Stars in Passing

Robert Jacobson

The global network that links the universe of computers is really many networks, each evolved in its own idiosyncratic fashion, whipped together like the frayed strands of cotton ropes. Along this network—which takes its name from the workings of a net, a tool devised to capture and hold prey—millions of human beings struggle to make themselves understood. It is not always easy to do, and the number of those dismayed by trying to communicate via the "Net" is exceeded only by those whose perseverance, taste for the novel, and need to be in touch (a fascinating metaphor in this context) overpowers their reticence to be trapped and held by the Net's allure.

The Net, like the human inventions before it, is not the product of any one mind. In chapter 3, John Quarterman has well documented the evolution of the Net as a collective, if not always collaborative, effort. Strand by strand, trunk by trunk, the Net has been built out of high technology and a dogged determination to let the email get through. The result has been ruggedly beautiful in a monumental way, and it works. But the average human being confronted with a communication task on the Net will recoil at the demands placed on her or him, the new behaviors and operations we must learn. The Net itself is forgiving, but this cannot always be said of the people who occupy the cyberspace it creates. And this applies as much to the professionals who design components of the Net as it does to the unabashedly nasty characters who occupy the deeper dens of communicative iniquity.

The Net has many identities: it can be a hard-edged place, a TRON-like evocation of electrons in eternal motion; a grey adjunct to the library, a virtual file cabinet for those who need to know; or a technological frontier town where entities shuffle their messages down an electronic boardwalk from the barbershop to the saloon. How one sees the Net is due largely to how one employs it: the Net appears differently to the power user blasting megafiles from site to site, the modest resident of USENET newsgroups and mailing lists, and the pedestrian email sender and reader who just wants to get her or his mail and then get out. The computer bulletin board system (BBS) appended to the Net via FidoNet or UUNET has a special relation to the sprawling web, a sort of second-class but spritely executed citizenship in the Network Nation.

What is generally missing from the Net, however (with a few exceptions), is hospitality; or, in a more extreme expression, humaneness. Individuals do what they can to humanize elements of the Net and provide safe havens for those sailing through cyberspace. Some newsgroups on the USENET are comfortable electronic homes away from home; I like to think that the newsgroup I moderate, sci.virtual-worlds, has that welcoming quality. The WELL (Whole Earth 'Lectronic Link), a Net-accessible computer conferencing system where sage advice and witty ripostes consume the memory core, is a unique example of a purposefully undesigned sub-network whose ambiance turned out to be surprisingly rich and warm. Around the world, individuals with a playful side have crafted MUDs, or multiple-user dungeons and dragons, where one can play at being a knight or a twenty-third century galactic trader.

Nevertheless, we can do more to make the Net a place where people want to visit, rather than where they are compelled to come. As an urban designer by education, trained in the semi-intuitive art of shaping physical space, I suspect that there is more art and craftsmanship than science and engineering to the design of a good cyberspace. The Net was created by scientists and engineers, with help from educators and others whose manifest duty led them to this uncharted realm—but the resulting melange of odd and uncomfortable places highlights the need for a more conscious aesthetic to bear on this unique, intangible environment.

Thus, in reconstructing the cyberspace in a humane form, I reject the harsh language and austere methods of science. I suggest that softer metaphors can better help us rebuild the Net brilliantly, to reflect the subtle pleasure of shared human experience. Words like *civility, conviviality, reciprocity, harmony, edification, artfulness,* and *spirituality* spring to mind as ideal concepts to guide us to our goal. I would further suggest that the resistance we sometimes encounter to using these meaning-laden words as design tools—claims that they are "not scientific," insufficiently rigorous, or have nothing to do with computers—reflects a parochialism and blindness to the fact that, after all, the Net is a social construct, just a bunch of wires and radio transmitters and computers if not for the human weaving of its elements into a rich tapestry of form and significance. The Net is what we experience it to be, and the language of common experience is ultimately more powerful as a design parameter than speculative cognitive science, tenuously stretched sociology, and mechanical usability testing combined.

Civility

The first law of effective communication is civility. It is the respect we manifest for another person's words, face-to-face or on the Net. Politeness is sometimes used to mean civility, but politeness only stands for the trimmings of the well turned-out courtier. Civility has a robustness born of the respect one citizen shows another, the common recognition that a community can exist only to the extent that it encourages many voices to speak from many points of view. In this way something akin to truth is deducible, and good decisions can be made.

Civility is a property of certain regions on the Net. In the better run newsgroups, for example, civility is a quality that almost always prevails. The minority and avant-garde viewpoint is not only tolerated but sought out, to raise alternative perspectives. In situations where civility is not present, conversation online degenerates into a keyboard fight as combatants toss ill-considered, bilious verbiage at one another. Being in the midst of one of these catfights is deeply embarrassing, perhaps because one cannot even have the satisfaction of knowing with certainty the first causes from which the dispute has arisen. Worse yet are those situations in which civility was once the house rule but now has vanished. The story is by now apocryphal, but for those of us living through it it was anything but pleasant, how a temperamental host of a threaded computer conference, enraged at the online presence of his lover's other champion, not only exited the system in a huff but also removed every one of his own contributions from the conference, leaving behind an empty shell of meaningless words. This sort of reckless disregard for what has been built over time by many minds acting together is the bane of community. A simple, civil rhetoric should prevail online.

Some argue that direct talk is necessarily uncivil; that civility isn't cool. The person who types invective, in their opinion, is honestly expressing what he or she feels, thus making for a more genuine dialogue. There are newsgroups on the USENET and more than a few BBSs where one can go and, as in the famous Monty Python skit, be abused. Occasionally wandering into one of these electronic snakepits, I wonder what attraction they hold. Maybe it is the easily felt testosterone-high among the teenage boys or neo-Nazis or out-of-work Red squads who inhabit these warrens that makes them so interesting. But uncivility is still too prevalent even in more genteel quarters. For example, women, many of whom are not disposed toward strong assertive rhetoric, often complain that on the Net, in newsgroups and other online activities, their desire for collaborative, emotive expression is slighted. They come looking for community, expect civility, and instead get uncivility flavored with masculine individualism.

One cannot design civility into the electronic infrastructure of the Net (except, perhaps, by disguising the participants so that everyone is anonymous and thus equally to be feared). Civility is a social phenomenon for which opinion leaders on the Net are ultimately responsible. Civility on the Net is a tribute to those who make it a point to bring it about.

Conviviality

The marketplace of ideas is an old concept said to predate the industrial age for which it became the perfect intellectual ornament. It conjures images of stalls presided over by merchants hawking deep insights. Watch out for the thumb on the Aristotelian scale! For me, a more appealing metaphor is the groaning table, the medieval feast, where one stuffs oneself with every morsel of information and swills a heady brew of knowledge. Conviviality is the joy we share at being somewhere unique, online, to meet many minds at the groaning table of shared understanding.

Can anyone forget the moment of discovery when, for the first time, we hooked up modem to phone line and computer to modem—and then discovered the incredibly wide world *inside?* The experience certainly shook me. Isolated in a relatively quiet town in California's Central Valley, in 1984, from my computer I dialed a number in San Francisco—and suddenly became part of one of the most raucous, convivial online communities I have ever known, the infant WELL. My circle of friends expanded magnificently, with my emotions warping through space to encompass personalities many tens and sometimes hundreds of miles away. The feast had begun.

Over the next nearly ten years I explored other online communities and, a few times, helped invent communities of interest where none existed. Each time there was the rush of pleasure at bringing together people of like mind or sentiment, who could find joy in each others' online presence and support. Most of these communities organized in-person activities to complement their Net dealings; those without such meetings often did not fare well. For those online communities for whom the act of coming together had been dramatic and relatively sudden, one or a series of face-to-face gatherings (f-t-f, in the parlance of the Net) proved crucial to stabilizing the relationships among the inhabitants of the communities and the longevity of their respective groups. More leisurely established online communities, like the various LISTSERVs (or list services, automated emailing lists) and newsgroups, may not feel the same need to assemble so that their members can examine each other. But this may only be an illusion; their gatherings may take place at larger, more formal conferences and events, in which case the f-t-f factor may be as significant as ever.

Another memorable aspect of online conviviality was learning just how wide is the spectrum of human experience. In our schools and media we are led to believe that the range of human behavior is relatively narrow; true deviance is the purview of criminals and crazy people. No. Online, I discovered that the range is virtually a universe wide. Even though there may be only five million of us on the Internet, a mere tenth of a percent of the world population, still we are a very large number of people with whom one may discourse. In the convivial groups I have been invited to join, there are a seemingly infinite variety of pairings, matings, and families (a tribute to the human Turing Machine, able to crank anything out of its binary genders) and a willingness to speak frankly about them. At first, I was taken aback by this honesty. After all, it is not the stuff of everyday conversation. But gradually I learned that there is no such thing as the "normal," unless by normal we mean the condition of suppressing the truly standard deviation.

Conviviality online is the act of sharing the mindfood spread on the table before us. It binds us. We become a community through the ritual of acknowledging difference and the fact that we are, nevertheless, together.

Reciprocity

It comes in the middle of my list, but reciprocity may be the single most important quality that can be designed into both the infrastructure and the operations of the Net. In short, reciprocity is the Golden Rule embodied in information technology: that which you can know about me, to influence or direct me, is also allowed to me about you, to influence or direct you. Reciprocity is also one of the scarcest of the properties of online experience, because the technologists who build the infrastructure do not think of it as a valuable property of communication media. In a world where movies, CDs, and videos tend to dominate colloquial thought about communication, one-way communication, from producer and director to audience, is thought natural and right. For example, it is not unusual for individuals to accept inequitable access to information technology even though it may be the result of correctable design oversights. Many of us have come to believe (perhaps rightly) that technology is inherently designed to reflect class biases and, since most of us are not members of the elite, we are lucky to have things work as well as they do. In a technological system designed with reciprocity in mind, such denial would not be tolerated. As a result of the participatory design movement in Scandinavia, workers (at least up until the last, most recent economic collapse) have had the ability to literally redesign their factories and the information technology that links the factories. There are no mysteries in the reciprocal relationship.

A popular stand-in for reciprocity is interactivity. They are not the same, however. Interactivity means simply the ability of two entities to exchange tokens, according to the rules. X does A, and Y does B. Reciprocity means to share in the making of the rules that govern our exchanges. X does to Y, and Y does to X. Interactivity appears to be a solution to the problem of equalizing relationships among humans and machines, but it is more likely a trap. At the behavioral level, the phone rings and it must be answered. At the systemic level, the ATM machine takes your debit card and gives out money, but without disclosing how it got the money or what will be done with the information about your transaction. Of course, the conventions of politics take nonreciprocal relations to the highest level of all, and if politics become embedded in the construction of the Net's infrastructure—as they show every sign of doing, as revealed in the recent U.S. debate over the NREN, the National Research and Education Network—then the chance of the Net user being able to learn about the Net institution, let alone circumvent or challenge its rules and operations, will become very slim.

Reciprocity is its own best argument. It is self-regulating and a necessary foundation for all the other characteristics of online environments that meet our test of humaneness. Without reciprocity, systems tend to go into imbalance and have much less strength for riding out stressful conditions. Online communities that succeed strive for reciprocity; in its absence, the communities fail. Going online becomes a chore.

Harmony

How does one design for harmony? It seems more a function of other factors, for which design may be a more appropriate endeavor, than a factor itself susceptible to design interventions. We achieve harmony through the successful advocacy of a particular behavior characterized, for example, as civility, and by the building of online systems and interfaces that make it possible for two or more people to collaborate easily. Then harmony results.

Or does it?

The disharmonious system is inherently incapable of sustaining healthy individuals and social relationships. One proprietary system, not yet on the Net but soon to join, was wracked by first one wave of turmoil and then many more as the story of an employee monitored and ultimately fired by management spread throughout the firm. Civility was not at issue; conversations were open and candid. People were convivial enough. There was some sense of epiphany in coming to grips with censorship, which before had only been a looming grey possibility. But the swells of emotion that swept the internal network of the firm led to an eventual high level of mistrust and finally the imposition by management of hard rules of use. One learns in political science that the application of force is the last recourse of the imperiled regime, but how can there be a revolution within a firm? In fact there cannot be a revolution without seriously jeopardizing the firm, so that the company to this day is a smoldering hotbed of ill feeling and lowered productivity. When it joins the Net, it may become a panspermatic infuser of bad vibes throughout the regions it affects (and infects).

To return to the prior question, how might one design for harmony? The easiest solution is to pursue stasis, which relates to harmony in the same way that interactivity relates to reciprocity. It is a cheap substitute. So we would design into the system various governors for keeping things in check, including (as discussed above) monitors for the people and software tools permitting surveillance of data. In a more liberal regime, we might give individuals tools, like online polls, to create a "public opinion" capable of running over any expressions of a highly individual nature.

But suppose our goal is not stasis but rather a dynamic harmony, a kind of movement in balance, like a dance company in a difficult but evocative performance. Then we need stabilizers of various sorts to tip the online interactions back onto a "carriage" capable of supporting the online community as it readies itself for and ultimately pursues forward progress. Usually these devices are human because of the finesse required to influence the course of a human activity. Censure, not censorship, becomes the means of disciplining the completely unruly who might otherwise destroy the electronic commons. Harmony, while it may be difficult to design *for,* is a parameter of online community that cannot be dispensed *with.*

Edification

The point of going online is to have experiences different from those one can have offline, in the material world. In one sense, this is an instrumental pursuit, the gathering of knowledge to do a thing. It is always surprising, however, to discover how many people come online simply for the point of doing so and the acquaintances and discoveries they will make. They come to edify themselves and others, and if the Net doesn't always deliver an ideal experience, at least they can come back another time and try again. Eventually, so it seems, many people do become broader, more tolerant, and more enlightened as a result of spending time online. This qualitative change may be just a hopeful figment of my imagination. As a designer, however, I am trained to empathize with clients, and the need for personal growth and expansion is strongly projected by the people with whom I have come into contact online.

The Net as it is constituted seems superbly situated to fulfill its inhabitants' need for edification. There are hundreds, even thousands, of archives holding terabytes and more of data about every conceivable subject; the willing explorer can spend a lifetime staying current on this treasure trove of information. All that is required is to locate this data, read or download it, and perhaps share it with others to test its validity. But somehow, for many people, the first step—attempting to locate the data—is also the last. There are several impediments to learning within the environment of the Net, not the least of which is simply knowing how to navigate around a space of complex dimensionality. When a database gets too big, as Donald Norman (Jacobson, 1992) has pointed out, the inclination is to want to "teleport" from place to place. Norman would dispense with the endless search routines that are finally too difficult for mere mortals to find their way and replace them with a smart environment that customized itself to the inhabitant, rather than the other way around.

Here we come very close to virtual worlds paradigms, of which I am quite fond and which I speak about in closing. If we can mold the Net to beneficially envelop the individual, so that in effect one "wears" the Net rather than travels it, we may solve the problems that normally defeat having an edifying experience online.

Artfulness

Things done well have an art about them. It is the visible invisible, a quality that speaks of excellence in execution. Developers of information technology seldom apologize for their more inartful creations; users are encouraged to learn various tricks—for example, to use absurd keyboards when better keyboards (and perhaps supplemental tools, like joysticks and mice) are available. Styling is too often confused with artfulness. Styling is the floss on the package or the line on the product that bespeaks of attention paid to the package and product *after* the sales item had already been frozen in form.

Artfulness, on the other hand, is a commitment to realizing a statement or a vision and manifesting it as a compelling experience. Regrettably, we can't say this very often regarding the Net. There are some compelling innovations on the USENET, for instance, that deserve the label of artful; in particular, one thinks of the WAIS, or Wide Area Information Service, maintained by Thinking Machines Corp. on its Cambridge-based hypercomputers. Today via WAIS one can access material on all subjects from many databases, with the additional benefit of the information being filtered by primitive agents (computer programs that act without explicit instruction to scout for or prioritize specific information). This is an artful implementation.

Most of the NET, however, does not have dramatic or sufficiently unique information to build around. At most sites there is the usual USENET package of offerings, including programs, calendars, and indexes to archived materials. Similarly, on most newsgroups there is a familiar banter. However, the quality and personalities of the moderators who manage the minority of moderated newsgroups tend to create variance among the newsgroups; these moderated newsgroups are considered to be among the best.

An artfully conceived Net, in terms of its structure and appeal, would probably generate an intense effort to find new applications for the Net, and these might incorporate some artful ideas as well. USENET's administrators might pay more attention to such small details as the way mail is routed about the system and such portentous questions like how email can be fused with fax, and so forth. We should also consider the quality of our online conversations and see if the Net is capable of supporting simultaneously data and voice, something that has been predicted for some time. Finally, we might ask participants to join in these design efforts, on the grounds that such participation makes for contented citizens during the design process and, as we are all pioneers in this process, provides many minds to double-check what it is we are doing (see Harasim, chap. 2).

Spirituality

With the exception of a few Ray Bradbury stories that have dealt with the concept of the soul of the machine (or perhaps, the ghost in the machine!), it is generally unpopular to speak about the spiritual nature of the online experience. However, like Peter and Trudy Johnson-Lenz, the Portland couple who have been so influential in restoring ceremony to the use of computers, many now understand that there may be something profoundly moving about online communications and being on the Net.

What is this magic? Is it the spontaneity of rapid and consecutive communication via email, or the more structured but equally quick exchange of information within a structured group—so that one can thoroughly appreciate and admire our deeply human capabilities for communication, capabilities that lie fallow in other contexts? Or is it simply that reconnecting with human beings en masse is somehow akin to reintegrating with the whole of humanity, with an evolving, dynamic collective memory, in a twist on Jung's frozen archetypes?

The spiritual dimension of online communication must be the one for which it is consciously hardest to design. But because, if it exists at all, it is so fundamentally a part of the online experience, then the spiritual is necessarily expressed by the artful designer's system designs. Staring at a Macintosh's blindly radiating, tiny screen in the early hours of the morning, it is hard to recall the power that drove the Macintosh development team to realize a truly novel departure in computing. I suspect a Zen priest would be able to find great meaning in the scrawling of the cursor across the screen, leaving small characters in its wake; he would be captured to a greater degree by the mystery of the Net which, invisible yet prolific, is like a soundless ocean. Like the giant goldfish in the still pond, the ebb and flow of personal energy across the Net evokes a certain awe. The challenge is to design online systems that recognize and respect these qualities. It is not trivial.

The Virtual World

The emergence of the virtual world releases us from the bondage of the computer terminal and its tiny window on the world. The virtual world, a general interface, embodies the paradigm of *virtuality:* that what we perceive is all we can know. The person is at the center of the information universe; it is according to her or his capabilities that our interpretive information systems must be organized. The virtual world grants easy access to chosen environments and selected data, in the form of natural objects or self-defined symbols. It promises to engender a vastly enlarged Net population and wholly new ways of using network technology.

Simply described, the virtual world is an information environment created and sustained using fast rendering machines and distributed data models of objects and relationships. Special I/O devices intimately serve the human sensory array—primarily through simulated sights, sounds, and tactile cues. Position sensors, voice input software, and built-in tools and controls adjust the virtual world to comply with the actions of the individual participant or multiple participants within. Today, laboratories in Asia, North America, and Europe are working hard to bring virtual world technology to market. We should see its full-scale arrival within the decade, as *televirtuality*, the sharing of virtual worlds transmitted over the wire, is made possible by the Net.

A person's ability in the virtual world to transcend space and time, to be anywhere, anytime, as or with anyone, is the principal attraction of the virtual world. It is very seductive. Paeans in the press and long lines to play virtual-world arcade games and to see films purporting to treat the subject attest to the attractive power of being able to slip one's earthly bonds. But transcendence is a tricky business. It leads either to greater awareness, insanity, or both. In medieval times, many saints came back from their ordeals as sanctified babbling idiots. Their gibberings were taken to be the inspired Word from on high. This does not seem an appropriate goal for travellers on the Net, although some would swear that the online population is already well inclined toward Bedlam.

Should individuals be systematically trained or given an opportunity to learn freely within the virtual world? This topic inspires heated debate among those who insist that participants must be provided with navigation tools and preconfigured experiences, as the first step toward mastery of the virtual world, and those who would follow the Taoist "uncut block" tradition of inviting participants into a void, where with "virtual construction kits" they would build their own worlds to fit. This ultimate design question remains unresolved and will probably remain so despite what is learned from the first early experiments of world inhabitation. Unfortunately, today's primitive technology can only support simple worlds, whether designed by experts or by the inhabitants themselves. Consequently we can only speculate on how human beings will take to these information environments when they become complex enough to pose perceptual problems.

Nevertheless, we can safely predict that when virtual world technology finally unmoors individuals from their accustomed physical and mental geographies, their desire to identify with online communities residing in novel worlds will expand the significance of the Net. The ability to mutate apparent reality may become a compelling educational experience and entertainment. What was once a technological means to an intellectual or emotional end—sailing through cyberspace—may become the end in itself. McLuhan's prescient axiom, that "the medium is the message," is totally relevant.

We may long for instruction in how to evaluate these phenomena that occur on many levels: psychophysical, social, intellectual, emotional, and even spiritual. One solution is to observe superficially simpler media, like novels and other literary forms, and how they abet people's ability to voyage in new realms. But examined more closely, literature is one of the most complex embodiments of human experience. In fact, literature's "subjectivity quotient" is so high that it is extremely difficult to share the experience of a literary expression except at a public reading, a storytelling, or as theatre. Another possibility is to look at more contemporary media and make comparisons with what we imagine the virtual world may become. However, the closer one gets to the appearance of the virtual world—for example, television, because it is video-based; or multimedia, because it relies on the computer—the more extreme are the differences between the actual experience of the media.

For now, we might as well think of cyberspace as the data-driven pseudospace, the "consensual hallucination" so vividly described by the writer William Gibson (1984). Our adventures may not be so extreme as those encountered by Gibson's characters, but they will certainly be quite different from what we know today. Our descendants will be surprised at our network naivete and the apparent sophistication with which we describe phenomena whose outlines are barely evident over the horizon.

What tools do we have to assist in constructing virtual worlds that comport with our rules for "good space"? What I have read of interface design suggests to me that we are torn between philosophical homilies and empirical anecdotes, neither an especially firm base on which to build a virtual edifice.

We might begin by first specifying the qualities sought in the virtual worlds we create. We might then move on to develop metrics by which the presence of these qualities can be determined. Is something sufficiently malleable or responsive? How shall we know until we have an information environmental yardstick that is capable of putting things in perspective. (Metaphors for experiential knowledge, like perspective, are readily available, but we have consigned them to the slightly irrelevant world of art. We need to reintegrate art with our work or at least reclaim the metaphors we have let slip through our figurative fingers.)

Cognate to our concerns are design methodologies from the fields of environmental design and information science. We expect sense-making to provide us with useful tools for estimating knowledge needs, and so to guide the crafting of virtual worlds. More surprising is the applicability of design methods from the material world, like wayfinding, that tell us how human beings locate and navigate themselves through virtual space. If we wish to build virtual worlds that work, that are more than the ad hoc product of technological accidents, then we are definitely in the business of information environmental design, and we should ply the tools of designers.

Finally, inherent to televirtuality—the experience of actually sharing virtual worlds—are crucial social and philosophical questions. For example, where are we when we transmit images of ourselves, but not our bodies themselves, to a distant place? The ability to virtually transcend limitations of time and space does not render these dimensions meaningless, only ambiguous. The traveling of virtual beings to a "place" that exists only in computers linked by a network—the classical definition of cyberspace—is an assembly of sorts, but is it endowed with the same political and social meaning as a crowd gathered in a street or the legal responsibilities of a group of business people who are making a contract? Suddenly, the world, real and virtual, has become more complex!

And these are just the simple questions, easy to pose because they are so obvious. More profound are the consequences of televirtuality on the individual as a member of a collective and as a self apart. The transmission of one's being, or at least a part of one's persona, to realms for which we still have few words, is certain to alter the perception of personhood . . . not least for the individual involved. Who am I if I am not only capable of being in multiple times and places, but also in multiple identities: male, female, other; old, young, or unborn; human, animal, plant, or inanimate object; or an atom, the universe, or a simulacrum of the godhead itself? These are not just heady speculations. Experiments with some of the less cosmic masques have already taken place, with sometimes startling results.

We cannot easily extrapolate from current media, although the lessons of drama tell us a bit about the means, value, and wisdom of assuming roles other than those we commonly play. The structured forms of communication forced upon us by our physical, timebound bodies (only rudely surmounted by video and other contemporary forms of synthetic presence) are all that human beings have known for thousands of years, with rare exceptions. That exception is the experience of altered states of consciousness found most fully in the trance of the mystic or the heightened awareness available to more of us in a transcendent moment.

Conclusion

There are ways of seeing the Net that are not common to the discourse of the scientists, engineers, and educators who first came to the online environment and whose professional predispositions and instrumental needs biased the way they built the Net. Their design parameters are stark and austere. There are guides more subtle, but perhaps more useful, by which we can measure the quality and value of the online experience. I have suggested a series of concepts—civility, conviviality, reciprocity, harmony, edification, artfulness, and spirituality—as one set of guides. Others may suggest different but equally valuable sets of design parameters. In any case, we should begin discussing how we can improve the quality of the online experience now, while the Net's infrastructure is still malleable and our own behavior remains flexible and capable of change.

21   *The Global Authoring Network*

Linda M. Harasim and Jan Walls

The very term *global networks* implies the existence or emergence of global systems, describable as different elements in a common relationship. Every system embodies expectations concerning the ways that its elements should relate to each other—for what purpose or multiple purposes, for how long, through what forms of mediation, using what language or languages, over what channels, using what protocols, with what levels of formality, to what degree of personalization, and so forth. A globalizing network consists of emerging relationships among elements whose expectations have been created by experience in different systems—relationships for different purposes, through different forms of mediation, over different channels, and using different protocols. This new situation may be viewed as an unprecedented opportunity to weave a greater diversity of elements into a richer texture of relationships with an expanded definition of mutuality. It may also be viewed as an unprecedented challenge to redefine our thinking about the norms—the behavioral expectations—that lend stability to human systems.

Epilogue

As observed in the Preface, this book is the product of a global network process that we named the GAN: the Global Authoring Network. The GAN was an effort to define, practice, and refine a new mode of relationship between editor and authors of an edited volume on the very subject of global networks. It was a global network focusing on globalizing networks and structured to encourage a sense of editorial unity while preserving a wide diversity of authorial perspectives. It required the addressing of such fundamental and broad topics as networlds, global matrices and virtual communities (chaps. 2–4). It also addressed such issues as the international legal implications of globalizing information exchange, applications and implications for the workplace in light of international, intercultural, and interlingual co-operation (chaps. 5–10). Naturally, the addressing of all these issues must be grounded in experience and articulated in such a way as to suggest a vision of where globalized networks are leading us, could be leading us, and should be leading us (chaps. 11–20).

The goal of the GAN was to use global networking of authors in the following ways:

- To arrive at a cohesive and interdependent whole

- To inform one another of the contents of the other chapters, and to refine our own thinking and cross-referencing

- To facilitate a process of interactive feedback, to enhance the creative/analytical process, and build a unity of vision in the book

Chapter authors were not obliged to incorporate all suggestions but were encouraged to use peer feedback to help edit and refine their own chapter and to link it to a vision of the book as a whole. Final editing decisions would be made by the chapter author(s) and volume editor.

What were the outcomes of the GAN? Given that (1) a traditional problem with producing a cohesive volume out of edited chapters written by diverse authors is the development of a shared perspective on the topic and subtopics, and that (2) electronic networking allows for cost-effective exchange of information and sharing of views in collaborative endeavors, we proposed the following hypothesis: *Computer-mediated networking of authors in a time-constrained collaborative discussion of each others' draft chapters will encourage a unified vision of the topic to a degree that would be very difficult and far more time consuming by nonelectronic mediation.*

The GAN Process

A total of nineteen contributors from three continents and four countries (England, Japan, Canada, and the United States) were linked by electronic mail to send and receive messages related to book chapters.

Nine others participated as readers, offering occasional comments. Five authors and coauthors were not able to participate on the GAN, and the process of integrating their chapters into the book was substantially different, as discussed in the Applications section.

The GAN began in January 1992, and discussion of the chapters continued regularly over a four-month period. Comserve, an email distribution list for communication professionals, was employed. Participants sent their message to one project address, at Comserve, which automatically distributed the message to the GAN participants on BIT-NET and Internet.

The nature of the networking technology, in this case email, was a critical factor in designing the GAN collaboration. The advantages were that the networks were global and hence familiar and accessible to most of the book contributors. The attributes of time and place independence augmented the opportunities for participation; the text-based archives facilitated review and consideration of comments received and sent.

Nonetheless, email services are recognized as limited, awkward, and "not really tuned or tunable" for collaborative work (Greif, 1988, 6). Unlike groupware such as computer conferencing or more powerful systems such as the TeamWorkStation being developed by Ishii (see chap. 8), email has few tools to organize a shared object for a group discussion. Only such cues as the address and the subject header provided clues as to the content of the message and distinguished that message as part of the GAN rather than any other source.

To organize the exchange around each chapter, and to coordinate/synchronize the discussion flows, a design based on sequential presentation of chapters was employed. Each week an author would present her or his chapter electronically, prefaced by comments about the objectives of the chapter and questions or requests for feedback that would be especially appreciated. The "host author" would then moderate the discussion for one week; fifteen chapters were discussed in this way on the network.

This model of group discussion is quite distinct from what would have been possible if the GAN had been linked by computer conferencing, which enables multiple topics to be discussed simultaneously. In the conferencing model, the system organizes the discussion around the various topics. In the "group email" model, the coordination or synchronization of group interaction was provided by the weekly schedule and a set of conventions for key words in the subject headers designed to organize the messages along a topical format.

Outcomes

Outcomes of the GAN are discussed in terms of the volume and quality of exchange, impacts on the authors and the book process, and issues in the design and implementation of a global network for group work.

The volume of communication exchanged on the GAN over the four-month period was high: over five hundred pages of text (125,000 words) were generated containing comments, questions, and critiques related to the chapters. This figure excludes the chapter contents, which constituted another two hundred and fifty pages of text. The volume of the exchange was double that of the book manuscript.

The high level of input throughout the sixteen-week period was somewhat unexpected given the voluntary nature of the task and the demanding professional and travel schedules that characterize the lives of contributors to the book. Participants communicated even while traveling, logging on from a hotel room using a laptop computer.

Most authors participated (i.e., both reading their group mail and contributing messages). The flows of discussion are presented in figure 21.1. The bar chart in figure 21.1 shows the weekly volume of communication on the GAN. The chapters were not presented in the book order, but primarily according to completion schedules. Week 1 was a general introduction, not chapter discussion.

There were ebbs and flows to the volume of discussion over the sixteen-week period of the principal GAN exchange. The total number of words indicates the combination of general interest in the chapter contents, participant availability (work and travel schedules) and, as discussed in the next section, host-author (moderator) proactive inspiration. A relationship between the level of input by the author/moderator and that of the discussants was suggested by the usage data.

Moderating

The author(s) of each chapter were asked to moderate the discussion of their draft manuscript over the period of one week. Moderating in-

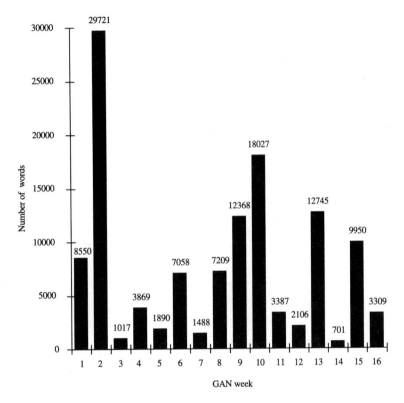

Figure 21.1
Communication volume on the GAN

volved launching the discussion with a brief statement of the goals of their chapter, followed by questions or issues that would help them in revising their chapter.

All authors complied and, despite their demanding work schedules, launched and concluded their discussion week in a timely fashion.

Moderators responded to each message and in some cases stimulated a discussion around common issues raised by discussants. The majority of the messages were focused on the issues in the chapter, but a few tangential discussions did emerge: a discussion on the definition of human community, on "flaming," and on the role of email in the Rodney King trial in Los Angeles that was then taking place.

Most of the weekly discussions suggest a relationship between the level of the author-moderator input and the level of GAN input into the discussion (see figure 21.2). Whether a causal relationship exists was not determined.

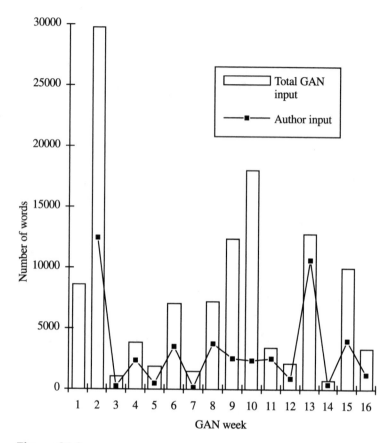

Figure 21.2
Relationship of author/moderator to total GAN output

Group Review

Feedback generated through the process of the GAN can be categorized as follows:

- Praise, interest, appreciation for the analysis
- Identification of common themes, different perspectives
- "I see links between my chapter and this one . . ."
- "I treat this same issue in my chapter, from a somewhat different perspective that examines . . ."
- Elaborations on themes in the chapter
- "My own experience . . ."

- Substantive critiques
- Disagreements
- Suggestions for new perspectives
- Identification of weaknesses in the argument
- Suggestions for new or additional content
- Suggested references
- Suggestions for corrections/stylistic improvements
- Vetting: seeking feedback on potential content or analysis
- Questions and requests for clarification
- Related tangents
- Informal social exchange

As would be expected, most commentators offered remarks from their own disciplinary or professional perspective. This produced the anticipated diversity of perspectives on each topic and also provided fuel for lively discussion, which the authors would consider in subsequent drafts and final revision of their chapters.

Most of the substantive discussion and nitpicking was offered and received in good humor, as illustrated in the following exchange:

>Well, you are sooooooo picky, indeed.

>I am wondering what's behind it. <grin>.

Well, as Eve said to Adam in the garden, "The snake made me do it!" But, speaking of the devil, you know how I do love to click into the old diablo advocati <smile>, I have also done my time as proofreader and editor, so that has had an effect.

Some comments, such as the following, were extremely helpful in providing a rallying point for a common definition of terms, such as "community," that tend otherwise to be used too loosely by committed telecommunicators:

Before we move on I'd like to suggest a brief definition of community. I think of community as essentially more than a utilitarian gathering to accomplish a task. Thus many groups are not communities in my sense. To qualify as a community a group must have solidarity plus history plus culture. By solidarity I mean sentimental bonds or identifications distinct from functional roles. By history I mean a shared past that plays a role in the group members' identity, not just in the time line of a task. By culture I mean shared codes that enable the members of the group to understand each other. Each of these elements, solidarity, history and culture may exist without the others, but only where all three come together do we find something we would want to call real community.

This motivated at least one author to devote more time and space than originally planned to matters of community, society, groups, mediated relationships, and goal achievement.

Impacts

The goals of the GAN were achieved: all the authors reported benefit from the network. The GAN helped to develop the book from chapters written by diverse authors into a more cohesive and interdependent whole, with a shared perspective on the topic and subtopics. The authors used the GAN to become familiar with the other chapters and contributors and to refine analysis and cross-referencing within the chapters. Participants reported that the GAN was valuable "in terms of understanding the work of fellow contributors and in structuring our own chapter." The GAN also was found to facilitate a process of interactive feedback, which enhanced the creative/analytical process and built a unity of vision in the book. The authors felt that the group review process "help[ed] us have a better sense of the topics and issues that others are addressing and encourage[d] the writers to think more globally about issues that are contained in other chapters." Since "a conference of people of diverse personal, professional, and network backgrounds can be a source of new ideas, styles, and professional and personal connections" authors found that they benefited from the exchange of perspectives and information gained on the network.

Electronic networking allowed for cost-effective exchange of information and sharing of views in collaborative endeavors. Participants noted that the GAN discussions had a valuable educational outcome: the exchange of perspectives introduced new ideas and viewpoints on the issues presented in the chapters.

I found the comments extremely helpful. My own strategy for revision was to copy the comments of the readers into the text of the paper at the appropriate place and then as I worked on the revision I had the comments in a written format. Once I dealt with them, I just deleted them. So personally I have [found] that my chapter is much improved as a result of the exchange.

Participation on the GAN contributed to building a unified vision of the book: "the discussion helped clarify several issues which were adapted into the final copy . . . and led to a shift in focus . . . to more of our global concerns and work."

The GAN exchange shaped not only the individual chapters but "served an extremely important role in helping us define the book as group."

Networking of authors in a time-constrained collaborative discussion of each others' draft chapters promoted a unified vision of the topic to a degree that would be very difficult if not impossible by nonelectronic mediation. No other medium could support the ongoing interaction and enable each participant to view comments from all others. The opportunity for reflection and thoughtful input that the asynchronicity provided was vital for such collaborative peer review.

Those authors unable to participate in the GAN could not reflect the unity of perspective evident in chapters of participating authors; the editor provided guidance on the themes and perspectives of the book and incorporated references to other chapters in the text. Moreover, the relationship of these authors to the book was subjectively different, since they did not have the extensive interaction with the authors of the other chapters nor the vision of the book as a whole.

Networking Technology

The choice of network technology for the GAN was viewed as significant and received comment. Many participants found the email mode awkward for the collaborative nature of the task.

I believe the use of mail permitted only some of the group to interact on a regular basis but for others it deterred participation . . . I receive some 100 plus mail messages per day because I regularly use CMC for teaching and research, and so [I] had to postpone large parts of GAN discussion due to immediacy of the other work.

Organizing the GAN messages was difficult. The lack of tools to organize messages available on systems such as computer conferencing systems or USENET newsgroups had a negative effect on participation for some authors.

I found that because of the mail use that many comments I ported to a file and did not give [them] as much attention to them as I would had they been in a conference for better access and response . . .

Yet for others, the use of email was facilitative.

I had no trouble with the e-mail arrangement and fear that if it were a conference, I would have been less likely to have read it as it would have been easier for me to have been too busy to turn to it. With it appearing with the rest of my work, I tried my best to make time.

The network format encouraged the participant to give some thought to each of the other chapters, even to those only remotely connected with her/his own area of special interest. Regular, unavoidable confrontation with coauthor perspectives contributes to what has been called *convergence* in a field of study known as *convergence theory,* which states that "if two or more individuals share information with one another, then over time they will tend to converge toward one another, leading to a state of greater uniformity" (Kincaid, 1988, 282). The implications for unifying perspectives between multiple authors are obvious.

On the other hand, by limiting focused discussion to one week for each draft chapter, the email format discouraged the kind of in-depth discussion that might emerge through multiple topic computer conferencing, wherein authors might naturally gravitate toward subtopics that were of special interest for in-depth discussion. The optimal solution likely lies not in "either/or", but in "both/and" strategies: it would not be implausible to have an email focus on one chapter each week, alongside multiple conference sections that would cater to the interests of subgroups among the authoring group. Or, as another participant suggested: "set up a reasonable network of connections of a mailing list into at least a USENET newsgroup, and probably into the conferencing systems of those who have favorite conferencing systems."

Design

We asked participants how they might reconstruct the GAN. Several suggestions were offered:

1. If financially feasible, a preliminary face-to-face meeting would be valuable—especially if participants did not know one another or hadn't worked together previously, and if the process was time-constrained. Such a meeting would help provide "the big picture" and enable people to connect with one another and with the spectrum of themes and perspectives—to help mentally organize the themes that emerged on the GAN.

2. Advance planning is essential. Implementing an online collaborative project requires extensive organizing of the networks, the agenda, and the anticipated workload on the individual participants. Estimating the workload is critical to participants with busy lives. Materials related to the technical and process activities need to be developed and distributed among participants. Substantive material, such as the book chapters, should be sent as far in advance as possible.

3. Select the networking technology that best fits the task and the user group. This can be a difficult decision, given such factors as accessibility, cost, and user preferences. Even while many authors in the GAN acknowledged that a conferencing system might be best suited to the task, selecting one specific system can be contentious. Users may not have the time nor the interest to learn a new system for a limited period. On the other hand, the potential benefits or specific demands of the task may warrant the effort of introducing a specific groupware tool for that period.

4. Design the group interaction: identify tasks, sequence, roles, and timelines. As one author observed: "the acts of authoring and of participating in an email exchange are quite different activities with their own peculiar behavioral requirements."

Various models are available: the sequential group review format used in the GAN; an online workshop (Harasim and Winkelman, 1990); a collaborative editing process in which authors have more editorial control over each other's chapter. A format based on the learning circle model was also proposed:

In the learning circle model, each of the writers would have sent their summaries at the beginning of the session and we would have posed a set of questions for each of the others to respond to. Each writer would have been responsible for sending at least one message for each of the authors reacting to their questions or chapter. The organizers (you guys) as circle coordinator would have created a matrix which would have included the chapters down one side and the authors initials across the top and x's to indicate that we have commented on someone's work. This would have been posted each week. In this way, you would see what you had accomplished and what you still needed to do. I would have [been] more inclined to return the favor of reading the chapter of someone who gave me comments as well as try to respond to everyone. This way all of the discussion would have run parallel with subject headers indicating the author and topic.

5. Provide moderating, whether by a specially designated facilitator or in a turn-taking model.

Prologue: Looking Ahead

The GAN experience offers a number of insights regarding how global networks of authors and educators might be used and developed most advantageously.

Selecting the network technology that best supports the required activity and group is key. Given the task, online exchange of manuscripts and mediating of group review, an asynchronous text-based medium is very appropriate. Asynchronicity enables the participation of people with different time schedules and in different time zones. Text-based communication supports considered response and can be archived for future reference.

Design of the interaction is equally key to effective collaboration. Specifically, how can we structure the benefits of holistic involvement offered to all coauthors by group email, while enjoying the equally important benefits of longer-term and more in-depth analysis and discussion of each separate chapter offered by the conferencing approach? The challenge may be seen as one of integrating the benefits of *synchronic* (dividing attention among several manuscripts at the same time) and *diachronic* (focusing attention on single manuscripts in a linear sequence over a period of time) approaches.

Group email offers the advantage of requiring all chapter authors to be involved in discussion of each other's manuscript, encouraging greater breadth of discussion than would likely occur if a smaller number of chapter authors participated in discussing only those topics that interested them most. Greater depth of discussion, however, is limited by the fact that each chapter is up for discussion only once and only for one week.

Diversity of perspectives is virtually required in group email discussion, thus encouraging each author to consider multidisciplinary angles on topics that might otherwise be seen only through the author's conventional discipline. Unity of vision is encouraged by the group email's requirement that all participants contribute and respond to the multidisciplinary discussions of issues raised in the book. These strengths and weaknesses may be visualized more graphically through a matrix (fig. 21.3).

The ideal global authoring network, as well as other forms of computer-mediated network collaboration of the future, will find ways to incorporate the advantages of both of the above modes. This may be

	Breadth of discussion	Depth of discussion	Diversity of perspectives	Unity of vision
Group email mode	Weekly chapter rotation encourages breadth	Some depth sacrificed in interest of holistic vision	All interests bring diversity of focus to each week's chapter	Group involvement in each chapter encourages unified vision
Conference mode	Limited in interest of in-depth discussions	Continual discussions develop depth	Interests tend to focus on different chapters	Limited in interest of in-depth discussions

Figure 21.3

done through using group email for discussing certain broader aspects of the collaborative project, while also maintaining separate conferences for each chapter or sub-heading of the collaborative project. Each chapter author would be encouraged to read and offer comments on each other's chapter-conference, with the understanding that each author will probably be more attracted to some chapter conferences than to others.

The unity of vision could be maintained by the editor, or an editorial group, reviewing and summarizing the salient points of each chapter conference and offering summary comments via the project group email each week. This would capture much of the benefit of everyone's involvement in every aspect of the discussion of everyone else's chapter without forcing information overload on colleagues who would rather keep control over the scheduling of their GAN work.

The GAN model and experience, or more likely a modified and improved version of it, can serve as a template for productive international, even intercultural, collaboration for mutual benefit, integrating a diversity of backgrounds, interests, and expertise into a synergistic whole, wherein the whole is truly greater than the mere sum of its parts.

We leave the last word to Shakespeare whose observation in *The Tempest* could well be heeded by global networkers of the late twentieth century.

what's past is prologue, what to come
In yours and my discharge.
—(Act II, Scene 1)

Appendix
A Sampler of Global Network Addresses

Chapter 1

To participate on the Internet, you must establish an account with a research or educational institution that connects to the Internet or subscribe to a network gateway such as UUNET (call (703) 204-8000), or CERFnet (call (619) 534-5087, (800) 876-2373, or send email to help@cerf.net). The WELL (see below) also provides Internet access.

To access BITNET, you must set up an account at a facility that is a member of BITNET. For further information, call the BITNET Network Information Center at (202) 872–4200.

To participate in FidoNet you must dial into a BBS that is part of the FidoNet. For the number of the host nearest you, call the Basic'ly Computers BBS at (604) 584-9811 and contact Bob Satti, the Zone 1 coordinator.

Chapter 4

To join the WELL, TELNET well.sf.ca.us or dialup (415) 332-6106 and follow the signup procedures, or call (415) 332-4335 and talk to a human. Rates are $15/mo plus $2/hr.

Chapter 13

For more information on the AT&T Learning Network, write P.O. Box 6391, Parsippany, New Jersey 07054-7391, or call, USA:1-800-367-7225 ext. 4158; Canada: 1-800-567-4671; United Kingdom: 44 071-

537-4115; Europe/Middle East: 322 676-3576; Hong Kong: 852 846-2800; Japan: 03-5561-3411; Australia: 02 256-6000.

Chapter 14

To join BESTNET, send a message to bestnet@bestsd.sdsu.edu. For an institution to be affiliated, the cost of membership is based on what value-added services they can provide to others on the network. To be an institutional member, one needs to run VMS on a VAX to be a distributed node, but affiliation is also possible by telneting into BEST-NET.

Chapter 15

TWICS
International Education Center
1-21 Yotsuya, Shinjuku-ku, Tokyo 160 JAPAN
tel: +81.3.3351.5997
fax: +81.3.3353.6096
Internet: twics@twics.co.jp

Chapter 17

Member networks of the Association for Progressive Communications:

AlterNex, IBASE
Rua Vicente de Souza 29
22251-070 Rio de Janeiro
BRAZIL
Tel: +55-21-286-0348
Fax: +55-21-286-0541
email: suporte@ax.apc.org
(serves Brazil, South America)

APC International Secretariat,
c/o IBASE
Rua Vicente de Souza 29
22251-070 Rio de Janeiro

BRASIL
Tel: +55-21-286-4467
Fax: +55-21-286-0541
email: apcadmin@apc.org

Chasque, Instituto del Tercer
Mundo
Casilla Correo 1539
Montevideo 11000
URUGUAY
Tel: +598-2-496192
Fax: +598-2-419222
email: apoyo@chasque.apc.org
(serves Uruguay)

ComLink
Moorkamp 46
D(w)-3000 Hannover 1
GERMANY
Tel: +49-511-350-3081
email: support@oln.com-
link.apc.org
(serves Germany, Austria, Switzer-
land, North Italy, Ex-Yugoslavia)

EcuaNex Intercom
Casilla 17-03-596
Quito
ECUADOR
Tel: +593-2-505-074
Fax: +593-2-580-835
email: intercom@ecuanex.ec
(serves Ecuador)

GlasNet
Ulitsa Yaroslavaskaya 8
Korpus 3, Komnata 111
129164 Moscow
RUSSIA
Tel: +7-095-217-6182
     +7-095–262–7079
email: support@glas.apc.org
(serves Russia, Commonwealth
of Independent States countries)

GreenNet
23 Bevenden Street
London N1 6BH
ENGLAND
Tel: +44-71-608-3040
Fax: +44-71-253-0801
email: support@gn.apc.org
(serves Great Britain, Western
Europe, Africa, Asia

Institute for Global Communica-
tions
(PeaceNet, EcoNet, ConflictNet,
LaborNet)
18 de Boom Street
San Francisco, CA 94107
USA
Tel: +1-415-442-0220
Fax: +1-415-546-1794
email: support@igc.apc.org
(serves United States, Mexico)

Nicarao, CRIES
Apartado 3516, Iglesia Carmen
1 cuadra al lago, Managua
NICARAGUA
Tel: +505-2-26228
Fax: +505-2-26180
email: support@nicarao.apc.org
(serves Nicaragua, Central America)

NordNet
Huvudskaersvaegen 13, nb
S-121 54 Johanneshov
SWEDEN
Tel: +46-8-600-0331
Fax: +46-8-600-0443
email: support@pns.apc.org
(serves Scandinavia, Baltic States)

Pegasus Networks
PO Box 284, Broadway
Brisbane, Queensland 4006
AUSTRALIA
Tel: +61 7 257 1111
Fax: +61 7 257 1087
email: support@peg.apc.org
(serves Australia, South Pacific,
Southeast Asia)

Web, Nirv Centre
401 Richmond St., Suite 104
Toronto, Ontario, M5V 3A8
CANADA
Tel: +1-416-596-0212
Fax: +1-416-596-1374
email: spider@web.apc.org
(serves Canada)

Chapter 21

Comserve can be accessed from any computer that can send and receive email over BITNET and Internet. Comserve can be contacted at either of the following addresses: Comserve@Rpitsvm (BITNET) and Comserve@vm.its.rpi.edu (Internet). To get started with Comserve, send a message with only the word HELP in the body.

Contributors

Linda M. Harasim

is associate professor, Department of Communication, Simon Fraser University in British Columbia, Canada. She holds a Ph.D. in educational theory from the University of Toronto and has been active for the past decade researching educational and organizational applications of computer networking. She has designed, implemented, and evaluated networking applications in Canada, the United States, and Latin America and was the organizer of the Global Authoring Network, which linked contributors for this book. She edited *Online Education: Perspectives on a New Environment* (Praeger, 1990) and, together with coauthors Starr Roxanne Hiltz, Lucio Teles, and Murray Turoff, is about to publish *Learning Networks: A Field Guide* (MIT Press, 1994). She has published many articles on computer communications and has presented her research at numerous international meetings. She conducts most of her teaching and her project work online, on various global networks.

Izumi Aizu

has a long experience in people-to-people communications and international marketing. As secretary general of the Networking Forum, he has promoted PC networking in Japan from its early stages. He is now committed to the establishment of a new research institute, the Institute for Hypernetwork Society, with Shumpei Kumon. He is a member of study groups on computer networks for a number of government ministries including MITI (Ministry of International Trade and Industry) and MPT (Ministry of Post and Telecommunication).

Armando Arias, Jr.

is dean of the College of Arts and Sciences at Texas A&M University-Kingsville and cofounder of BESTNET. BESTNET conducts an ongoing research program concerning the higher education application of computer con- ferencing and related technologies in the areas of instruction, interinstitutional cooperation, research, institutional service, and administration.

Beryl Bellman

received his B.A. and M.A. degrees in anthropology from the University of California at Los Angeles and his Ph.D. in social sciences from the University of California at Irvine. He is a professor of communication studies at the California State University at Los Angeles. He has conducted extensive cross-cultural and intercultural communications research in Africa and Latin America, which has resulted in the publication of three books and over two dozen essays. Dr. Bellman is a cofounder of BESTNET and has published extensively and presented numerous scholarly papers on computer communications and related technologies. He also frequently consults for various international and governmental agencies on communications, education, and intercultural issues.

Anne Wells Branscomb

is a legal scholar specializing in communications, computer, and intellectual property law. She is president of the Raven Group, a consulting firm specializing in strategic planning and policy analysis for high-technology firms. She is also a research affiliate of the Harvard University Law School and Program on Information Resource Policies. Her academic achievements have included appointments as adjunct professor of international law at the Fletcher School of Law and Diplomacy of Tufts University and adjunct professor of international telecommunications law at the Polytechnic Institute of New York.

Andrew Feenberg

is professor of philosophy at San Diego State University. He is the author of *Critical Theory of Technology,* and *Lukacs, Marx and the Sources of Critical Theory* (both with Oxford University Press), as well as numerous articles on philosophy of technology and social thought.

Howard Frederick

is author of *Global Communication and International Relations* (Wadsworth, 1993) and *Cuban-American Radio Wars* (Ablex, 1986). He is president of the international communication section of the International Association for Mass Communication Research (IAMCR) and the former director of PeaceNet, the world's largest computer network dedicated solely to human rights and peace. He currently teaches in the Department of Politics and Society, University of California, Irvine.

Hiroshi Ishii

joined NTT Yokosuka Electrical Communications Laboratories in 1980. He is currently a senior research engineer of NTT Human Interface Laboratories. He teaches human-computer interaction (HCI) at Chiba University. Since 1985 he has conducted research on computer-supported cooperative work (CSCW) and groupware design. His research interests focus on human-computer interaction, multimedia shared workspace design for realtime and asynchronous collaboration, structured groupware design based on human communication models, and the role of CSCW technologies in cross-cultural communication. He has a number of publications in the *Communications of the ACM* (CACM).

Robert Jacobson

is president and chief executive officer of WORLDESIGN, Inc., an information design firm specializing in the design and construction of virtual environments in industrial settings. Formerly associate director of the Human Interface Technology Laboratory at the University of Washington, Dr. Jacobson has maintained a long scholarly interest in the design of humane information environments.

Mitchell Kapor

received his B.A. from Yale College in 1971, holds a master's degree in psychology, and has studied management at MIT's Sloan School. He is the cofounder and chairman of the Electronic Frontier Foundation. Previously, he founded Lotus Development Corporation and served as its chief executive officer, president, and chairman. He is the designer of Lotus 1–2–3, Agenda, and many other software applications. Currently, he serves as chairman of ON Technology, Inc. of Cambridge, Massachusetts. He is the chairman of Commercial Internet Exchange (CIX) and serves on the Computer Science and Telecommunications Board of the National Research Council. He is an adjunct research fellow at Harvard's Kennedy School of Government in the area of information technology policy.

Sara Kiesler

completed a Ph.D. in social psychology at Ohio State University in 1965. In 1979 she joined the faculty of Carnegie Mellon University, where she is a professor of social and decision sciences and social psychology, as well as a member of the university's robotics institute. She has participated in national policy committees on the social implications of technology and written extensively on this topic.

Michael Kirby

is president of the New South Wales Court of Appeal. Between 1975 and 1984, the Honorable Justice Kirby was the first chairman of the Australian Law Reform Commission. From 1978 to 1980 he chaired an OECD Expert Group on Transborder Data Barriers and the Protection of Privacy. This produced the *OECD Guidelines on Privacy*, which were adopted by the Council of the OECD. The guidelines have been widely influential, including in the Australian Federal Privacy Act. Since 1991 he has been chairing the OECD Expert Group on Security of Information Systems. He holds many other international posts including chairman of the Executive Committee of the International Commission of Jurists, Geneva.

Shumpei Kumon

completed his B.A. and M.A. degrees in economics at Tokyo University. He attained a Ph.D. degree in economics at the Russian and East-European Institute, Indiana University. He translated a couple of Kenneth Boulding's books into Japanese and published books on social systems theory, international systems, and the network society. He coedited, with Henry Rosovsky, *The Political Economy of Japan, Vol. 3, Cultural and Social Dynamics* (Stanford University Press, 1992). Currently he is a professor and researcher in the Center for Global Communications (GLOCOM) at International University of Japan.

Marvin Manheim

is the William A. Patterson Distinguished Professor of Transportation at the J. L. Kellogg Graduate School of Management, Northwestern University. Previously, he founded and headed the transportation systems program at MIT, where he taught for nineteen years. His B.S. and Ph.D. degrees are from MIT. He teaches, does research, and consults on competitive strategy and the strategic uses of information technology, on globalization and strategic change in organizations, and on new forms of information systems such as team support and intelligent agents. Professor Manheim has lectured and consulted in more than fifteen countries, published over 130 papers and reports, lead the development of two major federal government regulations, and written or edited four books, including a well-known transportation textbook.

Robin Mason

is a lecturer in computer-supported cooperative learning at the Open University, U.K., supporting and evaluating the university's use of computer conferencing in mass distance education. Her research involves the integration of computer conferencing with other teaching media such as audio, audiographics, and video.

Catherine Murray

is associate professor in the Department of Communication at Simon Fraser University, teaching telecommunications policy and regulation. She is a frequent expert witness in the area of public demand for and valuation of new information services in the Canadian regulatory arena. Prior to joining Simon Fraser, she was vice-president of telecommunications for Decima Research, a consulting company in the field of public opinion and market research.

John Quarterman

is editor of *Matrix News,* a monthly newsletter about contextual issues crossing network, geographic, and political boundaries, and is secretary of Matrix Information and Directory Services, Inc., of Austin. He is the author of "Notable Computer Networks," (*CACM,* October 1986) and *The Matrix* (Digital Press, 1990). He is also a partner in Texas Internet Consulting, which consults in networks and open systems, with particular emphasis on TCP/IP networks, UNIX systems, and standards.

Howard Rheingold

is the author of *Virtual Reality* (Summit, 1992), *Tools For Thought* (Simon & Schuster, 1985), and several other books about technology, culture, and the human mind. He is the editor of *Whole Earth Review.* He is working on a book for Addison-Wesley about "virtual communities," for late 1993 publication.

Margaret Riel

is an educational researcher who has developed and assessed educational programs through telecommunications. She works with AT&T to design the educational structure and write the curriculum guides for electronic "learning circles" on the AT&T Learning Network. She also provides online training and direction to the circle and mentor coordinators on the AT&T Learning Network.

Jeffrey Shapard

is from Montana via Tokyo, where he lived and worked for over a decade. He trained in language and linguistics, with a B.A. in English from the University of Montana and an M.A. in linguistics from the University of Oregon. He became involved in electronic networking in 1984 in Japan and then developed and operated the TWICS system and service until 1992 when he returned to the United States for graduate studies in business at the University of California in Berkeley. He is a longtime "connect-activist" and global networker.

Lee Sproull

has spent more than a decade studying established electronic mail communities to learn about how they change patterns of communication within organizations. She received a Ph.D. in social science from Stanford University in 1977. Until 1992 she was a professor of social sciences and sociology at Carnegie Mellon University. She is now a professor of management at Boston University. She has written extensively about information behavior in organizations and social analyses of computing.

Lucio Teles

has his B.A. in sociology from the Johan Wolfgang Goethe University, Frankfurt, Germany, an M.A. in international development from the University of Geneva, and a Ph.D. in computer applications in education from the University of Toronto. He has conducted research on the use of computer networking to enhance classroom learning and professional development. Currently he works on the design and implementation of multimedia environments as manager, instructional computing, at the Open Learning Agency in British Columbia, Canada.

Alex Tindimubona

is program officer for the African Academy of Sciences in Nairobi, Kenya, and is editor of their scientific journal. He received his doctorate in chemistry from the University of British Columbia; prior to his current position he was a member of the chemistry faculty at the University of Nairobi. He is also involved in the development of AFRINET.

Jan Walls

completed his B.A., M.A., and Ph.D. degrees in Chinese and Japanese languages and literatures at Indiana University. He has published translations and studies of poetry and poets, presented papers and public lectures on cross-cultural communication, and continues to pursue ongoing research into the ways that differences in life experience, language structure, and cultural values impede interpersonal and intercultural communication. Currently he is a professor in the Department of Communication and director of the David Lam Centre for International Communication at Simon Fraser University.

Daniel Weitzner

is an attorney in the Washington office of the Electronic Frontier Foundation, where he is involved in a range of communications and information policy issues including infrastructure policy as well as free speech and privacy problems raised by new communications technologies. Previously he was a policy analyst at the American Civil Liberties Union Information Technology Project. Mr. Weitzner has a J.D. from Buffalo Law School and a B.A. in philosophy from Swarthmore College.

Notes

Chapter 2   *Networlds: Networks as Social Space*
Linda M. Harasim

1. A student describes her experience in an educational computer conference.

2. Akira Shinjo, cited in B. Schepp and D. Schepp, *The complete guide to CompuServe,* New York: Osborne McGraw-Hill, (1990) 12.

Chapter 3   *The Global Matrix of Minds*
John S. Quarterman

This book chapter is adapted and expanded from two articles in the newsletter *Matrix News* (Quarterman, 1991a; 1991b). For more information, send mail to mids@tic.com.

Chapter 5   *Jurisdictional Quandaries for Global Networks*
Anne Wells Branscomb

1. The word "cyberspace" originates from science fiction for the virtual world in which some "cyberpunks," or people addicted to computers, operated. The term has been more recently adopted by John Barlow to mean the electronic frontiers of computer networks.

2. Donald Ronstadt, "Cyberocracy, Cyberspace, and Cyberology: Political Effects of the Information Revolution," Rand, P-7745, (1991):77.

3. Statement in the first Ithiel de Sola Pool commemorative lecture at the Massachusetts Institute of Technology, October 1990.

4. Citation from *Harper's* magazine, April 1990.

5. From Robert S. Boyd, "Computers chip away at privacy," *The Chicago Tribune,* July 4, 1990, 1.

6. For an excellent analysis of these variances with respect to Financial Services, see Joel R. Reidenberg, "The Privacy Obstacle Course: Hurdling Barriers to Transnational Financial Barriers," *Fordham Law Review,* 56(6) May 1992.

7. See Fair Credit Billing Act, 15 U.S.C. Sec. 1666 (1988); Fair Credit Reporting Act, 15 U.S.C. Sec. 1681(1988); Fair Debt Collections Practices Act, 15 U.S.C. Sec. 1692 (1988) and Electronic Funds Transfer Act Sec. 1693 (1988).

8. OECD, "Recommendation of the Council Concerning Guidelines Governing the Protection of Privacy and Transborder Flows of Personal Data, OECD Document (C 58 Final) October 1, 1980.

9. Council of Europe, "Convention for the Protection of Individuals with Regard to Automatic Processing of Personal Data," January 18, 1981, European Treaty Series no. 108.

10. "First UK Ban on Data Exports is to Named Companies in the USA," *Privacy Law and Business,* Winter 1990/91, 5.

11. Vienna Convention on Diplomatic Relations, April 18, 1961, Arts. XXVII, XXIX 23 U.S.T. 3227, 3239, 3240, 500 U.N.T.S. 95, 108, 110.

12. 18 U.S. C.A. Sec. 2511 (3) repealed by Foreign Intelligence Surveillance Act of 1978, Pub. L. 95–511, 92 Stat. 1797 (1978), replaced by Exec. Order No. 12,333, 46 Fed. Reg. 59,941, (Sec. 2.5) December 8, 1981.

13. The International Telegraph Convention of Paris, May 17, 1965, 9 Recueil des Traites de la France 254.

14. Electronic Communications Privacy Act of 1986 (PL 99–508).

15. R. T. Piernchiak, "White Supremacists See Computers as Revolutionary Key," AP March 3, 1985, via NEXIS; S. Green, "Neo Nazis go High-Tech," UPI, March 9, 1985, via NEXIS.

16. United States v. Bank of Nova Scotia, 69 F. 2d 1184 (11th Cir. 1982); 740 F.2d 817 (11th Cir. 1984), 84–2 U.S. Tax Cas. (CCH) P9802; The logic of the court was that "the confidentiality laws of the Cayman Islands should not be used as a blanket to encourage or foster criminal activities . . . and even if the Cayman Islands had an absolute right to privacy" which it could bestow upon its own citizens "this right could not fully apply to American citizens," who could not be insulated against a criminal investigation since they are required to report such financial transactions as were in question pursuant to 31 U.S.C. Sec. 11221 and 31 C.F.R. Sec. 103.24 (1979). The court also relied upon the fact that the disclosure was to a grand jury investigation in itself a privileged and confidential proceeding. See also J. T. Burnett, "Information, Banking Law and Extraterritoriality," *Transnational Data and Communications Report,* January 1986, 17–18.

17. Dow Jones News Document, 860404-400, *Wall Street Journal,* April 4, 1986, 10.

18. On November 4, 1979, Iranian militants occupied the U.S. embassy in Tehran and took hostages. As one response to this indignity, President Carter declared a national emergency and froze all Iranian assets subject to the jurisdiction of the

United States. Pursuant to this authority, the Secretary of the Treasury promulgated Iranian Assets Control Regulations, 31 C.F.R. Sec. 535.101-904 (1979). Numerous cases were filed by claimants to these assets—see, for example, Malek-Marzban v. U.S., 653 F. 2d 1213 (4th Cir. 1981); Itel Corp. v. M/S Victoria U (Ex Pishtaz Iran) 710 F.2d 199 (5th Cir. 1983); Behring International Inc. v. Imperial Iranian Airforce et al., 712 F.2d 45 (3d Cir. 1983), 36 Fed. R. Serv. 2d (Callaghan) 391.

19. D. Tweedale, "U.S. Businessmen Complain about Sanctions against Panama," UPI, April 15, 1988, BC Cycle via NEXIS.

20. After the Soviet Union placed Poland under martial law, the U.S. government attempted to disrupt the construction of the Soviet gas pipeline from Siberia to Western Europe by placing an embargo on U.S. originated products and technology. This affected Dresser Industries, which relied upon data in the United States.

21. *Transnational Data Report,* February 1987, 7.

22. "Hacking" is a word originally intended as a compliment meaning a highly skilled and ingenious computer scientist. More recently it has been popularized by journalists to mean unscrupulous individuals who use their skills with computers to wreak havoc upon networks and databases. "Cyberpunks" or "crackers" are more acceptable words to describe transgressors who roam the electronic corners of cyberspace, exploring its frontiers and disregarding no trespassing signs.

23. The Computer Fraud and Abuse Act of 1986 (PL 99-474) covers only federal and interstate computer crimes, making it a federal misdemeanor to trespass intentionally to read or obtain data and a felony to access computers to destroy or alter computer data.

24. A tortfeasor is one who commits an actionable offense or civil wrongdoing for which compensation for damages incurred may be achieved through the courts. According to Black's law dictionary, a tort is "a legal wrong committed upon the person or property independent of contract."

25. Simon L. Garfinkel, "Computer Network Users Attempt a Mutiny," *The Christian Science Monitor,"* December 5, 1990, S&T Section, 12.

26. Cubby, Inc. v. CompuServe, Inc, 776 F. Supp. 135, 1991 U.S. Dist. LEXIS 15545; 19 Media L. Rep. 1525 (1991).

27. This amendment was first proposed by Professor Lawrence Tribe of the Harvard University Law School at a conference held in California, March 1991, organized by the Computer Professionals for Social Responsibility.

28. NAACP v. Alabama, 357 U.S. 449 (1958); Thornburgh v. American College of Obstetricians, 106 Sup. Ct. 2169 (1986); but see Buckley v. Valeo, 424 U.S. 1 at 71-72 (1976) requiring disclosure of the names of contributors to campaign committees.

29. "Computer as a Forum of Hate Poses Problem," *Los Angeles Times,* November 16, 1991, F13.

30. "UNCTAD Meeting on Technology Transfer Fails to Reach Agreement on Code of Conduct," BNA, Inc. Daily Report for Executives, June 7, 1985, DER no. 10, L-8.

Chapter 6   *Computers, Networks, and Work*
Lee Sproull and Sara Kiesler

This chapter appeared in *Scientific American*, vol. 265, September 1991. The chapter is published with the permission of Scientific American, Inc.

Chapter 7   *Integrating Global Organizations through Task/Team Support Systems*
Marvin Manheim

This chapter is an adaptation and extension of Manheim, 1992.

Chapter 8   *Cross-Cultural Communication and CSCW*
Hiroshi Ishii

A previous version of this manuscript appeared in *Whole Earth Review* (no. 69, Winter 1990) edited by Howard Rheingold (Ishii, 1990b). This chapter is published with the permission of *Whole Earth Review.*

1. The term "Computer-Supported Cooperative Work" (CSCW) was coined by Paul Cashman and Irene Greif in 1984 when they decided to use the term for a workshop they were running. CSCW is rooted in the pioneering work of Doug Engelbart of "augmenting human intellect," the explorations in the use of computer conferencing and computer networks (Engelbart, 1963).

Chapter 10   *Information Security: At Risk?*
Michael Kirby and Catherine Murray

1. United States, National Research Council, *Computers at Risk: Safe Computing in the Information Age,* National Academy Press, 1991, 7.

2. Japan Information Processing Development Center, Final Announcement of Symposium, Tokyo, October 1991, 3.

3. See, for example, the special issue of "Communications, Computers and Networks," *Scientific American* (September 1991), especially, V. G. Cerf, "Networks," 72.

4. See M. D. Kirby, "Information Security—OECD Initiatives," a paper delivered to the International Symposium on Information Security, Tokyo, October 1991. Reprinted in *The Computer Law and Security Report,* 8 (June 1992):102–110.

5. Liability of air carriers for losses to passengers and cargo as set out in the Warsaw Convention has totally failed to keep pace with inflation and the exponential expansion of international air travel. Despite attempts by various countries to ratify amending protocols to the Warsaw convention, no consensus in international reform has emerged. People who suffer loss to passengers and cargo are virtually forced to sue in the courts, seeking to circumvent the convention's arbitrary cap on recovery by proving willful recklessness. Families of victims of the Pan Am accident in Bali in 1974, and of the Korean Airlines or Lockerbie disasters are still waiting for settlement.

6. Universal Declaration of Human Rights, art. 12.

7. See Articles 8 and 17 respectively.

8. For a fuller discussion, see M. D. Kirby, "Legal Aspects of Informatics and Transborder Data Flows" in G. L. Hughes (1990) *Essays on Computer Law* (Melbourne, Australia: Longman Professional).

9. OECD *Guidelines on the Protection of Privacy and Transborder Flows of Personal Data,* Paris, 1981.

10. A double dissolution is the means provided by the Australian constitution, s 57, for resolving differences between the House of Representatives and the Senate. Where the Senate rejects or fails to pass a measure, the Governor-General may dissolve both houses simultaneously. Upon resumption, if necessary, there may be a Joint Sitting which, if it carries the disputed measure, will give it authority of law. The procedure has only been used once (1974).

11. Masao Horibe, "Access to Information Held by the State and Privacy in Japan," (paper for the XIII International Congress of Comparative Law, Montreal, August 1990, mimeo).

12. Ibid., 15.

13. The plaintiff recovered most of the requested damages of Y800,000 in the Tokyo District Court. See Horibe, ibid., 15.

14. Ibid., 17.

15. Ibid., 19.

16. Ibid., 22.

17. Ibid., 22.

18. M. D. Kirby, "Legal Aspects of Informatics and Transborder Data Flows" in G. L. Hughes (1990) *Essays on Computer Law* (Melbourne, Australia: Longman Professional).

19. Council of Europe, European Committee on Crime Problems, *Computer-Related Crime* (Strasbourg: 1990) 14.

20. Ibid., 15.

21. Ibid., 16.

22. Ibid., 17.

23. Organization for Economic Cooperation and Development, ICCP Report No. 10, *Computer-related Crime: Analysis of Legal Policy* (Paris: 1986).

24. See Council decision, 26 July 1988; O J No. C 288, 21 October 1988.

25. Ibid., 60.

26. Ibid., 83.

27. See M. D. Kirby, "Toronto Statement on the International Legal Vulnerability of Financial Information," (1990–91) 3 *Computer Law and Security Report,* 2.

28. Ibid. See also L. J. Hoffman, ed. *Rogue Programs: Viruses, Worms and Trojan Horses*, (New York: Van Nostrand Reinhold, 1990) 61.

29. See M. D. Kirby, "Toronto Statement on the International Legal Vulnerability of Financial Information," (1990–91) 3 *Computer Law and Security Report*, 2.

30. See International Standards Organization (ISO), "Security Architecture," Part II in *Information Processing Systems: Open System Interconnection: Basic Reference Model ISO-7498-2* (New York: American National Standards Institute, 1989).

31. Compare D. B. Parker, "Restating the Foundation of Information Security," confidential note (Applied Research Note 11—Revised).

32. OECD, Press Release (CSG/Press 91, 31, Paris, 5 June 1991) 1, 2, 4, 7, 20.

33. European Communities Council, Working Party on Economic Questions (Data Protection), "Outcome of Proceedings," (Brussels, 29 July 1991, mimeo).

34. Ibid., 2.

35. Ibid., 3.

36. National Council Report (n 1, above).

37. Ibid., 3.

38. "Current State of Computer Security-Related Policies and Measures," a document provided by the delegation of Japan to the OECD Expert Group (1991) 7.

Chapter 11   *Building a Global Network: The WBSI Experience*
Andrew Feenberg

1. For an analysis of that instance, see Feenberg (1992).

2. The Western Behavioral Sciences Institute was founded in 1958 as a nonprofit educational and research foundation in La Jolla, California. In the 1960s, while Carl Rogers was there, the institute became well known for its work on encounter groups, but when I joined the staff in 1981, not much remained to remind one of this early history; WBSI was seeking a completely new direction. For more on WBSI, see Farson (1989/90) and Rowan (1983) and (1986).

3. The predominance of English has something to do with the fact that WBSI was an American institution, but still more to do with the American dominance of international communications and business. After all, English serves as a universal medium because it is so widely spoken. However, under special circumstances, it is possible to arrange things more equitably. For example, in 1987 I taught an online course for the CELSA at the University of Paris that enrolled students from France, French-Canadians, and English-speaking Canadians. Each contributed in his or her own language; we were treated to a remarkable mixing of styles of writing and thinking.

4. This wider social significance of this clash of cultures is discussed in Feenberg (1991, chap. 5).

Chapter 14   **Technology Transfer in Global Networking**
Beryl Bellman, Alex Tindimubona, and Armando Arias, Jr.

1. This project stems from a series of meetings sponsored by Digital Equipment Corporation for the global extension of BESTNET into Africa. These meetings involved representatives from the National Science Foundation (NSFNET division), National Academy of Sciences, American Association for the Advancement of Science, the World Bank, Agricultural Cooperatives Development International, USAID, the African Development Foundation, and the California State University system. These representatives met with representatives from several organizations internal to Digital who support this effort. As a result of those meetings, it was decided that the African Academy of Sciences was the appropriate African organization with which to work and that the California State University and BESTNET should codevelop proposals with them to establish an African computer communications network and integrate it with the already functioning BESTNET project.

The African Academy of Sciences is a continentwide, nongovernmental, nonpolitical, and nonprofit organization of senior scientists, science policy experts, and science managers with its secretariat in Nairobi, Kenya. Started in 1985, it is dedicated to the promotion of science and technology for development. It does this through a vigorous program of activities spanning mobilization and strengthening of the African scientific community; networking; publication and dissemination of scientific materials; policy research; and capacity building in science and technology.

Chapter 17   **Networks and Emergence of Global Civil Society**
Howard Frederick

1. There are more than one hundred news agencies around the world, yet five transnational news agencies controlled about 96 percent of the world's news flows.

Words per Day of Major News Agencies, 1986–87 (Millions)

17,000	Associated Press (AP)
14,000	United Press International (UPI)
4,000	TASS
1,500	Reuters
1,000	Agence France Presse (AFP)
.500	EFE (Spain)
.300	Agenzia Nazionale Stampa Associata (Italy)
.115	Deutsche Presse Agentur (Germany)
.150	Inter Press Service (Rome, New York)
.100	Non-Aligned News Pool
.075	Telegrafska Agencia Nova Jugoslavya (Tanjug)
.025	Caribbean News Agency
.020	Pan-African News Agency
.018	Gulf News Agency

See Mowlana (1986: 28); International Journalism Institute (1987: 40); UNESCO (1989: 136–141).

Chapter 18   *Social and Industrial Policy for Public Networks*
                  Mitchell Kapor and Daniel Weitzner

1. The Electronic Frontier Foundation (EFF) is a nonprofit advocacy and educational organization established by Mitchell Kapor and John Perry Barlow. Mitchell Kapor is the chairman of EFF and Jerry Berman, an attorney and former head of the ACLU Information Technology Project, is the executive director of the Electronic Frontier Foundation's Washington Office. The EFF board includes John Perry Barlow, John Gilmore, Stewart Brand, Esther Dyson, and David Farber.

2. Professor Eli Noam has said: "Common carriage is the practical analog to [the] First Amendment for electronic speech over privately-owned networks, where the First Amendment does not necessarily govern directly." E. Noam, "The FCC as the National Systems-Integrator: The New Paradigm for the 90s," statement before the FCC Hearing: "Networks of the Future: Policy Implications—Challenges and Risks," May 1, 1991.

3. In 1991, the U.S. Congress passed a law creating the National Research and Education Network (NREN). See the High-Performance Computing Act (HPCA), Pub. L. No. 102–194, 105 Stat. 1594 (1991).

4. HPCA, Sec. 102(c)(4).

Chapter 19   *Co-Emulation: A Global Hypernetwork Society*
                  Shumpei Kumon and Izumi Aizu

1. The social game is a competitive game in which participants (social actors) compete for conventional prizes (say, prestige or wealth) by conventional means (say, following rules of international law, or civil/commercial codes).

2. Keiretsu-type organizations are business (economic, financial, or industrial) groups in postwar Japan (Abegglen and Stalk, 1985, 162). Keiretsu are networks of companies usually allied around major banks or trading companies. These alliances are linked by cross-shareholdings, common banking affiliations, and the use of the same trading company to procure raw materials and to distribute products (Prestowitz, 1988, 157). Imai (1992) argues that, as informatization of industry proceeds, Keiretsu will further evolve into a looser group called industrial networks.

3. A video of Apple's vision of computer networks in the year 2015.

4. "Ie" is a Japanese word usually meaning house and/or family, but it also means highly integrated and cohesive social groups with a high degree of self-sufficiency. Members of an Ie, particularly a large Ie, although they do not have any direct blood relation, usually describe their status and roles in the organization in terms of blood relations such as "parent" and "children." Concrete examples of Ie are Daimyo (feudal lords and warriors) and today's large Japanese firms.

References

Chapter 1   *Global Networks: An Introduction*
Linda M. Harasim

Clarke, A. C. (1992). *How the world was one: Beyond the global village*. New York: Bantam Books.

Gibson, W. (1984). *Neuromancer.* New York: Ace Books.

Chapter 2   *Networlds: Networks as Social Space*
Linda M. Harasim

Benedikt, M., ed. (1991). *Cyberspace: First steps*. Cambridge, MA: MIT Press.

Bikson, T. K., and Eveland, J. D. (1990). The interplay of work group structures and computer support. In J. Galegher, R. E. Kraut, and C. Egido, eds. *Intellectual teamwork: Social and technological foundations of cooperative work*. Hillsdale, NJ: Lawrence Erlbaum Associates.

Feenberg, A. (1991). *Critical theory of technology*. New York: University of Oxford Press.

Finholt, T., Sproull, L., and Kiesler, S. (1990). Communication and performance in ad hoc task groups. In J. Galegher, R.E. Kraut, and C. Egido, eds. *Intellectual teamwork: Social and technological foundations of cooperative work*. Hillsdale, NJ: Lawrence Erlbaum Associates.

Galegher, J., and Kraut, R. E. (1990). Technology for intellectual teamwork: Perspectives for research and design. In J. Galegher, R. E. Kraut, and C. Egido, eds. *Intellectual teamwork: Social and technological foundations of cooperative work*. Hillsdale, NJ: Lawrence Erlbaum Associates.

Galegher, J., Kraut, R. E., and Egido, C., eds. (1990). *Intellectual teamwork: Social and technological foundations of cooperative work*. Hillsdale, NJ: Lawrence Erlbaum Associates.

Greif, I. (1988). Overview. In I. Greif, ed. *Computer-supported cooperative work: A book of readings*. San Mateo, CA: Morgan Kaufmann Publishers.

Harasim, L. (1987). Computer-mediated cooperation in education: Group learning networks. *Second Symposium on Computer Conferencing and Allied Technologies*. University of Guelph, 171–186.

Harasim, L. (1989). Online education: A new domain. In R. Mason and T. Kaye, eds. *Mindweave: Computers, communications and distance education*. Oxford: Pergamon Press.

Harasim, L. (1990). Online education: An environment for collaboration and intellectual amplification. In L. Harasim, ed. *Online education: Perspectives on a new environment*. New York: Praeger Publishers.

Harasim, L. (1991). Designs and tools to augment collaboration in computerized conferencing systems. In J. Nunamaker, and R. Sprague, eds. *Proceedings of the Hawaiian International Conference on Systems Science, Vol. IV, Organizational Systems and Technology Track*.

Harasim, L., Hiltz, S. R., Teles, L., and Turoff, M. (1994). *Learning Networks: A Field Guide*. Cambridge, MA: MIT Press. Forthcoming.

Hiltz, S. R. (1984). *Online communities: A case study of the office of the future*. Norwood, NJ: Ablex Publishers.

Kiesler, S., Siegel, J., and McGuire, T. W. (1991). Social psychological aspects of computer-mediated communication. In C. Dunlop and R. Kling, eds. *Computerization and controversy: Value conflicts and social choices*. San Diego: Academic Press.

Kraut, R. E., Galegher, J., and Egido, C. (1988). Relationships and tasks in scientific research collaborations. In I. Greif, ed. *Computer-supported cooperative work: A book of readings*. San Mateo, CA: Morgan Kaufmann Publishers,

Licklider, J. C. R., and Vezza, A. (1988). Applications of information networks. In I. Greif, ed. *Computer-supported cooperative work: A book of readings*. San Mateo, CA: Morgan Kaufmann Publishers.

Rice, R. (1984). Computer-mediated group communication. In R. Rice, ed. *The new media: Communication, research, and technology*. Beverly Hills, CA: Sage Publications.

Rosenthal, A. (1992). Editor's Letter. *Online Access* 7(1).

Schepp, B., and Schepp, D. (1990). *The complete guide to CompuServe*. New York: Osborne McGraw-Hill.

Shapard, J. (1992). Personal communication (on the GAN).

Van Gelder, L. (1991). The strange case of the electronic lover. In C. Dunlop and R. Kling, eds. *Computerization and controversy: Value conflicts and social choices*. San Diego, CA: Academic Press.

Zuboff, S. (1988). *In the age of the smart machine*. New York: Basic Books.

Chapter 3   ***The Global Matrix of Minds***
John S. Quarterman

Asante, M. K., and Gudykunst, W. B., eds. (1989). Inquiry in international communication. In *Handbook of international and intercultural communication*. Newbury Park, CA: Sage Publications.

Barron, B. (1991). Libraries on the matrix. *Matrix News* 1(6) 1, 7. (Available from Matrix Information and Directory Services, Inc. (MIDS), Austin, Texas).

Bhushan, A., Pogran, K., Tomlinson, R., and White, J. (1973). *Standardizing network mail headers*. (September 5, Requests for comments 561, p. 3). ARPANET Working Group.

Blokzijl, R. (1990). *RIPE terms of reference*. (Network working group request for comments 1181). Menlo Park, CA: SRI International, Network Information Systems Center.

Bressler, R. D., and Thomas, R. (1973). *Mail retrieval via FTP*. (Requests for comments 458, p. 2). ARPANET Working Group.

Carl-Mitchell, S. (1991). X.400—fact and fancy. *Matrix News* 1(2) 1. (Available from Matrix Information and Directory Services, Inc. (MIDS), Austin, Texas).

Carl-Mitchell, S. (1992). Electronic mail demystified. *UniForum* (January) 31. Santa Clara, CA.

Carswell, S. A. (1988). *E-Mail*. Boston: Artech House.

Coombs, N. (1991). Reflections on the impact of the electronic classroom. *Matrix News* 1(5) 1, 1819. (Available from Matrix Information and Directory Services, Inc. (MIDS), Austin, Texas).

Couey, A. (1991). Cyber art: the art of communication systems. *Matrix News* 1(4) 4. (Available from Matrix Information and Directory Services, Inc. (MIDS), Austin, Texas).

Crocker, D. H. (1982). *Standard for the format of ARPA Internet text messages*. (August 13, Requests for comments 822, p. 47). ARPANET Working Group.

Deutsch, P. (1991). On the need to develop Internet user services. *Matrix News* 1(4) 1. (Available from Matrix Information and Directory Services, Inc. (MIDS), Austin, Texas).

Dillard, J. L. (1975). *All-American English: A history of the English language in America*. New York: Vintage (Random House).

Febvre, L., and Martin, H. J. (1990). *The coming of the book: The impact of printing, 1450–1800*. London: Verso. (First published as *L'Apparition du Livre* by Editions Albin Michel, Paris, 1958.)

GAO. (1991). *High-performance computing industry uses of supercomputers and high-speed networks*. (Report to congressional requesters, No. GAO/IMTEC-91-58, p. 30). United States General Accounting Office.

Habegger, J. (1991). Exactly what is the NREN? *Matrix News* 1(4) 5. (Available from Matrix Information and Directory Services, Inc. (MIDS), Austin, Texas).

Jackson, S. (1991). The top ten media errors about the SJ games raid. *Matrix News* 1(3) 1. (Available from Matrix Information and Directory Services, Inc. (MIDS), Austin, Texas).

Kapor, M. (1991a). Encouraging equitable competition on the Internet. *Matrix News* 1(3) 1. (Available from Matrix Information and Directory Services, Inc. (MIDS), Austin, Texas).

Kapor, M. (1991b). Civil liberties in cyberspace. *Scientific American* 265(3):158–164.

Leffler, S. J., McKusick, M. K., Karels, M. J., and Quarterman, J. S. (1989). *The design and implementation of the 4.3BSD UNIX operating system.* Reading, MA: Addison-Wesley.

Lottor, M. (1992). *Internet growth (1981–1991).* (Network working group request for comments 1296, January). Menlo Park, CA: SRI International, Network Information Systems Center.

North, J. B. (1971). *ARPA network mailing lists.* (Requests for comments 155, May, p. 5). ARPANET Working Group.

Partridge, C. (1991). How many users are on the Internet? *Matrix News* 1(3) 1. (Available from Matrix Information and Directory Services, Inc. (MIDS), Austin, Texas).

Postel, J. B. (1982). *Simple mail transfer protocol.* (Requests for comments 821, August, p. 68). ARPANET Working Group.

Presno, O. de. (1991). Children help change the online world. *Matrix News* 1(5) 1, 13–16. (Available from Matrix Information and Directory Services, Inc. (MIDS), Austin, Texas).

Quarterman, J. S. (1990). *The Matrix: Computer networks and conferencing systems worldwide.* Bedford, MA: Digital Press.

Quarterman, J. S. (1991a). Networks from technology to community. *Matrix News* 1(2) 2. (Available from Matrix Information and Directory Services, Inc. (MIDS), Austin, Texas).

Quarterman, J. S. (1991b). Networks across boundaries. *Matrix News* 1(3) 2. (Available from Matrix Information and Directory Services, Inc. (MIDS), Austin, Texas).

Quarterman, J. S. (1991c). Network applications. *UniForum* (January) 36. Santa Clara, CA.

Quarterman, J. S. (1991d). National network policy. *Matrix News* 1(1) 1. (Available from Matrix Information and Directory Services, Inc. (MIDS), Austin, Texas).

Quarterman, J. S. (1991e). Analogy is not identity. *Matrix News* 1(7) 6–9. (Available from Matrix Information and Directory Services, Inc. (MIDS), Austin, Texas).

Quarterman, J. S. (1991f). Which network and why it matters. *Matrix News* 1(5) 6–13. (Available from Matrix Information and Directory Services, Inc. (MIDS), Austin, Texas).

Quarterman, J. S. (1992). How big is the matrix? *Matrix News* 2(2). (Available from Matrix Information and Directory Services, Inc. (MIDS), Austin, Texas).

Quarterman, J. S., and Carl-Mitchell, S. (1991). Networks are volunteers. *Matrix News* 1(4) 6. (Available from Matrix Information and Directory Services, Inc. (MIDS), Austin, Texas).

Quarterman, J. S., Carl-Mitchell, S., Wilhelm, S., Boede, J., and Sheffield, B. (1991). *High-speed networks in domestic industry.* (Report for the U.S. General Accounting Office, May 28, p. 36). Austin: Texas Internet Consulting.

Sterling, B. (1992). *The hacker crackdown: Law and disorder on the electronic frontier.* New York: Bantam Books.

Terpstra, M. (1992). Re: RIPE DNS Hostcount November 28, 1991. Personal communication, February 3. Amsterdam.

Vittal, J., Crocker, D., and Henderson, A. (1977). *Proposed official standard for the format of ARPA network messages.* (May 12, Requests for comments 724). ARPANET Working Group.

Chapter 4   ***A Slice of Life in My Virtual Community***
Howard Rheingold

Kiesler, S. (1986). The hidden messages in computer networks. *Harvard Business Review* (January–February).

Licklider, J. C. R., Taylor, R., and Herbert, E. (1968). The computer as a communication device. *International Science and Technology* (April).

Oldenburg, R. (1991). *The great good place: Cafes, coffee shops, community centers, beauty parlors, general stores, bars, hangouts, and how they get you through the day.* New York: Paragon House.

Peck, M. S., M.D. (1987). *The different drum: Community making and peace.* New York: Touchstone.

Reich, R. (1991). *The work of nations.* New York: Random House.

Chapter 5   ***Jurisdictional Quandaries for Global Networks***
Anne Wells Branscomb

Aronson, J. D. (1987). Telecommunications negotiations in GATT. *Transnational Data Report* (February) 11–13.

Huber, P. (1990). Good tidings from Lotus Development. *Forbes* (December 24) 136.

Landweber, L. (1992). International connectivity. *The Internet Society News* 1(1):3.

Walter, P. A. (1991). Databases: Protecting an asset, avoiding a liability. *The Computer Lawyer* 8(3) 10.

Zachmann, W. (1990). Prodigy's myopic vision might hurt profitability. *PC Week* 7(49) 76.

Chapter 6   **Computers, Networks, and Work**
Lee Sproull and Sara Kiesler

Constant, D., Sproull, L., and Kiesler, S. (1992). *The kindness of strangers: Discretionary information sharing in a networked organization.* Pittsburgh, PA: Carnegie Mellon University.

Dubrovsky, V., Kiesler, S., and Sethna, B. (1991). The equalization phenomenon: Status effects in computer-mediated and face-to-face decision making groups. *Human Computer Interaction* 6:119–146.

Dunlop, C., and Kling, R. (1991). Social relationships in electronic communities. In C. Dunlop and R. Kling, eds. *Computerization and controversy: Value conflicts and social choices.* San Diego, CA: Academic Press.

Eveland, J. D., and Bikson, T. K. (1988). Work group structures and computer support: A field experiment. *Transactions on Office Information Systems* 6(4) 354–379.

Finholt, T. (1992). *Accessing organizational expertise through computer-mediated communication.* Unpublished doctoral dissertation, Carnegie Mellon University.

Galegher, J., Kraut, R. E., and Egido, C., eds. (1990). *Intellectual teamwork: Social and technological foundations of cooperative work.* Hillsdale, NJ: Lawrence Erlbaum Associates.

Greist, J. H., Klein, M. H., and Van Cura, L. J. (1973). A computer interview for psychiatric patient target symptoms. *Archives of General Psychiatry* 29:247–253.

Huff, C., Sproull, L., and Kiesler, S. (1989). Computer communication and organizational commitment: Tracing the relationship in a city government. *Journal of Applied Social Psychology* 19(16) 1371–1391.

Rule, J., and Attewell, P. (1989). What do computers do? *Social Problems* 36(3) 225–241.

Sproull, L., and Kiesler, S. (1991). *Connections: New ways of working in the networked organization.* Cambridge, MA: MIT Press.

Waterton, J. J. and Duffy, J. C. (1984). A comparison of computer interviewing techniques and traditional methods in the collection of self-report alcohol consumption data in a field study. *International Statistical Review* 52:173–182.

Zuboff, S. (1988). *In the age of the smart machine.* New York: Basic Books.

Chapter 7   *Integrating Global Organizations through Task/Team Support Systems*
Marvin Manheim

Bartlett, C. A. (1986). Building and managing the transnational: The new organizational challenge. In M. E. Porter, ed. *Competition in global industries*. Boston: Harvard Business School Press.

Bartlett, C. A., Doz, Y., and Hedlund, G., eds. (1990). *Managing the global firm*. London: Routledge.

Bartlett, C. A., and Ghoshal, S. (1989). *Managing across borders: The transnational solution*. Boston: Harvard Business School Press.

Benjamin, R. I., Rockart, J. F., Scott-Morton, M. S., and Wyman, J. (1984). Information technology: A strategic opportunity. *Sloan Management Review* (Summer) 3–10.

Biddle, G. J. (1990). *Global Information Technology*. Paper presented at Tenth International Conference on Decision Support Systems, May, Boston, MA.

Bollo, D., Hanappe, P., and Stumm, M. (1991). New means of communication to serve commercial carriers: An experiment on a European basis. *Proceedings of the 24th Annual Hawaii International Conference on Systems Sciences*. Los Alamitos, CA: IEEE Computer Society Press.

Cash, J. I., McFarlan, F. W., McKenney, J. L., and Vitale, M. (1988). *Corporate information systems management*. Homewood, IL: Irwin.

Clemons, E. K., and Row, M. (1987). Structural differences among firms: A potential source of competitive advantage in the application of information technology. *Proceedings of the 8th International Conference on Information Systems, December 1–9*.

Clemons, E. K., and Row, M. (1988). McKesson Drug Company—a case study of Economost—a strategic information system. *Proceedings of the 21st Annual Hawaii International Conference on Systems Sciences*. Los Alamitos, CA: IEEE Computer Society Press.

Coleman, D. A., ed. (1992) *Groupware 92, San Jose, CA*. San Mateo, CA: Morgan-Kaufmann Publishers.

COMPAT 90. (1990). *EDI Europe*. London: Blenheim Queensdale.

de Meyer, A., and Mizushima, A. (1990). Global R&D management. In H. Vernon-Wortzel and L. H. Wortzel, eds. *Global strategic management: The essentials*. New York: Wiley.

Earl, M., ed. (1988). *Information management: The strategic dimension*. Oxford: Clarendon Press.

Flaherty, M. T. (1986). Coordinating international manufacturing and technology. In M. E. Porter, ed. *Competition in global industries*. Boston: Harvard Business School Press.

Gabarro, J. J. (1990). The development of working relationships. In J. Galegher, R. E. Kraut, and C. Egido, eds. *Intellectual teamwork: Social and technological foundations of cooperative work*. Hillsdale, NJ: Lawrence Erlbaum Associates.

Galegher, J., Kraut, R. E., and Egido, C., eds. (1990). *Intellectual teamwork: Social and technological foundations of cooperative work*. Hillsdale, NJ: Lawrence Erlbaum Associates.

Hackman, J. R., ed. (1990). *Groups that work (and those that don't)*. San Francisco: Jossey Bass.

Hedlund, G., and Rolander, D. (1990). Action in hetarchies—new approaches to managing the MNC. In C. A. Bartlett, Y. Doz, and G. Hedlund, eds. *Managing the global firm*. London: Routledge.

Hopper, M. D. (1990). Rattling SABRE—new ways to compete on information. *Harvard Business Review* (May) 118–125.

Hudson, R. L. (1991). IBM again revamps European sector: It seeks to find proper mix as market grows tougher. *Wall Street Journal* (April 21).

Information power: How companies are using new technologies to gain a competitive edge. (1985). *Business Week* (October 14) 108–116.

Ives, B., and Jarvenpää, S. (1991). Applications of global information technology: Key issues for management. *MIS Quarterly* 15(1).

Ives, B., and Jarvenpää, S. (1990). Global information technology: Some conjectures for future research. *Proceedings of the 23rd Annual Hawaii International Conference on Systems Sciences, Vol. IV, Emerging Technologies and Applications*. Los Alamitos, CA: IEEE Computer Society Press.

Johnston, R., and Lawrence, P. R. (1988). Beyond vertical integration: The rise of the value-adding partnership. *Harvard Business Review* (July–August) 88(4) 94–101.

Keen, P. G. W. (1988). *Competing in time*. Cambridge, MA: Ballinger Publishing.

Keen, P. G. W. (1991). *Shaping the future: Business design through information technology*. Cambridge, MA: Harvard Business School Press.

Lamont, D. (1991). *Winning worldwide*. Homewood, IL: Business One Irwin.

Larson, C. E., and LaFasto, F. M. (1989). *Teamwork: What must go right, what can go wrong*. Newbury Park, CA: Sage Publications.

Levitt, T. (1990). The globalization of markets. In H. Vernon-Wortzel, and L. H. Wortzel, eds. *Global strategic management: The essentials*. New York: Wiley.

Magad, E. L., and Amos, J. L. (1989). *Total materials management*. New York: Van Nostrand/Rheinhold.

Manheim, M. L. (1988). Using information systems to compete successfully in today's world: A challenge to managers. In *Information systems for government and business: Trends, issues and challenges. Proceedings of the 2nd Kawasaki International*

Seminar on the Information Systems Challenge. Nagoya, Japan: United Nations Centre for Regional Development.

Manheim, M. L. (1989). *Strategy as process: Cognitive concepts and information systems support.* Unpublished working paper. Evanston, IL: Strategy Research Center, Kellogg Graduate School of Management, Northwestern University.

Manheim, M. L. (1990). Global information technology: Globalization and opportunities for competitive advantage through information technology. *Tijdschrift voor vervoerswetenschap* (Journal for Transport Science). Rijswijk, The Netherlands: Kwartaalschrift van de Stichting NEA, 1990 (2) 138–159.

Manheim, M. L. (1992). Global information technology: Issues and opportunities. *International Information Systems,* 1:38–67.

Manheim, M. L., Xie, Y., Chang, G. N., and Staples, R. (1992). *Using task/team support systems to achieve strategic objectives in globallycompeting organizations: A design methodology (preliminary).* Unpublished working paper. Evanston, IL: Northwestern University, Transportation Center.

Manheim, M. L., Elam, J., and Keen, P. S. (1989). *Strategic assessment: The use of telecommunications as an element of competitive strategy by the city of Amsterdam.* Cambridge, MA: Cambridge Systematics, Inc.

Manheim, M. L., and Mittman, B. (1988). *Strategic assessment of information technology's role in increasing the competitiveness of the U.S. steel industry.* Evanston, IL: Northwestern University, University Steel Resource Center.

Mills, D. Q. (1991). *Rebirth of the corporation.* New York: Wiley.

Mitsubishi Research Institute, Cambridge Systematics, and Shinko Research Institute. (1990). *Global business opportunities for Kansai.* Unpublished study. Tokyo: Mitsubishi Research Institute.

Miyazawa, N., and Koike, Y. (1991). Cases of developing strategic information systems at Nippon Steel Corporation. *Proceedings of the 24th Annual Hawaii International Conference on Systems Sciences.* Los Alamitos, CA: IEEE Computer Society Press.

OECD. (in press). *Report on integrated logistics.* Paris: Organization for Economic Cooperation and Development.

Ohmae, K. (1989). Planting for a global harvest. *Harvard Business Review* (July–August) 136–145.

Porter, M. E., ed. (1986). *Competition in global industries.* Boston: Harvard Business School Press.

Roure, J. (1990). *Integrated logistics management system.* Paper presented at the International Working Group on Strategic Informatics, Paris, France.

Sethi, V., and Olson, J. E. (1991). Information technology in a transnational environment. *Proceedings of the 24th Hawaii International Conference on Systems Sciences.* Los Alamitos, CA: IEEE Computer Society Press.

Sokol, P. K. (1989). *EDI: The competitive edge*. New York: Free Press.

Strassman, P. A. (1985). *Information payoff*. New York: Free Press.

Synnott, W. R. (1987). *The information weapon*. New York: Wiley.

Tanja, P. (1988). *EDI developments in The Netherlands: A short survey of critical issues*. Delft, Netherlands: TNO.

Wiseman, C. (1988). *Strategic information systems*. Homewood, IL: Dow Jones-Irwin.

Chapter 8   **Cross-Cultural Communication and CSCW**
Hiroshi Ishii

Ellis, C. A., Gibbs, S. J., and Rein, G. L. (1991). Groupware: Some issues and experiences, *Communications of the ACM* 34(1) 39–58.

Endo, T. (1992). Human interfaces in telecommunications and computers. *IEICE Transactions on Communications* E75B(1) 20–25.

Engelbart, D. (1963). A conceptual framework for the augmentation of man's intellect. *Vistas in Information Handling* 1:1–29. Washington, DC: Spartan Books.

Fuji Xerox Education Department. (1984). *ICC basic skill seminar text*. Tokyo: Fuji Xerox.

Galegher, J., Kraut, R. and Egido, C., eds. (1990). *Intellectual teamwork: Social and technological foundations of cooperative work*. Hillsdale, NJ: Lawrence Erlbaum Associates.

Greif, I., ed. (1988). *Computer-supported cooperative work: A book of readings*. San Mateo: Morgan Kaufmann.

Greenberg, S., ed. (1991). *Computer-supported cooperative work and groupware*. London: Academic Press.

Grudin, J. (1991). CSCW introduction. *Communication of the ACM* 34(12) 30–34.

Ishii, H. (1990). Cross-cultural communication & CSCW. *Whole Earth Review* 69 (Winter) 48–52.

Ishii, H. (1992). Translucent multiuser interface for realtime collaboration. *The IEICE transactions on fundamentals of electronics, communications and computer science, special issue on next generation human interface* 75(2) 122–131.

Ishii, H., and Arita, K. (1991). ClearFace: Translucent multiuser interface for TeamWorkStation. *Proceedings ECSCW '91*. Dordrecht, The Netherlands: Kluwer Academic.

Ishii, H., and Miyake, N. (1991). Toward an open shared workspace: Computer and video fusion approach of TeamWorkStation. *Communications of the ACM, Special issue on CSCW* 34(12) 37–50.

Johansen, R. (1988). *Groupware: Computer support for business teams*. New York: The Free Press.

Malone, T. (1988). Designing organizational interfaces. *Proceedings of CHI '86, ACM SIGCHI.* New York: ACM. 66–71.

Nittetsu Human Development. (1987). *Talking about Japan.* Tokyo: ALC Press Inc.

Schrage, M. (1990). *Shared minds: The new technologies of collaboration.* New York: Random House.

Chapter 9   **Global Networking for Local Development**
Jan Walls

Boulding, K. E. (1985). *The world as total system.* Beverly Hills, CA: Sage Publications.

Bullock, A., and Stallybrass, O., eds. (1977). *The fontana dictionary of modern thought.* London: Fontana Books.

Daly, H. E., and Cobb, Jr., J. B. (1989). *For the common good.* Boston: Beacon Press.

Dore, R. (1987). *Taking Japan seriously: A Confucian perspective on leading economic issues.* Stanford: Stanford University Press.

Goonasekera, A. (1990). Communication, culture and the growth of the individual self in third world societies. *Asian Journal of Communication* 1(1) 34–52.

Granovetter, M. (1973). The strength of weak ties. *American Journal of Sociology* 78:1360–1380.

Kincaid, D. L. (1988). The convergence theory and intercultural communication. In Kim, and Gudykunst, eds. *Theories in intercultural communication.* Newbury Park, CA: Sage Publications.

Leiss, W. (1989). *Under technology's thumb.* Montreal and Kingston: McGill-Queen's University Press.

Pasmore, W. A., and Sherwood, J. J., eds. (1978). *Sociotechnical systems: A sourcebook.* San Diego: University Associates.

Penzias, A. (1989). *Ideas and information: Managing in a high tech world.* New York: Simon and Schuster.

Ramos, A. G. (1981). *The new science of organizations: A reconceptualization of the wealth of nations.* Toronto: University of Toronto Press.

Rifkin, J. (1987). *Time wars: The primary conflict in human history.* New York: Simon and Schuster.

Thomas, W. I. (1966). *On Social organization and social personality.* Chicago: Chicago University Press.

Toennies, F. (1965). *Community and society,* C. Loomis, trans. New York: Harper and Row.

Watzlawick, P., Bavelas, J., and Jackson, D. (1967). *Pragmatics of human communication.* New York: W. W. Norton & Co.

World Commission on Environment and Development. (1987). *Our common future.* Oxford: Oxford University Press.

Chapter 11   *Building a Global Network: The WBSI Experience*
Andrew Feenberg

Blackburn, L., and Mason, R. (1991). *Draft report on the evaluation of DiSCII at the Open University.* Unpublished manuscript.

Eurich, N. (1990). *The learning industry: Education for adult workers.* Princeton: The Carnegie Foundation for the Advancement of Teaching.

Farson, R. (1989). Education's second computer revolution. *Edu Magazine* 52 (1989/90) 48–52.

Feenberg, A. (1986). Network design: An operating manual for computer conferencing. *IEEE Transactions on Professional Communications* 29(1):2–7.

Feenberg, A. (1989). A user's guide to the pragmatics of computer-mediated communication. *Semiotica* 75(3/4) 257–278.

Feenberg, A. (1991). *Critical theory of technology.* New York: Oxford University Press.

Feenberg, A. (1992). From information to communication: The French experience with Videotex. In M. Lea, ed. *The social contexts of computer-mediated communication.* London: Harvester-Wheatsheaf.

Feenberg, A., and Bellman, B. (1990). Social factor research in computer-mediated communications. In L. Harasim, ed. *Online education: Perspectives on a new environment.* New York: Praeger Publishers.

Harasim, L. (1991). Designs and tools to augment collaboration in computerized conferencing systems. In J. Nunamaker, R. Sprague, eds. *Proceedings of the Hawaiian International Conference on Systems Science, Vol. IV, Organizational Systems and Technology Track.* 379–385.

Hiltz, S. R. (1986). The virtual classroom: Using computer-mediated communications for university teaching. *Journal of Communication* 36(2) 95–104.

Rowan, R. (1986). *The intuitive manager.* New York: Berkley Publishing Group.

Rowan, R. (1983). Executive Education at Computer U. *Fortune* (March 7).

Chapter 12   *Computer Conferencing and the New Europe*
Robin Mason

Collis, B. (1991a). Telecommunications-based training in Europe: A state-of-the-art report. *The American Journal of Distance Education* 5(2) 31–40.

Collis, B. (1991b). Telecommunications projects in European secondary schools. *ISTE Update* 4(3) 3–4.

Davies, D., Davies, G., and Jennings, C. (1992). *The ELNET final report.* Southampton: CECOMM, Southampton Institute.

Davies, G. (1992). Case study 5: Language acquisition in ELNET. In D. Davies, ed. *The ELNET final report*. Southampton: CECOMM, Southampton Institute.

Gwyn, R. (1991). *A European platform to develop a mechanism for cooperation in the field of information technologies in education*. UNESCO seminar paper, Moscow (June) 17–21.

McLure, A., and Heap, N. (1990). European learning networks: A review of current developments. *Proceedings of the 3rd Guelph symposium on computer-mediated communication*. (May 15–17) Guelph, Ontario.

Majo, J. (1991). Closing address. In FUNDESCO, ed. *Telecommunications-based training for the 1990's*. Brussels: Commission of the European Communities.

Milligan, F. (1991). *Email and Europe: An Anglo-Dutch connection*. Coventry, UK: National Council for Educational Technology.

Nipper, S. (1991). Somewhere, over the rainbow . . . On satellites, distance education and EuroPACE. In FUNDESCO, ed. *Telecommunications-based training for the 1990's*. Brussels: Commission of the European Communities.

Rasmussen, T., Bang, J., and Lundby, K. (1991). When academia goes online: A social experiment with electronic conferencing for the Nordic media research community. *DEOSNEWS* 1(24).

Rebel, K. (1990). Modern learning technologies and their importance for the "European open learning"—the Delta example. *Research in Distance Education* 2(3) 2–7.

Robinson, P. (1991). Globalization, telecommunications and trade. *Futures* 23(8) 801–814.

Smith, K. (1990). Collaborative and interactive writing for increasing communication skills. *Hispania* 73 (March) 51–61.

Somekh, B. (1989). The human interface: Hidden issues in CMC affecting use in schools. In R. Mason, and A. R. Kaye, ed. *Mindweave: Communication, computers and distance education*. Oxford: Pergamon.

Walker, R. (1991). EPOS: Building a working open learning service. In FUNDESCO, ed. *Telecommunications-based training for the 1990's*. Brussels: Commission of the European Communities.

Chapter 13 **Global Education through Learning Circles**
Margaret Riel

Bredo, E. (1989). Supportive context for learning. *Harvard Educational Review* 59:206–212.

Cuban, L. (1986). *Teachers and machines: The classroom use of technology since 1920*. New York: Teachers College Press.

Hanvey, R. (1977). *An attainable global perspective*. New York: The American Forum for Global Education.

LaFrenz, D., and Friedman, J. (1989). Computers don't change education, teachers do! *Harvard Educational Review* 59:222–225.

Riel, M. (1992). A functional analysis of educational telecomputing: A case study of learning circles. *Interactive Learning Environments* 2:15–29.

Stapleton, C. (1992). *Assessing success of collaborative educational activities on globally distributed computer-based electronic networks.* Paper presented at the annual meeting of the American Educational Research Association, San Francisco, April 20–24.

Tye K. (1991). *Global education: From thought to action.* Alexandria, VA: Association for Supervision and Curriculum Development.

Winn, T., and Coleman, I. (1989). Urban and rural: A dialog about computers in schools. *Harvard Educational Review* 59:212–217.

Chapter 14   *Technology Transfer in Global Networking*
Beryl Bellman, Alex Tindimubona, and Armando Arias, Jr.

Adrianson, L. (1985). *Group communication via computer: Social psychological aspects of the Com system.* University of Goteborg, Sweden 15(4).

Adrianson, L., and Hjelmquist, E. (1985). *Small group communication in two media: Face-to-face communication and computer-mediated-communication.* University of Goteborg, Sweden 15(1).

Arias, A., and Bellman, B. (1987). International cooperation through interactive Spanish/English transition telecourses. *Technology and Learning* 1(2) 6–9.

Arias, A., and Bellman, B. (1990a). Computer-mediated classrooms for culturally and linguistically diverse learners. *Computers in the Schools* 7(1/2) 227–242. Special Issue on Language Minority Students and Computers.

Arias, A., and Bellman, B. (1990b). Pedagogical and research uses of computer conferencing: BESTNET communications. *Instructional Computing Update* 2(1) 2–5.

Bellman, B. (1988). A model for user interface and information server design. In E. Stefferud, O. J. Jacobsen, and P. Schicker, eds. *Message handling systems and distributed applications.* The Hague: North Holland Press.

FIPSE Technology Study Group (1988). *Ivory towers, silicon basements: Learner-centered computing in postsecondary education.* McKinney, TX: Academic Computing Publications.

Harasim, L. (1986). Computer learning networks: Educational applications of computer conferencing. *Journal of Distance Education* 1:59–70.

Harasim, L. (1990). Online education: An environment for collaboration and intellectual amplification. In L. Harasim, ed. *Online education: Perspectives on a new environment.* New York: Praeger Publishers.

Hiltz, S. R. (1990). Evaluating the virtual classroom. In L. Harasim, ed. *Online Education: Perspectives on a new environment.* New York: Prager Publishers.

Hiltz, S. R. (1993). *The virtual classroom.* Norwood, NJ: Ablex Publishers.

Hiltz, S. R., and Turoff, M. (1978). *The network nation: Human communication via computer.* New York: Addison Wesley.

Kerr, E., and Hiltz, S. R. (1982). *Computer-mediated communication systems.* New York: Academic Press.

Lakoff, R. (1975). *Language and women's place.* New York: Harper and Row.

Chapter 15   ***Language, Character Codes, and Electronic Isolation in Japan***
Jeffrey Shapard

Burkley, R. E. (1989a). *Implementing Kanji characters on VMS—a technical overview.* (Invitation to the KANJI Platform). Japan: DEC.

Burkley, R. E. (1989b). *Supporting Chinese, Japanese and Korean written languages.* (Invitation to the KANJI Platform). Japan: DEC.

Electronic Networking Forum. (1991). *Pasocom tsuushin you netto-kan kani messaaji koukan shisutemu (Simple message handling system for personal computer telecommunications networks) (ENF/MHS).* Presentation to the Electronic Networking Forum, Tokyo, October 1991.

Frey, D., and Adams, R. (1990). !%@:: *A Directory of Electronic Mail Addressing and Networks.* Sebastopol, CA: O'Reilly & Associates.

Kindaichi, H. (1979). *The Japanese Language.* Tokyo: Tuttle.

KKC. (1991). *Japan 1992: An international comparison.* Tokyo: Keizai Koho Center (Japan Institute for Social and Economic Affairs).

Kodansha. (1983). Kodansha encyclopedia of Japan. Tokyo: Kodansha.

Lunde, K. R. (1990). Using electronic mail as a medium for foreign language study and instruction. *CALICO Journal* (March) 68–78.

Lunde, K. R. (1992). *JAPAN.INF version 1.2: Electronic handling of Japanese text.* Available through FTP at ucdavis.edu (128.120.2.1). and msi.umn.edu (128.101.24.1), by contacting the author through email at lunde@adobe.com.

Lung, P., and Nakamura, T. (1991). *Japanization of software packages.* Presentation to the International Computer Association, Tokyo, Japan, July 1991.

MBM. (1991). *Waapuro/pasocom tsuushin BBS denwacho (Word-processor/ personal computer telecommunications BBS telephone guide).* Tokyo: Micom BASIC Magazine Publishers.

Mandelbaum, D. G., ed. (1970). *Culture, language and personality: Selected essays of Edward Sapir.* Berkeley and Los Angeles: University of California Press.

Miller, R. A. (1972). *Japanese and other Altaic languages.* Chicago: University of Chicago Press.

Murai, J. (1989). *JUNET and WIDE: Japanese academic networks.* Presentation to the International Computer Association, Tokyo, May, 1989.

Murai, J. (1990). WIDE Internet, JUNET, and other networks in Japan. In T. L. LaQuey. *The user's directory of computer networks*. Bedford, MA: Digital Press.

Murai, J., and Kato, A. (1987). Researches in network development of JUNET. *Proceedings of the ACM SIGCOMM '87 workshop* (Stowe, Vermont, 11–13 August 1987) 17(5) 68–77. New York: ACM SIGCOMM.

Quarterman, J. S. (1990). *The Matrix: Computer networks and conferencing systems worldwide*. Bedford, MA: Digital Press.

Rikitake, K. (1988). *A proposal for more flexible VAX/VMS terminal device drivers, to enhance Nihon DEC's share in the Japanese market*. Paper presented by TWICS to Nihon Digital Equipment Corporation, April, 1988.

Sapir, E. (1921). *Language: An introduction to the study of speech*. New York: Harcourt, Brace & World, Inc.

Shapard, J. (1986). TWICS BeeLine: From BBS to BeeJima. *ENA Netweaver:2:6:6*. (published electronically).

Shapard, J. (1990). Observations on cross-cultural electronic networking. *Whole Earth Review* (December) 32–35.

Shapard, J. (1991). A Japan BBS pioneer: Interview with Pete Perkins. *Boardwatch Magazine* (September).

Sheldon, K. M. (1991). ASCII goes global. *Byte* (July) 108–116.

Yoneda, K. (1986). Personal communications.

Yamada, J. (1990). Fido tte Nan Da (What is Fido?) *Networker* (Autumn) 137–144.

Chapter 16   *Cognitive Apprenticeship on Global Networks*
Lucio Teles

Brown, A. L., and Palincsar, A. S. (1989). Guided, cooperative learning and individual knowledge acquisition. In L. B. Resnick, ed. *Knowing, learning and instruction: Essays in honor of Robert Glaser*. Hillsdale, NJ: Lawrence Erlbaum Associates.

Collins, A., Brown, J., and Newman, S. (1989). Cognitive apprenticeship: Teaching the crafts of reading, writing, and mathematics. In L. B. Resnick, ed. *Knowing, learning and instruction: Essays in honor of Robert Glaser*. Hillsdale, NJ: Lawrence Erlbaum Associates.

Greenfield, P. (1984). A theory of the teacher in the learning activities of everyday life. In B. Rogoff, and J. Lave, eds. *Everyday cognition*. Cambridge, MA: Harvard University Press.

Harasim, L. (1990). Online education: An environment for collaboration and intellectual amplification. In L. Harasim, ed. *Online education: Perspectives on a new environment*. New York: Praeger.

Harasim, L., Hiltz, S. R., Teles, L., and Turoff, M. (1994). *Learning Networks: A Field Guide*. Cambridge, MA: MIT Press. Forthcoming.

Levin, J. (1990). *Teleapprenticeships on globally distributed electronic networks.* Paper presented at the Boston meeting of the American Educational Research Association.

Ong, W. (1982). *Orality and literacy.* New York: Methuen.

Teles, L., and Duxbury, N. (1991). *The networked classroom: An assessment of the Southern Interior Telecommunications Project.* Burnaby, BC: Simon Fraser University, Faculty of Education.

Rogoff, B. (1984). Introduction: Thinking and learning in social context. In B. Rogoff, and J. Lave, eds. *Everyday cognition.* Cambridge, MA: Harvard University Press.

Chapter 17   *Networks and Emergence of Global Civil Society*
Howard Frederick

Bagdikian, B. (1989). The lords of the global village. *The Nation* (June 12).

Frederick, H. H. (1993). *Global communications and international relations.* Pacific Grove, CA: Wadsworth.

Hamelink, C. J. (1991a). Global communication: Plea for civil action. In B. V. Hofsten, ed. *Informatics in food and nutrition.* Stockholm: Royal Academy of Sciences.

Hamelink, C. J. (1991b). *Communication: The most violated human right.* Stockholm: Inter Press Service dispatch.

Information rich vs. poor. (1991). *Global Electronics* 107 (March–April) 4. Referring to Bureau of the Census data cited in the *San Jose Mercury News*, March 27, 1991.

International Commission For The Study Of Communication Problems (MacBride Commission). (1980). *One world, many voices.* Paris: UNESCO.

International Journalism Institute. (1987). The mass media in the world. Citing UNESCO. (1989). *World communication report.* Paris: UNESCO.

Jussawalla, M. (1985). Can we apply new trade rules to information trade? In G. R. Pipe, and C. Brown, eds. *International information economy handbook.* Springfield, VA: Transnational Data Reporting Service.

Mowlana, H. (1986). *Global information and world communication: New frontiers in international relations.* New York: Longman.

Quarterman, J. S. (1990). *The Matrix: Computer networks and conferencing systems worldwide.* Bedford, MA: Digital Press.

UNESCO. (1989). *World communication report.* Paris: UNESCO.

United States Department of State. (1988). *International communication and information policy.* Washington, DC: Department of State.

Chapter 19   *Co-Emulation: A Global Hypernetwork Society*
Shumpei Kumon and Izumi Aizu

Abegglen, J. C., and Stalk, Jr., G. (1985). *Kaisha: The Japanese corporation.* New York: Basic Books.

Barlow, J. P. (1992). The great work. *Communications of the ACM* (January).

Bressand, A. (1989). Networld—draft report on emerging global networked society. In *Project PROMETHEE Perspective.*

Hiramatsu, M. (1990). Chiho karano hasso (Ideas from regional area). Iwanami Shoten.

Imai, K. (1992). Japan's corporate network. In S. Kumon, and H. Rosovsky, eds. *The political economy of Japan: Vol. 3, the social and cultural dynamics.* Stanford: Stanford University Press.

Institute for Networking Design, ed. (1992). *Proceedings of HyperNetwork '92 Beppu Bay Conference, 1992.* Tokyo: Institute for Networking Design.

Kumon, S. (1992). Japan as a Network Society. In S. Kumon, and H. Rosovsky, eds. *The political economy of Japan: Vol. 3, the social and cultural dynamics.* Stanford: Stanford University Press.

Malone, T. W., Yates, J., and Benjamin, R. I. (1988). Electronic markets and electronic hierarchies. In I. Greif. *Computer-supported cooperative work: A book of readings.* San Mateo: Morgan Kaufmann Publishers, Inc.

Nielsen, J. (1990). *Hypertext & hypermedia.* Boston, MA: Academic Press.

Prestrowitz, Jr., C. (1988). *Trading places: How we allowed Japan to take the lead.* New York: Basic Books.

Rheingold, H. (1992). *Virtual reality.* New York: Summit Books.

Rothschild-Whitt, J. (1984). The collectivist organization: An alternative to rational-bureaucratic models. *American Sociological Review* 44 (August) 509–527.

Sculley, J., and Byrne, J. (1987). *Odyssey—Pepsi to Apple . . . a journey of adventure, ideas, and the future.* New York: Harper & Row.

Chapter 20   ***Sailing through Cyberspace***
Robert Jacobson

Gibson, W. (1984). *Neuromancer.* New York: Ace Books.

Jacobson, W. (1992). The ultimate user interface. *Byte* (April) 175–176.

Chapter 21   ***The Global Authoring Network***
Linda M. Harasim and Jan Walls

Greif, I. (1988). Overview. In I. Greif, ed. *Computer-supported cooperative work: A book of readings.* San Mateo, CA: Morgan Kaufman.

Harasim, L., and Winkelmans, T. (1990). Computer-mediated scholarly collaboration. *Knowledge: Creation, diffusion, utilization.* 11(4) 382–409.

Kincaid, D. L. (1988). The convergence theory and intercultural communication. In Y. Y. Kim, and W. B. Gudykunst, eds. *Theories in intercultural communication.* Newbury Park, CA: Sage Publications.

Index